DISCARD

The Women I Think About at Night

Traveling the Paths of My Heroes

Mia Kankimäki

Translated by Douglas Robinson

Simon & Schuster
New York London Toronto Sydney New Delhi

Simon & Schuster
1230 Avenue of the Americas
New York, NY 10020

Originally published in 2018 in Finland by Otava as *Naiset joita ajattelen öisin.*
The English-language edition published by agreement with Mia Kankimäki and Elina Ahlback Literary Agency, Helsinki, Finland.

First Simon & Schuster hardcover edition November 2020

Interior design by Carly Loman

Manufactured in the United States of America

10 9 8 7 6 5 4 3 2 1

Library of Congress Cataloging-in-Publication Data is available.

ISBN: 978-1-9821-2919-4
ISBN: 978-1-9821-2924-8 (ebook)

You think you know what a journey can offer you, but in fact that is precisely what you don't know.

KAREN BLIXEN, A LETTER FROM AFRICA, JANUARY 18, 1917

elegant Graces and lovely-haired Muses, come

SAPPHO, CA. 600 BCE

Contents

I Night Women: A Confession

I'm M. I'm forty-three years old. On countless nights over the years I've thought about women—and it has nothing at all to do with sex.

I've thought about women on those sleepless nights when my life, my love, or my attitude is skewed, and it seems there is no end to the dark night of my soul. On those nights I have gathered an invisible honor guard of historical women, guardian angels to lead the way.

The lives of these inspiring night women have not followed traditional paths. They have transgressed boundaries and expectations. Many of them are artists and writers, people doing lonely, introverted work. Most have not had families or children, and their relationships with men have been unconventional. Many have traveled in or moved to foreign countries, and made massive life changes at an advanced age. Some have lived with their mothers their entire lives; some have suffered from diseases and mental disorders; but all of them have followed their passions and made their own choices. These exemplary women have been my plan B—the one I'll adopt if everything else goes to hell.

One of the women is Sei Shōnagon, a writer and court lady who lived a thousand years ago in Kyoto, about whom I wrote my first book. But there are many others. Some nights I lie awake thinking about Frida Kahlo, whose biography I read when I was eighteen. It transformed how I thought about womanhood. Other nights I think about Georgia O'Keeffe, who wound up alone in the New Mexico desert painting buffalo skulls and making her first trip around the world when she was in her seventies. I think about Yayoi Kusama, a Japanese woman who, deciding to become an artist, wrote to Georgia O'Keeffe to ask her advice, and later, after shaking up the New

York art world in the sixties, returned to Tokyo and asked to be allowed to live in a psychiatric hospital. I think of Karen Blixen, who followed her husband to Africa and ended up running a farm on her own. I think of Jane Austen, who, though she lived unmarried in her parents' attic in the English countryside, transformed the art of the novel. I think of the poet-artist Ema Saikō, who lived in Japan in the Edo period. It is her calm that finally brings sleep to the dark night of my soul.

I wonder where these women found their courage. What advice would they give me, if we could meet? And above all: Could I go exploring in their footsteps?

I've been on that journey for some time now. And the amazing thing is that I keep finding more and more forgotten night women who churn up my imagination, an ever-expanding network of women who lived in different centuries and different corners of the world, slicing the waves through my brain. They are Marys, Karens, Idas, Nellies, Marthas, Alexines, Sofonisbas, Battistas—they are writers, artists, explorers, depressed spinsters, war correspondents, wives of Renaissance aristocrats.

They are the women I think about at night. At first I thought about them on sleepless nights, in search of strength, inspiration, and purpose for my life; nowanights I stay up specially to think about them, my pulse pounding for them and with them. Why have they come to me, clung to me, swept me up in their lives? Why have I surrounded my desk with their faces? Why do books about them pile ever higher on my floor? Why do I collect facts about them like talismans?

Let me start at the beginning, one picture at a time.

But first let me pack my bag. I have a flight leaving soon.

PART 1

Africa

[LETTER ON A NAPKIN]

Dear Karen,

I'm writing this quick note to you on a KLM napkin. I'm sitting on an airplane en route to Kilimanjaro, afraid. I'm so afraid I'm trembling. I keep asking myself how the hell I've managed to put myself in this situation again. Couldn't I just have stayed home watching the Nature Channel?

The worst thing is, I'm not even sure where I'm going. I wrote to a certain Finnish man living in Tanzania, someone I don't even know, and he wrote back inviting me to come visit him in his home anytime I like. So I'm going. I'm hoping he'll be at the Kilimanjaro airport to meet my plane, because I don't even know where he lives.

This is your fault, Karen. Could you please send me a bundle of your famous courage? I could surely use it.

Yours, M

II White Fog, Winter–Spring

The long and the short of it—perhaps more long than short—is this.

It's November of the previous year. I'm lying in my ice-cold tatami-floored room in Kyoto, not particularly inclined to clamber up out of my futon bedding at all. My first book was published a couple of months ago, and I've come here to figure out what to do next. I've wandered aimlessly down the narrow alleyways of this beloved city, met friends, sat in tearooms, and visited temples glowing with fall colors, but my mind is sludge.

I think: *This is my absolute lowest point.*

I'm forty-two. I have no husband, no children, no job. I've sold my apartment, I've written and published my first book, and I've quit my job forever. I've stepped into white fog. I am free—and completely adrift.

I haven't the foggiest clue what to do next. Where should I go? Whom should I follow? What can a fortyish, familyless woman who has abandoned her work and her home *do* with her life?

The last few years, to be sure, have been the most wonderful time of my life. I've lived out of suitcases in Kyoto, London, Thailand, and Berlin. Whenever I've visited my native Finland, I've house-sat for friends or holed up in my parents' attic. I've worked on my book and floated in freedom, in that unfathomable feeling of being able to spend my time precisely as I choose.

When I watch my friends staggering about on the verge of burn-out, I feel vaguely guilty. No nine-to-five drudgery, no workplace negotiations, no one waiting at home for me to take care of them—it feels as if I've managed to escape from Alcatraz and am now bobbing along on my rubber raft watching the others slave away. It feels outrageous that I can decide what I'm going to do next all on my own. Life can't really be like this, can it?

In theory, everything is fantastic—but a worm of anxiety gnaws away at me somewhere deep inside.

It feels as if my life is moving in the opposite direction from my friends'. They decorate their homes, bake tosca cakes for their kids to take to the bake sales at their schools, run marathons, buy summer cottages, and pamper themselves with weekend trips to Central Europe. As a fortysomething I've returned to a twentysomething's life: no schedules, no duties, no job, and especially no money, and I've moved into a studio apartment so small that not even my college dorm room was a doghouse this tiny. I'm free, but an outsider.

In my darker moments it seems to me that I have absolutely nothing to show for the last twenty years of my life.

In my brighter moments I realize that I've managed to free myself from everything.

And now this expedition of mine, this whole life of a fortysomething woman, stands in need of a new direction and a new meaning. As I lie there not sleeping on that futon in Kyoto, a grandiose idea has begun to infiltrate my thoughts: Maybe I should begin to follow those exemplary women of mine, the ones I think about at night? I could become a travel writer, or a writer-explorer. I could follow them to Africa, Mexico, Polynesia, China, the New Mexico desert—could follow them around the world. But how might that be possible?

Then one evening I've been sitting up late drinking a cup of strong, bright-green matcha tea in this magical tearoom I've found, and my brain is racing. It occurs to me that the place that interests me most right now is Africa. It also occurs to me that it scares the daylights out of me to imagine traveling there alone. But that is where I have to go.

Upon my return to Finland from Kyoto, I decide to send my book on Sei Shōnagon to Tanzania. On the outside of the package I write the address I found on the Web: *Box 10, Arusha, Tanzania.* It is the address of a Finnish researcher on wild animals whose name I mentioned on page twenty-six of my book. I slip in a note telling him of my dream of traveling to the savanna. I think dreamily (and completely absurdly) of Sei, my envoy, my scout, my exotic decoy, yanking me along on the voyage with her.

And she does.

On New Year's Eve I get a text message from Olli, the wildlife researcher: Thanks for the book! I'll write more by e-mail, but you're welcome here anytime you like.

If I've been waiting for a sign, this is it. Dread twists my guts into knots, but damn it, if I don't work up the courage to go, I'll never forgive myself. I don't know this Olli at all, but on the basis of his books about Tanzanian nature and one phone conversation from three years before, I've gotten a sense of him as a straightforward (and very talkative) person. I read on the Internet that he has a house in the countryside near Arusha—is that where he's inviting me to visit him? (In my mind I see jacaranda lanes, cooks, and gardeners, but the place may well be a tiny clay hut.) And surely he isn't thinking, given my eagerness to visit him, that I have romantic designs on him?

Maybe now would be the opportune moment to dip into my Karen Blixen bank account—the savings account into which I've been stashing away money for my dream journeys. Those journeys that I either will or will not dare set off on.

For me Karen Blixen represents not only unfamiliar landscapes and Africa's wild nature, but also exemplary courage.

I've visited Africa twice. Both trips were dreams come true—and on both I was scared to death. Though frankly I can't figure out how it's possible to be scared in an organized tour group. Such things are institutionalized to the nth degree, and while on one a person feels like she is being institutionalized as well. On my South Africa tour, we sat in a minibus for such lengthy periods—some days we'd clock four hundred miles—that when I clambered groggily out of the vehicle to stretch my legs somewhere in the Swaziland countryside, I didn't even bother to remove the inflatable airplane pillow from around my neck. And yet—I was afraid. The first safari night I slept out on the savanna, I heard a lion roar, and was so terrified that my teeth chattered. (I'd had no idea that your teeth could actually chatter from fear.)

You can bet, though, that Karen Blixen wasn't afraid. She ran a farm on the high plains in East Africa and went out on hunting safaris that lasted weeks and even months, eating meals prepared by servants over campfires, drinking champagne from crystal glasses, and listening to Schubert on a gramophone. In my mind's eye I can see, stretching out to the horizon behind her, the yellow grasses of the savanna, acacia trees like umbrellas, zebras, giraffes—and a typewriter. Karen is wearing a long skirt, a white button-down blouse, and lace-up leather boots. If you've seen the movie *Out of Africa*, you will also have seen a handsome man leaning on his elbows with a safari scarf around his neck.

Reading Karen Blixen's memoir, on which the movie was based, it's obvious that she was a bold, cheerful, and wise person who got things done, and that she had an enviable ability to adapt and survive. Sometimes she seems like an unsurpassable superwoman. A random list of her merits gleaned from the book is impressive:

1) Karen farms coffee in East Africa.

2) Karen is a skilled hunter. Once the Maasai ask her to shoot a lion that has been preying on the village cattle; sometimes she shoots a zebra or two as a Sunday meal for the farmhands.

3) Karen goes on long treks. She travels alone with Gĩkũyũ and Somalis, and rides with her dogs through herds of antelope.

4) Karen is a famous physician who sees patients every morning. Her patients have plague, smallpox, typhoid, malaria, wounds, bruises, broken limbs, burns, and snakebites; the most severe cases Karen transports to the hospital in Nairobi or a mission station. Once Karen herself accidentally takes an overdose of arsenic, but thinks to check for an antidote in a novel by Alexandre Dumas, and manages to counteract the poison with milk and egg whites.

5) Karen is also a teacher, a judge, and a philanthropist. She has opened a school on her farm and serves as a judge in local disputes. Mornings Karen picks coffee alongside her workers, whom she loves. Sundays she passes out snus to the old ladies.

6) One day she finds old Knudsen dead on the path and gets a local boy to help her carry the body into the shed. She isn't afraid of the dead, as the locals are (and as I am). She isn't afraid of anything else, either.

7) Karen's an excellent cook. She has taken lessons from the French chef of a fine Danish restaurant, and her dinners are famous all across East Africa.

8) When the rainy season is delayed, Karen writes tales in the evening. You don't need me to tell you that she can write. Her writer's voice is calm, pellucid, and tender. This woman is strong; she knows who she is. She understands, she knows how, nothing fazes her.

If only I were Karen.

But obviously I'm not. I sit on the KLM airplane seat fighting back panic. I'll arrive in Kilimanjaro at nine in the evening, in the darkness of night. Will this "Olli" even be there to meet me? And what will I do if he isn't? Where will I find a place to spend the night?

I've exchanged e-mails with Olli about mosquito netting and "permethrin-impregnated clothing treatments," which the tourist guides emphatically recommend as protection against malaria, but Olli has told me not to worry: as long as I get my shots and pills, I can forget all about that stuff. Still, I could have sworn that the doctor I saw at the health clinic before leaving looked worried as she wrote me a prescription for malaria medication.

I can't help thinking that the entire Western world's understanding of Africa is precisely as lopsided and distorted as the Chilean artist Alfredo Jaar insisted in the exhibition I saw recently in the Helsinki art museum Kiasma. The *Time* magazine covers he collected showed devastatingly clearly what images are offered to us of Africa: wild animals, starvation, disease, and war. Cities, cultural life, and universities—the mundane realities of the African middle class—have been effectively airbrushed out of the picture. And this campaign of erasure has worked on people like me: when I think about Africa, I think of diseases, sanitary problems, and terrorist attacks. Robberies, rapes, kidnappings, traffic accidents. Mosquitoes, snakes, tsetse flies. Amoebas, bilharzia, cerebral malaria. Dysentery, heatstroke, yellow fever, cholera, HIV, and Ebola—that whole endless list of "dangers and annoyances" about which my *Lonely Planet* guidebook so solicitously warns.

Or even worse: I obsess about things that no longer even exist. When I've asked a couple of friends-of-friends who have worked in Nairobi for travel tips, I've realized I'm living in dreamland. They talked of the massive Kibera slum and the work being done by refugee organizations—it goes without saying for them that one goes to Kenya to work in development efforts, in refugee camps, and with street children. How could I tell them what I'm dreaming of: Karen Blixen–style safaris. I dream of flying over the savanna in a small plane and beginning to understand the elephants' language, of looking lions in the eye, of sitting on a camp chair in front of a tent typing on an old-fashioned typewriter, or reading a leather-bound book with a drink in a crystal glass within arm's reach.

Even apart from my travel preparations and my Karen research, the spring has been strange. In February I ended up having to have wisdom tooth surgery, after which I couldn't open my mouth for three weeks. I lay there in a drug-induced haze in my parents' attic, sucking in my mother's puréed food through a straw while reading Akseli Gallen-Kallela's *Africa* and feeling envious of the hippos I watched on TV, because they can open their mouths at a 180-degree angle.

In March I was hit with some kind of throat problem that put me in voice therapy, where I found myself doing all kinds of strange vocal exercises, like singing the Finnish national anthem, in two-part harmony with the therapist, by blowing into a glass tube inserted into a water glass. Most absurd of all, though, was the mapping of my vocal range, according to which I speak in my lowest possible voice, though in fact I'm a soprano. A soprano! Ridiculous. My whole self-image is based on being a gloomy and phlegmatic alto with a low voice—and now I'm supposedly someone else, this cheerful, enthusiastic, and energetic person who for forty-two years has been speaking with the wrong voice!

The symbolism is heavy-handed: after all, I'm going on this trip precisely in search of a new voice, the voice of the kind of brave woman who walks through life smiling nonchalantly.

Haven't found it yet.

I write Karen a note on a napkin. I'm not aware yet of just how conflicted my relationship with her will turn out to be.

KAREN

NIGHT WOMEN'S ADVICE 1

Go to Africa.

NIGHT WOMAN #1: *Karen Blixen née Dinesen*
PROFESSION: *Coffee farmer, later writer. Arrived in Africa in January 1914, at the age of twenty-eight. Spent a total of eighteen years in British East Africa, now known as Kenya, running a coffee plantation. Left East Africa for the last time in July 1931, at the age of forty-six, broke, depressed, syphilitic, having lost everything. Moved into her childhood home to live with her mother and began to write her first book.*

When Karen left for British East Africa as a twenty-eight-year-old in 1913, she too had one thing on her mind: changing her life. She was sick and tired of everything her world had to offer a young woman. Emigrating was her plan B.

Karen Dinesen was born in 1885 into an affluent Danish family and spent her childhood in an old rural manor house in the seaside village of Rungsted near Copenhagen. Called Tanne by her family, Karen was her father's girl, and no wonder: her father was a freethinker who had traveled in America and lived with the Native Americans. It was with his world of passions, heroic deeds, and distant wildernesses that Karen identified. But her father committed suicide shortly before Karen turned ten, and his death would haunt her throughout her life.

The women's world represented by her mother and aunts, by contrast, disgusted Karen. It was her lot to be stuck at home, surrounded by her aunts, who sat endlessly thrashing out questions of virtue and sexual morality. In that world, women were raised not to earn a living but to marry. Karen too, therefore, was given the private education appropriate for an upper-class girl, involving the reading of poems, writing in a beautiful hand, and speaking English and French. Subjects like mathematics were passed over as unnecessary for women. Life in the Rungstedlund house was so sheltered, so claustrophobic, that

Karen would later say that whenever she returned there she felt a stale, stuffy sensation akin to stepping into a train car jam-packed with people: the air was used up. Karen had no intention of staying in that train car, and under no circumstances was she going to live that idle life "appropriate to her station," devoted to family and charity.

At twenty Karen decided to become an artist and enrolled in the Royal Academy of Fine Arts in Copenhagen to study painting. In her free time she hung out in aristocratic circles, where the preferred activities included racing horses, shooting birds, playing golf, drinking whiskey, organizing balls, buying cars and airplanes, and having passionate affairs. Also hanging out in those same circles were Karen's second cousins, the aristocratic Swedish brothers Bror and Hans von Blixen Finecke. Bror was a good-natured, profligate, and irresponsible hedonist whose main goal in life was having fun. He was not particularly known for his intellect or his tact. Nor did Karen fall in love with him. She fell in love with his brother, Hans.

But Hans was not interested in Karen, and in 1910 she fled to Paris. There she polished her social skills, becoming a witty, sharp-tongued young woman, whose intensity made her a bit scary. She smoked cigarettes, spoke in a low voice, and began to pronounce Tanne Russian-style, as Tania. And when Bror von Blixen proposed to her a few years later, Karen said yes. With Bror, after all, another horizon opened up for her: she could go to Africa. Karen was twenty-seven.

When the banns for Karen and Bror's wedding were published in 1912, Karen's inner circle was not overjoyed at the news. Bror was not held in particularly high esteem, and the couple did not even seem to be in love. But Bror's uncle urged them to move to British East Africa: rumor had it the country was indescribably beautiful, and it had "fantastic economic potential." British East Africa had been established in 1895, and European settlers were flooding in to occupy that fertile high plain, which the British government was selling at ridiculously low prices. The indigenous people—the Gĩkũyũ, Maasai, and other tribes—had been evicted from their ancestral lands.

Karen's relatives provided the money to buy the land, and Bror traveled early to oversee the land purchases and equip the house—they planned to marry once Karen arrived in Mombasa in January 1914. Bror, however, who spent his time in Africa on safari, decided to give up their original plan to raise cattle. He sold the land he had bought and used the money to buy a much bigger coffee plantation. He was convinced coffee was the future.

Meanwhile, Karen was preparing for the move. She packed furniture, including a dining room suite and two bedroom suites as well as boxes of table silver, crystal glasses, porcelain, linens, paintings, framed photographs, jewelry, rugs, a French grandfather clock, her grandfather's entire library, a trunkful of medicines, and her favorite engagement present, a Scottish deerhound named Dusk. In early December 1913, Karen took the train with her mother and sister from Copenhagen to Naples, where a few weeks later she boarded the steamship *Admiral*, which would take her to Eastern Africa. The ship steamed from Naples through the Mediterranean and the Suez Canal to the Red Sea, and from there through the Indian Ocean down the Somali coast south to Mombasa. The sea journey took a total of nineteen days.

What did Karen know about her destination? She had, of course, seen bad prints of African scenes, read accounts in books and newspapers and Bror's letters; but she was on a voyage to the unknown in a whole other sense than I am. How did she imagine her future on those lonely nights? Though how do I know she was alone? The ship was full of emigrants from the east coast of Africa, South Africans, Brits, and Germans, who raised their glasses and danced and played bridge in the ship's salon.

The *Admiral* arrived in Mombasa on January 13, 1914, and Karen and Bror were married the next morning. The ceremony lasted all of ten minutes; after it was over, Karen was officially the Baroness von Blixen-Finecke. Then they jumped on a train that would take them from the hot, humid coastal region around Mombasa toward Nairobi and that vast, fertile high plain where their future life was to begin.

I arrive in Africa a hundred years and four months later, in May 2014. When my plane lands at the Kilimanjaro airport, Karen and I are separated only by the Kilimanjaro volcano, the beeline border between Tanzania and Kenya, two hundred-odd miles, and those hundred years. I do know that one thing at least has changed in the interim: 82 percent of the ice cover on the peak of Kilimanjaro has melted.

It would, of course, be ideal if I could marry someone just before setting off on the car journey to my lodging—but that's not likely to transpire.

III Tanzania–Kenya, May

My first day in Africa. It's morning. I'm sitting at a garden table eating Tanzanian porridge brought to me by Olli's wife, Flotea. The sky is cloudy and the air is fresh, humid but pleasant. Exotically colored birds twitter and chirp, and the banana trees swish in the wind—this morning when I awoke, I thought the swishing was rain. Somewhere on the far side of a fence a cow moos—apparently the same one Flotea went out and milked for Michell's breakfast. (Flotea asked whether I would like some, but I declined politely.) Incredible: I'm here.

I arrived late in the evening afraid, exhausted, underfed, with a migraine. I stepped out of the plane into a damp heat, the dark of the night, and that slightly clayey, spicy scent that I remembered from my previous trip to Africa. The Kilimanjaro airport was little more than a tiny dilapidated building, where I stood in line for my visa, dripping with sweat, watching the moths flapping about in the overhead lights. Lively American students stood in line near me singing out: *We're gonna see some li-i-ons*. I also spotted the beautiful kerchiefed Somali girl who'd sat next to me on the plane. She hadn't felt like talking then either. She had pulled a leather-covered iPad out of her Vuitton purse, which she'd wrapped in a YSL scarf, and spent the entire flight listening to the Muslim Pro app on earbuds.

Olli had been at the airport to meet my plane. The first thing he said was that I didn't look anything like the photo on the inside flap of my book's dustcover (definitely not!), but I could say the same about him. My memory of him from our phone conversation a couple of years before, on the other hand, was on the money: he talks like a house afire, hardly stopping to take a breath, on all kinds of subjects—so much information, in fact, that I wish I had a tape recorder to get it all.

We stuffed my bags in his green Land Rover, which according to Olli isn't a "car" so much as a "tool," and it looks it. (I later learn that Olli washed it specially for me.) It's thirty miles from the airport to Olli's place, and he said it would take us an hour to drive it—the Land Rover's headlights were weak, and it was pitch-black dark—but Olli managed to follow another car, now and then checking the temperature gauge with a flashlight, worried that the engine was overheating. The rich smells of nighttime nature flooded in through the open windows. We passed tiny villages and roadside bars, scarcely visible in the dark—no streetlights out here, of course, and the crescent moon that had earlier floated by on its back had apparently sunk. At last we arrived at a nondescript intersection ("Maybe it's this one?" Olli mused under his breath in the dark, as if not recognizing the road he lived on), and we turned onto an unbelievably potholed and muddy oxcart path that no other car could possibly have navigated—and at times I was sure this one couldn't either. We were in the countryside near Arusha, and everything looked very, very poor. Fortunately, Olli had e-mailed me a photo of his house, because all I could see in the dark was a collection of ramshackle huts made of clay and corrugated iron, and I would probably have started hyperventilating around then. The jarring ride ended at last at a house surrounded by walls and an electric fence. In the yard of the bungalow-style house waited Olli's Tanzanian wife, Flotea, and their almost-two-year-old daughter, Michell.

And so now here I am, in a Tanzanian village. My actual African Karen Blixen dream—savannas stretching out to nature-park infinity—is still far ahead of me, but of course I also want to see what ordinary people's lives here are like. I know that Tanzania is a poor country, much poorer than Kenya. I know that the area known in colonial times as Tanganyika was first part of German East Africa and then later belonged to the British Empire; that it gained independence in 1961 and was run on communist principles until recent years. There are more than 120 tribes here, and nearly 30 percent of the population lives below the poverty line.

And it shows. Olli's house is very comfortable, with its living room sofa suite and television, its tiled yard, its potted palms and one-way-mirror windows, through which no one can see in. But on the other side of the locked gate in the perimeter wall is a whole other world: muddy roads, scrap-iron huts and clay huts without window glass, electricity, or running water. The surrounding areas are so poor that I'm embarrassed to be unpacking outfit after outfit into the closet, my kimono-style bathrobes, my hair dryer, my energy bars, my jars of cosmetics—all the stuff that seemed so important as I was packing to leave but here seems obscenely excessive. (I didn't, however, bring crystal glasses or a grandfather clock.)

Nor would Olli's house be considered opulent on the Western scale. It was built a few years ago, but the paint is flaking off the walls and ceiling, and I see rust and mold in numerous places. Apparently the problem is low-quality materials, which only last a few months in this climate. The power is continually going out, and even when it's on the electric current is so weak that they haven't been able to use their washing machine for six months. Water pressure in the county pipes is practically nonexistent; the water drips out of the faucets so miserably that, as Olli says, "we have to rely on carried water." In the morning I see what that means when the neighbor "house girl" arrives with a gaggle of kids, each wearing a broad smile and dirty plastic sandals, carrying buckets of our shower water for the day on their heads. The water in the buckets is pumped up into the tank on the roof, from which it flows down into the faucets for us to use. But the water that comes out of the faucets is not usable even for cooking: there is a separate bucket in the kitchen filled with water for boiling. I've read somewhere that you need to brush your teeth with bottled water, and that's what I intend to do.

At ten to nine in the morning, Olli tells me that the power usually goes off at nine, to charge my phone and take a shower now, before the hot water runs out. I rush into the bathroom, as instructed, and then try to read my e-mail, but Olli's dongle only works intermittently, and eventually I give up. As the local saying has it, this is Africa.

A "house girl" named Mama Junis arrives at the house. I notice that Flotea leaves the leftover *mchanyato* stew pot on the table overnight, and Mama Junis takes it with her in the morning. She cleans and does laundry and keeps Flotea company—Flotea is often home alone with Michell during the day. Mama Junis lives next door in much more primitive conditions: her clay house has a dirt floor and no water or electricity, so perhaps it's nice to spend her day in a house where occasionally you can flop down on the sofa to watch TV. Besides, as all the neighbors know, you can charge your phone here. Everyone in the village seems to have a phone but no electricity, nor necessarily money to buy talk minutes. Mama Junis is cheerful and lively in Flotea's company, but never once smiles at me. I wonder whether I'm just another irritating rich white person.

In the afternoon Olli and I head into Arusha to run errands. There is, in fact, a restaurant right in front of our house—actually a scrap-iron shack with a grill out front—and a kiosk-type stand where you can buy bottles of water and bags of chips. On the potholed road Olli lives on, there's a meat stand where, to my horror, Olli plans to buy ingredients for dinner: from the ceiling of the open-air hut hang assorted slabs of meat, with no refrigeration. At the next stall Olli buys talk minutes for his prepaid phone. He doesn't even get out of his car, just calls out to the vendor, who sends a little girl over to the car window with the goods. It's Sunday, which means there aren't a lot of people out and about. At Moshono Stand in one corner of the village, moped taxis wait for passengers. On the muddy road to Olli's place, everyone is dressed in their Sunday best. I see colorful Tanzanian costumes, complexly knotted head-kerchiefs, and suits on men: it's important for the people here to be stylish in public, even if they have no money.

The traffic today is light; Olli tells me there are usually nightmarish traffic jams. Arusha used to be a tiny village, but over the last few years it has exploded into a population center with a million and a half inhabitants—and traffic arrangements haven't kept up with the growth. The road into the center is lined with jacarandas and African tulip trees, whose blossoms glow orangish-red. En route we pass a restaurant where Olli tells me he and Flotea will sometimes buy a goat leg as takeout; and then a bell tower, Africa's midpoint, equidistant from Cairo and Cape Town. Arusha is chaotic: I have no desire to be out walking along the street. We buy food at a supermarket, where European-style products are obscenely expensive, and avocados at a roadside stand, where Olli dickers in Swahili. (I can't get over how disproportionate prices are: a manual car wash inside and out costs 6,000 shillings, or less than three euros, but then some things, like baby diapers, are so insanely expensive that most locals can't afford them.) We agree that I'll eat with the family while I'm visiting and then at some point Olli will bill me for food, transport, and miscellany. Then we drive to the lot where Olli is building his own house—the one they're living in now is a rental. The rooms are nearly finished on the inside, but Olli says he can't afford to finish the external walls. They plan to move in June. I don't know whether I'll still be here then, but Olli says he has arranged other lodgings for me if I am.

Olli and Flotea are both incredibly friendly and hospitable, and Michell is, of course, cute enough to eat—though she's still quite shy. Flotea, who is thirty-six, belongs to the Chagga tribe and grew up in Kilimanjaro; her father was once the director of the Kilimanjaro National Park. She is tall, calm, and mild, and doesn't say much, but smiles as if you and she are sharing a secret. Olli, on the other hand, is this incredible information center—facts come pouring out of him at such a mind-boggling pace that there's no way I can process it all. Over the last twenty-four hours I've heard just about everything one could possibly want or need to know about Tanzanian traffic culture, national characteristics, child-rearing, house construction, drilled wells, the water supply system, explosive population growth (the worst problem in these parts), the dysfunctionality of the postal system (it's a miracle that he got my Sei Shōnagon book), the importance of telephones (nothing here is more important than keeping in contact with friends and relatives), Tanzania's stunning nature and nature reserves, Africa as a canary in the climate-change coal mine (in a very short time weather conditions and rainfall have changed dramatically, and frighteningly), and of course his own personal history. Olli is happy to share his many difficulties with me. He is most stressed out about his house-building project, which with all its setbacks, communication difficulties, and struggles with cultural differences sounds, to put it mildly, like a nightmare.

As we drive around Arusha, I keep feeling the impulse to snap photos, but for some reason it doesn't seem right. So instead I log the photos I would have liked to take in my notebook:

The reddish-brown clay roads.

The banana trees, their verdant freshness, their lush green foliage.

The motley rows of corrugated-iron shacks: stores, bars.

The clay houses, the half-built houses. Concrete walls around the skeletal house frames.

The clotheslines with laundry hanging on them.

The fires burning in backyards.

The trash, piles of trash everywhere.

The children peeking out from behind houses.

The men sitting behind Singer sewing machines outside the market.

The nooks and crannies of the market, with fruit stalls, spice mountains, tilapias, gigantic Nile perch, dried fish in imaginative shapes, woven baskets, chemical canisters sold to carry water in.

Traffic cops with nameplates on their chests saying LIVINGSTONE.

The men in car repair shops.

Herds of goats in the street.

Men riding mopeds with mountains of egg cartons strapped to their backs.

Women walking barefoot through mud and sludge.

White men in their large SUVs.

The mamas sitting in front of corrugated-iron bars.

Beautiful young girls with brown teeth.

In the evening the power goes out and we sit in the dark house with flashlights. We eat the stew Flotea fixed from the meat Olli and I bought at the village stall. It's tasty. In the dark kitchen Flotea keeps a battery-powered radio switched on, singing along with the music. Olli cracks open a Serengeti beer with a picture of a leopard on its label. Michell bounces to and fro while I sit writing at top speed, jotting down words like *takeout goat leg*. The mood is wonderfully homey—what on earth was I afraid of?

Oh, right: malaria. The instant dusk begins to settle in, I start to see mosquitoes in the house; and despite the antimalarial medication I can't help obsessing about all the horrors they bring. My eyes scan the mosquitoes hysterically, since I am generally their number-one favorite, and it stands to reason that they'll be all over me here as well. And so at exactly 6 p.m., as the dark descends, I am swathed in the outfit recommended in the guidebooks, white clothing with long sleeves and long trouser legs. To that outfit I've added long white compression socks to the knees, and have sprayed myself with my evening perfume, namely Off! It doesn't matter that the sweat runs down my spine. Olli, of course, is in shorts, as usual. I just hope he doesn't notice my strange garb.

As I climb into bed I notice that a lone mosquito has managed to infiltrate the mosquito netting over my bed. And of course there is absolutely no way I'll be able to fall asleep without tracking it down and slaughtering it. It doesn't help one bit that Olli has explained that the mosquitoes that carry malaria *look* different from regular ones—that their attack position is *quite different*. How the hell am I going to know which kind is zeroing in on me? And wouldn't it be too late then anyway? I thrash around inside my mosquito net with my headlamp, my whole body wrapped in a thin film of sweat, but the bloodthirsty devil will not show itself. In the end I can no longer stay awake hoping to ambush the theoretical mosquito. I sleep like a log.

[KAREN WRITES]

January 20, 1914. My own little Mother -- I am sending this by runner -- so you get an idea of this great new life -- I am in bed, not on account of illness but of night hunting, in a little log cabin -- and all around on every side the most magnificent and wonderful scenery you can imagine, huge distant blue mountains, and the vast grassy plains before them covered with zebras and gazelles, and at night I can hear lions roaring like the thunder of guns in the darkness. -- Out here it is not too hot at all, the air is so soft and lovely, and one feels so light and free and happy.

April 1, 1914. Dearest Aunt Bess -- When I observe the various races here I feel that the superiority of the white race is an illusion. -- We have 1,200 young men on the farm here, who live ten or twelve to a wretched little grass hut, and I have never seen an angry face or heard quarreling, but everything is always done with a song and a smile -- I go riding almost every day in the Masai Reserve and often try to talk to the tall, handsome Masai.

July 14, 1914. My own beloved Mother -- We have had an absolutely marvelous time, I have never in my life enjoyed myself more. -- It was a tremendously successful safari -- I shot one lion and one big leopard. Bror has taught me to shoot and says that I shoot well. . . .

December 3, 1914. Dearest Mother -- I am very busy training a completely ignorant cook. As I can't cook myself, and it has to be carried on in Swahili, it is hardly easy -- My cook and I can now make perfect puff pastry of different types, custard flans, meringues, pancakes, layer cakes, various kinds of soufflé, cream horns, apple cake, chocolate pudding, cream puffs—and he is also good at all kinds of soup, bakes good bread and scones. . . .

When in January 1914 Karen arrived at her new home, a small brick bungalow a dozen miles from Nairobi, all of the plantation's twelve hundred African workers were there to greet her. Off in the distance loomed the Ngong Hills like the blue crest of a wave, and around them the Swedo-African Coffee Company now owned 1,800 hectares of land. In the first photograph she sent to Europe, Karen poses all in white: a long white skirt, a white blouse, white heels, long white stockings, and a white floppy hat. In the photo Karen is the only one smiling. All eight African servants stare solemnly into the camera.

It seemed to Karen as if she had "come to a quiet country." Back then Nairobi was a primitive, gray, decrepit little town full of corrugated iron, but the high plains were a paradise. The terrain was a dry-yellow savanna; the undulating hills were dotted with dark-green coffee plants. The wildlife in the region was abundant: flamingos nested in the mountain lakes; buffalo, rhinos, and eland antelopes grazed on the hills; elephants, giraffes, and monkeys lived in the forests; and large herds of zebras, wildebeests, gazelles, and large cats lived in the savannas. Yes: a paradise. The air in the high plains was so pure and clear that whites reportedly experienced such a powerful euphoria that they were not quite responsible for their actions. The settlers indulged so freely in affairs of passion that women were asked in steamship bars whether they were married or lived in British East Africa.

On the brief honeymoon Karen and Bror spent on the savanna, staying in a primitive log cabin (game was plentiful; the lions roared through the night; only the flies and the fleas were an irritation), Karen felt that her new life was a splendid thing. "Here I am where I ought to be," she wrote. Here she found the wide-open spaces, the freedom, and the passion of which she had dreamed in Denmark.

But in February, one month after her arrival, Karen contracted malaria, and spent weeks in bed, nauseated and depressed. Bror was out on safari, or in Nairobi in the club favored by settlers, the Muthaiga, "taking care of business," and Karen wrote home that "it's a little tedious as Bror is out a lot." In fact, Karen was bedridden all spring. Whenever she felt a bit better, she planned a large-scale remodeling of the house (it was badly built and the porch was impractically situated on the sunny side of the house), went for rides, participated in the planting of coffee bushes (it would be three to five years before they would begin to produce enough to harvest), and taught her Somali cook how to prepare food. She wrote to her mother in Denmark, asking her to send an 1830 cookbook, since that would roughly match the equipment she had at hand.

When her doctor prescribed a change of climate, she and Bror went off on a monthlong hunting safari on the Maasai reserve. They took along three mule-pulled wagons and nine servants: it was easier to travel with such a small entourage. The safari was a memorable one. Karen had never slept in a tent before, or sat in a *boma*—a protective enclosure built of thornbushes—or even held a rifle in her hands, let alone shot game for meals. Bror taught Karen to shoot, and they ate antelope they had killed for dinner. Karen loved hunting—was positively enraptured by it. On their trip they shot six big lions, four leopards, a cheetah, and massive quantities of elands, impalas, wildebeests, dik-diks, zebras, wild boars, jackals, and marabou storks. They posed for countless photographs with their prey, and the high point of the safari for Karen was encountering a lion for the first time and watching the life fade from that noble creature's eyes.

When they returned from the safari, the First World War had begun. Bror rode his bicycle to Nairobi to join the army, and Karen moved to safety in the Kijabe mountain station, occasionally driving supply caravans through the Maasai reserve. Then she returned to Ngong to oversee the plantation.

By the end of the year Karen was still ill. Eventually it became clear that what she'd been fighting wasn't malaria after all. Bror had given her syphilis.

*

[KAREN WRITES]

Paris, May 28, 1915. My own dear little Mother, do not be the slightest bit worried. All is well. – – I am here in Paris on my way to London to talk to a specialist in tropical diseases there. I have actually been rather ill again and the doctor in Nairobi prescribed a change of air at home for me. – – It seems that in London they give some kind of injections for malaria that cure you completely. . . .

Karen lied to her mother. The syphilis diagnosis had been made early in the year, and according to the doctor in Nairobi it was fierce as a sailor's. Apparently Bror had had numerous affairs in Nairobi. Once this was revealed, Karen, in despair, swallowed too many sleeping pills and almost died. "There are two things you can do in such a situation," she wrote later: "shoot the man, or accept it." She accepted it.

And so, in the spring of 1915, Karen traveled to Paris for a cure. According to the doctors, she would need a lengthy and painful course of mercury and arsenic, and even then there was no guarantee she would ever fully recover. Because of the war Karen couldn't remain alone in Paris, so she traveled to Denmark, where she spent three months in the hospital, discreetly installed in the general ward. "Now I've endured that too," she said later, "and now I'm even nearer to experiencing really great things."

I would add to the tally of Karen's exemplary bravery:

9) Suffering malaria and syphilis in Africa, a hundred years ago.

10) Traveling alone into the very heart of war-torn Europe to obtain treatment.

11) Ingesting mercury and arsenic as medicaments. Withstanding their toxicity.

12) Accepting the situation.

13) Returning to Africa and Bror.

*

[KAREN WRITES]

March 24, 1917. My dear beloved Mother, this is my first letter from [our new house], we have now moved in and I am extremely glad to be here—despite living in a temporary state of chaos. The workmen have not done a thing since I gave them their orders two months ago – – but it is still lovely to be here.

March 27, 1918. Dear Ea – – We are experiencing a drought here that exceeds anything one can imagine at home. The whole country will perish if it goes on much longer – – [We are short of everything], butter, milk, cream, vegetables and eggs – – All the plants are withering, the plains are on fire every day and are completely black and charred, and when one drives to Nairobi, the town seems to be enveloped in a vast conflagration—an impression caused by the dust that hangs over it day and night—with the wind blowing from the Somali town and the bazaar, you feel that plague and cholera germs are whirling merrily around. There is a hitherto unknown mortality rate among small white children in Nairobi, and this scorching hot, perpetually drying wind gets on adults' nerves. . . .

When Karen returned to Africa in January 1917, after her eighteen-month sojourn in Europe, the coffee plantation should have been ready to produce its first harvest—but the seasonally unusual heavy rains and the long drought that followed whittled the harvest down to almost nothing. What was now called the Karen Coffee Company, financed by Karen's maternal uncle Aage Westenholz, was in the red, and Karen and Bror were now in dire financial straits. Karen wrote to her relatives in Denmark to ask for a pay raise: everything was so expensive that they spent everything they had on living, and "we constantly have to entertain guests as well." The following year's harvest was catastrophic as well: the drought continued, Africans starved, and starvation led to the plague, the Spanish influenza, and smallpox; then followed a strangely frigid and humid drought. The farm was not producing a penny, and it was racked with shortages. Nor was this a brief or unusual state of affairs. Though Karen didn't know it yet, this was the beginning of years of endless financial straits and floods of desperate letters she would send to Denmark begging for additional funding, for the entire period she was in East Africa, until the coffee plantation finally went belly-up for good in 1931. It would never produce properly. Bror had created it in a climate that was too cold and too dry for coffee.

Even so, Karen and Bror moved into a new, larger house, which they called Mbogani. There Karen founded the "oasis of civilization" of which she had dreamed since leaving Denmark. Of course, it wasn't a perfect oasis. The look was right, complete with flower-patterned sofas, Gustavian-style dressing tables, lace-lined lampshades, and crystal carafes; but according to Karen, the reality was more like eighteenth-century Denmark: the roads to Nairobi were impassable in the rain; they had to hunt to put food on the table; all entertainments had to be improvised; and good books and stimulating conversation were scarce as hens' teeth.

In 1917, Karen learned to drive a car, and would later recommend that all women acquire this skill. She desperately missed books, music, and art, and feared that in their absence she was descending into idiocy. She dreamed of painting, of studying art, and would occasionally paint the sere colors and bright light of the high plains, or portraits of the Africans (she complained that the locals were terrible models, and once while painting a young Gĩkũyũ she had to threaten him with a pistol during the entire session to make him sit still). When Bror was away—and that was often—Karen was lonely, depressed, and homesick. She could lie in bed for a week on end—but then would dissemble cheerfully to her mother that she had only suffered a mild heatstroke. She also wrote to her mother that she had not yet given up hope of having a child—indeed, that she was certain it would still happen. One day their neighbor, Sjögren, gave her a gun, and she burned with a desire to go out hunting. For lack of a better outlet, she picked off doves in the yard ("yesterday afternoon I shot twenty-one"). Another day Bror shot a fifteen-foot python; Karen made plans to send the snakeskin to Hellstern in Paris to have shoes made out of it. She hung out with Somalis, and wrote to her family that all her best friends were Muslims, and that her Somali servant and right-hand man Farah was "truly an angel," so wise and sensitive. (In fact, Karen had read so much about that fascinating religion that Bror had "refused to hear anything about Mohammed between twelve and four.") Karen didn't get along with the other European settlers very well; she hated how smugly superior they felt to the Africans. She felt a spiritual kinship with her "black brothers," and over the years they became increasingly important to her. She began to plan the founding of a school for the plantation's children.

Every Sunday Karen sat down at her desk and wrote a long letter to her mother, or her brother Thomas, or her sister or Aunt Bess, who received long reflections on the day's burning issues concerning marriage, sexual morality, contraception, and the women's movement. ("Dear Aunt Bess," Karen wrote once, "what a frightful idea of yours, to publish my letters. If I knew this was going to happen, it would be impossible for me to write.")

And when after two years of drought and gnawing suffering the rains finally commenced, Karen wrote: "This is a paradise on earth. I have a feeling that wherever I may be in the future, I will be wondering whether there is rain at Ngong."

Glossary

Asante sana. Thank you.
Karibu. (You're) welcome.
Maji. Water.
Ndizi. Banana.
Nyama. Meat.
Samahani. Sorry.
Usiku mwema. Good night.
Na wewe pia. Same to you.

Peaceful life.
I had planned to interview Flotea about all sorts of things relating to a woman's life, her dreams and female role models, but I find that it's not so simple. First there's the language barrier—I don't understand everything she says in her Swahili-accented English—but it also becomes very clear that I don't know how to ask the right questions. My own point of view suddenly seems wildly irrelevant (no one here has ever heard of someone named Karen Blixen), and many of my problems are patently first-world problems. I'm still embarrassed to think of the panic I'd felt when Olli responded to my e-mail question about what to bring for them by suggesting that I bring Flotea some perfume. *Some perfume!* I'd replied that I would *never* buy perfume for another woman. It's such an intimate choice, such an expression of a woman's identity, that I had searched for just the right perfume *for myself* for the last ten years—and still hadn't found it. Absurd. I don't know whether Flotea liked the scent that I ended up bringing her, but I quickly realized that if a woman here manages to get her hands on a perfume that costs twice her monthly salary, her most pressing concern will not be how well it expresses her identity.

I do find out a few things, though. One is that Flotea would like to do something else with her life than to be a housewife. But it's almost impossible for a woman to get a decent job here without connections or sexual favors. Once Flotea had applied for office work at a large international organization, but she would have had to discuss the hire first with the boss "over dinner." Many women, I heard, would very much like to start their own businesses, and Flotea too dreams about opening a children's clothing store; but a woman often has to agree to become the boss's lover in order to feed her children. I ask about marriage, male-female relations (apparently, earlier many husbands treated their wives extremely badly), polygamy (for example, men in the Arusha tribe traditionally take three wives, who all live in the same compound), and divorce statistics. Flotea believes that once you marry, you stay married, even if you fall in love with someone else. True, Flotea doesn't really seem to consider falling in love to be all that important in life. More important to her is a "peaceful life": one's own money and freedom.

Mzungu.

Flotea and I go out to buy groceries from a village woman who has set up tables with fruit and vegetables for sale in front of her house. The children stare at me curiously and wave at me as we leave: "Bye-bye, *mzungu* (white person)." This is something I have to get used to: when Olli and I ride around in his car, every single passerby points at us and shouts, "*Mzungu, mzungu,*" as if warning the others of an approaching danger. I can't always tell whether the name-calling is good-natured curiosity or somehow hostile. The villagers call Olli "Papa Michell," and Flotea is "Mama Michell": it is polite to use the name of the family's oldest child in addressing those who have been so lucky as to have a child.

Michell herself has begun to recover from her *mzungu*-shock. When I arrived, she clung to the walls looking stunned, her lips zipped; but now, with the help of the Moomin book I brought, we've made friends. We also have the same diet: for breakfast I follow my fried eggs and sausage with a bowl of Michell's porridge, which Flotea boils every morning.

Kanga.

Flotea gives me a beautiful *kanga*, a square of cotton fabric with an orange flower pattern on a blue background. *Kangas* come in packages of two, one to wear as a skirt, the other to tie around oneself for a top—which latter is, in fact, rather cumbersome in everyday use. Mama Junis often wears a short-sleeved shirt with her *kanga*-skirt; Flotea typically wears a sweater, since it's so cold (only 70 degrees Fahrenheit!). A *kanga* always has writing on it, for example a proverb, with which one can send a message to the neighbors or one's husband. My *kanga* says: "*Mungu hamtupi mja wake,*" God's blessing. I need one that says: "Not for mosquitoes," or "Lion sighting desired." Or "Fortyish woman seeks meaning of life."

Cold chain.

On a shopping trip we pass the butcher's hut on the village road, with its thick cuts of meat, and Flotea points out that this is where she buys meat. Fortunately, I already knew that. I try to explain that we don't do things this way in Finland—that meat is sold in refrigerated sterile portions. I want to tell her about what we Finns call the *kylmäketju*, but at the moment I can't think of the English term for that. Later I remember it's the "cold chain."

Olli later tells me that on tent safaris the meat purchased for the trip is transported for days in the car without refrigeration, and no one gets sick. I wonder how this is possible, and consider the possibility that the whole cold chain is just Western overprotectiveness.

Mtori.

I hang out in the kitchen, wearing my *kanga*, watching as Flotea fixes *mtori* stew for lunch. It's a traditional dish of the Chagga tribe. It has meat, bananas, and carrots in it, and it is delicious. I'm told *mtori* is a traditional fattening-up food for women who have recently given birth, to help them produce milk. When a Chagga woman gives birth, she has to eat nothing but pot after pot of *mtori*, for three whole months. During that time the woman never leaves home; and when she does finally step outside the home at the end of her three months, she had better be impressively fat, or everyone will think her husband isn't taking good care of her, or—most shameful of all—has no money. To celebrate the coming-out event, the new mother's female relatives and friends throw a baby party. The husband is not invited, but he has to procure massive quantities of food and beer, which the old women guzzle down by the bottle. When Michell was born, tradition dictated that Olli had to slaughter a goat with his own hands. In the olden days the new mother was given milk and cow ghee, used in cooking—but nowadays people bring money in small bills. Each guest throws the bills in the air, so that the whole house is covered with bills.

I'm told that many women would prefer to have just one or two children, but poor people often have seven or eight. Abortion is illegal, but it's still performed, in secret, using traditional medications. The procedure is painful and may cause extended illness, but nearly every woman has experienced it, many of them numerous times.

Kachumbari.

One day Flotea makes *kachumbari*, a salad made fiery with lots of vinegar, containing cucumber, avocado, tomato, carrot, and spicy *pili-pili*, and, to go with it, homemade french fries. I remember the stern warnings I had read in travel guides saying under no circumstances should you eat vegetables or salads uncooked—and I eat it anyway. *Kachumbari* is heavenly. It becomes my favorite local food.

Another day Flotea fixes *ugali*, a firm cornmeal porridge that you cut with a knife and eat with your fingers, dipping it in a meat gravy. Olli hates *ugali*, but I think it too is delicious. It occurs to me that Flotea has probably decided to cycle through all the prime Tanzanian culinary experiences.

One day at dusk we head off to buy the takeout goat leg that I've been lusting after. A little shack on the corner of the Arusha road has grilled goat legs lined up. We choose one, and the cook slices it and packs it with chili sauce and toasted banana. At home we wolf down the delicacies off a common plate.

WhatsApp.

Flotea and I become friends on Facebook. Flotea is amazed that I don't have WhatsApp. She says it would be nice to send each other photos that way. It's true, I don't have it—unlike Flotea, I don't own a smartphone—and I've never even heard of the app. I tell her that in Finland we don't have WhatsApp (turns out we do, I'm just ignorant), so it must be some African thing.

I ask Flotea for some more Swahili vocabulary and write the most important words and phrases down in my notebook. *Asante sana*, thanks. *Karibu,* welcome, or you're welcome. *Usiku mwema*, good night. *Lala salama*, sweet dreams.

As I'm getting ready for bed I notice that Flotea has sent me a DM through Facebook: Lala salama, Mia.

Urban Maasai.

One afternoon Olli and I eat at a lunchroom favored by the locals in Arusha. Lollygagging at the tables are Maasai men decked out in red-checked *shuka* fabric and tire-tread sandals. If the impression of Maasai that I've gotten from Karen's descriptions is noble, beautiful, and brave, these urban Maasai are a whole different story. Their eyes are dull, their sandals down-at-heel, the jackets they've thrown on over their red-checked capes ragged and dirty. They have come into Arusha to sell tanzanite, the local gemstone, to tourists. They are a sad sight—and I wonder whether this is the fate of all nomadic tribes driven off their traditional lands. Sitting there at our plastic table, I spoon in my rice pilaf quickly and leave the bony piece of meat uneaten.

Hair salon.

When I arrived, Flotea had a pretty braided hairdo, but one day Mama Junis sits on the steps undoing her braids so Flotea can go get her hair treated. It's very expensive to get your hair done up in a braid do in a hair salon, and it takes all day. After you have it done, you can't wash your own hair yourself; you have to go to the salon to have it washed. Same thing with straightened hair: if you wash it yourself, it frizzes up and is ruined. So women here go to the hair salon often.

We leave for the salon in the late afternoon. Flotea changes out of her home wear—her *kanga*—into tight black jeans, a pretty shirt, green ballerina slippers, and a big gold watch and earrings, and spritzes herself with a little of the perfume I brought. Then we walk all the way to Moshono village and continue from there along the highway to Arusha. It's glorious to walk on the red sand road in the calm and mild evening sun surrounded by all that green. The schoolchildren stare at me and some shout "Good morning," though they mean "evening." On the road we meet school buses, cows, goats, chickens, mopeds coming the other way.

The hair salon is on the road to Arusha. A girl hanging out in the doorway points at me, shouts, "*Mzungu,*" and doubles over with laughter. They probably don't see whites in these hair salons, ever. Compared with its surroundings, the salon is truly fancy and trendy: the floor is shiny, and the hairdressers have unbelievably long neon-colored gel nails on their toes. Flotea points to the jar with the goo she wants in her hair: "Hair mayonnaise, best treatment for hair," she explains. I stand in the doorway looking out at the people walking by: from the salon I have a direct view of Mount Meru, which is shrouded with a thin cloud layer. Along the road outside pass yellow school buses, children in green school uniforms, working men, and mamas with their burdens—some with wide plastic tubs on their heads, some carrying huge bunches of bananas. I try to photograph the schoolchildren, but they all spot my white face from afar, like some kind of beacon, and start pointing and laughing, and I can't bring myself to snap the pictures. You really can't just come here as a tourist and expect to be an outside observer. Here you're always the center of attention.

An orange-haired stylist sits weaving a mass of loose hairs into thin braids and tying them to a string anchored on the arms of the customer's chair. A young man with booze on his breath has come in to charge his phone; he dozes in another chair. A boom box blares Dolly Parton, Rihanna, and Tracy Chapman. Flotea gets mayonnaise in her hair, which is then dried straight with some kind of steam dryer. It's five thirty; dusk approaches.

It's pitch-black dark when we finally head home, groping our way down the potholed road. We use the lights of passing cars and mopeds to guide our way, but once I nearly crash into an oncoming cow. It's dark brown, and it has no lights.

Mr. Hauli.

One day Olli and I head into Arusha to run errands, and find ourselves in the middle of absurd events that seem to come straight out of a *No. 1 Ladies' Detective Agency* novel. We're looking for a certain Mr. Hauli, whom Olli paid weeks ago to run electricity to the construction site—but still there's no electricity. Now it turns out that the man does not even work for the Tanzanian state electric company. His business is to dress up in Tanesco coveralls and impersonate a representative of the electric company, and, once he's been paid, to do absolutely nothing. After we've first spent an eternity waiting in line at the electric company, then called in the general contractor, then collected him and two more guys in the Land Rover and set off in search of Mr. Hauli (word is he's a dangerous man who is known for his underhanded dealings, so we need backup); having found him at long last in his house at the end of a labyrinth of potholed alleys (in the muddy yard there are piles of trash, an open fire in a pit, and ragged laundry hanging on a line; in the crack that the door is open stand two kids and a wife in a *kanga* and a fancy braid do), having then hauled our prey back to the electric company (three big men bouncing about in the Land Rover's cargo area), having witnessed Mr. Hauli's casual attempt to sneak away out of the electric company's yard and then listened to his promise to come to the office the next morning at nine to return the money; but then having driven back to the electric company the next morning and waited two hours for Mr. Hauli (every time he answers the phone he insists he's "en route"), and having experienced the pleasant surprise of him actually showing up with the electric company papers but without the money, which he goes to "get at the bank" but never returns, I begin to realize what Olli meant when he said that he spends all his time and energy dealing with practical matters.

A week later the electricity still hasn't been hooked up, the workers have vanished, and the general contractor is no longer answering his phone. Olli rages and tears his hair, saying the house will never be finished—at least not by the June moving day.

SPF 50.

It's pouring rain. It's been raining nonstop all week, and it's starting to feel damp even indoors: the clothes in the closet, the pages of books. Olli shows me a leather belt he found in his drawer, blanketed with mold. The damp and the sun here gradually eat everything, and the termites and pharaoh ants handle the rest. Mama Junis sweeps the floors and airs out the rooms as much as she can in an effort to prevent that.

Despite the rain, I'm so afraid of the equatorial sun that I smear myself every morning with the highest possible SPF sunblock. After a week in Africa I am just as pale as when I arrived. I'm afraid that the savanna, when I finally get to it, will burn me to a crisp.

Supu.

One afternoon Olli suggests that we go eat a bowl of *supu* nearby. We walk a little way down a muddy path and arrive at a shack where some men have a boiling cauldron of broth out front. In the hut's window-hole hang fly-covered chunks of meat, and one man fishes in the cauldron and picks out a cooked piece for me. The cut-up meat is placed in a small aluminum bowl, with meat broth in another bowl. The meal costs 1,500 shillings, or around sixty-five cents. The men stare curiously and urge us to go inside and sit down. The tiny room is black with flies, and I sit down at a filthy table to work my spoon with one hand and shoo flies with the other. (Olli says that the hand movement for shooing flies has become such an integral part of old people's gestural language that they automatically wave one hand around whenever they eat, even if they're in a fancy restaurant.) It occurs to me that if I'd been alone, I would have starved to death before daring to eat in a place like this.

Ten-day magic.

When you travel, everything is always strange and scary at first—the food, the huts, the people, the animals, the smells, the sounds. But then at some point you begin to adjust, your organism says *Okay, fine*, your eyes open, and you begin to see past the strangeness. That's why I want to stay on this trip for a long time. I want to wait till I start *seeing*.

That usually happens around the tenth day.

We're not there yet.

Safari for one.

Olli tells me about the luxury-tent safaris he's led, and they sound insanely wonderful. I had hoped to visit a national park with him, but it turns out that the house-building project makes it impossible for him to go anywhere. Olli also warns me off the backpackers' safaris, saying that I would lose my temper with one of those groups before I could blink an eye. The absurd truth begins to dawn on me: I'm going to have to go on a safari for one. Or, well, for two: myself and a guide.

That means several scary things: It'll be 1) expensive, and 2) a social challenge for an introvert like me, not being able to hide in a group. In addition, 3) the guide will most likely be a man. I'll be spending a couple of weeks on the savanna alone with a man I don't know. The gears start turning in my head. Could that mean problems?

Olli doesn't understand the question.

The proposed itinerary for my safari for one includes twelve days in national parks, two nights in each place: Arusha National Park; Lake Manyara; Seronera, Lobo, and Ndutu in Serengeti National Park; and finally the Tarangire ecosystem. The Ngorongoro Crater has been dropped from this itinerary, because the daily entrance fee per car is $250, exorbitant for a single passenger. On the agenda on safari days are morning and evening drives through the nature parks. Sounds good, but I have to admit I'm a bit disappointed when I realize that I won't be taking a tent safari—and therefore not having the authentic Karen Blixen safari experience—because that would be way too expensive to arrange for one. Instead I'll be staying in nature park lodges, hotel-like inns. Darn it, I really wanted to sleep in tents!

Olli surprises me by saying that he went on his first safari when he was almost forty. Until then he had done other jobs with his PhD in biology and environmental science; but when he won the award for the best nonfiction book in Finland for his book on butterflies, he decided to make a childhood dream come true by going on safari—and he got hooked. Nowadays he knows the Tanzanian nature parks like the backs of his hands, has written numerous books about them, leads safaris to them, and, at long last, a few years ago, moved to Tanzania to live. But Olli spent his very first night in Africa in a tent at the Tarangire Safari Lodge—and apparently was scared to death.

We drive to Arusha to talk to Andrew, Olli's business partner, about my safari, and it turns out that it will cost an arm and a leg, much more than I had budgeted. But, dammit, what else am I going to do? This is what I came for!

That evening I lie in bed fretting about money matters and then comfort myself by eating Flotea's *ndizi rosti*, roasted and salted banana (heavenly). I think about Karen writing that *there is something about safari life that makes you forget all your sorrows*, and how on the savanna *one feels the whole time as if one had drunk half a bottle of champagne*. Maybe, drunk on champagne, I would forget how much that magic was costing me?

Washing machine.

For the safari I'll need clean clothes, so we start doing laundry by hand. The washing machine is out for the count—and anyway, Flotea doesn't trust that gizmo to get the clothes clean. Out in the yard Flotea pours a little cold water and laundry detergent at the bottom of three tubs, and we start rubbing and rinsing. It takes us three hours, after which my hands are red, stinging, and blistered, and my back and shoulders are knotted up from squatting on the ground. I realize that Westerners would never get anything done if they had to do all their laundry like this. It may also be that globally laundry is the greatest enslaver of girls. Who would have time to go to school if the whole family's laundry has to be washed by hand?

Crazy.

Flotea and Olli's friend Eutropia has invited us over for dinner, so we get ourselves gussied up in our Sunday best and head out the door. Eutropia's half-built house sits on a mountain slope with a to-die-for view. We drive as far up the bumpy village roads as we can, and then climb up the last steep cart path on foot, past simple clay huts with yards full of ragged children, stray dogs, and clothes drying on the line.

Eutropia used to work in the lodge of a nature park, but has since opened an interior decorating supply shop and is building her house. The living room looks great, with sofas and cowhide-covered rattan tables, but there's no electricity or plumbing yet in the house, or, say, a refrigerator, and the room that seems to serve as a makeshift kitchen is full of huge water tubs. Also living in the house are Eutropia's sister and mother, and the mother, an old hard-of-hearing Chagga woman, sits silent on a sofa dressed to the nines: along with a colorful *kanga* she is wearing an orange jacket with fringes and a flower-pattern shawl. Eutropia has fixed us an *mchanyato* stew and offers us beer; she and her family have already eaten. The view of the valley out the windows is stupendous, and the stereo—powered by solar panels—blares Patsy Cline's "Crazy."

We drive home through villages bathed in late-afternoon sun, dodging chickens and goats on the muddy potholed road. We decide to celebrate Mother's Day by stopping for a moment in the patio restaurant at the luxurious Meru Hotel. The contrast between the clay huts and the glass-walled hotel could not be more glaring. At the gate there's a security checkpoint, where the undercarriage of our car is checked with extendable mirrors. The hotel garden has a vast lawn surrounded by palm trees and a stylish restaurant with poolside bars. In the patio restaurant sit rich, well-dressed locals and whites, who relate the details of their safari experiences halfway around the world over Skype. By the pool someone still lies in his swim trunks with a drink in his hand. We order strawberry milkshakes and lychee juice, and the check comes to roughly what a salesperson in Eutropia's shop would earn in a week.

Minefield.

Yes, it has begun to dawn on me just how different are the realities in which people live here. There is the locals' life, and then there is the life of white people. There is the life of the poor and the life of the rich. There are chaotic cities, poor rural villages, and problems with poverty, hygiene, health, petty crime, corruption, and a lack of security. And there are the walled, gated, and security-checked areas for the rich, right in the middle of ordinary poverty. And then, way off somewhere else, there is the Nature Channel world, the world of untouched landscapes and wild animals, that dream Africa to which tourists are shepherded. Ordinary locals never see that world at all.

I also notice that it's not easy to situate myself on this map. Here all of a sudden I'm a "rich" white person (which I am certainly not in Finland) who draws everyone's attention wherever she goes—and not necessarily positive attention. I am annoyingly conscious, every single moment of my stay, of everything that distinguishes me from the locals: the color of my skin, my clothes, my wallet, my assumptions about hygiene, my safari dreams, my absurd Karen Blixen project. I'm interested in everything around me, I want to see everything and understand everything—but how can I? Even taking photographs doesn't feel right. How can I even begin to write any of this? How can I write about a middle-aged Finnish woman's arrival in Africa without descending into *exoticization*—when everything is exotic to me—or *the colonial gaze*? I can't help being white or coming from the Western world; and try as I might there's bound to be lots I can't understand about the local culture. But somehow I need to write about this, since I've set off on this journey. Over and over as I edit what I've written, I censor my phrasings—and then reinstate them. Can I use the word *black*? Can I write about the dishonest electrician, or is that racist? Should I pretend not to have noticed the poverty all around me, or not to have devoted a single moment to worrying about amoebas and dysentery? (Like the time when I couldn't eat the wonderful-looking popcorn-tasting roasted corn that Flotea bought from a roadside vendor, once I'd watched the old woman sitting there on the ground in the muddy yard sprinkle salt on the corn with her whole palm.) Am I allowed to look at everything through the eyes of an outsider, a foreigner, an alien? Will I be forgiven anything on the grounds that I at least *try* to understand?

When I wrote about Japan in my first book, none of these concerns even occurred to me. I just wrote whatever came to mind, without censoring anything, without worrying about political correctness. But now, writing about Africa, it feels like I'm walking in a minefield.

Most likely no matter how careful I am, I'll somehow manage to blow myself up anyway.

F.

We finally go to Andrew's office to nail down my safari plans. Behind the desk sit Andrew's two beautiful daughters, and I hand one of them a grip-lock plastic bag containing the complete contents of my Karen Blixen account. It's crazy, I know, but it seems I really am going to squander the money I had budgeted for two months' subsistence on a two-week trip.

Also in the office is my future guide and driver, a thirtysomething Chagga man with a friendly smile. I will, in other words, be spending twelve days and nights on the savanna with this Fazal, far from civilization, the Internet, and telephone signals.

It occurs to me that Karen's closest African companion, the man she spent eighteen years with on the farm, often just the two of them, was named Farah.

F: that has to be a good sign.

[KAREN WRITES]

April 6, 1918. Dearest Mother -- I went to a very enjoyable dinner yesterday at Muthaiga Club [in Nairobi] -- We were just four, the previous Governor's daughter and an unusually charming person, Denys Finch Hatton, whom I have always heard so much about but never met before. . . .

Karen met Denys Finch Hatton for the first time in April 1918, shortly before her thirty-third birthday. The thirty-two-year-old Denys was an aristocratic British big-game hunter who arranged safaris in East Africa for VIP guests, such as the British royal family. He was tall, thin, cultivated, and supposedly "impossibly handsome"—though frankly what I see in the photos is a rather ordinary-looking balding man. Perhaps he had a charisma that the photos didn't catch. When Denys and Karen next met, on a hunting trip a month later—the party bagged thirty antelopes, two jackals, and a leopard—Karen was hopelessly smitten. Denys came over for dinner and spent the night, and the next morning Karen drove him to Nairobi. "It is seldom that one meets someone one is immediately in sympathy with and gets along so well with. What a marvelous thing talent and intelligence is," Karen wrote to her family back in Denmark.

It seemed to Karen that she had finally met the man of her life, and as Bror sniped, she freely admitted that the only thing she cared about in this world any longer was meeting Finch Hatton again. Denys was the very embodiment of her ideal man, and she was happy, she said, to be finding a treasure like this "at her advanced age." Denys was self-confident, intelligent, and cultured, and he had excellent taste. He played Stravinsky on the gramophone and quoted Shakespeare, the Greek classics, and famous poets from memory. At the Muthaiga Club, anyone looking for a white hunter would be told: *You need the best, old sport; get Blixen, if you can, or Finch Hatton.* On his safaris Denys had the best cooks, ironed linens, crystal glasses, excellent wines, and, of course, a gramophone; and at dinner, which was served under lantern light precisely at seven thirty, one ate soup, freshly shot game, and bread baked that morning. (In 1928, when Denys arranged a safari for the Prince of Wales, they also stopped every afternoon at four for tea.) Denys also seems to have had a decent sense of humor. Once he flew from Africa to London just to hear a certain opera performance, then flew back the next morning without meeting a single relative. (Though in those days the flight to London took six days in each direction, so perhaps the story isn't quite true.) Another time a friend sent him a telegram from London to ask whether Denys knew so-and-so's address; and when the courier had finally, after traveling for weeks, delivered the message to the remote place where Denys was on safari, Denys sent the courier back with the reply: "Yes." He didn't care what others thought about him, and always did exactly what he wanted—and it went without saying that he wasn't the marrying type. But he was held in high esteem wherever he went. Even Bror was proud of his wife's "high-level" crush, and introduced Denys as "my good friend and my wife's lover." Denys was so precious to Karen that she hardly even mentioned him in her books. Some other sources boringly dismiss him as a "playboy."

In February 1919, Karen wrote to her mother ecstatically: "We had a shoot here on the Sunday after the races. . . . Finch-Hatton was ill with fever and stayed here, he is still here now, and I am delighted to have him. I don't think I have ever met such an intelligent person before, and one does appreciate that here. I must stop now as I am going out with Denys. There are big clouds promising more rain. . . ."

In August 1919, the Blixens—yes, they were still married—traveled to Europe to relax in postwar London and Paris. (The First World War had finally ended in November 1918.) They bought crystal glasses, drank champagne, had evening wear tailored and dress shoes made from the snakeskins they'd brought—since apparently it was impossible to get anything fashionable in Nairobi. "It's amazing how much clothes mean," Karen wrote. "Perhaps I value them too highly, but nothing—be it illness, poverty, loneliness, or other misfortunes—distresses me more than having nothing to wear."

In Denmark Karen was laid low by exhaustion, the kind that strikes a person when she no longer has to take responsibility for anything, and can just lie around eating her mother's food. Karen spent a whole year at Rungstedlund, getting more treatment for her syphilis, but also suffering the Spanish flu and blood poisoning. The future of the coffee farm hung in the balance, and Karen despaired. Bror traveled to Africa to see to affairs in March of 1920, among other things to borrow money for the plantation. Karen didn't return to Mombasa until New Year's 1921.

What she found when she arrived home was an abomination. Bror had kicked over the traces. All manner of people had been living in the house, and much had been destroyed. Bror had sold or pawned Karen's furniture and silver, used her porcelain and crystal glasses as targets for shooting practice, hosted all manner of orgies, and even hauled the dining room table and chairs out onto Ngong Hills for an exotic dinner. The plantation's financial state was also catastrophic. In the spring the company's CEO, Karen's uncle Aage Westenholz, arrived in Kenya with a mandate from the investors and relatives to sell the estate, which was hemorrhaging money. Karen, however, desperately wanted to continue, and in pleading her passionate case may have slightly exaggerated her own competence, claiming for example that she was the only one who knew how to fertilize the coffee plants or how to treat the tenant farmers' burns. In June 1921, therefore, it was agreed that Karen would begin running the plantation—with the condition that Bror, who had proved utterly irresponsible, could have nothing to with either the coffee farm itself or the Karen Coffee Company.

Bror vacated the farm for good. Karen's relatives urged her to get a divorce as well, but Karen didn't want that. Whyever not? Bror had cheated on her, infected her with syphilis, and devastated her assets—and Karen herself had fallen in love with Denys. But Bror had for years been her most intimate companion, and as a divorcée she would lose not only her social status and title as baroness but, paradoxically, her freedom to be with Denys. It was a terrible blow to her that in the end Bror wanted a divorce. Bror wanted to marry a certain "English lady" who wanted to "help him financially," and the divorce decree was handed down in January 1922. Karen was thirty-six. She had been married for eight years.

"These are difficult times for me, far, far more difficult than, for instance, when I was ill," Karen wrote. I do know, Karen, how hard it is to leave even a bad relationship. Even a difficult person becomes so close, your lives are so intimately and intricately woven together, like the root systems of trees, that it feels as if you are tearing your own self out of your life.

*

[KAREN WRITES]

January 1923. Dearest Mother – – I should like to give all young women two pieces of advice: to have her hair cut short and to learn to drive a car. These two things completely transform one's life. For centuries long hair has been a sort of slavery; suddenly one feels freer than words can express, with a short mane that can be tidied in a moment and that the wind can blow through. And as nobody wears corsets out here you can really move as a man's equal. If it suited me I would wear trousers here, "shorts" as so many ladies do; but alas, alas, I do not have the legs—or the moral courage—for that. . . .

April 1, 1923. Dearest Mother – – There is absolutely no reason for you to be sorry for me because I'm alone. To begin with I'm not *alone – – My situation here, with my boys and dogs and white people, has grown up around me naturally and been created by myself; it suits me and I am happy in it. . . . Nor should you think that I am in need of "peace and quiet," as you say – – You must never feel sorry for me about such things as loneliness or illness; I consider them of no account.*

May 28, 1923. My dearest Mother – – You would all laugh at me if you saw me in my wet weather outfit—at present I nearly always wear long khaki trousers and a kind of blouse reaching to the knee, and bare legs and clogs; now my hair is short I fancy myself as Tolstoy, without the beard. I have also taught myself to plow, so that I did not need to feel inferior to Tolstoy in a photograph. . . .

July 22, 1923. Dearest Mother – – I am writing with a little tame bushbuck, "Lulu," lying under my desk; I have had her for a fortnight and hope she is going to live. – – Unfortunately there are a great many leopards around the house at the moment – – It is strange to hear them roaring around the house at night just as they did thousands of years ago.

August 2, 1923. Dearest Elle – – I think that there is a really fine time ahead for women and that the next hundred years will bring many glorious revelations to them – – I think it will be truly glorious when women become real people and have the whole world open before them.

September 10, 1923. Dear Tommy – – Since I received Uncle Aage's letter the scent has gone from the roses and the radiance from the full moon in my life here and – – my strength has gone. – – Will you help me to make a new start in life? – – I could make a very good marriage as things are at present; but I have become absolutely convinced that I would not marry except for love or in order to achieve a position that I was really suited to fill. – –

The way in which girls are brought up is really shameful. I am quite certain that if I had been born a boy I would now, with exactly the same intelligence and other abilities that I have, have been able to look after myself really well. But even now I would surely be capable of it if I only had some help to start with.

February 24, 1924. Dearest Tommy – – I am sorry to write to you so often about my woes. But on the other hand I think that if I should die now – – you might perhaps wish that I had written in time. Of course it is not certain that I am going to die; but it is a good deal more likely than anyone at home believes.

If I had thought that Karen's life in Africa was peaceful and harmonious, as the calm narrative voice of *Out of Africa* might lead one to believe, I was wrong. Her letters reveal a very different reality. Karen was depressed, racked with anxiety, stressed out, fearful, and often ill. Occasionally Denys, her mother, or her brother Thomas would visit the farm, and then all was wonderful; but for long periods she was alone, with only her faithful Farah for company. And all the while the threat of having the farm sold hung over her like a guillotine blade.

In fact, Karen seemed to spend the next nearly ten years riding a hellish emotional roller coaster that either plunged her into the depths of despair or raised her to the heights of ecstatic joy, depending entirely on whether Denys was there with her.

Even now Denys was mostly away for almost two years, but whenever he did come around, Karen's depression vanished as if by magic. In August 1923, Denys decided to give up his own bungalow and moved his things into Karen's house at Ngong. From then on he spent time at Karen's between safaris, a week or two at a time, between monthslong absences. Karen had a bookcase built in her house for Denys's enormous book collection, and Denys brought wines and records from Europe, and if Karen was out riding when he arrived, he would open the doors and play Schubert on the gramophone at full volume, to let her know he was there. Evenings they would sit by a blazing fire on the hearth and Karen would tell stories. One day they agreed that they would both be buried in a certain slope of Ngong Hills that could be seen from the farm. Karen was beside herself with joy.

To her brother, Karen wrote: "Denys Finch Hatton has been staying here for some time, and is probably staying on another week, and I have been really completely happy, indeed, so happy that it is worth having lived and suffered, been ill, and had all the shauries to have lived for this week." I understand, Karen: if you can just be with that amazing, the most amazing man (how lucky one is to have that), nothing else matters.

But she also urged her brother never to tell anyone what kind of effect Denys had on her: "By the way, if I should die and you should happen to meet him afterward, you must never let him know that I have written to you like this about him!"

For Karen played it cool with Denys. The conditions were stringent: no commitments, no demands. Denys was happy at the farm, but he came only when he wanted to come. Denys didn't believe in marriage, and maybe declarations of love and the tiniest hints of codependency made him feel anxious. . . . Karen knew that if she showed Denys just how important he was to her, if she hinted that, in fact, her whole life depended on him, he might get a whiff of her desperation like some wild animal on the savanna and vanish forever. So she adapted. She made Denys's fear of commitment a virtue, even wrote a critical essay against marriage, praised "the love of the parallels," and began to despise those lovers who gazed into each other's eyes and took possession of each other's lives.

When Denys was at the farm, Karen came to life, and played the consummately strong and independent woman, the unneedy companion who would never ask how long her lover planned to stay. She adjusted to Denys's daily rhythms, woke up early to go out hunting with him, but was so revved up that she couldn't sleep at night, and maybe chewed on a little stimulant like *miraa* in the morning to keep going. . . . And then when Denys left, she would collapse and lie in bed for weeks, ailing and depressed.

*

[KAREN WRITES]

August 3, 1924. Dearest Tommy – – I have been feeling so dreadfully down, so—as you write—"desperately unhappy" during the last few months, since Denys left. – – I have felt it to be so utterly – – meaningless – – that I exist at all, – – that I was out here, that I was painting, getting up in the morning – – I would really like to be married and am tired of always being alone. – – I believe that for all time and eternity I am bound to Denys, to love the ground he walks upon, to be happy beyond words when he is here, and to suffer worse than death many times when he leaves. . . .

When she was alone Karen would think about the future. What would she do if the farm was sold? Would it be possible "at her age" to train herself for some profession? At least she could travel, to China perhaps, or study art in Rome or Florence, maybe manage a small hotel for Africans in Marseille or Djibouti, or else "marry well" (unfortunately, Denys wasn't an option). Or should she enroll in a cooking class in the Danish royal kitchens?

Karen was thirty-eight and it seemed to her that her life was at a turning point. "I *must* have a change. I really do want to try to get a clear idea of my future—whether I should stay out here or get started on something quite different," she wrote. It seems incredible that Karen still didn't know what her thing was. She had no inkling that she would become a world-famous writer.

In January 1925, her divorce from Bror finally took full effect, and in March Karen left for Europe. "I am looking forward more than I can say," she wrote to her mother, "to everything that awaits me: buying clothes in Paris, looking at pictures and listening to music again, the countryside at home, fruit and rye bread and shrimp—and please will you buy a real Norwegian goat-cheese to greet me with; I have been dreaming of that time and again."

But in Denmark, Karen sank into despair. Her future was uncertain, Denys was only around at random intervals, and everything was so damned burdensome alone. Karen began to say that she hated Africa and planned to remain in Denmark forever. Of course, it would be crazy to live in Rungstedlund with her mother—she would be turning forty next spring—but it was still tempting. Living in her mother's attic would mean no need to struggle. Everything would be as easy and pleasant as a walk in the garden! Karen saw her own life as an exhausting attempt to climb a steep mountain, as if she were constantly striving to attain some potential greatness in herself, something that *could be*—and she envied her siblings their contentment with ordinary everyday life.

Right, Karen. Do we really have to be constantly striving for something difficult and scary? Why can't we just lie in bed in our parents' attic and watch the Nature Channel?

[KAREN WRITES]

February 14, 1918. Dearest Mother – – There is something about safari life that makes you forget all your sorrows and feel the whole time as if you had drunk half a bottle of champagne – bubbling over with heartfelt gratitude for being alive. – – One only feels really free when one can go in whatever direction one pleases over the plains, get to the river at sundown and pitch one's camp, with the knowledge that one can fall asleep beneath other trees, with another view before one, the next night.

Day one of the safari. Fazal picks me up at 10 a.m. in a stretch Toyota Land Cruiser the color of dry grass. The car is huge: there's room for six people in the passenger area. We had specifically talked about not taking this big a car on a trip for two, but now here we are. I climb into the front seat, and Olli, Flotea, and Michell stand in the yard and wave good-bye.

We head off toward Arusha National Park, and I set myself the task of interviewing Fazal. He is thirty-four and has worked as a driver-guide for fourteen years. He has studied at a wildlife institute, where among other things his training covered botany and zoology, environmental issues, geology, cultural knowledge, customer psychology, and leadership, and at present he is chair of the Tanzanian tour guides union. He says he loves off-road gigs like this. Fazal is clearly ambitious—he tells me he's planning to write a book. He would like to publish a collection of safari stories, and asks me detailed questions about everything related to the process: writing, publishing, selling, and marketing books. He seems to be a little unclear about the fact that the writer of a book *actually writes the book*—that that part of the job isn't handled at the publisher's, say, and that, in fact, the very first thing he would need to do in order to write a book would be to start writing. (Only later does it occur to me that earlier, people would dictate their letters to professional scribes, which gives me a better idea of what he might have meant.) Fazal is also shocked to learn that I don't have a lawyer protecting me against the publisher cheating me on sales figures and trying to hide royalties from me. "You just *trust* their word?" he says, as if this were the most incredible thing he had ever heard.

It's raining when we arrive at the entrance gate to Arusha National Park. The only other visitors at the gate are a young American couple smacking gum. They've ridden up to the gate on bikes and now are planning to take a taxi into the park. Fazal shakes his head: an ordinary taxi has no business on these roads. When the ringtone on the taxi driver's phone goes off, the American girl starts grunting rhythmically and doing mini dance steps to the beat of the ringtone—and I think, *Thank God I'm on this trip alone in my own car.*

Arusha National Park is lovely and green, with rolling hills. Just beyond the gate opens a paradisal meadow where zebras, bushbuck, and warthogs graze. The rain drifts down gently; everywhere I look, nature is green and peaceful and glistening with rain; as we drive through evergreen mountain forests the only sound I hear is bird cries. On our way to a viewpoint we get stuck in the mud on the first steep hill. As Fazal rocks the car back and forth for what seems like an eternity, I think of those taxi tourists. I would be no use at all, trying to push a car out of this ankle-deep mud. But we get to the top at last and eat a picnic lunch on the edge of the Ngurdoto caldera: inside the brown cardboard lunch box Fazal brought is a drumstick encased in shrink-wrap, an apple, chips, juice, and a bun. Down in the caldera, the crater of a collapsed volcano, we can see a herd of buffalo. All around us are butterflies and *mkindu* grass. The weather has cleared up, and the play of light and shadow casts a dreamlike film over the caldera.

In the early evening we stop at a flat space with a breathtaking view: in front, snowcapped Kilimanjaro, framed in clouds; in back, Mount Meru, bathing in the sunset; down below, the Momella lakes, the grassy spits between them dotted with giraffes; rolling green hills all around us as far as the eye can see. One side of volcanic Meru collapsed long ago, making it look strangely flat and concave, like a façade. But if I were to climb to its peak, twenty-two thousand feet above sea level, it would take me four days. And a single climber would be accompanied by six bearers—or, on a luxury tour, twelve. Fifty bearers for a four-person luxury tour, carrying tents, food, water, toilets, and clothes up the mountain.

In the evening we arrive at our accommodations, Momella Lodge, on the edge of an emerald-green savanna. Howard Hawks filmed *Hatari!* here in 1962, and there are photos on the reception wall to prove it. In the movie John Wayne hunts rhinos and giraffes on the savanna for zoos, and apparently many a heart-stopping scene had to be dubbed after filming, because you could hear him cursing as he lost his temper. Now there's a spectral air of some long-forgotten time hanging over it. It seems deserted, since now is the off-season; I later learn that I'm the only guest. I am promised that the electricity will be on for a couple hours every evening; if you want your shower water warm, you have to let it run for at least fifteen minutes; and Olli has warned me not to swim in the pool, where hippos like to bathe. Crisscrossing my floor are black hairy millipedes, and I'm already afraid of what dinner will bring—I just hope not food poisoning. But as if to compensate, someone has arranged bougainvillea flowers on my bed, under the mosquito netting, in the shape of a heart.

As I unpack my things, I reflect again on the ludicrous quantity of clothes, cosmetics, and other junk I've brought along to the savanna that I absolutely cannot do without. My bag is overflowing with guidebooks, diaries, headlamps, binoculars, chargers, salted nuts, potato chips, water bottles, sun and night and eye creams, malaria pills, diarrhea pills, pain pills, sleeping pills, spare glasses, spare antibiotics, spare batteries, and, of course, piles and piles of clothes in the prescribed colors, beige and camo-green: visored caps, cargo pants, thick-fabricked safari skirts and shirts (no flimsy fripperies, and least of all red running shoes, which would attract the animals' attention). But as Olli reassured me, hauling stuff with you gives you a sense of security. Maybe if I run into a buffalo, I can bang it on the head with my toilet kit.

And yet this place is amazing. From my cabin window I can see the savanna, and behind it Kilimanjaro glinting in the evening sun—the same Kilimanjaro that Karen could sometimes see on a clear day from her plantation. The evening darkens into night and the cosmos plants glow in the full moon's light. The savanna warbles and trills; the mosquitoes awaken. Somewhere out there in the darkness are buffalo. All around Kilimanjaro rages a thunderstorm. In the lodge's vast empty dining room, Fazal and I eat dinner alone.

In the morning it's raining buckets, but we still head off on a drive through the park. Not a sign now of either gigantic mountain—they've vanished overnight like a dream—and as we drive through the deep lagoons that have taken over the road, I wonder whether the taxi tourists are still around, maybe stuck in one of these mud pits. But all around us everything is incredibly lush, and the land rolls almost neon-green against the dark-purple sky. Maybe this is the landscape Hemingway was thinking of when he titled his book *Green Hills of Africa*.

Sometimes we drive through grass so tall we can't see the road at all, but Fazal seems to be sure that under it all is a road of some sort. We don't see any other humans, but we do see giraffes, zebras, and antelopes. Buffalo stare at us mutely. Fazal goes on for some time about poachers, who are a serious problem here. A single buffalo will yield 450 pounds of meat, and if you sell that as beef you can earn a million shillings, or more than $500. That makes poaching incredibly tempting—even though the punishment if you're caught is life in prison. As we drive, the roads are sometimes blocked by troops of baboons, and the big males in each troop eye us sternly as if confirming their safety. You smell their pungent stench, they grunt softly as they galumph off into the bush, and then you hear the tearing of leaves and the smacking of lips. We see blue monkeys with their quizzical faces, long tails, and fur that looks crimped with an iron, and black-and-white guerezas with their long fur. On the far shore of Lake Momella there are pink flamingos, but the soil here is volcanic, and the fluoride-rich water rushing down from the mountains darkens the flamingos' feathers—as well as the locals' teeth.

Near Lake Momella we stop to watch two giraffes necking in the tall grass along the lakeshore. It's quiet—only the birds chirp somewhere off in the distance. The giraffes stand silently side by side for a long time, and then suddenly arch their long necks forward or to the side and make hypnotic serpentine movements, each responding to the other, dodging as if anticipating the other's movements. It is a touching sight. It's like a mystical, mute dance.

Our presence here in this off-road vehicle is likewise a kind of half-mute shadow dancing—but there's nothing particularly touching or mystical about it.

Fazal is, to be sure, an infallibly friendly, cheerful, polite, and service-minded guide who is clearly working every moment to read my mind. When we stop to look at animals, he reads every shift in my position as a clue to when we should get moving again. (If I want to keep looking, it's best to sit still as a statue.) If I take my pen out to write while we're bumping along on a particularly potholed road, he stops—and if I put my pen away, he drives on. Every time I make the tiniest movement on the seat, he asks whether everything's okay (it is). He picks bugs off my clothes, slaps tsetse flies off my skin, reminds me to drink and to smear myself with sunblock—even if the sky is cloudy. He asks at regular intervals whether I need to pee, and if I don't, he warns me that I have not been drinking enough, and passes me another bottle of water. He also tells me every evening what I should wear the next day—long pants or shorts, sandals or lace-up shoes—and warns me to put a hat on when we are riding along with the sunroof open. The client's well-being is his alpha and omega.

Still, I feel sorry for him, having to spend nearly two weeks cooped up with a taciturn introvert like me. I wonder whether his customer psychology class dealt with untalkative Nordic clients who aren't constantly gushing *Oh wow, that's amazing,* even when they're impressed (to tears, in fact). Fazal keeps asking whether I'm okay—I am, yes, I am, even if I'm not the motormouth type. "How can you write stories?" he asks. "I think you must be like a girlfriend I once had.

Always when we were together she sat quiet, and then later wrote me notes where she said what she wanted to say."

Touché. That's exactly who I am.

In the morning we pull out of Momella Lodge under cold, rainy skies. The drive to our next destination, Lake Manyara National Park, is long, and we must go through Arusha, where there happens to be a seminar organized by the nature guides union—of which Fazal is the chair. He has asked me whether we could make a quick stop there. I agree.

The seminar is held in a decrepit former hotel; in attendance are maybe two hundred guides, all but two of them of the male persuasion. The meeting is already in progress when we arrive: men speak into microphones in turn and occasionally raise their fists in the air and shout slogans, as if at some revival meeting. I am offered a seat at the panel table up front, but the curious stares of two hundred men are too much for me, so I ask to sit at the back instead. I have no clue what is being said in Swahili, but judging from the mood in the room the topic is almost certainly guides' rights and enhancing their professional pride. After a while Fazal asks for the floor, and I hear him introducing me in Swahili. Every face in the room turns to gaze upon my specialness with great interest, and suddenly a microphone is thrust into my hands. Tongue-tied with surprise, I am only able to squeak out a tentative "hi." Two hundred men applaud and cheer at this dazzling brilliance of mine.

Later one of the two women in the hall, Maggie, comes to interpret the speeches for me. The topic is client experiences, and how the safari companies treat their guides. The guides feel they are the key to the whole operation, since they know the parks and interact with tourists on a daily basis, but many companies treat the guides badly and are not the tiniest bit interested in environmental protection or the condition of the parks. On the other hand, clients often expect the same conditions on safari that they have at home—asphalt roads, running water, electricity—and when they don't get it, they complain to the safari companies, and the guide responsible for the negative feedback gets sacked.

Maggie also tells me that there are only two female guides in all Tanzania, herself and her sister. Maggie thinks that's unfortunate, because women are perfectly suited to this work: they are natural leaders with the intuitive skills to take care of a family, and a group of clients is like a family whom the guide serves for the duration of the safari as mother, doctor, and friend. Maggie also believes that a female guide is better able than men to manage the middle ground between being too intimate and too distant, and better at reading situational psychology.

Maggie is obviously a fiery and plucky feminist, and she argues fervently for more educational opportunities for Tanzanian girls. She tells me that girls' schooling is often interrupted by female biology: girls miss an average of five days a month due to menstruation. They are too ashamed to go to school, because they can't afford proper sanitary napkins—they use corn husks and cloths instead—and they have no way to wash. These missed days add up over the school year, and the girls fall ever further behind in their lessons. Maggie, in fact, directs a volunteer organization called Dare Women's Foundation, which offers girls sanitary napkins and guidance in hygiene and a healthy diet, as well as information about environmental protection. They also take orphaned children to the national parks, because most locals can never afford to visit one.

It is shocking to realize that efforts to improve women's educational levels might depend on such a basic need as sanitary napkins.

Someone comes to tell me that after the event, they want to offer Fazal and me lunch, because "everyone loves me." This is patently an exaggeration, but it nicely reflects the prevailing level of friendliness: every single guide we meet greets me, introduces himself, welcomes me, and wishes me a good trip with a big smile. But I can't help but reflect on how long this is going to take. Olli would no doubt be tearing his hair out if he knew that a client who has spent fat wads of dollars for every day on this trip is being treated to generous hospitality when she should be in the car looking at lions. Fazal, for his part, has decided to milk the occasion for everything it's worth: his complimentary speech has gone on for at least half an hour. He has almost certainly forgotten entirely that I exist.

At lunch we are served whole stuffed and baked fish with rice. Maggie and her sister eat it deftly with their fingers: they take a flake of fish and mash it together with rice into a ball. The fish is delicious. Fazal's meal never arrives, but he eats my leavings. Our third day on safari, and we're already like an old married couple.

On the drive toward Lake Manyara the ten-day magic kicks in: I begin to *see*. The roadside vendor shacks that looked so frightening at first are no longer just shocking, ramshackle piles jerry-built out of corrugated iron—I see now that they hum with business. Each vendor is an entrepreneur, and a person can find anything she's looking for here. Here's a stationery store called Perfect Stationery, offering copying, printing, and writing services. There are dozens of phone stores and places that will top up your prepaid minutes. There are hair salons (Hair Cutz, Brotherhood Hair Cutting Saloon), pharmacies (Hope Medics), and clothing stores, and in one village we pass a vending cart labeled Mr. Barack Obama Mobile Shop. There are car parts stores (Perfect Motors), auto mechanics, and building supply stores, and if outside there's a sign saying FUNDI, that means that they hire workers for day labor.

In addition, everywhere you look you see half-built houses, many of them like ghostly hulks with only the brick walls standing. I'm told the poorest build their houses out of clay and branches; the materials for a house like that can be gathered in the woods for free and assembled into a dwelling with neighbors' help in a week. But if money is available, people begin to build with brick and concrete. It takes a long time to build that kind of house, because it's a sure thing that at some point the money will run out—but the project is always resumed as soon as additional funds are secured. Looking at these gray skeletal houses, it's impossible to know whether they'll ever be built—whether, for example, the builder has already permanently run out of money.

We finally reach the Maasai Steppe, and drive seventy miles on a perfectly straight road through a vast green plain. Ahead of us glimmers the mist-ringed edge of the Great Rift Valley: it looks like something out of a fairy tale.

This area belongs to the Maasai tribe; here they maintain their traditional culture. There are no fixed dwellings on the steppe, but now and then we see Maasai boys herding goats and cows with sticks. To these nomadic people, cattle are everything: they buy and sell them, sleep on their hides, use their milk and blood as nutrition. The number of cows, wives, and children a Maasai man has is the measure of his wealth. A rich Maasai might own two thousand cows. (The price of one cow is a million shillings, or about $500.) A man with fewer than fifty cows is considered poor. We pass Maasai villages, *manyattas*, divided off with stick fences; the houses, built out of cow manure, are arranged in a circular pattern. In the shade of the trees men have gathered for a meeting. The men, warriors, are dressed in red-checked *shuka* fabric; the women, children, and uncircumcised boys wear blue checks. Traditionally the warriors colored their skin, hair, and cowhide capes bright red with ochre to frighten away their enemies—that is, wild animals. A blood-red Maasai warrior is powerful and strong—he symbolizes danger.

We stop for a moment at a Maasai marketplace. Fazal urges me to keep my camera hidden: Maasai don't like having their pictures taken. In the dusty square are hundreds of Maasai, young and ancient, men and women, many of them toothless or with yellowing eyeballs; most will have walked here from dozens or even hundreds of miles away. This is no tourist display. The women's shaved heads turn away from me; they have babies strapped to their backs, and their big ear jewelry and piercings hang heavily. Their proud gazes act like a mirror: when I look at them, I see only my own whiteness, my assumed wealth, my stupid tourist stare. I come from a different world. That world could not interest them less.

Just before the gates to Lake Manyara National Park we stop in the village of Mto wa Mbu. The village's name means "mosquito stream"—and in this malarial region, I can't imagine a less inviting name. A guide Fazal knows wants to show me the village and its tourist activities, so I follow along docilely to check out a wood carver who makes animal figures out of ebony, mahogany, rosewood, and teak. A couple of schoolchildren follow us, giggling, as we walk through the banana groves. The guide explains that in this region alone there are thirty varieties of banana: soup bananas, sweet fruit bananas, and varieties used for making beer. At one intersection grow quinine trees, whose leaves are used to treat malaria. In the yards we see clothes drying on the line and children peeking through the narrow openings of doors. Every family has a goat and a cow. I'm told they are the family's bank: if something happens, you can always sell the goat. At the end of the tour we step into a small banana-beer brewery and bar. In the tiny hut sit three women around a single *mbege* plastic tub, out of which each drinks in turn. When the tub is empty, the next drinker buys a round. The beverage is a ghastly-looking thick brown gruel. I'm already frantically trying to come up with a polite reason to refuse any offer to taste it, when the guide fortunately says that under no circumstances should I touch it: it would certainly make me sick. The mamas, though, agree to be photographed, and they hold up their bucket of beer with satisfied looks.

We don't arrive at our Manyara hotel until six in the evening. I'm about to faint with hunger. The place is amazing: poised on the edge of the Great Rift Valley, the hotel has an unreal view of the national park spread out below. Olli has made me promise to insist at all costs on a room between 48 and 54, since those rooms have the best view. Number 12 was reserved for me, and when I ask to be moved, they shift me up a floor to 24, which does have a nice view of the pool and the garden with its lounge chairs. I try to push for number 48, but I'm told that that whole wing has been closed for the off-season. No hot water is available there, which would mean that they could not offer me their accustomed "standard of comfort." Still, they let me go look at the room. It's thick with dust and spiderwebs, but the view is indeed breathtaking: straight out of the bed, the bathtub, or the balcony you have an unobstructed view down the Rift Valley as far as the eye can see over the green Manyara groundwater forest. To my surprise Fazal begins to put pressure on the staff, and in the end they agree to clean the room and bring up hot water by some means at an agreed-upon time. I burn with shame.

I'm even more ashamed when I learn that it is against hotel rules for Fazal to eat dinner with me, as he did at the previous place. They don't even have rooms for driver-guides: for his night lodging he has to drive to a village a half hour away. He complains that he will not be able to find a breakfast he can stomach there—and it later turns out that the lodging in that village is too filthy for his standards, and he has to drive even farther away.

I don't know what to think. Here in this hotel owned by the Tanzanian government, local guides are not to be seen in the restaurant—though a Finnish guide, say, would not bother them in the slightest. As a paying customer, would it have been in my power to demand a different kind of treatment? After all, to satisfy my request for a view, I'm making their staff run up and down with hot water! I'm ashamed to enjoy my suite and the luxurious buffet dinner, served to the accompaniment of African drum music. I'm ashamed to be ensconced here in this beautifully landscaped, fenced-in hotel territory, which shields the best view in the region from the locals' eyes—the people who live in clay huts just outside the fence, without electricity or windows. I'm so ashamed that although, despite the staff's best efforts, no warm water ever comes out of my shower, I lie that everything works as promised.

I wonder whether Karen was ever ashamed to live in her beautifully furnished house in her finery. Or had liberal guilt not yet been invented back in colonial days?

And yet as the sun sets I park myself out on the balcony hanging over the edge of the Rift Valley, and can't help but feel powerfully moved. Hell, here I am, in wild African nature. What could possibly have brought me to a place like this? Once darkness has fallen, a gigantic orange full moon rises from the horizon. Bats swoop and dive in the corridor leading to my room; the crickets sing their nocturnal song. The sounds of the distant night animals echo off the valley below.

The dawn is not particularly rosy. My head had begun aching in the evening, and I couldn't sleep; I suppose I was anticipating the orange moon and the coming sunrise, and so had left the curtains open on the picture window in my divine-view room. And I had mosquitoes in the room. And for the very first time, my stomach is rocky. How is it possible that I've been here nearly two weeks, and have survived who knows what fly cuisines, and now the buffet table at this fancy restaurant is the thing that finally does me in? Still, Olli's safari itinerary has me heading out for a drive around Lake Manyara National Park first thing this morning, so there's nothing to do but suck it up and get by somehow—with medicine, if need be.

I complain to Fazal of my headache, and he says it's because I don't talk—because I keep all these experiences inside. Gotcha. Somehow I doubt talking would help; in my experience, migraines strike when I'm inundated with impressions, and if one day too much happens (as is typical on trips), the next day I should stay in bed and process it. But Fazal is right about one thing: I can certainly sit in the car for an hour saying absolutely nothing. Why not?

We drive down to the Manyara groundwater forest. From down here the hotel looks like a tiny white dot high on the cliff's edge. Fazal keeps noticing things: now elephants in the woods on the slope, now baboons or monitor lizards that are so far away I can't spot them even with binoculars. It's a matter of professional skill: I can spot an extra space between words in a text I'm proofreading from a hundred meters away. I also reflect on the fact that it's not so strange after all traveling alone with a safari guide. After two days it feels like I'm traveling with a friend, that perfect kind of friend who knows everything about everything, handles all the plans and reservations, and speaks the local language—and I don't even have to haggle over whose turn it is to drive next. The only thing we disagree on is the desired amount of social interaction.

The cool of the morning has faded. The sun blazes through the cloud cover. Everywhere we hear the buzz of insects and the chirping of birds. There are a few yawning hippos in the pond; another is still wandering through the tall grass looking for food, with a white bird on its back. Four elephants lumber along next to the road. From the meadow wafts a heady herbal scent. On the lake we see pelicans and marabou storks; on the horizon surges a vast flock of pink flamingos, like a dream, or a mirage. Beaks in the water, they step rhythmically through the lake like ballerinas in a long line, following some precise choreography—only Tchaikovsky's music is missing. The place we stop for lunch is situated on a slope and has a view out over Lake Manyara. On its misty, paradisal shore are grouped zebras, buffalo, stately solitary giraffes, and wildebeests galloping with shoulders hunched. Is a sight like this even possible?

This place alongside the Great Rift Valley turns my imagination to the globe, the scope and scale of everything, bigness and smallness. Significance, insignificance, the incredible multiplicity of nature, the creation story—how this amazing ball streaks through space with us on its surface. The vista before me is simply incomprehensible.

I watch the tourists hanging out of the open sunroofs on their jeeps, and think they look ridiculous, a little scared, somehow out of place. That's how I look too: stupid as hell. We drive from giraffe to giraffe and the cameras whir—*wow, wonderful, ama-a-zing*—and the country-counters can check another item off their bucket lists. I turn away from them and think that I'd like to curl up on that sublime shore amidst the giraffes and just stay there, somehow mystically fuse with it all. I know, of course, that I can't. If what you come here for is a primordial experience, some kind of connection with origins, with creation, you can get it—well, in the sense that you can look at it through glass. But you can't join it. You can only look at it.

I try to look with everything I've got.

At night, then, as I lie in my viewpoint bed, I think of Karen, and the boundless joy she too felt in these wild landscapes. In my mind I scroll through pictures of Karen from a century ago, getting them confused with the landscapes I've just seen here.

In my favorite photo, a young Karen is sitting by a table on safari. She's wearing a practical shirt, a scarf tied at the throat, and a felt hat. Food is about to be served, for the table is set with a plate and a fork. Karen is smiling, perhaps at Bror. She looks free and happy, somehow light. It feels as if she is *precisely where she ought to be*.

There are other wonderful photos. In one, Karen is wearing a long white dress and pearls and is feeding Lulu the antelope milk from a bottle. Lulu has moved into the house and sometimes sleeps under the desk while Karen writes her letters.

In another, Karen sits at a table smoking a cigarette with a tame owl on her shoulder.

In yet another, Karen is dressed in a riding outfit, sitting on her horse Rouge, with her two Scottish deerhounds next to her. They are about to go galloping out on the savanna, where the dogs will scatter the herds of buffalo along the grassy plain.

In another, Karen sits on the porch with a lap full of white lilies as long as she is.

There's also a photo in which Karen and Denys sit in the tall grass with a picnic basket. They do not look like they're in love. They do not look at the camera, or at each other.

[KAREN WRITES]

July 4, 1926. Dearest Aunt Bess – – Mother writes in her letter that she is considering whether it would not be better to use the money intended for her journey out here for a trip home to Europe for me. – – I will begin by saying that in no possible way and under no circumstances will I go home before the spring of 1928. It is partly because I can see that things cannot go *so well – – here when I am away, and partly because I will not* break up my life *in such small pieces. Besides the considerable amount of time that goes in travel preparations and in the journey itself – – it takes one – – three or four months before one gets used to affairs and conditions out here again. After my return this last time it is only just now that I am beginning to feel really at home here again.*

November 7, 1926. Dearest Mother – – [There is a stork here] – – it is completely tame, walks about on the veranda and comes when it is called – – I am feeding it on frogs, which the totos bring in buckets for 3 cents a piece. – – Lulu – – is keeping it company. I think I have quite a gift with wild animals—do you remember how tame the owl became, too, in quite a short time? It must be the same ability I have for getting on with the natives—and the same that gives me my aversion to marriage, if you understand what I mean! I have no desire to capture and shut in and appropriate them, and they can feel that.

Karen returned to British East Africa in February 1926, after spending eight months in Denmark. She was alone and depressed, and could not seem to shake her depression, her exhaustion, or her hopelessness about the future. She tried to pull herself together, and to start painting or writing, but could not concentrate. She had no strength for anything. To top it all, the high plains were suffering from famine, a troop of monkeys had settled in at the farm and were decimating the cornfields, and there was a new disease ravaging nearby villages called the blackwater fever, among whose casualties was a boy that Karen adored named Abdullai. Karen cared for patients on the farm and in emergencies made house visits, and her reputation as a miracle-working physician grew.

In March, Denys returned, but only for two weeks; after that he planned to travel to England. Karen tried to enjoy his visit, but couldn't help constantly thinking that only five days of his visit were left, only two hours of this evening were left—and then Denys would be gone, and she would be plunged once more into the black pit of loneliness. Karen wrote a desperate telegram and letter to her brother, which she did not send. The telegram read: "Will you help me to get to Europe, I shall die if I remain here." And the letter: "I *must* write and I don't know whom else to write to, besides you. To be forced to silence . . . feels as if one is buried alive, and you must imagine me as if you saw me lying in the darkness with the weight of the earth on my breast, and forgive me for this screaming." Karen wrote that she had been thinking perhaps it would be best if she killed herself. If she didn't, what would she do? "Do you think, Tommy, that I can still 'become something,' and that I have not thrown away all the chances life has offered me?"

In May, Karen's emotional turmoil took a new form: she thought she was pregnant. Karen passionately wanted a child, and immediately sent Denys a telegram in England, using the code name Daniel for the possible baby. Denys's reply was brief: "Strongly urge you to cancel Daniel's visit." To Karen's reply he sent a new telegram: "Do as you like about Daniel as I should welcome him if I could offer partnership but this is impossible STOP." Karen's response: "Thanks cable I never meant to ask assistance consent only Tania."

This was Karen's last pregnancy. Apparently she miscarried, as before. She did not write a word to Denys for the rest of the summer.

Karen was forty-one and unmarried. She had syphilis and no money. She was in love with a man who would not commit to her. She would have liked a child to give her life some purpose, but that wasn't happening either. She was at rock bottom. In the fall Karen wrote a seventeen-page letter to her brother, revealing the conclusions she had reached in her self-study. Ordinary "happiness" was clearly not for her. She must accept her fate, "run parallel" with her lover, not seek to possess him—though loneliness was a heavy burden. She would focus her efforts on raising the farm's children. She would think of Denys as an old trusted friend and of herself as a wise older woman living alone—sort of like a nun.

Maybe this was Karen resigning herself to her fate. Maybe she was rationalizing. But does any unmarried, childless woman in her forties have any other option but to build her life out of the cards she has been dealt? "It's not the cards you're dealt, it's how you play them," Karen wrote. There really are just two choices: either you lie around feeling sorry for yourself, or you realize that those cards are your entry into a special, wonderful future that would not have been available to you otherwise, and start living accordingly.

*

[LETTER, UNSENT]

The only thing I have to say to you, Karen, is that I've been in love with Denys too, that charismatic, compelling, absent man who came and went as he pleased. Who, when he was leaving, never even said where he was going, or when he would be back, or how much he hated having to leave when he would rather stay with you, who just got up, walked into the front hall, pulled on his jacket, and said, "I'm gone." And then there was something in that man, Denys, that always made it feel like the lights had gone on in the room when he returned. It always felt then like I was where I was supposed to be. Always – – though I knew that all too soon he would be gone again.

Denys can make you wait for him a long time—but when Denys is no more, Karen, when Denys is over, then we have to start doing something else. Writing, traveling, reflecting on how we want to live the few remaining moments in our lives.

And the fact that we are finally free of waiting for anyone, even Denys, is a gift.

*

And lo: her next years were happy ones.

[KAREN WRITES]

July 13, 1927. My own dearest Aunt Bess -- I believe that most people -- would be happier travelling around from one fair to another with a monkey, if that would enable them to gain some experience and have new impressions and movement, than sitting with a secure income in an insured house, where one day is just like another. -- I think that most people have an unconscious feeling that there is more nourishment for soul and spirit in danger and wild hopes, and in this: hazarding everything, than in a calm and secure existence.

November 11, 1928. Dear Mother -- On Saturday -- after dinner I drove in to a dance at Muthaiga; Denys didn't want to go, and I meant to go home early, but one never does that from Muthaiga, I didn't get back until half past five. Lady Delamere behaved scandalously at supper -- she bombarded the Prince of Wales with big pieces of bread, and one of them hit me -- in the eye, so I have a black eye today. . . .

It was also in these years that Karen's most significant encounters with lions occurred. To Karen they were important experiences as metaphors for something else, and later as grist for her literary mill—but I truly do not know what to make of these lion killings. It's hard for me to read how on New Year's Day 1928, Karen and Denys met "an absolutely splendid, big black-maned lion," the finest they'd ever seen, and decided that they just "had to have it"—and then, once they'd shot and skinned it, feeling "very proud and happy," they sat down to breakfast and drank a bottle of red wine. "I don't think I have ever had a more delightful New Year's morning," Karen wrote to her mother ecstatically.

It is equally difficult to read about another incident that became even more significant to Karen. One day in April of the same year, the foreman came to tell Karen that two lions were harrying the bulls, and asked permission to poison them. Karen forbade this, calling it unsportsmanlike conduct. Instead, Karen and Denys dragged a bull carcass up onto the hill as bait for the lions, and when they returned in the dark of the evening, the light from the lantern Karen was holding revealed, about twenty yards away, a "supernaturally large" lion staring at them—and soon another as well. The situation was life-threatening, but Denys managed to shoot both of them. Then they skinned both lions and returned home "as from the wildest adventure," and, excited, opened a bottle of champagne. "They were two young male lions, both with black manes and enormous paws—they looked beautiful even dead, and I'll never forget how they moved in the midst of the black of night," Karen wrote.

After this incident the locals began to call Karen "Honorable Lioness," and somehow the whole episode confirmed for the forty-three-year-old that her choice between "the lions and family life" had been the right one: lions were her thing. She wrote to her aunt Bess that the foreman would have gone up and shot the lions himself, but then had reflected on the fact that he was a married man with one child at home and another on the way, and decided that he couldn't take a risk like that. "Yes, I understand perfectly," Karen had replied. "Denys Finch Hatton and I can go after them instead." "Come now then," she had said to Denys, "let us go and risk our entirely worthless lives." To Aunt Bess she continued that she had come to the conclusion that you have to choose, and that those who plan on marrying should be very clear on whether they are choosing lions or married life. "A good deal of [the value of my life], if it exists at all, is due to the fact that I shoot lions. Or that it is possible for me to live free and do what I like in my life. There are many people of this kind in the world and I consider that they are just as entitled to their rights and their place in it as family men and women."

Yes, Karen, I understand the metaphor. What I simply cannot fathom, however, on these paradisiacal plains of Manyara, is that killing animals gives you such a rush that you feel like downing a bottle of champagne.

—

But perhaps things were somehow different a hundred years ago. After all, safari hunting was extremely popular back in Karen's day. The craze had been started by former US President Teddy Roosevelt, during whose nine-month-long safari in 1909 a shocking eleven thousand animals were killed. After that, rich upper-class tourists flowed into East Africa and shot so many wild animals that by the 1920s there was a danger that the whole abundant range of wildlife in the high plains would be driven to extinction.

Karen had first caught the hunting bug on her honeymoon safari with Bror back in 1914. Before that she had never quite grasped the idea of hunting. But then everything changed, and she became euphoric: animals were shot; carcasses were dragged, skinned, and butchered; the hides and horns were admired. . . . It was almost as if she and Bror had become addicted to a kind of gambling, and the bigger and more beautiful the individual was, the more points the shooter racked up. In 1914, Karen wrote that she did not believe that "any normal person can live in lion country without trying to shoot them." Photographing wild animals, by contrast, was to Karen's mind just a "pleasant platonic encounter"—not a matter of life or death, and therefore not particularly interesting.

When I think of Karen at night, my mind begins to be flooded with disturbing images as well—the ones in which she poses with lions.

One photo shows Karen and Bror holding rifles with two lionesses at their feet, looking like they are dozing in the midday heat. But they're dead. Karen looks pleased.

In another photo, six lion skins and three leopard skins have been stretched over the safari tent. In front of the tent sits Karen, with one unskinned dead leopard at her feet.

In yet another photo, Karen and Ingrid from the neighboring farm pose with a zebra they've shot. The women are wearing practical dresses and floppy hats and holding rifles. They've set off on a Sunday jaunt with the dogs. Behind them the grassy savanna extends to the horizon.

In another, Karen smiles broadly, having just shot a leopard.

*

[A LETTER WRITTEN ON MANYARA HOTEL STATIONERY]

Dear Karen,

As much as I admire you, I find it difficult to look at those photos where you pose triumphantly with dead lions. Please don't send me any more.

Your M

*

In the fall of 1928, the Prince of Wales, the future King Edward VIII, visited East Africa. Denys had been asked to arrange a safari for the prince, and at one royal lunch the prince invited himself to dinner at Karen's house, where he wanted to see a *ngoma*, a traditional tribal dance performance. Karen became completely stressed out: she would have only a few days to plan the menu, "find some ladies for the party," and persuade the tribal chiefs to send their warriors to perform the *ngoma*.

But the dinner was a success. The royal meal served at Karen's house on November 9, 1928, began with Kamante's famous clear broth, followed by Mombasa turbot in hollandaise sauce, partridges (bought from the Maasai) with peas, creamy truffle pasta, wild leeks, tomato salad, wild mushroom croustades, savarin cake, and strawberries and pomegranates. Karen and Denys sat at the ends of the table (as we know from the seating chart that Karen drew in a letter she sent her mother), and after dinner they all went outside to watch the *ngoma*, that amazingly stirring spectacle in which Gĩkũyũ men who have painted their bodies with red chalk dance wildly in ostrich feathers and ape-hide leggings to ecstatic drumming by firelight.

Later when I watch the documentary of the safari arranged for the Prince of Wales, in the photos I see, posed alongside the prince, both of his guides: Bror and Denys. Denys is tall, thin, and somehow sturdy-looking, with a ghastly old-man hat on his head; but his stock rises fast in my eyes when I learn that he was the one who started talking about putting an end to the out-of-control hunting in East Africa. With Prince Edward's support, Denys began to campaign in England to ban hunting from cars—he hated that practice, which made it possible for a tourist with lousy aim to shoot twenty lions a day—and ultimately all hunting was banned in the Serengeti. The new fashion, launched by Prince Edward, was the photographic safari.

Karen, too, later softened. At seventy-five she wrote in her book *Shadows on the Grass*: "When I first came out to Africa I could not live without getting a fine specimen of each single kind of African game. In my last ten years out there I did not fire a shot except in order to get meat for my Natives. It became to me an unreasonable thing, indeed in itself ugly or vulgar, for the sake of a few hours' excitement to put out a life that belonged in the great landscape. . . . But lion-hunting was irresistible to me; I shot my last lion a short time before I left Africa."

In the morning we set a course for the lions: we have a whole day ahead of us driving from Manyara to the Serengeti. The weather on the high plains is foggy and chilly. We drive through Karatu, our last "city" before the end of civilization—a cluster of huts coated with red sand and dust at a crossroads. It doesn't invite closer acquaintance. When we stop to tank up, a little boy comes and knocks on the window to ask for a dollar for a school uniform, or a lunch, or even just a cup of tea. This is the road all the rich safari tourists take to their destination. Hence the huts.

We drive along the rim of the Ngorongoro Crater, and stop for a moment at a viewpoint. The crater is a holy place for the Maasai, and it looks like something straight out of a fairy tale—or like something from the kingdom of dreams in a Hayao Miyazaki film. Olli complained that he was sick of "that whole damn crater"—nothing ever happens there, he said—but to the random tourist it looks like the earthly paradise. From the crater's rim we drive down into the idyllic mountain valley, with its rolling hills. The land is blanketed with yellow flowers. Here and there we see Maasai *manyattas* and gigantic herds of cattle.

Then all of a sudden the land turns into a parched, flat desert, and the temperature shoots up thirty degrees. We'll be driving this straight road for another sixty miles to our Serengeti lodgings. Here is the Olduvai Gorge, the cradle of human life, where our ancestors *Homo habilis* and *Homo erectus* lived over a million years ago—but this desert certainly doesn't feel like a Garden of Eden. The aridity is fierce, the heat is like a sledgehammer, and the air is gray with dust. The thorny bushes alongside the road are blanketed in white dust, and every car raises a cloud behind it that extends several hundred yards. Soon everything inside the car is likewise coated with Olduvai dust. The dirt road is washboarded from beginning to end, and Fazal blasts down it as fast as the car will go. Every instant our bodies are subjected to an infernal pounding. I understand now what Fazal meant this morning when he said that we had a tough drive ahead of us. I tie a scarf over my mouth and nose so as to be able to breathe—the dust floods through the windows, which must be kept open to make the furnace-like heat bearable. Now and then we pass Maasai women sitting under a lone tree, and I wonder how it is possible to live here: there can't be water within a radius of dozens of miles.

Finally, before dark, we reach Seronera, in the middle of the Serengeti. I am nauseated and suffering from some sort of dehydration and heatstroke—though I've been drinking constantly. The heat is strange: normally I sweat like a waterfall, but here my skin is dry and burning hot, as if I had a fever. It's as if the scorching heat and the bone-dry land had greedily sucked every drop of moisture out of my body for its own use. I lie in my room in the Seronera Wildlife Lodge racked with the shakes. I guzzle down water by the quart, eat crackers, and in desperation mix a bag of rehydration powder (meant for replenishment after the intestinal flu) into water and swill that down as well. I can't even look out my window at the savanna scenes, or listen to the dark, where the hyenas will soon begin their cackling. The Serengeti is a rough place for a small human being.

By morning I have more or less pulled myself together, and we set off on a safari drive at 6 a.m., in the dark. I'm told that this year the Serengeti's rainy season ended earlier than usual, so the large wildebeest herds are already heading north. The great migration of the gnu antelopes, or wildebeests, is one of this area's unsolved mysteries. Millions of them migrate each year in search of rain and green grass in a circular route from the southern Serengeti up to the Maasai Mara in Kenya. I'm also told that the migrating herds might still be in Kirawira, in the northwestern Serengeti, but that's quite far from here, at least a two- or three-hour drive. But we head in that direction, and quite soon we reach a largish herd of wildebeests crossing the Grumeti River. An endless stream of them emerges from the woods on one side of the river, dozens, hundreds, and crossing with them in the same herd are zebras too, and even baboons. They are all determined to get somewhere—perhaps Kirawira. One wildebeest lies dead farther off, in a dried-up channel of the river; near it stands a lone calf, looking lost.

We stop in the middle of the herd and climb up on the roof of the car to eat the breakfast boxes sent along by the lodge. The wildebeests bleat rhythmically; their mooing and moaning all around us forms a constant comic sound carpet. I wonder whether their endless and seemingly brainless bleating ever irritates the silent zebras that migrate with them. For the first time on this trip, I squat behind the car to pee. Hundreds of wildebeests stare intently.

After breakfast an elderly American couple drives up in their Land Rover. "Wha-aat, are you all alone in that bii-iig car?!" the man crows to me, sticking his head up through his sunroof. "She's not alone, I'm here too," Fazal mutters, annoyed. Later he returns to the topic with a snort: "How could that couple be sure we weren't married?" I understand his annoyance: guides are often treated like invisible servants. The people in charge of our lodgings like to keep up the same pretense.

I now learn why I'm being driven around in this huge stretch jeep, when the American couple has squeezed into one half its size. Fazal tells me that many women making this trip without a companion want privacy. They don't want to be alone with a male driver in a small space, let alone in the front seat, and this car gives me that option of distance. I just haven't figured out that I'm expected to climb into the back row of seats. It would seem silly, in fact. And Fazal and I would have to converse by shouting.

We ditch the Americans and set off driving north through a tall yellow untouched field of grass that waves as we pass. There could be cheetahs here. Instead we spot a leopard, resting in the branches of an umbrella acacia. It stares at us with its yellow eyes but does not flee, though we creep along through the tall grass, closer and closer.

Sometime after midday we return to the lodge for lunch. The plan is for us to spend the remainder of the day resting. I'm beat, feeling nauseated again, and it seems to me Fazal is a bit under the weather as well. Absurd as it may sound, I've been waiting to get online again, after six days cold turkey, but it turns out that the lodge's computer room, with fifteen workstations for guests, is closed for the off-season. (Of course.) I'm so exhausted that I almost throw a teary hissy fit. It's a violation of my human rights not to let me get online in the Serengeti! After many complicated and embarrassing demands, arrangements, and technical difficulties, I do finally enter cyberspace on the laptop of the friendly Indian chef.

This momentary umbilical link to civilization is gossamer-thin and keeps breaking. I do manage to read a few e-mails before sinking back into a queasy depression that resembles homesickness, but probably has more to do with intestinal disorders and dehydration. I labor to post an ecstatic squib to Facebook, then retire to my room to collapse in bed.

I wonder what it is about the Serengeti that takes the stuffing out of a person. The heat, the dust, the endless dry plains, the furnace-like blast of the sun, which you cannot escape . . . I am painfully aware that if I were left alone on these plains for a twenty-four-hour period, I would die. If I didn't end up as lion food, I'd die of the heat and thirst, and no one would notice or care. The herds of wildebeests would wander past me, the vultures would gnaw on my remains, and the only thing left would be a pile of white bones, an insignificant detail in the flatland extending to the horizon in all directions.

The Serengeti has me reflecting on how transitory life is—how abundant, but also how fragile. Everything we do to protect our existence—work, money, clothes, goods, technology, security locks, insurance, data communications, Facebook posts—is meaningless here. The Serengeti sets its own priorities, and they are shade and water. In fact, I've thought of nothing else for the last couple of days.

I'm also starting to understand how people go crazy here, from the sun, the heat, these conditions—how they lose control, go off the deep end, start to see things and behave strangely. I've begun to understand how people get the feeling that there is no escaping this place, that the rest of the world has faded into nonexistence.

I think about the lion we saw yesterday, our first: a male lion who walked around under the open car window so close that I could hear his heavy panting. I sat without moving a muscle, remembering what Karen had said about the admirable economy of a lion, how there is nothing superfluous on its incredible body. Maybe now I have a better sense of why people shot lions a hundred years ago. If it's just the lion and me, a choice has to be made. One of us is going to die.

[KAREN WRITES]

October 23, 1918. My own beloved Mother – – I am sorry not to have written for so long, but actually I have been ill most of the time. As you will know from my telegram, I developed a blood poisoning after my fall from a mule – – [then] *I got a high fever – – the doctor – – gave me chloroform – – and cut open my leg from the knee right up to the hip, and took out a lot of "dead flesh" – – Spanish flu is raging out here to a most worrying extent; last week 22 people died of it. – – There is also a lot of small pox. . . .*

January 14, 1919. Dearest Mother – – My leg is not nearly healed up yet after almost five months – – Otherwise I have been very well recently – – I am taking some arsenic, which does wonders for me.

December 4, 1920. Dearest Mother – – My disease consists of constant vomiting and dizziness, but I do not know whether it is a kind of poisoning. . . .

May 6, 1923. Dearest Mother – – I have not been feeling well for some time; recently I consulted a new young Doctor Anderson in Nairobi, he thought that I was suffering from malaria. . . .

May 4, 1926. Dearest Mother – – I am annoyed because I have had to stay in bed again, and because I am really not at all well – – I cannot say that I am actually ill, but so immensely tired, and not fit for anything at all. I have never felt anything like it before, it is as if it's too much trouble to live, and I can't tell how it is going to develop. Except for the time when Denys was here I have been feeling like this [all spring].

Damn this unrelenting physical weakness! A slightly stronger physique would suit an explorer better. Then I could just ignore my external conditions. Then every new environment wouldn't plunge my organism into shock, and I wouldn't have to collapse so often with headache, nausea, exhaustion, insomnia, tension, stomach problems, dehydration, heatstroke, or blood sugar fluctuations. Evenings I'm so tired I hardly have enough strength to open my bag; I can just barely reach in there and grab some (any!) clean shirt. Woman, you're so weak!

But if I'd imagined that Karen, unlike me, was enviably energetic, healthy, and strong, I was wrong. She wasn't. In fact, she was frequently ill. She too handled the heat badly; she suffered from malaria, sunstroke, suppurating wounds, and nausea. She vomited. She was afflicted with dizzy spells and food-poisoning-like symptoms. She was often hospitalized for terrible inexplicable pains that felt like an acute toothache had struck her heels, hands, or ears. She complained that clumps of hair were falling out of her head, and took to wearing a turban.

She also suffered from depression, and later began to get panic attacks. Whether because of her syphilis, Denys, unrelenting financial problems, the threat of having the farm sold out from under her, loneliness, or just mood swings, she was often bedridden for weeks on end with anxiety. Weeks, months, years. Karen lay in bed for years!

At first I was almost angry at Karen: What kind of exemplary woman is this? But as I lie nauseated in bed with my pharmacopeia in the middle of the dry-as-dust Serengeti, I can hardly imagine what it must have been like to lie ill in these conditions a century ago. I reflect on the fact that *despite everything* Karen stuck it out in Africa for nearly eighteen years, and that sometimes it took her *more than a year* to get back to Europe for medical treatment.

Probably the lion's share of Karen's mysterious symptoms were caused by the degenerative developments of her syphilis, which perhaps was not after all, as had been thought, cured in 1925. Her medical history would seem to confirm this: at the time of the original infection, a rash and high fever, easily confused with malaria (*check*); in the second stage, diminished appetite, insomnia, nausea, headache, pain like being struck by lightning appearing suddenly in odd places, pain in her bones/joints/hands/feet, intestinal problems, eye infections, hair loss, feeling poisoned (*check, check, check*). Intermittent respite from symptoms, during which the disease continues to wreak its havoc in internal organs, the brain, the nerves, bones, and joints . . . and then the strange symptoms resurface, and the patient is dismissed as a hypochondriac and neurotic (*check*).

In Europe and Africa at the end of the nineteenth century, syphilis was extremely common, but it was taboo, much as HIV remains today: one did not speak or write of it, not even in private diaries, except with code words. During the first years the disease was extremely contagious and condemned its carrier to loneliness, as well as endless physical suffering, for the side effects of the mercury and arsenic treatments were almost worse than the disease itself. The upside was that after two years the danger of contagion began to decrease, until at around seven years it was no longer contagious at all. If I had wondered how Karen and Denys's sex life was possible, this is the explanation.

As I read about the horrors of syphilis, I begin to see Karen's lonely years in Africa in a new light. Maybe her despair, her depression, her emotional roller coaster, the manic highs and the depressed lows were partly caused by syphilis—not just by Denys. Just thinking about the disease must have been crushing—enough to send anyone to bed for days.

And yet there was also a paradoxical glamour to syphilis. It was the disease of heroes and artists. It was contracted by notables from Columbus to Beethoven, from Nietzsche to Baudelaire, and from Oscar Wilde to Vincent van Gogh. In 1926, Karen wrote to her brother: "If this didn't sound so beastly, I might say that it was worth having syphilis in order to become a baroness." Still later she believed that the disease made her a writer: "I promised the devil my soul, and in return he promised me that everything I was going to experience hereafter would be turned into tales."

It could also be, however, that Karen's multifarious ailments arose not from syphilis but from a constant state of toxicity—from the fact that for years she medicated herself against all her diseases in the way she thought best: with a tiny dose of arsenic.

I leverage myself out of bed in the morning, ready to head out on a drive around the national park, but the woman at the reception desk tells me that Fazal is ill and has been taken to the hospital. What!? Fazal was, in fact, complaining about his stomach yesterday, but I had no idea it was this serious. And what hospital, exactly? How far is it to civilization from here, anyway? The woman doesn't know. She says a technician who works in the lodge has agreed to take me out for a morning drive. The rest is TBA.

Fortunately, it's my seventh safari day, and I don't spook easily. I'm sure things will work out. And if I die on the savanna, well, I'm ready for that too.

While Fazal lies ill, then, I'm sent out with the technician to drive through a grassy plain that stretches in all directions as far as the eye can see. The plain is exactly the color of a lion. It's so quiet I can hear the grass swishing in the wind. We see an endless line of zebras wandering in the golden morning light toward a watering hole, following the leader. We see jackal couples, warthogs grazing down on their knees, hyenas returning from slaughter with their smiling lips red with blood, impalas running full-tilt with their tails up. We study cheetahs through binoculars—they sit in the tawny grass so far away that we can just barely make out their heads sticking up above the stalks—and wait in vain for them to start stalking the Thomson's gazelles hiding in the vicinity. We find a leopard trying to stalk the impalas by creeping through the tall grass, but the ten tourist vehicles stalking it with their cameras bring that whole effort to naught.

We return to the hotel for lunch, and after lunch I watch as a big baboon galumphs about the deserted dining room and manages to snag some freshly baked buns and cart them off. Nature rolls on all around us, and we tag along as best we can.

Fazal returns in the afternoon. He's had food poisoning and was up all night vomiting, so he spent the morning in the lodge clinic to make sure it was nothing worse. "We can get a cell phone signal here and they have a small-plane connection to the city," he says. There will be no such luxuries in Lobo, the far-from-everything area on the northern border of the Serengeti where we're headed next.

During the off-season nobody bothers coming to the Lobo wilderness, so I am once again the lodge's only guest. I have a view from my room straight out onto the open savanna, but the lodge itself was inventively built on top of a kopje, a large rock formation. The kopje is also a favorite hangout for leopards, which means that going for a walk on the rocks after dark is strictly forbidden: the leopards stalk baboons and rock badgers, and have been known to climb the steps to the restaurant; a few months ago some leopard cubs were found playing in the lodge swimming pool. The hotel manager makes me promise not to climb up to the viewpoints alone, and insists on accompanying me to the peak of the kopje—though I don't see how this rather chubby Indian man in his checked suit with a glass of beer in one hand is going to save me from a leopard attack.

Between sunset and dinner there is a half-hour period during which hot water will come out of the shower and I'll be able to wash my hair. I'm drying my hair after my shower when the electricity goes out. This is par for the course, so I stand there in the dark waiting for the lights to come back on, holding the hair dryer in my hand. But nothing happens, and I realize that it must not be the whole lodge. A fuse has probably blown in my room alone. The lights will not come back on, because no one even knows they're out.

I wonder what the hell I should do. I'm naked, and it's pitch-black in the room. (When it gets dark in Africa, it gets *really* dark.) I haven't a clue where my headlamp is. I consider opening the door to my room—maybe enough light would come in from the corridor that I could see to put something on—but I've been specifically warned about the brash baboons that lurk outside and will push right into my room if they get even a whiff of food (somewhere I have a bag of crackers and fruit). The last thing I want right now is a dance with a baboon, which would send me out of the room screaming (naked) for help. Fighting down panic, I fumble about in the inky darkness (how *can* it be this dark!?) for the landline, but it's dead (of course), and anyway I can't see the number to dial for reception, which I know is written right next to the phone. Finally, after an eternity of groping about, I find my cell phone, by the light of whose display I manage to locate my clothes and at long last my headlamp—which I now remember I placed on the nightstand immediately upon my arrival for just such an emergency. Sheesh.

I do finally manage to make my way to dinner, which is served in the gorgeous and vast (but empty and echoing) dining room. The only diners being served by white-gloved waiters are Fazal and me.

*

[KAREN WRITES]

February 5, 1928. Dearest Mother – – Everything about safaris is so indescribably fascinating to me, even starting in the dark in the cold, clear night air.

We head off on a safari drive at six the next morning. I've learned that the morning drives are the best: it's still cool, the morning slant of light is beautiful, and it feels as if we're seeing the animals at their private morning business. Hyenas with bulging bellies pad about in the dark, on their way home from their nocturnal feasts. As the daylight comes up we see an elephant family at breakfast, follow lion tracks in the sand, and eat our breakfast on the roof of the car, watching lion cubs tumble and play in the tall green grass.

A little farther along we come upon two lions on their honeymoon. They lie spent in the grass, until the female gets up and goes to lie next to the male. This is the signal for the male to get up and do his business. At the climax he roars and bites the female on the nape of the neck; she flops over onto her side and strokes him a little with her paw. It looks idyllic, but in fact it takes four hundred of these couplings to fertilize the female. That's why a lion couple will be at this for a week, almost without a break, day and night, every quarter hour or so, without eating or drinking, toward the end sinking into darkness, exhausted by love.

After the fourth round we're still sitting in the car watching the lions. It's ten o'clock. We've been out for four hours, unhurried. It occurs to me that if I recall nothing else from this trip, what I'll remember will be this: the yellow grass swaying in the wind, the green hills of Lobo in the background, as two lions go about their long, life-sustaining labors. Me, the Land Cruiser, the red-checked Maasai *shuka* protecting the dashboard, and on top of it my binoculars, my camera, my notebook, my water bottle. Fazal is reading a book. I'm in love with Lobo. It's green, radiantly rolling, fresher and more merciful than the dry flatlands of Seronera. And more private: there's no one here. I stand up through the open sunroof and Fazal snaps a photo of me. With my visor cap, sunglasses, and white scarf, he says, I look like a Taliban girl—only the rifle is missing.

Driving on, we arrive at the ultimate Eden. Hundreds of zebras graze on the undulating green grassy plain. I take dozens of photos, but none of them can capture more than a pale ghost of this feeling—the feeling that this sublime vista goes on forever, 360 degrees around us as far as the eye can see, and in the middle of it all just us.

I think, as the Finnish painter Akseli Gallen-Kallela did when he arrived on the savanna in 1909: *When I reached this place, time stopped.*

After a seven-hour drive, we return to the lodge to eat. I try to freshen up my sweaty appearance for lunch, and apply melon-colored lip gloss. "What happened to your mouth?" Fazal asks, looking worried. "Oh, I think something bit me," I answer. In the empty dining room we are served an inconceivable five courses. At the end of it we bulge like those hyenas this morning.

I spend the afternoon sitting on the balcony with a view of the savanna. I watch the yellow-green grass waving, as if the wind were running across the plain, or like a thousand yellow snakes.

I think about Fazal, and how unusual it is to spend so much time alone with a person I don't know. Today, when we sat on the savanna waiting for the lions dozing under a tree to head off to hunt zebras, Fazal was reading a book and I was staring off into the distance. It was very quiet, and the mood in the middle of all that vastness was somehow strangely intimate. It occurs to me how lucky I am that

Fazal is not at all my type: under no circumstances would I want to be drifting into awkward, unpredictable situations. He, on the other hand, is so professional, and has spent so much time with sweaty and sunburned tourists wearing silly sun hats, that he probably isn't thinking anything about me at all.

I'd rather not leave Lobo's verdure at all, but I must. We set off on a full day's drive through the rattlingly dry Serengeti toward Ndutu in its southern corner. We stop for lunch at an information center, where Fazal chats with a friend of his who gives tourists rides in a hot-air balloon. (The friend is so stunningly handsome that I thank my lucky stars I'm not riding with him.) In the parking lot there is also a safari truck full of boisterous backpackers, and when they climb down out of the bed of the truck a guy in dreads and shades begins drumming coolly on the spare tire. Fazal tells me that the man in one couple walking past me had clucked pityingly about me having to travel alone, until the woman shushed him, saying, "Watch out, there comes the husband." Good God, get me out of the earshot of other human beings.

I get a lump in my throat when we arrive at our accommodation for the night, Ndutu Safari Lodge. At the end of a stone path sits my thatched-roof hut, glowing golden in the evening sun. Everything screams that this place is owned by Europeans: every tiny detail is an absolutely perfect rendition of a white guest's dream of Karen Blixen's Africa. It's also "green"—ecologically sound. The drinking water is rainwater collected during the rainy season and then filtered and purified. The lodge owners also remarkably resemble my night women. One of them, Aadje Geertsema, a cheerful-looking seventy-ish woman, came here back in the 1970s to study the servals in the Ngorongoro Crater. I hear her mention, in passing, in a subordinate clause, that she spent *three years living in her car* in the crater, never seeing other humans—except when she went to buy food supplies from Margaret Gibb, with whom she eventually bought and renovated the dilapidated Ndutu camp.

Before dinner I sit for a moment beside a campfire, staring up at the starry sky curving above us in the darkness. Sometimes dik-diks come up to the campfire, I'm told. One part of me is expecting Karen's antelope Lulu to walk up.

It's still dark on the drive the next morning when we spot a lone male lion out on the plain. He clearly feels the need to establish his territory, because he launches into a long and multifarious series of roars. It begins with low growls and various grunts and snorts, but when it reaches its full metallic volume, I can't help myself: my hand goes instinctively to my throat, and a shudder shakes my whole body. The lion fixes his yellow eyes directly on me; when I stare back through my binoculars, my blood nearly curdles. His head and muzzle are huge, his mane dark brown, his body sinewy—a lion of precisely the sort Karen described. He roars with his whole body. The chilling series of sounds rolls up from the depths of his being like an earthquake from the bowels of the earth, or like a rumble of thunder. His whole massive body launches that penetrating sound, lower than low, that resounds for miles across the savanna.

It feels as if I have never before heard a lion's roar—though I would have thought the thousands of nature documentaries I've watched, not to mention the MGM lion's iconic roar, would have infused my whole being with the sound before now. I remember Karen saying that the distant roar of a lion wasn't really a sound at all, but rather *a deep vibration of the air*. Later Olli tells me that the roar is emitted at such a strangely low frequency that not all recording devices pick it up. Apparently he has tried numerous times to record a lion's roar, but all that gets left on the track is the chirping of birds.

We drive along the shore of Lake Ndutu, and see a bat-eared fox taking care of its morning business next to its lair. On the shore we see the remains of wildebeest calves—perhaps they didn't yet know that the water in this soda lake is poisonous if consumed in large quantities. We see an elephant family picking yellow flowers by the trunkful off the meadow. We see giraffes drinking from a small pond—splaying their forelegs wide to get their long necks down close to the bright-blue ribbon of water in the middle of this dry plain. On the plain we see antelope skulls and scarab beetles struggling with their balls of dung. The morning is fresh and cool, with a pleasant breeze.

At last we come upon three cheetahs basking in the morning sun, and Fazal begins to dig out breakfast. He says he made an executive decision about breakfast, because just yesterday I happened to mention that it was my favorite meal of the day. Apparently I will have to pay six whole dollars extra for this "pampering breakfast basket," whose buns the Ndutu cooks woke up at four this morning to bake. "I hope you're not angry," Fazal says.

I'm not angry. On the contrary, I'm speechless with happiness. On the checked tablecloth spread out on the car's roof appear plates, forks, knives, napkins, metal tea mugs, and a thermos, then fresh bacon, boiled eggs, a basket of freshly baked banana bread and pancakes, plus yogurt, fruit salad, butter, marmalade, honey, and orange juice—all this in the midst of the cheetahs, in the slanting light of the morning sun, a mixed choir of songbirds in the background. I'm so moved I'm choked up. Fazal warns me that cheetahs sometimes like to jump up on a car's roof to check out the scenery. I have no idea what would happen then, but I don't care.

When we finally pull out of Ndutu and the Serengeti, we have a long drive ahead of us to Tarangire National Park. On the miserable, jouncing drive through the hot, dry Olduvai desert, we come upon numerous expeditions whose cars have broken down. Some are changing a tire, some trying to fix their engines, some waiting for spare parts. Our trip is repeatedly delayed as Fazal stops to offer aid to every stranded group: he helps one get the car started, gives another the remains of our lunch boxes and water bottles. I understand completely. If I were stranded on this hellish plain, I would fervently hope someone would stop.

Once when we stop to offer a stalled car help, a young Maasai woman runs up to our car with a baby strapped to her back. She wants to sell us bracelets made of colorful beads strung onto metal wires. When she sees that I'm traveling alone, she is so overjoyed that she decides to give me one of her bracelets. "I love her!" she shouts in

Swahili (as interpreted into English by Fazal), and hops on one foot with excitement before running off.

Tarangire: the last day of my safari. From in front of my half-tent-like hut I have a stunning view down to the animals' watering hole in a gorge, and I think I've reached my destination. But as we drive into the refreshing quiet green of Tarangire, I realize that twelve days on the savanna is also quite a substantial journey into yourself. At first you're afraid; then at some point you relax; and finally you inevitably come face-to-face with your own deepest essence.

As we pass some ancient baobab trees, Fazal once again raises the issue of my "taciturnity." This is really starting to annoy me, frankly. For twelve days now I've been working damn hard to be as chatty as I can possibly be. What, is it my job to keep him company?

It turns out that along the journey he has frequently had to explain my "uncommunicativeness" and "strangeness." Apparently in the local culture silence is rude, and if I'm not running my mouth nonstop I'm thought to be grumpy, dissatisfied. If I sit quietly writing, people think I'm writing up complaints! For example, in Arusha National Park Fazal warned the ranger in advance that I wouldn't say much on the walk to the falls, so he wouldn't wonder. Later the man thanked Fazal for the warning: without it he would have thought that the outing was a flop. In fact, he was surprised when I tipped him. What the hell! What should I have talked to this game warden about? He himself didn't say a word—just tramped ahead of me with his rifle!

I am seriously ticked off. I know I'm not the most socially gifted individual on earth, especially with people I don't know—but this is too much.

Nor is that all. I've been so happy that our interactions throughout the trip have been professional but friendly—and now Fazal has to go and ruin everything, and (dammit) *whine*. I can hardly believe my ears.

He and I have spoken about human relationships before, but to my mind on a relatively abstract level. The fact is, if you spend twelve days in the same car with someone, conversation is bound to turn to something other than the savanna ecotype currently out the car windows, including fairly personal matters. I know that Fazal is divorced, that he lives with his four-year-old daughter. I know that he would like to adopt more children, at least two more. I know that he has made friends with many of his clients, and that he is planning a trip to Sweden and Denmark to visit some of them. In the same way, I've told him all sorts of things about my own life—my work, my travels, my family situation. But now the questions start moving into new territory: Could you ever imagine yourself dating a foreigner? What qualities would your ideal man have? If someone took you out to dinner, what kind of restaurant would you like best? You know, hypothetically, in general. Could you imagine yourself living in Africa? What standard of living would be enough for you? Oh, and by the way, forgive me for saying this, but you look at least ten years younger than you actually are, how is that possible?

I'm agog at all this. First: for the whole two weeks, I've looked precisely as sweaty and saggy and middle-aged as I am. In response to Fazal's new line of questioning, I shut down completely. Play all your cards on the same day, was that your plan? Go for broke? *Faa-zaa-aalll, not like this!*

I try to answer the hypothetical questions as tactfully as I can.

"Listen, twelve days in the same car is a long time. I would hope we could remain friends, professional friends."

"Couldn't we drop the adjective?"

"No, because I suspect that you and I have different ideas of what friendship might entail."

"You don't leave me many chances," he complains.

But he doesn't give up.

"I'm wondering where I could take you. Not to clubs, you wouldn't like that. But maybe to Arusha National Park? They have a cottage for workers with fantastic views of Kilimanjaro, we could spend the night there."

Yeah, sure we could. God damn it to hell.

Why do you have to spoil the whole thing, this whole glorious

Karen–Farah dynamic, this story of trusted men whose names start with *F* (about which you of course know nothing)? Does it always have to come down to this? Why do we have to even start playing this stupid game?

Fazal goes on and on. I sit mostly quiet, as apparently is my wont.

He tells me straight out that he has deliberately left the whining—or, well, as he puts it, "the talk about friendship"—for the last day. Apparently it often happens that at some point on the safari, white women traveling alone fall into a kind of sublime euphoria. The experience is so vast and all-encompassing, and the rest of the world is so far away, that these women start wanting to intensify the experience with sex, and many guides gladly jump at the chance—you know, for the sake of customer relations.

I stare out the window, pointedly *not* mentioning my stray thoughts in Lobo, the fact that one day out on the paradisal savanna I did, in fact, think about sex. Apparently that is the epitome of hackneyed biological conditioning.

Fazal continues that unfortunately these feelings and thoughts are more or less the same as the ones you experience at three in the morning at a dance club after one too many drinks, and they never seem so great the next day. *He* for one would *never* exploit this kind of situation on safari. On the other hand, he thinks it's entirely appropriate for him to put out feelers on the last day of the trip, as things are winding down, to see the lay of the land. Who knows where our friendship might lead? he says.

I don't have the heart to tell him what I already know: he's not my type, I'm not looking for a relationship, and time is not going to make the tiniest bit of difference in any of that.

Evening is falling as I reach my tent. Once inside, I burst into tears. I cry out of twelve days' exhaustion, but also because this unbelievable trip is ending, and on this clear, starry night in Africa something is being offered to me that I surely do not want. I cry because I don't know how to live this life—because I seem to be in some intolerable way the prisoner of my own self—because I don't seem able to milk things for everything they might offer. I cry because I'm just now realizing that this was my last evening on the savanna, far from civilization, in this place that I've always dreamed about. Could I have used my time more effectively? Maybe not. But I do know that being plucked out of the world for two weeks pits a person against herself—and, well, perhaps also makes a person cling to whatever other person happens to be nearby.

And now it's my last morning. Lying in bed I look out through my mosquito net as the sun's rays slant down and light up the green acacia savanna of Tarangire. And I think: *Dammit, I may not be the kind of woman I'd like to be, but then neither was Karen.*

[KAREN WRITES]

September 5, 1926. Dearest Tommy -- Last year -- I came to the conclusion that what was making life so hard for me was the fact that I am so poor. It sounds so despicable and it took some time before I could really admit the truth of it -- I would consent to lose a leg in order to have 5,000 pounds a year -- because I think I could be myself without a leg, but it seems to me to be so extraordinarily difficult to be myself without money. -- Is it worse to admit that one suffers through poverty than that one suffers through loneliness or fear?

September 13, 1928. Dearest Ellen -- I myself have come to the conclusion that happiness does not depend on exterior circumstances but is a state of mind -- As the years go by one learns to understand and sort out the minor phenomena of life, that are necessary to enable one to be oneself. For instance, I know that I must not get fat; it is preferable for me to suffer the pains of hunger, because being overweight "cramps my style." I also know -- I am -- [a] *snob, and if I cannot be with the aristocracy or the intelligentsia I must go down among the proletariat or, what corresponds to that out here, the natives, because I cannot live with the middle class.*

Right from the beginning of my reading about Karen, this unpleasant suspicion kept creeping into my mind: What if she wasn't as exemplary as I've taken her to be? The woman who speaks in her memoir *Out of Africa* is calm, brave, and wise—but her letters and biographies reveal quite a different person. Many sources mention her pretentious and histrionic behavior. Her relationship with Denys was desperate. It's putting it very mildly to say that she was subject to mood swings. Her passion for hunting was shuddersome. Then there are all the letters that make it clear just how many different versions of events she told different people, how often she flat-out lied. And if you ask contemporary African writers, Karen's colonial attitudes do not earn high marks. Is this really someone I should be thinking about at night?

Readers of Karen Blixen's books are familiar with that self-confident, wise, competent, and equitable woman who accepts everything life throws at her with a Buddha-like calm and a warm sense of humor.

But there are other Karens.

Her letters to her brother Thomas reveal a less-filtered Karen. This Karen was an unsure, sickly, and depressed woman whose emotional life was a constant roller coaster and who was afraid of a whole grab bag of things: financial difficulties, losing the farm, losing her lover, traveling alone, living alone, her own weakness. This woman had panic attacks and wanted to die. This Karen's world was totally dependent on Denys: when he was around, she was ecstatically happy; when he was away, she collapsed into bed, useless.

The Karen featured in her letters to her mother, by contrast, was a fun-loving and lighthearted Karen whose problems were minuscule and fleeting. To her mother, Karen put a positive spin on her marriage, pooh-poohed her illnesses, and even lied about them (*just a little heatstroke!*), keeping up a cheerful and good-natured façade. But then—who among us wouldn't do the same?

Then there is the biographers' Karen: a conflicted, unpleasant person, self-centered, capricious, and fake. These writers have dumped all seven cardinal sins and more into her debit column:

1) Karen was proud and ambitious.

2) Karen was unstable—now in utter despair, now gushing with rapture—and easily depressed. She always took the servants' negligence and forgetfulness as personal affronts and abandonments.

3) Karen always got her way, because no one dared oppose her. People were afraid of her. As one friend remarked, "You had the feeling that she might suddenly shoot someone."

4) Karen was always playing some role. With her friends she was open and relaxed, but if someone she knew less well joined them, she might begin to speak in a pretentious voice that no one recognized.

When she wanted to make an impression, she became an exaggeratedly charming and conceited woman of the world. Apparently her "intellectuality" and "insane-seeming intensity" made men nervous. To people she considered insignificant, she was an iceberg, and she didn't really love children either—she studied children greedily, like a traveling salesman, to see what she could get out of them with a minimum of effort.

5) Karen lied and embellished stories. Sometimes about her age, sometimes about the social status of her companions; sometimes she took credit for other people's heroic actions. For example, once she claimed to have shot a lion that Denys had shot. She distorted events in her books to spin them more positively. While reading how brave and calm she was riding alone onto the savanna in *Out of Africa*, you have to remember her brother Thomas's remark that she was unable to mount a horse unaided, and threw a temper tantrum if the "boys" she called in to help her couldn't hold the horse still.

6) Karen was selfish. When her sister Ea died, she demanded that her mother come to Africa, and refused to understand that it was more important for her mother to care for Ea's little daughter. In Karen's mind, her niece would have years to spend with her grandma, but she would not.

7) Karen was a snob. She wanted to be unique, and fervently wished to be rich. In certain circles she became famous for her dramatic way of dressing and for shooting her own pelts for furs.

8) One source even claims that Karen didn't contract syphilis from Bror, but brought it home herself from a trip to Paris.

A difficult broad. The devil's consort. A mythic writer. Or the brave and calm Karen of her books? At least she knew how to brand herself.

As I finish reading her biography, I'm confused, flustered, and frankly angry at Karen: Is she really this unbalanced bitch? But later, as I reread her letters from Africa, it begins to seem to me that maybe her biographer Judith Thurman made her out to be worse than she was. Thurman seized upon every sentence written in a weak moment and took it out of context to make Karen sound thoroughly off-putting;

but as I reread the letters all the way through, those same sentences begin to sound understandable, yes, and quite human. Damn it all, Judith, *you* go to Africa and live there alone, broke, and sick for eighteen years, communicating only through letters that take weeks or even months to get through, and then see whether you have any moments of weakness, selfishness, depression, or despair—times when it feels like you're the only person on earth and no one will help! Sure, Karen was possessive and selfish, and had mood swings. Definitely she wanted to hide her weaknesses in every way she could. But wouldn't we all?

And then when I go back one more time to Karen's book *Out of Africa*, everything looks different. As the book's epigraph, she has taken the elevated quotation from Herodotus: "To ride, shoot with the bow, and speak the truth"; but now I know that the book is *literature*—a semifictional condensation of reality. I know that her calm is a bluff. "When times were dull on the farm," Karen says lightly in passing, as if those troubles had been just a brief subplot in an otherwise happy narrative. In reality, they refer to the whole eighteen-year struggle with a climate unsuited to coffee farming, nerve-racking droughts, locusts, a chronic lack of funds, loneliness, illnesses, crises in love relationships, miscarriages, and the constant threat that it will all be brought down into nothing.

And yet at the same time her Africa is a paradise lost, a perfected ideal image of what could have been, and maybe what at times even was. This Karen isn't afraid, isn't lying in bed for weeks, sobbing. This Karen is wise and brave. This Karen has survived her losses and surveys her life calmly, as if from the air—like Denys from his airplane, from enough of a distance that even suffering looks beautiful. This is the Karen that I've been thinking about at night. This is the Karen I followed to Africa, the better to admire her.

And maybe this is the Karen that Karen herself thought about at night. Her *exemplary self*, the ideal toward which she strove her whole life, without ever reaching it. That exemplary self that we all wish we were.

Missing in Action

I return to Olli and Flotea's guest room exhausted and already nostalgic. Things here are as they were before: nothing has happened at the construction site; the electricity still hasn't been hooked up. Flotea has had new reddish braids put in her hair, woven prettily around her head. But I'm still elsewhere, in another universe, with absolutely no desire to return. Olli understands how I feel. As consolation he shows me his treasure, a lion's hairball, bought years ago off a Maasai. It's amazing, a tight dark-brown sphere the size of a golf ball, which the savanna wind has worn perfectly round. I take a deep mournful whiff of it. It is saturated with the ancient scent of the wild.

Olli wonders how the trip went, asks about highlights, and I try to tell him something, but it all seems like a dream. The most important moment and why it became etched on my consciousness I can't even explain: the time when we stopped in the middle of an endless grassy savanna on the way from Ndutu to Ngorongoro, got out of the car, and walked so far that the car became a tiny speck on the horizon. As far as we could see in all directions there was nothing but us, a gentle breeze, zebras, antelopes, some jackals lying somewhere in the grass, and in the background misty Mount Ngorongoro, where time has stopped. In the photograph I have shrunk to an insignificant being in the midst of a grassy sea extending in all directions to the horizon.

That moment, on the third to last day. The microscopic scale of a human being. The refreshing thought that I am just a minuscule detail in the landscape.

I had planned to spend my last week in Kenya, but there have recently been more terrorist attacks there, and I'm not feeling tempted to go. I read in the news that the US has placed a travel ban on Kenya, the Brits have evacuated their tourists and canceled their flights, and

Finland's Kenyan consulate urges travelers to be extremely cautious, because the threat of new strikes and kidnappings is high. All this makes me feel very anxious. I decide to limit my stay in Nairobi to just a few days and spend a bit more time here.

After Olli has listened to my safari stories for a while, I can tell he's feeling the urge to get back out into the bush himself, and I begin to wonder whether I might not somehow tempt him to take us on a camping trip, just for a couple of days, now that I have this extra time. The day after my return Olli begins to calculate, just for the fun of it, how much it would cost to head over to Mkomazi National Park for a couple of nights. We'd take along a cook and a mechanic, tents, forty gallons of water, food, maybe a field shower. Three nights and four days, including gas, park entrance fees, the men's pay, and food would cost $800. Could I afford that? He gives me two hours to think about it—because we'd leave day after tomorrow. Help! But would this mean I'd get a Karen-style tent safari after all?

I've wanted to camp out in tents the whole time, but I have to admit that now, when push comes to shove, I'm afraid. I'm not exactly a camping kind of person. I don't have a great deal of experience with tents. Olli says there aren't a lot of animals in Mkomazi, so probably I wouldn't have to be afraid of them, but it would be hot there, maybe even hotter than in the Serengeti, where fighting dehydration was a full-time job. And what about toilets? He didn't put any on the list, and I'm afraid to ask. I know how to drop trou and pee on the ground, but on a four-day trip I'd have to do other kinds of business as well. I'd really like to know whether Karen had some kind of porta-potty on her safaris, or even just a pot. I'm annoyed that she says nothing about such matters in her letters. And hey, note to biographers: this is the sort of basic stuff people want to know! How did people go to the bathroom out there?

Olli confirms my suspicions: no toilet. There's a shovel that you carry with you into the bush. But this begins to seem like the least of my problems. Olli mentioned before that you hardly see any animals in Mkomazi, and I thought that meant that there aren't any. But there are. The place is just so wild and untouched that they don't show themselves to humans. In Mkomazi if you come within a hundred yards of an elephant, it starts gearing up to attack, because it feels threatened. In the Serengeti, the lions are used to tourist cars; but in Mkomazi, Olli has never seen a lion, though you hear them roaring at night all the time. Not only that: Olli tells me cheerfully that the lions there are the "famous man-eating lions"—the same lions about which Karen wrote a hundred years ago, after reading a bloodcurdling book called *The Man-eaters of Tsavo*. "Sure," Olli says to reassure me, "you hear stories about lions dragging people out of tents and eating them, but they're rubbish. In every single one of those cases somebody left the tent zipper open, or somebody was sleeping with their head out of the tent! We'll be fine. What, go outside for a pee at night? We-e-ell, yeah, it should be relatively safe." God help us. How the hell do I find the courage to go on a trip like this? The only thing pushing me to risk it is the desire to get closer to the conditions Karen experienced when she was sleeping in a tent a hundred years ago. No lodges, no animals used to tourists, no shelter but the car—which they didn't always have either.

I tell Olli that I'm scared. He says that fear is part of a person's natural emotional range, but that a Western person typically doesn't even know what real fear feels like. In African cities and on the savanna sleeping in a tent, on the other hand, you know what it's like to fear for your life. The only question is whether you can control your fear. He tells me he doesn't feel afraid in nature at all, but he does in Arusha—he's been mugged so many times.

I don't know whether Karen was afraid on safari. I don't remember her ever writing about that. But maybe with Bror and Denys, she wasn't able to be afraid. Maybe you don't feel fear if you're traveling with a man you worship and trust implicitly.

Olli starts making travel plans. He goes through the car quickly with the mechanic and works with the cook to plan grocery purchases. He packs the car with the tents (including the mess tent), sleeping pads, sleeping bags, camp chairs, pots and pans, dishes and utensils, camp kitchen equipment, washtubs, lanterns, tap water, drinking water, spare tires, a jack, tools. I wash clothes in a bucket and pack my own things. The queasiness that started stirring things up in my stomach a couple days ago is getting worse, so I take an antibiotic pill Olli offers—the situation must be gotten under control before tomorrow morning. The pill tires me, makes me logy, but I tell myself it doesn't matter what pills I pop, as long as they keep me more or less alive.

Early in the morning Flotea sends us off with a hefty breakfast. Wishing us a good trip, she confesses that she would never in a million years dare go camping on the savanna. She's deathly afraid of lions.

I just try to think that *everything about safaris is so indescribably fascinating.*

The Dindera campground in Mkomazi National Park is on top of a hill, on a little bluff with a view out over the green savanna spread out below and a small lake covered with water lilies. It's cloudy, but on a clear day the peak of Mount Kilimanjaro would be poking up between the other mountains. At the entrance to the park we're told that we are the only visitors. This is truly no tourist trap. They only have a handful of visitors every year. The area is wild and pristine, maybe a little like all the East African savannas were a hundred years ago. There is no connection with the outside world. Everything you need you have to bring with you.

As soon as we reach our campsite, Alois, the cook, a shortish Pare man, sets up his kitchen equipment on the bluff-stone revetment. He lights a charcoal fire and starts boiling water for tea, peeling vegetables, and marinating chicken legs. It turns out that Alois has been operating on the assumption that the trip is for two nights, and has only bought groceries for three days instead of four. As a blood-sugar neurotic, I'm about to lose it—I picture our last dinner consisting of a single egg and a cup of water . . . or would we need to bag an antelope for meat, like Karen did? But after a little more thought the cook says the food will suffice. He does complain about the stingy food budget overall, though—he is used to working for deluxe safari companies, where you don't have to scrimp on ingredients. Besides, the trip is too short for his talents, which really come most fully into their own on a ten-day safari. Alois defines the style of this trip as *budget luxurious*, and when I sit down to his food at dinner, I understand what he means.

From a Finnish perspective, hiring a cook for a camping trip seems a bit absurd, but here it seems to be standard operating procedure. Here you don't just open a can of pea soup and heat it over the Trangia stove, and even Olli in his sixteen years of working gigs like this has never traveled without a cook. He tells me he may have spent seven weeks in the bush without a shower or a toilet, but he isn't going to settle for fewer than three dishes on the table at dinner. And I understand that: if you're going to work, you don't have extra time and energy to waste on cooking. Besides, labor is cheap. The pay for the cook and the mechanic is 20,000 shillings each, or less than $9 a day.

And even if some budget-conscious northern European might decide to save by not hiring a cook, the car mechanic is life-or-death. We don't leave the campsite for even a short drive without Max the mechanic and at least a gallon canister of water. If the car breaks down—and in these conditions, that's a pretty common occurrence—it's no use waiting for help to arrive. The phones don't work, and there isn't another human being within dozens of miles. The temperature in Mkomazi climbs well into the nineties during the day, so you're not going to sit in a broken-down car for very long, and you can't get anywhere on foot.

Olli and Max set up the tents. The mess tent is really just a simple canopy above a cloth-covered dining table and some chairs, set with pitchers of juice and tea. The two hired men share a tent; Olli will sleep in a one-man gauze tube tent. He can admire the stars all night if he wants. The tent is so open to the elements, he tells me, that none of the men he hires for trips like this would ever agree to sleep in one. Before we left, Olli asked me whether I wanted a tent like that as well, but I said I wanted the thickest and toughest tent fabric he could find. So they set up a four-person Fjällräven tent for me, with an inner tent and an outer tent. Even that wouldn't stop a herd of elephants, of course, if one decided to rampage right over the top of me, but at least it feels safer than sleeping in a transparent tube.

And that's about it for the facilities. There's a towel hanging on a branch and a basin of water under it for washing. On the rock in front of my tent there's a roll of toilet paper for the quickie outdoor pee. Olli also shows me the proper latrine, a little walk from the campsite in the middle of tall grass: a concrete slab with a hole in it, covered with rocks, which you can apparently arrange into a seat.

Before sunset, we go on a little drive—hoping to reach what Olli calls Tanzania's most beautiful viewpoint. But we don't make it: the river is flooding and the road is out. Alois remains behind to fix dinner, though he doesn't seem happy to be staying in camp alone without the safety of the car. If a lion were to wander in for a visit, his only slim chance of survival would be to climb the tree next to the kitchen. But the dinner Alois serves up is fantastic. The sun sets at around six thirty, and suddenly it's pitch-black. The screaming of crickets and frogs is deafening. We sit in the mess tent in the dim light of a small field lantern, and for starters Alois brings in bread and a leek and coriander soup in small steel bowls. The main course is a huge platter of fried tilapia, coriander potatoes, heavenly *kachumbari* salad, and beans and carrots sautéed in butter. Dessert is sweet slices of pineapple. Later I hear that this is where the penny-pinching budget Alois complained about intervened: Olli had crossed off the cook's grocery list everything "useless and silly," such as chocolate mousse for dessert. "We don't need any *chocolate mousse* out there in the bush!" Olli had chuffed. "Or would you have wanted some?" he asks me now.

It's just gone eight o'clock, but we've retreated into our tents and I'm writing this with my headlamp—not much else to do in the dark. I change into my sleepwear and lie down on top of my sleeping bag, sweaty. It may of course turn chilly enough at night that I'll want to clamber into the sleeping bag. From the other tents I hear Olli yawning and the boys' quiet chatter. I feel surprisingly safe in the tent. As if I were in the womb, in the middle of everything and yet in my own (imaginary) safe haven.

At one in the morning I begin to hear the roaring of a lion—that low, metallic, blood-curdling, earth-rumbling thunder. It seems to be coming from a long way off, down on the plain. The male lion patrols his territory throughout the night, and the complex series of pronouncements on that topic drifts up to us at quarter-hour intervals till morning, moving slowly from east to west around the base of our bluff. I don't sleep a wink, and don't dare to go out for a pee. In addition, the tent is full of ticks. I wage endless war against them.

In the morning I learn that this is high tick season in Mkomazi. Our passage through waist-high grass to the latrine has worked its magic: the ticks jumped onto our clothing and rode it back into our tents. Olli tells me he's gotten tick-bite fever here twice; he did finally find an antibiotic that cured it in Finland—"but they stopped making it," he says. I'm consoled by the knowledge that ticks don't bury their heads in your skin right away: they hide in a fold of your skin for a day or two first, so if I can pluck them off in time, there shouldn't be any danger.

At five in the morning, Alois begins starting fires for breakfast. Olli didn't sleep a wink either, thanks to the lion and the ticks. Before the sun comes up, he heads out to the latrine hill shouting and clapping his hands, because at night he heard leopards growling on the slope. Once I start thinking about leopards, I no longer have the slightest desire to traipse out to the latrine. A quick pee in the middle of the road will have to do.

The sunrise is gorgeous. The eastern mountains bathe in a reddish-orange glow, while a mist blankets the western mountains, making them look coated with a soft white fur, or maybe a furry mold. From the kitchen area we see the peak of Kilimanjaro looming. Alois makes a vegetable omelet, fried sausage and tomato, toast, and slices of avocado and fruit for breakfast. If we make it through the trip alive, at least we won't die of hunger.

The sky is partly cloudy; the air is already hot and humid. We break camp and get on the road by eight.

The green rolling Dindera landscape soon turns into a dry red-sand desert where the acacias and impenetrable thornbushes glow in gray and silver shades. En route we see lesser kudus, kongonis or hartebeests, impressive straight-horned beisas, and long-necked gerenuks, which graze on the tops of trees by climbing the trunks with their front hooves. Many of these species in Tanzania are found only here in Mkomazi.

We're on our way to Maore, right on the Kenya border; the drive will take many hours. Olli wants to stop en route in Kisima to fill our water canisters and see whether his friend Tony is in. He is, and the guards—armed with Kalashnikovs—tell us to drive on in and up the hill, where a stone house stands, blending in with the landscape. It must be the only such house around here.

Tony Fitzjohn is nearly seventy and a character. As a young man he worked for eighteen years with George Adamson in Kenya, where they lived with wild lions in harsh conditions in the Kora nature reserve. George Adamson was a legendary lion man who devoted his life to protecting lions and returning ones raised in captivity to the wild; his wife, Joy Adamson, wrote *Born Free* and two sequels about Elsa the lion. Tony was twenty-six and living a shady kind of life in Africa in 1971 when George hired him as his assistant, upon the fatal mauling of his previous assistant by a lion. The good-looking, bare-chested young man shown wrestling lions in the unreal photos looks like Tarzan.

When political conditions heated up in Kenya and George Adamson was killed by poachers in 1989 (Joy had been murdered almost ten years before), Tony too became persona non grata and had to leave Kenya. He moved to Tanzania, to the Mkomazi nature reserve, which was in terrible shape back then, and began to develop it. He launched a project aimed at restoring the park's African wild dog population, which had been reduced almost to extinction; and later built a fenced-in protected area for rhinos—an area so large a whole mountain fits inside it. The first endangered rhinos were flown in from South Africa, and nowadays the population consists of around twenty-five individuals. The area also has an educational center where children come to learn about nature conservation and rhinoceroses, and next to the watering hole an underground viewing station has been built so that visitors can watch the animals. The man has accomplished an unbelievable amount almost on his own, with that inconceivable tenacity and iron will that one must have to promote nature conservation and fight the eternal problems here, such as corruption, poaching, and illegal cattle grazing. It was largely as a result of his two decades of work that Mkomazi was gazetted as a national park in 2008. These days Tony employs four dozen local workers with whom he stays in contact by radiotelephone—every now and then I hear him giving instructions in Swahili, in a quiet voice that brooks no opposition.

Tony is a nature conservationist heart and soul, but he is no sweet-tempered do-gooder. He's known for his difficult, choleric temper and no-nonsense straight talk. The locals either fear him or hate him. The first time Olli came to his place years ago, Tony's words of welcome were "Fuck off—*now*," backed up with an armed guard. Tony especially hates researchers, who show up here with their theories without understanding the first thing about practical circumstances—and in fact, if Tony has any say in the matter, researchers aren't allowed on the premises. "I don't do people," he says, but admits that these days he's domesticated, and no longer "drinks, steals, does drugs, or beats his wife." He still can't stand intruders or extra guests, so Alois and Max have to sit in the car for our entire visit. Tony knows he's hated, and doesn't want locals to see how he lives. Maybe he's been marinated in too many sauces: nature conservation is not always popular with locals evicted from their living areas, especially if irascible *mzungus* are behind the whole thing. That may be why Tony takes his foundation's most important task to be educating children's attitudes toward nature conservation.

Charismatic, Tony certainly is. His humor is black as night, and I could almost swear he's flirting with me. "Who's she?" he snaps without looking at me when we arrive, but at least he doesn't point a gun at me. When later Olli repeatedly refers to me as "she" or "that lady," Tony says, "You could at least use her name, it's Mia. We have to treat her nicely," he adds with a devilish grin, "so she'll feel comfortable and we can boil and eat her later." When I ask whether I might buy his autobiography, *Born Wild*, which was published a couple of years ago—and which Olli has begun to translate into Finnish, but so far without placing it with a Finnish publisher—he grumbles, "Do I look like a bookseller to you?" But then he growls into a radiotelephone, telling someone to bring one, and dedicates it with the words: "For

Mia (Missing in Action?). If you don't get my book published in Finnish, I want this back!" When Olli mentions that our experience here today will probably give me material for a nice chapter in my book, Tony groans: "I don't need any nice chapter!" I promise not to write anything nice about him.

In a rare show of hospitality, Tony invites us to lunch, and before lunch drives us out to the rhino reserve. He drives his open-top Land Rover like a crazy person—I hold tight, afraid he's going to bounce me out into the thorny acacia bushes headfirst. I was disappointed at first when I heard that Tony's airplane is in Nairobi being serviced, because I was hoping to get a little demonstration flight Karen-style. But when Olli tells me that Tony's flying style is even worse than his driving style—he might flip the plane upside down just ten meters above the ground—I'm relieved.

Tony lives with his wife and four children in their attractive, rambling, hilltop-hugging stone house, with a breathtaking view. His wife is currently visiting their children at school in England, so in place of his family Tony introduces us to a two-year-old baby elephant that has lived with them since it was a week old. Its mother had died, and one night it just appeared at the guard shack and woke the guard, as if asking for help. The elephant is bronze-colored from the red dirt; it is a bit cautious with Olli and me, but lets us pet it. In years past we could also have met Tony's lion Jipe, whose handshake, I'm told, was a lot scarier.

We eat lunch in a large mess tent on the vista balcony. "Use your hands, Mia," Tony says, and begins to gnaw on the grilled chicken drumsticks brought from the kitchen, occasionally stopping to lick his fingers clean. We throw the bones to the mongooses, who come right up to the balcony and throw themselves greedily at the bones, which are almost their size. After lunch Tony says without ceremony that he's going to turn in for a nap. "On your way out, check out the African wild dogs," he says. "And stop by on your way back day after tomorrow."

Then he walks into the house talking on his radiotelephone.

We set up camp in the evening in Maore, in the middle of a broad savanna, under the shade of a large tree. Before sunset Olli and I take a little walk down to a nearby lake. When Olli notices animal tracks—look, there's a zebra track, there's a buffalo, there's a fresh lion track—I try to keep my eyes on the horizon and my breathing steady. Without the car for shelter, it suddenly feels strangely as if I'm naked.

After dinner we go straight to bed. Above us curves the clear, starry sky with its nebulae, its Milky Way, and the upside-down Big Dipper. Surprisingly enough, I'm no longer afraid at all: I sink immediately into the depths and sleep like a log. No ticks, no lion roars, nothing. Now it's seven in the morning, the clouds are burning off, the sun is up. Olli is predicting it's going to be a hot day.

I've only been washing my face in the basin mornings, and yesterday evening I rinsed the red dust off my arms. Tomorrow morning I am going to have to wash at least my hair. Every morning I change my shirt, socks, and underpants, but I'm still beginning to stink—though Olli assures me that in the savanna wind, no one will notice. We have periodic conversations about the intestinal functioning of each member of the expedition—that seems to be de rigueur in these conditions—and in his role as an expert on biology and medicine, Olli is constantly asking me pointed follow-up questions about the state of my gastrointestinal tract. Every time I head off into the bush with the roll of toilet paper, he asks whether I need the shovel. I don't. My GI tract has shut down for its own psychosomatic (leopard-related) reasons.

We set off for a morning drive before eight, going all the way to distant Kamakota Hill. Alois remains in camp, Max drives, I stand in the open sunroof, and Olli sits in his favorite spot on the car roof. The thornbushes and dry acacia skeletons shine silvery in the sun. The soil here is lateritic with iron oxides, and glows in orange, rust, and even pink shades; it reflects the sun so brightly it dazzles the eyes. Sometimes the landscape is as spectral as in some sort of horror movie, or a postapocalyptic science-fiction film. I begin to understand why they call this place Mkomazi: the name means "no water."

Every once in a while we see big birds, including secretary birds, common spoonbills, vulturine guinea fowl, and southern ground hornbills—Olli feeding me the names. Every group of animals turns as if on command and flees us on sight: common elands, giraffes, zebras, warthogs, all of them reddish-orange like the soil here. The black-and-white ostrich is black-and-orange here; the warthog with its tail in the air as it scampers away is orange; the zebras have orange stripes; the giraffes look like they've been cast in orange bronze. Our car is orange. So are we, and all our things. Everything is covered in orange dust.

We stop occasionally to take photos or to collect twisted pieces of driftwood from the road—pieces of wood dyed by fire and red dirt and hardened over time into concrete by the savanna wind. On Kamakota we climb to the top of a massive kopje, from which we have a fantastic view in every direction. On the savanna we see a straight line, a boundary extending all the way to the horizon. On the right side of the line, the bushes are silver and dry; on the left, green and leafy. That line is where the rains have stopped.

When we return to the campsite for lunch, it's already blazing hot. After the meal Olli dozes in the tall grass under the shade of the tree, and I sit in my folding chair flipping through Tony's memoir. I think about Joy Adamson, who appears in the book—about how, like Karen, she "chose lions," and how in one documentary I saw the narrator said that her relationship with Elsa the lion was so close because Joy didn't have children. I reflect on why a woman's childlessness is always considered a tragedy, and why her actions are so often interpreted as compensation for a lack of children. It's not necessarily a tragedy. It's just that if you take one road, you don't take another. If childlessness closes some doors, it also opens others. And why aren't men's actions interpreted along the same lines? At least, I've never seen it claimed that George Adamson devoted his life to lions because he didn't have any children.

All morning I soaked in the views so greedily, standing too long in the sun with my head up through the refreshing sunroof, that now I'm headachy and nauseated. Even so, I force myself to go along on the evening drive, because the evening light is the most beautiful and colors the landscape gold. We see a martial eagle preying on a kori bustard chick, and drive for a long way along the Kenyan border, which runs just a few hundred yards from our campsite. The border is marked by a clear-cut roadway that runs straight as an arrow through the rolling terrain to the horizon. If I have sometimes wondered about the borders between African nations, which look like they were drawn with a ruler, now I understand: if there's nothing but savanna or desert in the borderland, there's no reason for the border itself to twist and turn.

When we return to camp, we wash our hair. There isn't enough water for a shower, but with a single basin of water you can wash two people's hair, and I feel refreshed.

To feel better, in the evening I drink large amounts of water as well, with the result that at night I'm about to explode. I try to talk myself out of it for a long time, but there's no help for it: I undeniably, absolutely have to pee. I sit up in my tent, listen to the dark intently, and hear nothing. I open the zipper to my tent and scan my surroundings with my headlamp like a guerrilla, on full alert for a Tsavo man-eating lion. Then I squat quickly just outside my tent, drop my pants, do my business as fast as I can, throw my legs into reverse, back into the tent, zip up the zipper lickety-split, and breathe. My heart is pounding.

Not particularly classy, I'll admit. But this is a matter of life or death.

Morning dawns foggy and indescribably beautiful. We are so close to the Indian Ocean that the humidity condenses off the ocean at night as a heavy dew and in the morning as fog. The tents and all our things are soaking wet, as after a cloudburst. The slant light of morning also reveals hundreds of spiderwebs spread everywhere in the yellow grass. They sway gently in the breeze like tiny, round, lacy cloths hung to dry on stalks of grass.

It's our last morning, and I'm already starting to miss tent life. (My leopard constipation has surrendered, and now I could last for another week.) Everything is simple, and therefore also a shade inconvenient, but in the main clear and relaxing. Mystifyingly, there's more time at a tent campsite than in a lodge, where you're always in a hurry to meet deadlines: dinner, electricity, hot water, sunset. You have to watch the clock so you'll have time to take a shower, dry your hair, make up, dress for dinner, and climb up to a special balcony to enjoy the sunset and/or sunrise. Here there's no regimen. You just sit in your tent chair enjoying the scenery, reading or writing, hair dirty, in whatever clothes you happen to have on, letting the sun set and rise, the light increase or decrease, the fog lift or fade away; and then you walk into the mess tent to eat when dark has fallen or day has dawned. Everything is here, all around us, and we are right in the middle of everything. Even though on a lodge trip you might spend the whole day on the savanna without seeing a single other human being, you still have that civilizational intervention waiting for you in the evening. Here no one comes between you and nature. I get it, Karen: I understand that happiness.

Upon our return home, I take a shower and rinse the color of the Mkomazi animals off myself. The water rolling down my body colors the floor of the shower orange.

[KAREN WRITES]

September 21, 1930. Dearest Mother -- I have had a few of the loveliest days, for Denys came last Thursday and left again yesterday. -- I went up flying with him yesterday, and I think it is doubtful whether a greater happiness could exist for me than to fly over Ngong with him. -- One ought to see Africa from the air -- then you really see the enormous expanses and the play of light and shadow over them. -- Denys wanted to try various maneuvers and turned the machine on its side once or twice, so I was glad I was strapped in. . . .

In May of 1930, Denys wrote from England that he was looking for an airplane that he could land on Karen's lawn over on the Ngong side of the house—and in September he did indeed arrive in his new plane. Its name was *Nzige*, meaning "grasshopper," and the road passing Karen's house to where Denys would always land is still named Nzige Road. On their first flight together, Karen and Denys flew over the Ngong Hills, checking out the coffee plants and African huts, and saw great herds of panicky zebras and impalas. Sometimes they would go up for just fifteen minutes, so that when they returned the tea in the pot was still hot; other times they would fly over Lake Natron, or to Naivasha, or to the Indian Ocean shoreline as far as Takaungu, and spend the weekend there. Denys told Karen that he had bought the plane just so he could show her this country from the air. It seemed to Karen, in fact, that from the air she at last *understood everything*. And to be sure, in those days—before the Nature Channel—flying must have seemed miraculous: they saw for the first time the entire vastness of the East African plains.

*

[KAREN WRITES]

October 12, 1930. Dear Ellen – – I have been up almost every day with Denys – – I can really picture to myself what it must be like to be an angel.

Those were their last happy times together.

Until now I have stalked Karen only from the other side of the border, and truth be told, Kenya could not tempt me less. I have been following the news with growing panic. Because of the threat of terrorist strikes, while in Nairobi one should stay away from shopping malls, international hotels, taxis, slums, and popular gatherings, and avoid being out and about during rush hours and weekends. What does that leave to do? My problem is that my return flight departs from Nairobi.

So now I'm sitting on a bus on the three-lane freeway leading to Nairobi, surrounded by endless lines of semis. Around me are smoke-belching factories, miles and miles of roadside ugliness: trucks stopped on the shoulder, car repair shops, warehouses. The air is thick with exhaust fumes and the reek of strange chemicals. Industry, traffic, vehicles, pollution, crowds of people—all rolling stupefyingly right over me, on a whole other scale from anything I saw in Tanzania.

It's far from idyllic. But I guess this is where I had to come if I am truly to find Karen.

My last days at Olli and Flotea's after our return from Mkomazi are spent preparing for travel. I scrub my laundry clean in a bucket—there is still so much savanna dust in my clothes that even the third rinse is reddish-orange. Flotea comes with me to help me buy presents to take back to Finland: I buy a few cotton *kikoi* cloths, though I end up having to pay at least double the local prices for them. Flotea's friend Prisca stops by, bringing me a dress she picked out for me in her shop—I had mentioned that I kept dreaming of getting a simple earth-colored *kanga* dress, but Prisca's taste is obviously much more flamboyant than mine, so now I am the proud owner of a garishly patterned Mama Africa outfit and head scarf to match. Flotea takes me to a shop nearby to have it tailored to fit. The seamstress spends an hour doing the job on her foot-pedal sewing machine. For that I'm charged 1,000 shillings, or just under fifty cents.

We go on one last little walk, eat *supu* in a swarm of flies, and in my notebook I describe the last photos I don't feel comfortable taking. Against the outside wall of one clay hut sit women of various ages, all wearing variously patterned *kanga*s and red woolen stocking caps; in the evening sun they make a lovely picture. I record their grim bronzed faces in my mental photo gallery, along with many others.

In the evening I lie on the sofa in my *kanga* skirt and a T-shirt, and we watch a couple more Africa-themed documentaries from Olli's extensive library. Michell putters about good-naturedly and calls out to me *moi moi* ("bye-bye" in Finnish). Flotea, wearing a fleece jacket and woolen socks, is boiling ginger tea. She tells me it helps protect you against the cold: winter is coming. It occurs to me that if I didn't have a return ticket, I could easily just put down roots right here. Olli interjects that then we could make another trip to Mkomazi. I feel like a member of this wonderful family.

Besides, if I lived here, I wouldn't have to choose between lions and family life. The family is in here, the lions out there.

On my last morning, I wake up at five thirty. Flotea has been up since four preparing a lunch—chicken and french fries—for my six-hour bus trip. I try to explain to her that a single drumstick will be plenty, I couldn't possibly take along a *whole* chicken. Flotea has been sobbing over my departure since yesterday, so the mood is not particularly cheerful. Flotea asks me once more whether I couldn't possibly cancel my return flight and stay here. Forever. I assure her that I would like nothing more.

Then Olli drives me to the Impala Hotel in Arusha, where my bus to Nairobi is already waiting. I'm the only white-skinned passenger on the minibus; but if I had been expecting an exotically noisy and chaotic trip in an overcrowded old rattletrap bus, I was wrong: the whole trip is as quiet as in church, and the bus stays on schedule to the minute.

After a two-hour drive, we stop at the Kenya border. Everywhere I look, I see dozens of locals in line for a stamp on the crumpled, faded, tattered paper that is patently their ID. I am standing in the line for passport control on the Tanzania side when my cell phone rings. The line crackles, and then I hear a familiar voice from some great distance: "You got a grant to support your book, congratulations!" Olli shouts the information he's found online into the phone. Then I walk across the border into Kenya.

My accommodations in Nairobi are situated far from the center, in a district named after Karen, only a few kilometers from Karen's house. Apart from me, the place is deserted: everybody else has canceled their trips due to the terrorist strikes and travel bans. The guy at reception agrees to find me a car and driver for tomorrow (it isn't safe to take regular taxis, and walking would be out of the question); then I carry my things up to a gigantic, ice-cold room. For dinner I eat a tough lamb chop alone in the inn's empty dining room. It's all a bit bleak, but what else can I expect for the price—I couldn't have afforded the glorious Karen Blixen dreams that would have cost me hundreds of dollars a night. On top of everything else, it's bone-chillingly cold and raining, and the same is expected for the next three days.

It takes a moment before it sinks in.

It's raining in the Ngong Hills.

*

[TELEGRAM]

KAREN I'm here stop the whole district is named for you stop there's Karen Road Karen Country Club Karen Blixen Coffee Garden Karen Shopping Center Karen Hospital Karen Police Station stop there is no Nzige airstrip stop where the coffee plantation was there's now a golf course stop I'll be there tomorrow stop M

*

I had a farm in Africa at the foot of the Ngong Hills.

Dear Karen, that's how you start your story, and when I finally stand in the yard of your house, your sentences begin to flow through my head like visions. Here it is, finally, your house. It's smaller and more modest than I'd imagined, but this is it: Mbogani. Here the oxen wandered across the plain *in the golden dust of sunset*, as you write in your book. From this lawn you and Denys took off in his airplane, you in your goatskin aviator's cap, flying over blue Ngong. Here you rode on horseback into the virgin forest that bordered the farm, as if *into the depths of an old tapestry, marvellously rich in green shades*. Here the morning air was *clear as crystal*, so bracingly fresh that it seemed to you that you were *walking along the bottom of the sea*. Somewhere over there stood the *round, peaked huts* of the Gĩkũyũ families that lived on the farm, and to the south began the world of buffalo, antelope, and lions, that big-game kingdom that *gave a particular character to the farm, as if you had been the neighbours of a great king*. And so when the sun set it felt as if the air had filled with animals, and downstream came the sound of hyena howls. Here you felt a part of it all, so that your breath was *one with the night wind's rustling in the trees*. And when the coffee bushes blossomed in the beginning of the rainy season, it was a radiant sight: *like a cloud of chalk in the mist and the drizzling rain over six hundred acres of land*.

You tapped the young stalk of what is now this gigantic, hundred-plus-year-old African tulip tree with your palm, and on this stone bench you sat mornings discussing things with the farm staff, and evenings smoking and looking over to the Ngong Hills, which you could still see, because the trees didn't block your view the way they do now. Sometimes the Gĩkũyũ chief would sit here dressed in an ape hide, with a skullcap made of a sheep stomach on his head, along with other tribal elders, who came to make important decisions. *Speak again like rain*, the Gĩkũyũ boys would say to you, meaning read some poems to us again, because to them the rhymes sounded like rain.

Here you enjoyed your Saturday afternoons, which to you were the most blessed time of all: *there would be no mail until Monday afternoon*, so you were all safe from the distressing business letters till then. In between their safaris came Denys and your friend Berkeley Cole; they supplied your house *brilliantly with wine and tobacco, and got books and gramophone records out from Europe for you*. Here on lonely evenings you gazed in the direction of Nairobi, and that *luminous haze on the sky above the town at night*, which set your thoughts in fierce motion and *conjured up images of Europe's great cities*.

And on those lonely nights *when the minutes dripped from the clock, life seemed to be dripping out of you with them.* But even then you felt *the silent, overshadowed existence of the natives*, which ran in parallel with your own, *though on a different plane.*

I wander through the house in no particular hurry. I'm told that in earlier days the wood-burning oven in the kitchen was kept alight around the clock, and because of the heat and the danger of fire, the kitchen was set in a separate building, at the end of a connecting walkway. In the kitchen there is a mahogany counter that is more than a century old, a manual butter churn, a Beatrice-brand meat grinder, and the drying rack for Karen's stockings. What isn't there is a refrigerator: all the food was stored in a normal pantry. Here Kamante cooked for royalty and beat whites of egg with a weeding knife so that they *towered up like light clouds.*

From Karen's study open glass doors the size of the entire wall onto the front yard and patio. On one side table stands the gramophone Denys gave her, and before the fireplace is a leopard skin. One wall is covered by a bookcase with a metal plaque bearing Denys's initials; atop the shelf are two ship's lanterns, red and green, the ones Karen employed to send messages to her closest friends, such as Denys and Berkeley Cole. On the desk is Karen's Corona travel typewriter; it's tiny, almost like a modern mini-laptop, except that this one contains its own printer. I picture Karen sitting here amidst all her piles of papers talking to Kamante about writing a book: *Msabu, do you believe yourself that you can write a book?* Kamante asked, pointing dubiously at the heavy leather-bound volumes on the bookshelf. *But what you write is some here and some there. When the people forget to close the door it blows about, even down on the floor and you are angry. It will not be a good book.*

Karen and Bror had separate bedrooms, and Karen spent a good deal of time in hers, as I know well: now sick, now writing letters, now reading her "real" books with hard covers, those rare pearls that washed up here from Europe. In Karen's bedroom almost everything is white: the cabinets arranged around the walls, the bed, and the dressing table, on which white lilies from the garden may have been set. I picture Karen lying here in her white nightgown: exhausted, sick, depressed, desperate, but sometimes happy as well. Here, if anywhere, existed that true, private inner Karen, the night woman that I want to know, and I put out feelers, hoping there might be something left of her that I can sense, maybe a scent. I imagine lying in that bed myself. Lying on my right side, I'd see the garden; lying on my back, I'd be staring up at the dark rafters. Karen stared at them endlessly.

The tour ends in the dining room, where Kamante's offerings were served to the Prince of Wales on November 9, 1928, as the guide who follows close on my heels tells me proudly. Yes, Kamante's famous clear broth, then Mombasa turbot, partridges with peas, creamy truffle pasta, wild leeks, tomato salad, wild mushrooms in turbinate shells, savarin cake, strawberries, and pomegranates. . . . I nod attentively and furiously jot down notes. Evidently the guide is sick of answering my questions about the origins of each object and whether this or that was here during Karen's time, because he makes a point of mentioning that "the ashes in the fireplace are not original."

I remain in the dining room alone. It's chilly in here. The room is decorated in dark; only the porcelain pieces the table is set with glow brightly. Through the windows I hear bird sounds and the rattling of cicadas.

I travel back in time a hundred years and imagine what life was like here during those endless lonely evenings, weeks, months, years. I know now that equatorial nights are black as the grave, that there are twelve hours of darkness on every day of the year; I know what it feels like when there is no electricity and dinner is lit up only by dimly flickering oil lamps. Darkness all around, the boundless vastness of the savannas, and forty-four days of hard travel to Denmark.

[KAREN WRITES]

March 17, 1931. Dearest Mother – – You must not think that I feel, in spite of it having ended in such defeat, that my "life has been wasted" here, or that I would exchange it with that of anyone I know. I feel – – that it is astonishing, how much – – I have been able to achieve. – – [Africa] *may be more gentle to others, but I hold to the belief that I am one of* [her] *favourite children. A great world of poetry has revealed itself to me – – here, and I have loved it. I have looked into the eyes of lions and slept under the Southern Cross, I have seen the grass of the great plains ablaze and covered with delicate green after the rains, I have been the friend of Somali, Kikuyu, and Masai, I have flown over the Ngong Hills. – – I believe that my house here has been a kind refuge for wayfarers and the sick, and to the black people has stood as the center of a friendly spirit. Lately it has been somewhat more difficult. But that is so all over the world.*

April 10, 1931. Private. – – Dear Tommy – – I think that these difficult times have helped me to understand better than before how infinitely rich and beautiful life is in every way and that so many things that one goes around worrying over are of no importance whatsoever. – – For instance, it seems to me that it would in no way be terrible or sad if I – – were now quite calmly to retire from life together with everything that I have loved here. – – It was terrible for Mother and so on – – [but] *to me it would seem the most natural thing to disappear with my world here. – –*

In all sincerity, it is really very difficult to see what if anything I can do in this world. – – Would you, for example, be prepared to take a job – – for two or three years in order to help me to educate myself or get started on something or other? – – Now you must not – – take this as a sort of threat; help me and sustain me, or I will die. – – As far as I myself am concerned, the most reasonable and easy thing to do would be to die. But if you feel – – that there is some meaning in making yet another attempt to live, then give it some thought.

December 1930 was the beginning of the end: the shareholders of the Karen Coffee Company decided to sell the farm at auction. The mortgage had not been amortized for a couple of years, and the shareholders had lost large amounts of money. Karen appealed to Denys, trying to borrow enough money to save the house and land, but to no avail. After seventeen years of struggle, the dream had dead-ended.

The buyer was a young Nairobi real estate entrepreneur named Remi Martin, whose intention was to convert the farm to a stylish suburb, its points of attraction being a golf course and a country club for whites. He planned to name the place Karen in honor of Baroness Blixen, and even offered Karen the chance to go on living in her house until the land was sold as construction lots. "I would rather live in the middle of the Sahara Desert than on a twenty-acre lot in the suburb of Karen," was her reply.

In April of 1931 Karen began to dismantle her household and sell her furniture and porcelains, which were spread out on the dining room table for people to view. In Nairobi it became a fashionable activity to drive out to the farm to see and finger the items on sale; Lady McMillan bought most of the furniture. Denys moved to Nairobi to stay with a friend. It was more comfortable for him there, he said: he had a telephone he could use and a dentist nearby. He was, therefore, mostly out of the picture as Karen's whole world came crashing down. Karen herself was in a state of nervous collapse. She didn't sleep or eat, and could not think clearly. She said she wanted to shoot her dogs and horses and then herself. She had terrible nightmares, and was so frightened that she asked the small son of a servant to sleep with her.

What would Karen do with her life? Exactly: *What can a fortyish, familyless woman who has abandoned her work and her home* do *with her life?*

In May, Denys was going to fly down to the coast to fix up his house, and in the pages of her book Karen paints an idyllic picture of their last encounter, where Denys walks out, comes back in to get a book of poetry, and then, as his last words to Karen, recites a poem.

In all likelihood the scene was not quite that serene. According to some sources, Karen and Denys were not getting along; in fact, they'd had such a bitter fight that they'd broken up. It was around that time that Karen tried to kill herself. There was a suicide note too, but it has disappeared.

News of the crash reached Nairobi before it did the farm. Karen was running errands in Nairobi and wondered why people turned their heads away from her on the street and didn't want to talk to her. "I began to feel as lonely in Nairobi as on a deserted island," she wrote. Finally at lunch, Lady McMillan took her into a side room and broke the news to her. The instant she heard Denys's name, the truth was revealed to her, and she "knew and understood everything," she later wrote.

Denys was buried the next day in the Ngong Hills near the spot they had chosen together. Karen wired her brother: "Denys killed flying fourteenth buried Ngong hills today Tania."

*

[KAREN WRITES]

July 5, 1931. Dear Tommy – – I am very tired, I have had so much to do.

All summer Africans came every day to sit in front of the house. They didn't want to believe that Karen would actually leave. They were also waiting for word of what would happen to them. Unbelievable as it may seem, Karen managed to negotiate enough land on the Gĩkũyũ reservation for her tenant farmers: all 153 families and all 3,000 of their cattle were able to relocate there. Everyone treated Karen like a widow, and it may be that Karen got her way because the new governor felt sorry for her after Denys's death.

At the end of July 1931, a group of settlers and Africans saw Karen to the Nairobi train station, where she set off on her last trip to Europe. In Mombasa, Karen boarded a steamship named the SS

Mantola, in steerage—all she could afford. Karen was forty-six years old.

It was five years before she could begin writing about her life in Africa, and twelve years before she managed to unpack the wooden crates she'd brought from Africa, containing her books and other remembrances from her life in the Ngong house.

My time in Africa is running short as well, but I'd still like to see the famous Ngong Hills over which Karen and Denys flew in their last year, and Denys's grave site there. It turns out that a man named Johnny who works at Karen's house can take me up to the hills—that is, if it doesn't bother me that his four-year-old daughter, Beyonce, comes along. And so Beyonce sits in the backseat looking stern while Johnny drives this white tourist up to Ngong.

Johnny seems to be well-versed in Karen-related matters; he even tells me he's done his own research. He talks about how influential and respected Karen was here, how she paid well and founded a school, despite resistance from the tribal chiefs. Karen's name is still known to both the Gĩkũyũ and the Maasai, Johnny assures me. In addition, he says he knows the children of Karen's servant Kamante. They are now in their sixties, and he has collected their stories of Karen. He offers me his notes to use in this book—they've never been published anywhere. "Next time you come to Nairobi," he says, "call me and I'll bring the papers over." I wonder whether this is true or whether he's just telling me what I want to hear. Backseat Beyonce doesn't weigh in.

In fact, a book has been published containing Kamante's memories of Karen, a moving picture book titled *Longing for Darkness: Kamante's Tales from Out of Africa*. It was compiled by Peter Beard, an American who in the 1960s found Kamante still living on the Gĩkũyũ reservation on the outskirts of Nairobi. And indeed Kamante does depict relations between Karen and the Africans as warm. In the chapter titled "The Goodness of Mrs. Karen," he describes how everyone in the region liked Karen. When people were evicted off their land, Karen would give them jobs in her garden and a place to build a house and farm the land. "She was indeed an excellent woman, because she never hated anybody or doctrine, even Mohammedans."

Also featured in the stories is one "Mr. Pinja-Hatern," and one chapter is titled "Mr. Pinja-Hatern Never Feared." When Mr. Pinja-Hatern died, Kamante wrote that "Mrs. Karen cried very much for the death of that man. They were very long friends and they liked each other. . . . Many came to beseech Mrs. not to do harm to herself, for death is awaiting everyone."

The nine-mile drive to Ngong and Mr. Pinja-Hatern's grave is not the minor excursion I had expected. It takes us more than an hour. Traffic snarls up at the shopping malls in Karen, as every car driving into the area has to be checked for bombs. This apparently is entirely routine, and has nothing to do with the recent terrorist strikes.

We pass the house where the screen adaptation of *Out of Africa* was filmed. I instantly recognize the shady jacaranda lane with the house at the end. We also drive past the house of Karen's servant Juma. Karen had the house built before she left in 1931, and it's still standing. Then we cross the river that a hundred years ago was the border of Karen's land. On the other side of the river began the Maasai reservation. When Karen and Denys rode to Ngong, this was still wild forest, but now the streets are lined with burning trash piles, construction sites, shacks, dump-like areas, and dilapidated houses about which it is hard to say whether they're half-built or half-torn-down. The shoulder is blanketed with trash, and herds of goats graze in the trash piles—as we drive past, Johnny says proudly that the goat meat from this area is the best. Ngong Township, behind which rise the hills, is a particularly ramshackle place. It's market day, so there are lots of people out and about, and the souped-up *matatu* buses blare out their music full-blast. Johnny says I should keep my window rolled up. If I'd imagined an idyllic drive to the mythic Ngong Hills, I was wrong.

Closer to our destination, we begin to rise up into the hills, and the scenery becomes lovelier. We drive through tiny villages, till the final muddy and rocky path is nearly impassable. Then the woman who takes care of Denys's grave site comes to open the iron gate around which grows a bougainvillea. Inside the fence is a monument and a small well-tended garden, but the trees block the view of Karen's house, Mount Kenya, and Kilimanjaro. Legend has it that lions used to frequent the grave, so I'm not surprised to see the gatekeeper's yellow mutt dash in and flop down at the base of the monument.

At this point, after five weeks of traveling, I'm almost as broke as Karen was in 1931 after her eighteen years in Africa, and I truly cannot afford to spend the night at the Karen Blixen Coffee Garden on the grounds of the old farm. Upon my return from Ngong Hills, however, I do stop in there, famished, for a late lunch. If Nairobi is a city of extremes, this is one of them: inside rigorously guarded gates (all cars are again checked for bombs) there is the perfect spot for Nairobi's affluent to relax in the lap of luxury. Around the original Swedo House—Karen's foreman's house—a restaurant and lodging complex has been built that is pure Karen Blixen dreamland. In the stylish "huts" around the garden, one can stay in the old colonial style, and the idyllic garden restaurant is full of rich whites, super-trendy blacks celebrating a birthday, and unctuous white-coated servers who carry trays of drinks and beautifully arranged plates of food. I order lunch at my garden table—sesame-seed-coated tuna in wasabi sauce—but I can't help feeling irritated. Everything seems grotesque, excessive, a smug charade, right down to the big-screen TVs blaring in the bar. I'm revolted. Maybe I've been away from people too long, out on the savannas that extend all the way to the horizon, or else surrounded by too much extreme poverty. Or else I'm just out of my mind with hunger.

Or maybe it's as Olli says: you experience all your feelings more powerfully in Africa, for good and bad. Everything is extreme: stunning nature, abject poverty, and the insanity of the whites.

More evidence of that last is on offer at the Muthaiga Club, the settlers' oasis to which Karen too rode or drove for lunch—but I have no way of getting in there. To this day you don't just walk into that mecca for the beautiful people. Applying for a membership, with proper endorsements, sounds like such a Stone Age upper-class process that the whole place gives me the heebie-jeebies.

I am able, however, to visit the Norfolk Hotel, which was opened in 1904. In Karen's day you could find all the British generals, majors, ladies, counts, and countesses; it was here that she spent her first night upon her arrival in Nairobi as Bror's new bride in 1914. Karen's arrival was written up in the society column of the local paper—*Baron and Baroness von Blixen-Finecke arrived in Nairobi Thursday*—but my arrival is completely without fanfare, so I'm able to slip past the reception desk to check the place out. Unfortunately, the hotel was so thoroughly remodeled after a 1980 bomb strike that the old-timey atmosphere I'm looking for no longer exists.

When I eat lunch in the famous colonial-style Lord Delamere bar in the Norfolk Hotel, with a Finnish friend of a friend named Hilkka, I get some inkling of what white people's life here is like these days. Hilkka works in Nairobi for a Finnish aid organization, and often travels on business to extremely dangerous areas—she is apparently accompanied on her trips by armed guards, two soldiers for each white worker, and conditions in the roadless deserts are difficult: the food is often inedible, and sometimes they have to live on the crackers and canned beans they bring with them, so that after a week on the road they are weak with malnutrition.

If Karen's life here meant the maximum imaginable freedom, these days foreigners' lives seem to be severely circumscribed by extreme restrictions and security directives. No walking in the city center. No taking a taxi. The chance of getting mugged is so high that if you go jogging, you should leave not only your watch but your glasses at home. If you want to have a picnic, it's best to do it in a fenced and guarded security park where they charge admission.

I ask Hilkka whether she's afraid. She shakes her head. "I'm not the scaredy-cat type," she tells me.

I reserve my last day for white tourists' Africa dreams. I visit an elephant orphanage, and before I head out to the airport I manage to arrange a lunch for myself in a high-end English-style manor house, where a night's accommodation will set you back $800. The exterior walls are covered with ivy, and rare Rothschild's giraffes graze on the lawns. Mornings, I hear, they come up to beg for goodies from guests' breakfast tables, and stick their long necks in through the windows.

The maître d' welcomes me and asks whether he can bring me

something to drink. I settle back in my chaise longue with a view of the giraffes. The rain we've had for the last two days seems to have stopped. The sun begins first to peek, then to blaze, between the bruise-colored clouds. I have the tiniest spiderweb-thin afternoon buzz as I sit here on my last day at this dreamlike giraffe manor house, which positively reeks with history.

It occurs to me, Karen, that maybe you weren't quite like I imagined. Maybe you weren't the endlessly brave, strong, independent, wise, and good superwoman I'd pictured. You were more human, weaker, sicker, vainer, more depressed, more at the mercy of your emotions, more selfish, more desperate, more possessive, more obsessed with shooting beautiful animals.

But that's okay, Karen. That's just the way we are.

Copenhagen, January

[KAREN WRITES]

January 22, 1928. Dearest Mother – – I think that I myself have come to the conclusion in life that all fear in reality is nervous, because there is nothing to be afraid of. That is to say: naturally one may be afraid of being killed, of getting pneumonia, driving one's car into the ditch and so on – all these risks naturally exist in life – but one must not be terrified *of them, because there is nothing in life to be terrified of. – – All terror is more or less terror of the dark: bring light, and it must of necessity pass, because it will be shown that there is nothing to be feared.*

A year and a half after my departure from Africa, I stand before Karen's grave in Rungstedlund. It's a gray January day, slush on the ground, a frigid storm wind blowing straight off the sea. The large, flat memorial plaque is under a huge three-hundred-year-old beech. When I stop at it, a solitary dog-walker passes by.

Greetings from Ngong, Karen.

The vast beech begins to sough in the storm wind, as if in response.

To this house, her childhood home, Karen returned from East Africa in 1931, penniless, depressed, syphilitic, having lost everything: the farm sold, Denys dead. And here, in this room, at her father's old desk, she began to tap away on her little typewriter.

And so began her third life, as a writer.

It wasn't easy at first for an unknown writer in her late forties to find a publisher for *Seven Gothic Tales*, but when it was at last published in January 1934 in the US under the pen name Isak Dinesen, it was an instant success. A year and a half later it was released in Danish, in Karen's own translation. Exhausted from the effort, Karen did not believe she could ever write anything as good again, but at the age of fifty-one she did start writing once more. *Out of Africa* appeared in 1937, first in English, then in Danish. The rest is history. Especially in the US, Karen's books were runaway sellers and critical successes. Her 1942 book *Winter's Tales* was so popular that the publisher brought out a special thin-paper armed forces edition that would fit in a uniform jacket pocket. Several times there was public speculation that Karen was nominated for the Nobel Prize for Literature, but lost in 1954 to Ernest Hemingway and in 1957 to Albert Camus. And after the screen adaptation of *Out of Africa* was released, she came to be known even by people who don't read books.

There are many legendary tales about Karen during the last quarter century of her life. She became a famous baroness, a *grande dame*, and a mythical storyteller who was "three thousand years old and had dined with Socrates." She threw elegant dinner parties where oysters, truffles, soufflés, and perfect broths were served. She gathered around her a circle of young literary men and entered into a dramatic love affair with a writer thirty years her junior. When in 1959 she traveled to America, a worshipped literary star, she drank champagne and danced on the table with Marilyn Monroe. She suffered from so many ailments, presumably syphilis-related, and had so many stomach and spinal-cord surgeries, that she could consume nothing but oysters, juices, and *gelée royale* ampules, and at eighty-four pounds was so skeletally thin that at age seventy she looked a hundred. She was, however, so greedy for life that she could spend the whole afternoon in Paris vomiting and lying in a semicoma, and then go out to a scintillating party, maybe with the help of amphetamines. "Thoroughbreds keep on running until they drop," Karen wrote about herself.

Karen died at home at the age of seventy-seven, in September of 1962, only one month after Marilyn. I think about how at the end she could no longer walk or stand, but continued writing nevertheless, and dictated her last works to her secretary while lying on the floor or in bed. She signed her last publication contract only two days before her death.

—

Standing in Rungstedlund at Karen's desk, looking out at the stormy sea, I decide that Karen's true exemplarity may not have been her adventurous life in Africa, let alone the less attractive sides of her personality that have come to light. No: what makes her truly exemplary, I think now, is that as *a fortyish, familyless woman who has abandoned her work and her home*, she was able to reinvent herself.

That at forty-six she finally began doing what we remember her for today.

That she *began to write*.

That after all that, she became a writer—one of the great ones.

*

Night women's advice:

Be brave. It doesn't matter if you're afraid.

Play the cards you're dealt.

Even if you're sick, you can still live full-tilt.

If you lose everything, start writing.

PART II

Explorers

[HANDWRITTEN LETTER, COPIED ON CARBON PAPER]

Dear Isabella, Ida, and Mary,

I'm writing to you from up here in my parents' attic, because I'm so upset I'm about to burst. I'm a forty-two-year-old unmarried woman who suffers from insomnia, headaches, general frustration, and the occasional blues, and wonders what on earth women like me are supposed to do with their lives. Live selflessly without drawing attention to ourselves? Decorate our homes and accrue pensions? Do our civic duties as taxpayers? Look after sick relatives and volunteer for charitable organizations? Have hysterical meltdowns at not being able to fulfill our primary functions as wives and mothers? Hope that, long as we are in the tooth, we'll still find a man who'll marry an aging spinster?

Well, of course not, I'm exaggerating. This isn't the nineteenth century! But maybe precisely because "everything" is possible for the modern woman, it seems surprisingly difficult to get one's own life in order. How can I possibly know how to live this one life I've been given? I need inspiration, role models, practical tips! Night women to show me the way!

And that's why I've felt so feverish since I heard about you. The answer to every question in a forty-two-year-old unmarried woman's head is: travel. TRAVEL!

(to be continued)

IV Kallio–Vihti, Summer

Strange things:

Drinking water straight from the tap. Walking in the street without clutching my purse tightly. A cool sun. Middles and muddles.

Upon my return from Africa, I sink into the abyss. My transition from Nairobi to the Kallio district in Helsinki is as creaky as an old rattletrap machine. I'm left hanging in a weird kind of middle-muddle. It feels like I just can't handle the sudden shift from one world to another. My head throbs with pain, and I'm so torn up I constantly feel like crying. I lie in bed for days on end, wiped out. Everything rubs me the wrong way: the light summer nights, the newspaper headlines, the overflowing shelves in the supermarket. I no longer know how to live here, but Africa is already fading like a dream. I study the photographs in which I stand in the middle of some endless savanna, a tiny, insignificant dot, or sit writing in my journal outside my tent in the Mkomazi morning mist. How can something that I have lived so passionately disappear so quickly?

I spend most of the summer holed up in my parents' attic in Vihti in the countryside outside Helsinki. I've rented out my city apartment to help me out of the financial hole my Africa trip has left me in. Southern Finland is blasted with record high temperatures for week after week. I'm down in the dumps.

At night I make mental lists of women. I draw diagrams. I place women with different kinds and levels of achievement on the world map, in different time zones; I group them mentally by profession, century, and geographic location. I sort them into married and single, mothers and childless. I list their professions, accomplishments, diseases, causes of death. I chart who influenced whom, until the women seem chained one to another, forming rhizomes that proliferate into messy spatiotemporal skeins too complex to draw. I ask my friends whom they think about at night, and the list lengthens. I think about women who float out on the peripheries of my consciousness, so that I still have no idea how they might be connected to me. I think about the places I'd need to travel in pursuit of my women; but for some strange reason my exemplary women and the places I'd like to visit don't meet.

But they all drift and float around me, in night-woman space.

Then one day my gaze happens to fall upon a large coffee-table book that my editor gave me ages ago, an inspirational gift. Somehow it's gotten buried under piles of other books. It's about female travelers in history; on the cover is a photo of a young woman sitting on a saddled zebra in Africa, probably in the 1920s. My pulse quickens. Who is she? How did she get there in that bob haircut and those safari shorts and knee-highs, with that stylish hat? She stares straight ahead, holding the reins as if she is about to set off on a gallop across the savanna—but a zebra cannot be broken!

She's Osa Johnson, a wonderful and crazy American adventurer. And the book is chock-full of night women.

The mood in my parents' attic is suddenly charged with electricity. I flip feverishly through the pages, and my fingers fly across the keyboard, filling page after page with notes. Then I begin to hunt down the books listed in the bibliography—the book quickly proves to be an unreliable source in many places—hauling them home in great piles from the university library, ordering the biographies of the most interesting women online, wading through the digitized Web copies I find of forgotten travel books. I follow my nose like a bloodhound, but it takes me days and weeks before I finally realize what I've stumbled upon. The perfect subject. A group of exciting historical and exemplary women I've never heard of. I've found the nineteenth-century female explorers.

Or rather, to be precise: a group of *perfectly ordinary middle-aged women* who, having seen their familial duties through to their natural conclusion, decided to defy propriety and follow their dreams by traveling around the world alone, decked out in corsets and long dresses.

Take, for example, the Scotswoman Isabella Bird, who as I read about her seems like my doppelgänger: a fortyish, depressed spinster who suffers from headaches and insomnia, but who is fed up with the narrow confines in which her society has trapped her. When in 1872 a doctor prescribed a change of climate—thinking that his patient would set off on some little cruise, to Brighton, say—Isabella bought a passage to Australia, found herself cured as if by magic, and ended up dawdling through the globe's dismalest dives alone for almost thirty years, writing ten or so travel books, and becoming in the end the first woman to be granted membership in the Royal Geographical Society.

Or the Austrian Ida Pfeiffer, who in the 1840s, at the age of forty-four, after her children had flown the coop, decided to see the world in her respectable lacy bonnet on a shoestring budget—and ended up writing wildly popular travel books.

Or British Mary Kingsley, who took care of her parents like a dutiful daughter till they were both pushing up daisies, then set off alone for the West African jungles, where she made friends with cannibal tribes and European merchants.

*

[THE LETTER CONTINUES]

Dear Isabella, Ida, and Mary—I'm thrilled! What unbelievable courage! You didn't let depression, headaches, bad marriages, or the deaths of parents get you down—you decided to start doing exactly as you pleased, never mind what anyone else thought about you! And the way you went about it! You couldn't go online before you left, to google lodging options in the Himalayas or the canoe timetables in the Congo jungle. You couldn't fortify yourselves with antibiotics, energy bars, or cell phones with global SIM cards. You didn't want travel companions. You packed your long black dresses, writing paper, a few cans of food, and ample armfuls of attitude, and set off on tramp steamers and farmers' horse-drawn carts to see the world, over weeks, months, sometimes years. Evenings you sat by candlelight, ignoring the exhaustion you felt in your bones, writing down the day's events in your notebooks or in letters, which then wended their laborious way back to those waiting at home, so that I and all the other women now and years from now might read about your travels.

Isabella, Ida, and Mary—you were middle-aged, world-weary women who cut loose a century and a half before that became fashionable. Inspired by your example, I am going to try to make my move out of this attic as soon as humanly possible.

August xx, your M.

*

I decide to follow Isabella Bird's recipe for curing depression immediately, and buy two plane tickets: one to Kyoto in September and another to Florence in November. I instantly feel better.

To be sure, it's become very clear to me, while reading through my piles of books, that traveling alone has not always been an easy or self-evident thing for women to do. I can just pack a bag and leave—assuming that my bank balance, schedule, and courage will allow it. But in centuries past, women could not travel without a companion, or for that matter without a husband's or father's permission. (History has stories of women whose only recourse was to travel disguised as men, as soldiers, say, or sailors.) That situation did improve in the nineteenth century, when Europeans began to travel more, but even then it was best for a woman to take along a chaperone (perhaps a maiden aunt), or else to join one of the group tours that had begun to be arranged by Thomas Cook. For British women it was respectable to travel alone even outside Europe, since the empire extended to every continent, and even in the most far-flung reaches of the globe one could expect to encounter one's compatriots and be treated well by them—as long as one had sufficient funds and proper letters of introduction.

But beginning in the 1850s, there also began to appear women who could be called explorers. "Exploring" in the sense of traveling for study was increasingly fashionable, as there were still uncharted regions on the globe, and sending expeditions into them could also promote colonial aspirations. Explorers (basically men) returning from their travels were national heroes, and the news reports and books about them were devoured greedily. This sort of travel began to sound tempting to women as well. But could a respectable woman just up and walk away from her duties and sail out beyond the pale of civilization?

Right: respectability. The most important consideration for a nineteenth-century European woman was *respectability*, and its key component, *concern for one's reputation*. Second most important was *shouldering one's responsibilities*—and there were always plenty of those, for as long as a woman had a husband, father, or brother, she was responsible for the daily chores in the household. In addition to cooking and cleaning, she had to manage the household, raise children, tend to the sick, and even, if she was unmarried, look after more distant relatives as well. But if she no longer had any of these responsibilities—if she was a spinster and her parents were dead—a woman could give thought to satisfying her own desires. That is, of course, if she wasn't overly encumbered with vague but pressing feelings of guilt.

It seems likely that even today women's attitudes have not been entirely freed from this messy skein of duty and guilt. I haven't raised any children or been responsible for my parents' care (yet), but it seems to me that I have nevertheless spent my entire life to date living according to unspoken expectations—under the sway of conditioned obedience and conscientiousness. I took the expected university degree, entered the profession for which I was qualified, strove ambitiously to advance in that profession for nearly a decade and a half . . . all quite willingly, even enthusiastically. But then, somehow, it began to pall on me. Was this all there was to life? Did life have nothing *new* to offer me? (Probably it was at this juncture that many of my friends started families.) I began to feel that I'd had enough of doing the things I was *supposed* to do. I'd been conscientious, decent, obedient, and sensible long enough. I didn't want to be sensible any longer! (Isabella, Ida, Mary—you all know the feeling.) And because I was tired of being sensible, I first went on sabbatical—and then didn't return to work. I decided I'd try to keep writing and traveling: I invented a profession of my own, writer-explorer. I know, over-the-top, right? That, I thought, would allow me to explore, travel, and write as much as my heart desired and my bank account would permit. (All right, agreed, "explorer" in the original sense of a person who traveled to study unknown and uncharted territories was no longer literally feasible, as there are no uncharted territories left; but I think of explorerdom as a kind of spiritual attitude, as my own personal mission to push the limits of my life as a middle-aged woman.) So I sold my apartment and bought another one half the size, divested myself of all my excess stuff and expenditures, and started applying for grants and planning trips.

And, yes: I feel guilt. About all of it. When friends ask me what I'm doing, I tend to emphasize the negatives (the meager and uncertain income, the project-like feel of my whole life, the constant packing and unpacking). It always seems to me that this freedom I have to fulfill my own desires is not quite socially acceptable. I mean, it can't be—right?

And in the nineteenth century, it wasn't. If a woman decided to set off on a journey, she had to justify it on some socially acceptable grounds. It wasn't enough to be interested in travel—that sort of excessive curiosity wasn't "fitting" for a woman. And so, after buying plane tickets to Kyoto and Florence, I began, with considerable concern, to study the "List of Socially Approved Reasons for a Woman to Travel" that I'd written based on the pile of books I'd been studying in the attic:

1) *Husband's work*. (Of course that would have to be Reason Number One, since a dutiful wife cheerfully follows her husband into even the most primitive corners of the world.)

2) *Health reasons*. (Approving murmurs.)

3) *Missionary work, religious pilgrimages*. (Definitely approving murmurs.)

4) *Landscape painting*. (Flowers and insects to be accepted as well.)

5) *Collecting plant samples*, and

6) *Scientific study.* (Assuming we consider women capable of such. Isn't a woman's interest in geography or the natural sciences a ludicrous thing, and at the very least unnatural? And how would such a woman even be able to complete her primary chores, such as sewing?)

At this stage I'm already a bit desperate, but fortunately number 7 saves me:

7) *Collecting materials for a travel book, and eventually using that work to enlighten readers.*

Enlightening readers! This was, in fact, the straw at which Isabella, Ida, and Mary grasped. Besides, back then the advantage of travel books was that you could make good money writing them [*sic!*], which meant that each book and the lecture tour based on it could easily finance the next trip.

Once these nineteenth-century women had come up with good enough reasons to travel, nothing could hold them back. Sitting in that attic in my parents' house, surrounded by growing piles of books, I realize that these traveling women are legion: female travel writers, female explorers, all kinds of adventuresses and other variously meritorious travelers. Why didn't I know anything about them before?

And so now I begin mercilessly to prune the list of inspiring women. For example, on my list of travel writers I draw a coldly determined line through the filthy-rich aristocratic heiresses, the missionaries, the governesses, those who traveled with their husbands, and those born after 1900. Without a second thought, I cross off the hunters (one book published in 1893 is titled *How I Shot My Bears*), mountaineers, aviators, sailors, car and motorcycle enthusiasts, and pirates (yes, there were women in that line of work too). I also reject the wives of explorers, though their experiences do interest me. Some I reject purely because of their destinations, even if their titles seem to promise a formidable reading experience (*Unprotected Females in Norway*, 1857); others I cut only with great reluctance, because the titles awaken delectable expectations (*To Lake Tanganyika in a Bath Chair*, 1886, or *A Year's Housekeeping in South Africa*, 1877). I also bypass the whine-fests, which is to say those traveling against their will with their husbands, or reports of women seeking a cure for their ailments—though it's entirely possible that it is precisely among such fearful travelers that I would find my soul sisters. (I have to remind myself sternly that I am seeking *role models.*) I absolutely reject politically active female travelers, spies, and secret agents, because I just can't bring myself to think about them at night, no matter how significant their achievements might have been. Excessive religiosity too dampens my interest depressingly. I have to grit my teeth a little to toss the entomologists and flower-painters overboard—all these endearingly nerdy aunties who traveled far and wide in pursuit of their passions and wrote such felicitously titled books as *Time Well Spent* and *Recollections of a Happy Life.* Then there is a group of Victorian women travel writers journeying alone in Africa; it requires a steely determination to cut them. I shelve their books in the end because they just seem to lack that certain undeniable spark that I demand from my most exemplary night women, that supernatural ability to inspire me to follow in their footsteps, even without knowing where that will take me. Women like Isabella Bird, Ida Pfeiffer, Mary Kingsley, and a few others.

For the fact is that I feel an overwhelming urge to follow in the footsteps of these particular women. They didn't have money, they weren't physically fit, they didn't have scientific training, they lacked all societal support, and they often weren't even young or healthy. But they went anyway.

And that's why I love them.

ISABELLA

NIGHT WOMEN'S ADVICE 2

If you suffer from depression, frustration, or headache, set off on a journey.

NIGHT WOMAN #2: *Isabella Bird*

PROFESSION: *Spinster, later a world traveler and travel writer. Suffered from depression, spinal complaints, and insomnia, until a doctor recommended a short sea voyage as treatment. Ended up circling the globe; once she started traveling, she couldn't quit.*

> *"It's a perfect infatuation. It is to me like living in a new world so free, so fresh, so vital, so careless, so unfettered, so full of interest that one grudges being asleep. . . . No door bells, no 'please ma'ams', no servants, no bills, no demands of any kind, no vain attempts to overtake all one knows one should do. Above all no nervousness, and no conventionalities. . . . I cannot tell you how much I like my life!"* —Isabella on board ship in the middle of the stormy Atlantic, 1871

Isabella Bird (1831–1904) was born in Yorkshire, Great Britain, into a world where a woman's most important qualities were virtue, industry, and selflessness. Her father was a vicar and her mother taught Sunday school, and the family followed the father from parish to parish. At home Isabella's mother taught her and her little sister, Henrietta, to read and write and to draw and sew. Isabella was also interested in Latin, Greek, and microscopes, but there was no chance of schooling for girls. Girls' schools didn't exist nearby, and universities weren't open to persons of the female persuasion.

Isabella was a sickly child and complained constantly of fatigue, back pains, headaches, and general weakness. A tumor was surgically removed from her spine, but the only treatment available for her other ailments was a change of climate. And so when the doctor recommended mountain air for the young Isabella, her father moved the family to the Scottish Highlands; and when the doctor recommended a long sea voyage, the twenty-two-year-old Isabella sailed with her cousins to America. Isabella wrote a book about that journey as well—*The Englishwoman in America* appeared in 1856—but because she considered it unfitting to earn money with her book, she donated her royalties to charity, buying fishing boats for poor fishermen. She also made another doctor-recommended trip to America, but when upon her return her father took sick and died, she decided, racked with guilt, that she would never again do anything as selfish as travel.

After her father's death, her mother moved the family to Edinburgh. Life there was, to put it kindly, stupefyingly boring. Isabella, twenty-eight, spent her mornings writing newspaper articles on topics related to spirituality and charity, and devoted her afternoons to making social calls, as was proper for a woman's social sphere. She wasn't exactly hounded by suitors. When a few years later her mother died, her options were limited. Isabella was thirty-four, Hennie thirty-one. Yes, they could live as many old maids did, moving from house to house without their own permanent home, caring for ailing relatives and helping with child care. But Isabella wanted none of that. Perhaps they could get by on their meager inheritance, and Isabella could supplement that by writing on parish matters?

That plan worked well for a couple of years, but then Isabella began to be fed up. Was this to be the entire scope of the rest of her life? Was there really *nothing* else an unmarried woman could do? At thirty-eight, a frustrated Isabella wrote to her publisher from thirteen years before, John Murray, who published a popular series of travel books, saying that she was looking for more challenging literary work: "If you can suggest anything to me, I shall be very glad." Murray urged her to travel abroad and find interesting new material—but Isabella hesitated. She passionately wanted to go, but how could she? After all, she had promised never to travel again! One work-around she came up with was to set off on a pilgrimage to Jerusalem—but no, that too felt excessively selfish.

While Isabella wrestled with the rules of propriety, her body seized the reins: she fell prey once again to her old back pains, headaches, and insomnia, as well as countless other ailments, including rashes, fevers, chest pains, muscle spasms, nausea, hair loss, nervousness, and depression. She would often spend the entire day lying in bed, unable to sleep, anxiously monitoring every feeling in her body, certain that each one was deadly serious. She would run to doctors but get no diagnosis. One doctor prescribed a steel net to be wrapped around her head, to take the weight off her spine, and urged her to spend time on a ship, as its rocking motion would ease her pain. The doctors drew blood from her with needles and leeches, and prescribed calming drugs such as opium-based laudanum, alcohol, and fashionable chlorodyne drops (a mixture of opium, cannabis, and chloroform), all of which have the side effects not only of addiction but of the very symptoms they were supposed to relieve. Isabella followed all the advice obediently, and even went up into the Highlands to rock in a boat, but nothing helped.

Probably many of her symptoms were psychosomatic. Like other intelligent and capable women, she would have preferred to do *more*, and somewhere away from home. That was precisely why so many frustrated women ended up in the state that in those days was diagnosed as "hysteria." For God's sake, I'd get hysterical too if I had to lie in a boat with a steel net on my head, when what I really wanted was to *do* something! But in Isabella's case, her ailments also offered an escape route: for a single woman, health reasons were among the precious few socially acceptable excuses to travel. When Hennie pressed her to take the sea voyage another doctor prescribed, after months of dithering she did finally buy passage to New York—and, once she had returned from there, another to Australia.

Health reasons—what a glorious excuse! Isabella used that as a smoke screen to justify her adventurous exploring trips for the next two decades. I can almost hear the clicking of the telegraph as the telegrams hurtled around the globe: *My back pains require a sea voyage around the world. . . . Owing to my headaches I am forced to stay here in Hawaii for a half year, due to the favorable climate, to ride, swim, and climb volcanoes. . . . To treat my depression I climbed to the very top of Long's Peak in the Rocky Mountains with a known ruffian and outlaw, who incidentally was remarkably good-looking. . . . Owing to my insomnia I am forced to ride a camel through the Sinai Desert as the only woman among twenty Bedouins. . . .* Genius, dear Isabella.

So now, in 1872, Isabella buys passage to Australia. She has had an awakening aboard ship in the middle of the Atlantic (*"It's a perfect infatuation. . . . I cannot tell you how much I like my life!"*), and now plans, *for health reasons*, to travel around the world: first from Great Britain to Australia, then to New Zealand, on to California, then finally across the continent of North America and the Atlantic back home. Isabella packs boots, a tweed dress, underclothing, warm socks, and a black silk dress for special occasions, as well as medicines, lined notebooks, sketchbooks, pens, ink, and paper and envelopes for writing long letters to her beloved sister. She boards a ship in Liverpool in July 1872.

She is forty years old.

Her first trip around the world will take a year and a half to complete.

In fact, Isabella didn't recover immediately. After the three-month sea voyage, Australia was a disappointment: everything was like at home in England, except that it was shockingly hot. Isabella felt alone and not keen on anything. She was homesick and depressed, suffered from heatstroke and headache, and couldn't sleep; she wrote long letters of complaint to her sister. She lay in her lodging, popped various pills three times a day, drank too much (wine and beer at lunch and in the afternoon and evening), and was continually fatigued (no wonder). Around that time the English papers were full of stories about how there was a surfeit of marriageable men in the colonies, and especially Australia, and how it was therefore a good idea for single Englishwomen (of whom in England there were at least a million more than single men) to make their way there. One organization even helped "desperate" women find husbands from across the sea. Some have speculated that Isabella's trip was motivated by a search for a husband, but she herself doesn't seem to have undertaken that mission. She wrote to her sister that she had not seen a single thing worth seeing or met a single interesting person on her entire trip.

Since it was no cooler in New Zealand, Isabella decided in desperation to push on immediately to America, and booked passage on the next ship heading for San Francisco. The steamship *Nevada* had truly seen better days; the leaky bucket barely stayed afloat. The very idea that this particular sea voyage was somehow dangerous, however, finally brought Isabella back to life. Inconceivably, she made a miraculous recovery on board ship. Her letters were suddenly charged with enthusiasm, and she herself was amazingly elated—even though they hit a typhoon, the food served on board was awful (there were ants and weevils in the bread), the ship's engine broke down, the air temperature in tropical waters rose well into the hundreds, the salon's ceiling leaked so badly that when it rained they had to wear slickers and rubber boots even indoors, and the cabins were overrun with cockroaches and rats.

Halfway across the Pacific a passenger's son took ill, and the captain decided to make a stop in Honolulu, in what were then the Sandwich Islands. Isabella went ashore to help find a doctor, and realized at once that she had found that paradise of palm-studded beaches, coral reefs, and volcanoes that she had looked for in vain in Australia and New Zealand. She decided to stay—and in the end spent more than six months in Hawaii. Naturally, in her preface to the book that appeared a couple years later, *The Hawaiian Archipelago*, she insists that she stayed on the islands because she had found "the climate favourable for health."

Hawaii blew her mind. She began to live the kind of life that she could not even have dreamed of at home. She climbed the world's tallest volcano and began to ride horses astraddle, as the local women did—something unheard-of in the "civilized" world. She lived with the locals and studied the island on her own, and drank deep of the surprises offered by her carefree life. She was afraid of nothing. She rode around the island without a map or a plan, spent the night in straw huts, ate fruit and poi, swam and washed in rivers, dried her clothes in the sun, and declared that it was the most wonderful thing she had ever experienced. In a letter to her sister, she gloried in her skill at cooking, darning, washing clothes, and budgeting money, and described how she could saddle, bridle, and otherwise tack up a horse all by herself. "No man now ever says of any difficult thing that I could not do it!" she proclaimed. When she looked at herself in the mirror, she saw a changed woman: where once had stood a haggard, sickly forty-year-old there now stood a glowing, tanned woman with shining eyes who looked ten years younger. Isabella was so radiant that a certain respectable Mr. Wilson even asked her to marry him. (Isabella turned him down.)

She wrote: "I am doing what a woman can hardly ever do—leading a life fit to recruit a man. With my horse and gear packed upon it, I need make no plans. I can fall into anything which seems feasible. . . . I feel energy for anything except conventionality and civilization." But she couldn't reject the "civilized" world entirely: her umbilical cord was Hennie, who waited for her at home, and she had no desire to cut that cord. Once, in a world-embracing derangement, she wrote to her sister suggesting that Hennie come live in Hawaii with her: *We can start a new life here!* But when Hennie took the suggestion seriously and began making arrangements, Isabella got cold feet and listed all the negatives of living there. It was out of the question for Hennie to travel! Hennie should stay at home. Whom else did Isabella have to write to?

In August of 1873, Isabella reluctantly left Hawaii and journeyed on toward San Francisco, where she caught a train for Colorado and the Rockies. There she rented a horse and set off to explore. Her greatest wish was to get to Estes Park, which was famous for its stunning landscapes; and the owner of one inn enlisted two young men to take her along with them on their journey there. The men were reluctant, as they truly did not want to be burdened with some woman, but agreed in the hope that the woman in question would at least be "young, beautiful, and vivacious." (Their hopes were dashed when "Miss Bird arrived in the morning wearing bloomers, riding cowboy-style.") Isabella was completely indifferent to what the men thought of her. She had lain awake all night, worrying about her ability to ride twenty-five miles a day.

The journey proved transformative. At the mouth to the gulch leading to Estes Park, they pulled up at a log cabin that to Isabella looked like the den of a wild beast. Laid out all across its roof were lynx and beaver hides, stretched out there to dry; off one corner hung a deer carcass; scattered around the house lay deer antlers, old horseshoes, and the remains of recently slaughtered animals; and the yard was guarded by a growling dog. Out of the cabin came a burly man in ragged deerskin pants, a knife on his belt and a revolver in his chest pocket. This "shocking figure" was the notorious ruffian and desperado Jim Nugent, known as Rocky Mountain Jim. Despite his scary reputation, however, Mountain Jim was strikingly handsome—at least on one side of his face. On the other side he had lost an eye in a scuffle with a grizzly bear. He was also surprisingly polite and cultured. Against all odds, Isabella was smitten—and so was the desperado.

Isabella had planned to stay in Estes Park only briefly, but the weeks and months went by, and she could not bring herself to leave. She stayed in a cabin on the Evans family's ranch and met Mountain Jim almost daily. They rode for hours on mountain routes and raced at a gallop in the crisp air. Some days Isabella helped her host family drive cattle, alongside the men; and when the weather turned cold, she wore a bearskin vest over her riding outfit and procured a man's woolen sweater and gloves. Come winter, she spent weeks living with the cattlemen in a cabin, writing that there was no woman within twenty-five miles, and when the mercury plunged into minus territory everything in the cabin froze: the milk, the butter, the bread, the syrup, the letter-writing ink, and Isabella's just-washed hair. She wrote that she ate and slept like a hunter, owning only the clothes she had on and a single pair of woolen socks that she had worn for six weeks straight. "I have almost forgotten that there are such things as women," she wrote. "On one day I rode 51 miles and thought nothing of it. I shall have been 10 months [in the open air and] on horseback."

When Isabella wanted to climb Long's Peak, sometimes referred to as America's Matterhorn, Rocky Mountain Jim came along as her guide. Mrs. Evans baked them enough bread for three days, sliced meat off the ox carcass hanging in her kitchen, and packed them tea, sugar, and butter. They slept outdoors with their saddles as their pillows ("I could not sleep, but the night passed rapidly"), and when no one else was around, Rocky Mountain Jim dropped his gruff manner and spoke to her tenderly. The actual mountain-climbing was almost too much for her, and she realized that she was not properly equipped for the ordeal in her Hawaiian riding dress and Mr. Evans's boots, which were too big for her. But she did it. "It is so sad that you can never see me as I am now with an unconstrained manner, and an up-to-anything free-legged air," she wrote to her sister.

As the months passed, the dude ranch began to gossip about a romance, and Isabella wrote to Hennie of "Mr. Nugent" in the throes of impassioned enthusiasm. He was brilliant company, charismatic, funny, sharp, and cultured, and you could talk with him about everything. Of course, he put on a rough swagger to keep up his image as a wild outlaw, and some believed that his nickname referred to the fact that his lies were so colossal. But under the rough exterior hid a lively and caring mind with a strikingly broad knowledge of literature. Isabella had never written so openly about her feelings for a man. "He is a most extraordinary man. His appearance is frightful, but [his gentle cosy manner] . . . his low musical voice . . . his infinite grace of manner. . . . For five minutes his manner was such that for a moment I thought [love] possible, but I put it away as egregious vanity unpardonable in a woman of 40," she wrote to her sister.

Just before Isabella departed for home, Mountain Jim told her the darker episodes in his life story and, in a dramatic encounter, declared his love for Isabella. Isabella was shocked and wept, but remained firm and turned him down. Wonderful as he was, she couldn't overlook his wild past, his mood swings, and his predilection for heavy drinking. "He is a man whom any woman might love but no sane woman would marry. . . . My heart dissolves with pity for him and his dark, lost, self ruined life. He is so loveable and fascinating yet so terrible. . . . I miss him very much."

Then Isabella did what she believed every well-brought-up woman from Edinburgh society circles would do: wrote him a formal letter. "Dear Sir, in consequence of the very blameworthy way in which you spoke to me on Monday, there can be nothing but constraint between us. Therefore it is my wish that our acquaintance shall at once terminate. Yours truly . . ."

*

[EXPRESS LETTER, SENT TELEPATHICALLY]

Friday, November 21, 1873

Dear Isabella, sweet Isabella, I'm standing here at the tippy-top of Long's Peak sending smoke signals and messages in Morse code, throwing rocks and shouting into a megaphone: D-o-n-t-s-e-n-d-t-h-a-t-l-e-t-t-e-r! But of course you send it anyway, or rather hand it to Mountain Jim when you run into him while riding, even though you see that he's already in pain and sick.

Dear Isabella, why a ridiculous letter like this, after all those experiences you've had? You became a new Isabella in Hawaii, didn't you, an independent woman who swam in rivers and climbed volcanoes and saddled her own horse and didn't give a fig for conventionality—so why would you cling tooth and nail to your image as a respectable lady? Why, oh why do we hold on to these old ways of behaving? Why can't we change our self-image, even when everyone else already sees us differently?

Yeah, yeah, you insisted to your sister that you were never seriously in love *with the guy, heavens no, you just went on and on about him with your cheeks burning and grasped at every possible chance to mention his name. Once you even dreamed that you were sitting by the hearth when Jim came in carrying a revolver and shot you! Of course, he was exciting to you precisely because he was "dangerous," as you admitted, but it doesn't take much psychology to interpret that as your secret wish that he come in and—well—shoot your respectability to hell.*

Sure, he drank too much and was probably depressed, or even bipolar, I do understand that very well. But you two had a connection nevertheless, of a kind that rarely forms between people. If you, Isabella, had been able to see yourself as that new woman that you were, you would at the very least have written a different kind of letter.

Your M

PS I really wish you had cut loose with Mountain Jim, and with others as well, if there were any. I would wish the same for myself, if I happened to bump into a good-looking, one-eyed desperado. You don't meet that many of them.

*

Isabella and Mountain Jim met a few more times. Isabella thought back on the wedding proposal she'd received from respectable, modest Mr. Wilson, and why she found this gloomy desperado so much more attractive, but didn't go back on her decision. On Isabella's last evening, this odd couple sat for a long time talking of poetry and writing.

They never met again. Only a half year after Isabella left, Mountain Jim took his last bullet.

Isabella's round-the-world trip had lasted nearly a year and a half, and it had transformed her radically. As she was about to board her ship in New York to cross the Atlantic, however, she wrote to a friend: "I still vote civilization a nuisance, society a humbug and all conventionality a crime, but possibly I may fall into the old grooves speedily." And indeed, as soon as she returned to Edinburgh, this is exactly what happened. Once again she became respectable Miss Bird, who lived with her sister, practiced charity, and devoted her days to writing. John Murray was interested in publishing her experiences in Hawaii in book form, so Isabella edited her letters to her sister into a book manuscript, and *The Hawaiian Archipelago* appeared in February 1875, equipped with a preface proclaiming *health reasons*. It was received with great enthusiasm, so Isabella also wrote up her Rocky Mountain experiences as a series of magazine articles. Around this time a certain doctor named John Bishop set his eye on Isabella, who was ten years his senior, and proposed marriage, but Isabella absolutely refused to even discuss it. The popularity of her book and series of articles also weighed on her conscience: surely it couldn't be proper to benefit financially from something that had been so much fun!

Almost overnight Isabella was transformed from the wild, free, transgressive, life-loving woman who rode through Hawaii and the Rocky Mountains astraddle the horse like a man back into a respectable old maid who cared way too much about what was proper. And the same pattern recurred every time she returned from a journey, for the next thirty years. Isabella lived a double life: while out traveling the world she was one person, but she was completely unable to bring that persona home with her. The pattern held even as her journeys grew wilder and wilder, her books more and more popular, and she herself was accorded the official status of an explorer.

As much as this annoys me, can't I find some way of understanding her, at least a little? Understanding how easily you sink back into familiar routines after a life-changing journey? How hard it is to sustain a change, a new self, that radical and invigorated being, when at home nothing whatsoever has changed? How difficult it is to avoid feeling like an outsider for having changed your priorities in life? Even if you've begun to think of society as "a humbug," conventionality as a crime, and the ideal of starting a family, owning your own home, and burning out at work as a nauseating norm, it's difficult to live any other way. It's hard to hold on to that transformative feeling.

And so a few years after her return, Isabella was sick again. She went to several doctors, but not one of them could understand why at home in Scotland she was a feeble invalid who could scarcely drag herself out of bed, but while traveling she became fearless, tireless, and utterly irrepressible. Be that as it may, as the doctors couldn't think of any other treatment, they prescribed a new sea voyage for her.

But where would she go? What corner of the world would be exotic enough to yield grist for her writing mill? For though *health reasons* were still her official smoke screen for travel, her true motivation was to gather material for a new book. She wrote to Charles Darwin (who else?) to ask for advice on mountain climbing in the Andes, but Darwin's reply was not encouraging: South America was not suitable for women. Then Isabella got interested in Japan. It had just opened to foreigners, and almost nothing was known about it.

Isabella, aged forty-six, sailed from England to New York in April 1878, took a transcontinental train to San Francisco, and then boarded a steamship for Yokohama, arriving there in late May. This time she traveled with "very little luggage"; in addition to her riding outfit and saddle, she carried with her letters of introduction to give to the people she would meet in Japan.

She did not take to Japan immediately. She found Yokohama unattractive, gray, and dull, and her depictions of Japanese people are shockingly racist: the people in the harbor were small, withered, bowlegged, flat-chested, poor-looking, and in general ugly, though they seemed friendly. (She mentions Japanese ugliness and other "national defects" several times in her almost-five-hundred-page book.) The climate in May and June didn't please her either: the weather was hot, humid, and drizzly. In addition, this was the first time Isabella found herself in a country where people didn't speak English and she couldn't read the papers, books, or street signs. As a result, everything felt alien to her. Nor was the famed "Oriental magnificence" anywhere in evidence: the buildings were gray wood, the people's clothes dull blue, brown, or gray, and no one wore jewelry; everything was poor and monotonous, and the only color and gold could be seen on temples. The women clattering and tottering on high clogs had clear skin and shiny hair, it was true; but their shaved eyebrows and blackened teeth made them look strange. The way women painted their lips red and powdered their faces thickly with pearl powder displeased Isabella, but she notes nonetheless that it's difficult to criticize women who have so much kindly grace of manner. In sum, she says that the people are the ugliest she has ever seen, but also the neatest and friendliest.

Isabella spent some time in Tokyo, where at last she found some eye candy: among other things, she admired the gorgeous kimonos on the people strolling through the imperial garden. But she was burning with desire to get out into the countryside to see "the real Japan." To the British consul, her plan to travel into the interior sounded extremely ambitious, but, he said, it would be entirely safe for a woman to travel on her own: her worst problems would be the fleas and the poor horses. He gave her a map, which unfortunately was seriously deficient: whole sections of it were blank. But Isabella could gather more information as she went along. "That will be all the more interesting," the consul declared cheerfully. In many isolated mountain villages, Isabella was, in fact, the first European woman anyone had ever seen.

She needed the assistance of an interpreter and servant; having interviewed applicants, she chose eighteen-year-old Itō, who could speak and write English and cook. He had visited the interior and by his own account could walk twenty-five miles a day. Isabella herself would travel partly on horseback, partly in a rickshaw, to pull which she hired a group of runners. She packed two wicker baskets full of things to take along: a few clothes (her traveling outfit was a dust-colored tweed dress, sturdy lace-up boots, and a traditional Japanese bamboo hat resembling an overturned bowl), an inflatable seat cushion for the rickshaw, a folding chair, a canvas stretcher bed (the only way to sleep without a flea infestation), a rubber bathtub, sheets, a blanket, candles, writing implements, an English-Japanese dictionary, Mr. Brunton's large map of Japan, and her own Mexican saddle and bridle. Everyone had an opinion on what kinds of food supplies she should take on a journey into the uncharted interior, but Isabella ended up packing only a small quantity of Liebig's meat extract, five pounds of raisins, a little chocolate for eating and drinking, and brandy for emergencies. (In a footnote based on her experience, Isabella encourages travelers in Japan not to burden themselves with any other food supply than Liebig's extract of meat. Developed by a German professor named Justus von Liebig, meat extract was a highly concentrated meat stock that was very popular everywhere in Europe. It was advertised with depictions of extreme conditions like crossing the Egyptian desert or living with indigenous peoples; for example, the famous explorer Sir Henry Morton Stanley used it to travel through the African jungles in search of Dr. Livingstone. Liebig's meat extract is still on the market today, and I'm wondering whether I shouldn't immediately order a can of it online for my next trip.)

On the day of her departure, Isabella was racked with nerves, mentally going over everything that could go wrong: "I often wished to give up my project, but was ashamed of my cowardice when, on the best authority, I received assurances of its safety." But why the shame? She was heading alone into unstudied territory without a map! Who wouldn't be nervous?

The first leg of her journey was a ninety-mile trip to Nikkō, done in three days by rickshaw and one set of runners. En route they stopped to rest in teahouses, where in addition to tea they could buy sweets, dried persimmons and fish, pickles, and sticky *mochi* rice cakes, as well as rain hats and a change of straw sandals for the runners. Isabella was immediately introduced to the "real Japan" she'd been longing to see: the houses in the countryside were flimsy huts, everything smelled bad, and the people were "ugly, shabby, and poor." Their night lodgings were horrifyingly austere. In the first place they stayed, Isabella was shocked when the room she was shown was, as was customary, completely empty except for a tatami mat crawling with fleas and swarms of mosquitoes. Itō set up a bed for her with a canvas mosquito net, prepared a bath, and brought her tea, rice, and eggs for dinner. She tried to write a letter about the day's events, but the relentless bug attacks made that impossible—as did the pairs of eyes peeking at her through the gaps in the *fusuma* sliding doors. She didn't sleep a wink all night, and the strange smells and sounds had her on the verge of panic: "The lack of privacy was fearful, and I have not yet sufficient trust in my fellow-creatures to be comfortable without locks, walls, or doors! . . . My money was lying about, and nothing seemed easier than to slide a hand through the *fusuma* and appropriate it. Itō told me that the well was badly contaminated, the odours were fearful; illness was to be feared as well as robbery!"

The ten-day magic was still in her future.

The next day, however, Isabella had collected herself, and wrote to her sister: "Already I can laugh at my fears and misfortunes. . . . A traveller must buy his own experience, and success or failure depends mainly on personal idiosyncrasies. Many matters will be remedied by experience as I go on, and I shall acquire the habit of feeling secure. But lack of privacy, bad smells, and the torments of fleas and mosquitoes are, I fear, irremediable evils." Later, back in England, Isabella added another observation in a footnote: "My fears, though quite natural for a lady alone, had really no justification. I have since travelled 1,200 miles in the interior, and in Yezo, with perfect safety and freedom from alarm, and I believe that there is no country in the world in which a lady can travel with such absolute security from danger and rudeness as in Japan." Amen.

Isabella knew, of course, that the trip would be rough, and had prepared for discomfort. In Nikkō, however, she was able to rest for nine days in the perfect Japanese idyll: she was lodged in the beautiful house of a man named Kanaya, with gardens and *tokonoma* alcoves. "I almost wish that the rooms were a little less exquisite, for I am in constant dread of spilling the ink, indenting the mats, or tearing the paper windows," she wrote to her sister. She was so taken with Nikkō that she considered it one of the most beautiful places in the world, and devoted page after page in her book to descriptions of exquisite temples, shrines, and Tokugawa Ieyasu's burial monuments. In Kanaya's house she also watched the local women's life, and gradually began to understand the aesthetics of sparsity and empty space. For example, she was delighted with ikebana, and once her eyes had been opened to this art form she declared almost word for word my own reaction a hundred and thirty years later: "Can anything be more grotesque and barbarous than our 'florists' bouquets' . . . in which stems, leaves, and even petals are brutally crushed, and the grace and individuality of each flower systematically destroyed?" She never did make friends with Japanese music, though. Kanaya's work—conducting the music in a Shintō shrine—consisted to her mind of "leading the discords," and listening to Japanese singing made her feel as if she were "among savages."

Leaving Nikkō, Isabella began an arduous journey through the interior to Niigata on the Sea of Japan, and from there north through the mountains to Aomori. They covered around seven hundred miles to get there, and it took them nearly two months, with stops. Isabella kept a meticulous log of the villages through which they passed, and the number of houses in each; she also noted down distances like any explorer hoping to be taken seriously. (There is a theory that Isabella's journey was undertaken at the behest and under the protection of the British consul, and that its purpose was to map out opportunities for missionary work in Japan.) Isabella and Itō proceeded on horseback, riding endlessly through mountain passes, valleys, and forests and past rice paddies, villages, temple ruins, poverty, dirt, and silent staring crowds of people. Both the children and the adults stared openly at her, for no one had ever before seen a foreign woman—or, for that matter, a fork or spoon. Many took her for a man, because her eyebrows had not been shaven nor her teeth blackened. In one valley Isabella was asked to give Itō a public command, so people could hear how a foreigner talked. Isabella was surprised at the extreme poverty in the mountainous regions, for "poverty of the squalid kind is usually associated with laziness and drunkenness," but here people were constantly working hard. In many places they were almost naked—in one remote village, the women wore only cotton pants, and one woman staggered about drunk. Itō was overwhelmed with shame: he didn't know that things could be so primitive in Japan, and it was shocking for a foreigner to witness such things. The inns were hideous—sometimes no more than half-falling-down shacks full of fleas, mosquitoes, noise, and stench. Sometimes they were black with smoke and soot from the hearth, and the room a dark, stifling space separated only with a paper screen. Often there was nothing to eat but rice and eggs, or black beans and boiled cucumber. One day Itō promised to slaughter a chicken he'd found for Isabella, but the chicken escaped and Isabella was desperate: she hadn't tasted fish, meat, or chicken in ten days. (Apparently she'd already run out of Liebig's extract of meat.) Once she gave a sick boy medicine, and before she knew it a crowd had lined up behind the screen, mothers and fathers carrying naked children in their arms with horrible diseases, each worse than the last.

Whenever they came to a blank area on Mr. Brunton's map, they forged ahead blind.

Isabella was often utterly exhausted. They were traveling through the heat and stifling rainy season of the summer, and sometimes they were impeded by torrential downpours that washed away roads and bridges. They were tormented by fleas and mosquitoes. Isabella's arm was inflamed with wasp and horsefly stings; her feet were full of ant bites; and swarms of hundreds of hornets drove the horses crazy. Some days Isabella was so racked with back pain that she was unable to ride. "Only strong people should travel in Northern Japan" was her summary of the situation.

But there were wonderful moments as well. They were traveling through breathtaking scenery, often the most beautiful Isabella had ever seen.

Isabella took meticulous notes on everything she saw, trying to be as scientific as she could. When their route took them to hot springs or *onsens*, she jotted down their temperatures and described the locals bathing, but never dared enter one herself (or perhaps just didn't consider it respectable to describe it in print). When she found herself in the middle of a local festival or *matsuri*, she described the festive atmosphere and the decorated portable shrines. She took detailed notes on the stores in Niigata, wrote extensive accounts of the manufacture of paper and silk, reported on the state of Christian missionary work in Japan, and tsked at people's "superstition." Into her book she inserted an analysis of Japanese cuisine, noting that even the finest Japanese food was an acquired taste. For example, she said, the daikon or Japanese radish was so disgusting in both smell and taste that "it has made many a brave man flee!" On the other hand, she found the Japanese way of making tea pleasant, though the tea wasn't black and it wasn't served with milk: to her the clear, straw-colored beverage smelled and tasted delicious and was always amazingly refreshing.

In mid-August Isabella reached Aomori at last, and continued on to Hakodate on the northernmost island of Hokkaidō, where her goal was to meet the "hairy Ainu"—representatives of that little-known indigenous bear-worshipping people. In the Hakodate consulate, she met men who were also mounting an expedition to the Ainu villages. These men were equipped with such massive quantities of food and other goods, mounted on pony caravans to carry it all, that Isabella predicted to her sister that "they will fail, and that I, who have reduced my luggage to 45 lb., will succeed!" And she did succeed. She spent a month in Hokkaidō, enchanted with its stunning scenery, and ended up spending several days in an Ainu village, observing their way of life.

From Hakodate Isabella returned through stormy seas by ship to Yokohama and Tokyo, and then spent another three months in Kyoto and surrounding areas. The majority of the letters she wrote from Kyoto were left out of the published travel book, because Isabella felt that the city did not match the attribute "unbeaten tracks" promised in the book's title. Fortunately, however, some of those letters were printed in her book, and I feel a warm glow of shared experience, as she fell head over heels in love with Kyoto in November, much as I did when I lived in that city for a longer period while writing my first book. Isabella adored the city's devotion to art and beauty, the brightly colored kimonos and enchanting obi belts worn by the women, the beautiful teahouses, the delightful temples and palaces and gardens splashed across the slopes of the purple mountains that surrounded the city. . . . Isabella admitted that she went crazy in the hundreds of little shops full of beautiful objects beautifully displayed. (Me too.) She wanted to buy things for all her friends back home, but suspected that they either wouldn't appreciate them or would unceremoniously jam them in between other knickknacks. The exquisite refinement of Japanese treasures only comes into its own, she thought, if you arrange them on a black lacquer tray on a shelf with only a few objects. (Agreed.) Isabella's final judgment, based on a ten-day stay: "With its schools, hospitals, lunatic asylum, prisons, dispensaries, almshouses, fountains, public parks and gardens, exquisitely beautiful cemeteries, and streets of almost painful cleanliness, Kyoto is the best-arranged and best-managed city in Japan."

Finally, on December 19, 1878, after a seven-month adventure in Japan, Isabella cast off from the Yokohama harbor on the steamship *Volga* to begin her journey home—this time through Asia toward the west, in order to make a complete circumnavigation of the globe. The snowy peak of Mount Fuji glowed red in the sunrise as the ship glided past it toward the ocean, carrying the letter-writing Isabella on board.

But Isabella did not head straight home. Why rush? After all, she was traveling for her health. The ship stopped in several places, including Shanghai, Hong Kong, Saigon, and the Malay Peninsula; after the Suez Canal, Isabella disembarked and traveled to Cairo. One of her most beloved childhood memories was her pastor father's story of how Moses received the Ten Commandments on Mount Sinai, and that's where she wanted to go. The route there from Cairo ran 270 miles through the Sinai Desert, and would take her eighteen days to traverse; the manager of her hotel in Cairo assured her that it would be impossible for her to undertake. He did, however, agree to round up some Bedouins, camels, and a servant and guide named Hassan. And so she packed a small amount of food (including Liebig's extract of meat, of course) along with medicine, brandy, and an umbrella for the sun. Also included were a big tent for her, a small one for Hassan, a mattress, blankets, a folding chair, a basin for washing, and kitchen implements (the Bedouins would light fires in the desert with the camel droppings they collected along the way). Unfortunately, in her books Isabella does not tell us how she managed bathing, relieving herself, and other intimate activities with unsullied respectability, but on this trip she realized just how convenient having her own tent made these things, and from this point on she always packed one on her trips. (On the other hand, being the only woman among twenty-odd Arab men didn't seem to pose any kind of obstacle to respectability.)

The trip was just as awful as the hotel manager had promised—and to top things off, Isabella got sick. On the very first morning she was feeling weak and nauseated, but she decided to tough it out across the furnace-like desert. When they stopped during the day to rest, Hassan showed her how to wriggle under a rock for a little shade—and if there were no rocks, Hassan dug a pit, in which Isabella crouched under a blanket for shade from the sun, reading the Bible and nibbling raisins. The daytime temperature was 105 (and higher) in the shade, and even in the evening it never dropped below 90. That first evening, after ten hours on a camel's back, her throat was sore, her head ached, and she had blisters and a rash—and she realized she had typhoid fever. All through the night she tossed and turned on her mattress in agony, but in the morning was ready to push on. "I feel this glorious desert," she wrote to her sister of her pains, is "worth them all."

One evening Hassan brought her bad news: one of the Bedouins had stolen all the water from the goatskin bags; they only had about a cupful left. That night she was desperately thirsty and nearly delirious: Bible verses and lines of poetry about water churned obsessively in her head, and at some point, thinking she heard the sound of rain, she rushed out of the tent, but it was just the desert wind thrashing the dry branches on nearby gnarled trees. Hassan showed her how to put pebbles in her mouth to relieve her thirst, and the next day the caravan continued through the merciless heat of the desert. Isabella could scarcely stay on the camel's back with her headache and itchy rash; she felt faint, and would have asked Hassan to stop, but couldn't get her mouth to work. When they finally reached an oasis, all she could make out was a man running up to them with a container of water in his hand.

Isabella had thought that her pilgrimage to Mount Sinai would be the high point of her travels—she was satisfying her wanderlust, yet her motivation was religious—but after the oppressive and tedious journey, her destination was a disappointment: Mount Sinai had not a single trace of spirituality to it. The monks at the monastery were flagrantly mercenary with tourists; and as they also distilled hard liquor, they were also drunk.

Isabella returned to Scotland on a ship from Alexandria to Liverpool, and arrived at Tobermory on the Isle of Mull (where Hennie had rented them a small house) in late May 1879. She had traveled around the world and been away for more than a year. Once again, after refusing to let typhoid fever and intolerable conditions stop her even in the Sinai Desert, upon returning home Isabella collapsed. "My body is very weak," she wrote, "and I can only walk about three hundred yards with a stick."

Isabella worked all summer on her series of articles on the Rocky Mountains, which had been received with such enthusiasm that John Murray wanted to publish it as a book as well. Her daily routine was enviably efficient and disciplined: she wrote all morning, ate lunch at one-thirty, went for a long walk with her sister, and then continued writing in the evening. Hennie took care of the house and worked with the cook to plan meals. (I can't stress strongly enough what a luxury it is to have someone else taking care of meals when you're trying to write.) When the Rocky Mountain manuscript was finished, she began to work on her Japan book, but worried in advance that it would be boring compared with her previous work. When *A Lady's Life in the Rocky Mountains* was released in October 1879, the first run sold out in a week. The reviews were glowing as well, and John Murray threw a party in Isabella's honor in London. All of a sudden she was the center of attention: she was praised as a "literary lion" and introduced to writers, politicians, and reporters.

A scandal of sorts arose, however, when the *Times* reviewer hinted that Isabella had ridden a horse in the Rocky Mountains dressed in men's clothing. It was the epitome of shameful behavior for a woman to imitate a man in any way, especially in dress, so Isabella took grievous offense. Her worst fear was that she would be taken for some sort of radical or, worst of all, a *feminist*—and that lampoons and satirical cartoons would be published about her, as had happened to other traveling women. And so, to reinforce her image as a respectable woman traveling *only for health reasons*, to the next edition of the book she added an explanatory footnote about her riding attire. It consisted—just so we're clear on this—of a jacket, an ankle-length skirt, and full Turkish trousers, which, according to Isabella, was "a thoroughly serviceable and feminine costume for mountaineering and other rough travelling, in any part of the world."

*

[LETTER TO TOBERMORY, ISLE OF MULL]

Dear Isabella,

Sorry, but I just have to write to you. Forget about the dad-blame respectability already! What difference does it make whether someone thinks you were wearing pants or not? What if you were? It makes me want to tear out my hair, reading all the contradictions in your behavior. Think about it: you ride all over the Rocky Mountains with a one-eyed outlaw; you drag yourself across the Sinai Desert with Bedouins while suffering from typhoid fever; later you slog for forty-two days through the snow in the Persian mountains; you're incredibly brave, tough, and, on top of everything else, over forty, and by the end of it all even over sixty—why do you give a rat's hind end what anybody thinks about you? Stuff their respectability! Wear pants if you feel like it!

I'd appreciate it if you could give my words a thought or two—maybe you'll get what I'm driving at.

Your M

*

But the fact is, *I'm* the one who doesn't get it. I just can't understand how important this whole clothing issue was for female travelers of that day. Because exploring was such an unfeminine pursuit, women who undertook it had to prove that while exploring they were still both 1) feminine, and 2) respectable. Women's travel attire became a serious, even political issue, the outcome of which was that a woman had to deck herself out *in all conditions* in an outfit that she would have worn at home: a corset, a long dark skirt, boots, and a hat or bonnet beneath which her hair was tied up in a bun.

And so, with smoking pen, let me jot down some night women's tips:

If you want to straddle the horse like a man, under your skirt wear bloomers (which were launched around 1850 by a feminist named Amelia Bloomer). Then do what Isabella did: while riding in the Rocky Mountains, say, whenever you approach a dwelling, no matter how dilapidated, dismount, put a skirt on over your bloomers, and ride into the village sidesaddle.

If need be, disguise yourself as a man. Especially aboard ship, this may be unavoidable—for example, captains of whaling ships, warships, and pirate ships have strict rules against allowing women on board. (One nineteenth-century woman, however, managed to serve twenty years on a British warship without her gender being revealed.) Another reason for disguise is that then you can travel without fear of being harassed or raped.

You want to wear pants for no particular reason? Consider whether you can afford to follow a certain Lady Hester Stanhope's example. She traveled dressed as a man in the Middle East in 1810 just because she found pants more convenient. Her behavior shocked the British. (The Arabs just thought it was some strange foreign quirk.) Be that as it may, the lady in question died in the mountains in Lebanon alone, deranged, and impoverished in her thirty-six-room house, which stories say was full of trash, old medicines, and moth-eaten Arabian saddles. Just saying.

The next summer Isabella's beloved sister contracted typhoid fever, and though Isabella and her doctor, John Bishop, cared for her day and night for weeks on end, Hennie died at the age of forty-six. Isabella was completely crushed. She tried to edit her Japan book, which was in the home stretch, but all inspiration had vanished. *Unbeaten Tracks in Japan* did appear in October 1880, in two volumes—and was an instant sales success—but when the box containing her author's copies came in the mail, Isabella couldn't even open it. What would she do now? She couldn't travel, certainly, or enjoy her popularity; from now on, she decided, she had better devote herself exclusively to charitable works. *(Goddammit, Isabella, not again!)* At forty-nine Isabella saw no other solution than marriage, and at last said yes to John Bishop, who over the years had proposed to her many times. The wedding was held in March 1881, nine months after her sister passed. Only a few relatives were in the church for the ceremony, and no wedding reception was held. (I think of Isabella in the photo that was taken on her wedding day: it shows a woman dressed in black staring blankly at the camera.)

When Bishop died in 1886, after only five years of marriage, Isabella refused to collapse. The inheritance left her by her husband ensured that she could afford to live comfortably and travel wherever she pleased. When her publisher John Murray asked what her plans were, she answered like a proper night woman: "I feel I should be an unworthy heir of many blessed memories if I did not try to make my life useful and interesting. *My needs are simple and I am absolutely without any ties, so that I can, if any measure of strength returns, shape my remainder of life as I please.* Such travelling as I am best fitted for involves very much hardship, many risks, the deprivation of all comfort and ease and for the most part complete isolation, and I must have an object worth the deprivations and hazards."

And Isabella did truly spend the rest of her life as she pleased. First she decided to head for the mountains in Central Asia. At the age of fifty-seven, Isabella first fulfilled a long-held dream by exploring the Himalayas on the back of a yak, then accompanied a certain Major Sawyer to Persia—by the end of an extremely dangerous six-hundred-mile journey in intolerably frigid conditions, Isabella had lost thirty pounds and her hair had turned gray. Despite that, and despite the horror at her plans expressed by the missionaries she met, she continued alone through Syria, Turkey, and Armenia, where hideous dangers and encounters with cruel nomadic tribes likely awaited her. But for some reason, Isabella was not afraid.

She returned to England from her nearly two-year journey in late 1890. Her diary had been stolen en route, and only a pocket-size notebook with brief notations survived from the end of the journey; but fortunately, the letters she had sent home from Persia had arrived. She holed up in a certain Miss Clayton's house (she no longer had a home of her own) and once again began the meticulous work of forging a travel book out of her experiences. ("I am frightfully busy, I make no visits, don't read, and only go out for exercise.") Her industry paid off: her new best-seller *Journeys in Persia and Kurdistan* was released in December 1891, in two fat volumes.

By this time Isabella enjoyed considerable respect. Many reviews of her books full of high praise had been published; she dined with the prime minister, she was introduced to Queen Victoria, and the king of the Sandwich Islands even gave her a medal of honor for her Hawaii book. She was invited to speak to Parliament, and the legendary Royal Geographical Society invited her to give a talk—the first woman ever to receive such an invitation. Isabella was reluctant to accept it, however, as she knew that the society did not accept women as members. She chose instead to address the Royal Scottish Geographical Society, since a woman *could* become a member of that body. This was an embarrassing turn of events for the Royal Geographical Society, and they decided to accept Isabella as a member—the first woman in history to be accorded this honor. At the society's meeting in November 1892, in fact, fifteen women were inducted as members. Some of the older RGS members, however, were vehemently opposed to this innovation. Enraged squibs on the subject were published in the *Times*, and men in cigar rooms discoursed on the scandalous new developments with mustaches a-quiver. One member who had recently published his own book on Persia—less successfully than Isabella's—wrote: "We contest the general capability of women to contribute to scientific geographical knowledge. Their sex and training render them equally unfitted for exploration, and the genus of professional female globe-trotters . . . is one of the horrors of the latter end of the nineteenth century." In *Punch*, women were lampooned in verse: "A lady an explorer? A traveller in skirts? / The notion's just a trifle too seraphic. / Let them stay and mind the babies / Or hem our ragged shirts / But they mustn't, can't and shan't be geographic." The society's opposition organized a new vote in April 1893, and now the provision of membership to women was rescinded. Those who had already been inducted, however, were allowed to remain.

Isabella was annoyed at this treatment, but decided to keep working, her next destination China. At sixty-two she had numerous health problems, and the doctors advised her to work less, rest more, preferably at a spa; many felt that at her age it was time to retire from the strenuous work of exploration. But Isabella went full-bore till the end: she still had nearly a decade left of active traveling time. In January 1894, Isabella left Liverpool on a ship bound for China, carrying her new tripod camera—she had learned to take photographs. For the next three years she studied Korea, China, and Japan, and her hundreds of painstakingly snapped and developed photos show villages, temples, and sugarloaf mountains along the Yangtze, as well as water buffalos, leprosy patients, and opium smokers. Isabella traveled the Yangtze in a small riverboat and mountain paths in a sedan chair with the curtains drawn (open curtains could have meant the other kind of curtains for a woman). She contracted malaria, broke her arm, and suffered the hurling of abuse and stones by the locals, for the Chinese hated foreigners and especially women traveling alone. In some inns, holes were drilled through her walls at night for locals to peek through, giggling. Once villagers even rioted: in Liangshan, Isabella sat barricaded in her room with a revolver, until soldiers were sent to protect her. Many European women had had nervous breakdowns and even died in attacks mounted by locals, but Isabella did not give up: by this point she was an extremely competent and experienced traveler whose determination was not easily shaken. Besides, despite everything she felt a deep passion for China and its citizens. When her book *Korea and Her Neighbours* appeared in winter 1898, and *The Yangtze Valley and Beyond* a little later, reviewers no longer called her a "traveler," but rather described her as an expert on the political situation in Korea. Not bad for an unschooled woman who'd started traveling in her forties for health reasons!

Isabella made her last trip to Morocco, where she rode horses and camped in tents alone in the Atlas Mountains. This unbelievably energetic world traveler died peacefully in her own bed in Edinburgh one October morning in 1904, at the age of seventy-two. Her travel trunks were packed at the time, ready to head off for China once more.

When I think about Isabella at night, my feelings are conflicted. I think of course of her wildly radical courage and admirable resilience—the thing that, despite all her illnesses, gave her strength in extreme circumstances. But I also think of how she always collapsed when she returned home. I think of the alienating effects of her religiosity, her sometimes uncomfortable racism, and how bizarrely important it was to her to maintain the façade of conventional respectability and virtue. I think of her deep-seated good-girl syndrome, the fact that she never was able to untangle the contradiction that while traveling she was someone else, *some free and courageous new woman*, but at home surrendered again to others' expectations. She felt guilt about her traveling till the end.

When I study the sepia-toned photographs she took in China at the end of the nineteenth century, I imagine her carrying her camera box along the shores of the Yangtze, developing her photos in the river's current at night, in that *dark room supplied by nature*, as she so beautifully put it. Her photographs always remained a bit grainy, because no matter how she filtered the final rinse water, some fine-ground Yangtze sand always clung to their surface. I run my fingers over the cool pages of the picture book: they are smooth. The sand rubbed off somewhere along the way.

Other images float through my mind:

Isabella riding in an ecstasy of freedom in Hawaii—experiencing for the first time the core of her own self, with no thought of what a woman *should* be.

Isabella sitting in the Rocky Mountains in the spark-flecked glow of a campfire, sharing a connection with some utterly unlikely person. In the air hovers an awareness of how right it all is—and how impossible.

Isabella lying in a sandpit in the Sinai Desert, sick and delirious, reading the Bible, at once brave, miserable, and lonely. (Because that's exactly how bravery often feels.)

Isabella writing her meticulous letters with an even and close hand, on paper that is so thin you can see right through it; and those letters traveling through the decades to be finally read by me.

Then I think of myself buying a plane ticket to Japan as a cure for depression, following Isabella's example.

I think that, despite all, I love Isabella because as a sick, depressed, middle-aged woman, she still *left*, again and again, for realms that were not even on the maps.

Because she succeeded in her goal: to travel and still be taken seriously.

*

Night women's advice:

Travel alone, preferably in the roughest conditions possible.

Travel even if you're sick. Travel especially if you're depressed, frustrated, or tired of your life.

It doesn't matter if you aren't aristocratic, rich, beautiful, brilliantly talented, young, or even healthy. You can take your toughest trips in your sixties.

Don't be afraid. Be tough. Be industrious. Write ten books.

Learn to take photographs and use scientific instruments if you need to.

Write about whatever you have to—never mind what: botany, say, or ethnography—even though you have no training in it.

Be buoyant as hell.

IDA

NIGHT WOMEN'S ADVICE 3

You don't need a reason to travel.
Travel on a shoestring budget.
Bum lodgings, if you can.

NIGHT WOMAN #3: *Ida Pfeiffer, née Reyer*
PROFESSION: *Wife and mother, later world traveler and travel author. Obediently raised her children and dumped her husband, while secretly studying a terrestrial globe; set out on her first journey at forty-four. Circled the planet twice on a very small budget. Earned her travel funds by writing books, which were translated into seven languages.*

> *"And now, dear reader, I would beg you not to be angry with me for speaking so much of myself; it is only because this love of travelling does not, according to established notions, seem proper for one of my sex, that I have allowed my feelings to speak in my defense. Judge me, therefore, not too harshly; but rather grant me the enjoyment of a pleasure which hurts no one, while it makes me happy."* —Ida, in the preface to her travel book about Iceland, 1846

When Isabella Bird was only ten years old, Austrian Ida Pfeiffer (1797–1858) left Vienna on her first voyage. In the black-and-white daguerreotype I have pinned to my corkboard, someone's severe-looking aunt sits in a Biedermeier-style day dress from the mid-nineteenth century with a frilly bonnet tied under her chin. Next to her is the explorer's emblematic object, a terrestrial globe, but also a blank sheet of paper and a book. The photograph is both absurd and enticing, because it sends conflicting messages. The woman it depicts is Ida Pfeiffer, a woman I do truly think about at night.

Ida grew up in an affluent family, the daughter of a cotton-factory owner. Her father raised her alongside her five brothers as one of the boys, dressed her in boys' clothing, and joked that one day Ida would be trained as an officer. The goals of her spartan rearing were courage, determination, and the ability to tolerate harsh conditions, minimal food, and pain—traits that came in handy in Ida's later life. But after her father's death when Ida was nine, her mother began to restructure her upbringing in a direction more suited to a girl, trying to get Ida interested in dolls and to wear a skirt, but with scant success: Ida became so anxious that she got sick, and a doctor finally recommended that she be allowed to go back to boys' clothing. Still, at thirteen Ida was forced to transfer to the world of women. She had to learn needlework, cooking, religion, foreign languages, and, of course, playing the piano, an essential skill for all girls—which Ida, however, hated so much that she cut her fingers and burned them with sealing wax so she wouldn't have to practice. Science and math were out of the question: the whole idea was to raise Ida to be a good wife and mother. But it was in those days that she began to dream of foreign countries and to devour travel accounts—inappropriate as such excessive reading was for girls. Around that same time Ida also fell madly in love with her tutor, who asked her to marry him, but her mother declared that relationship out of the question. Ida announced that she would either marry this man or never marry at all, and for a few years managed to keep all other suitors at bay. At twenty-three, however, a reluctant Ida was married to Dr. Anton Pfeiffer, a widower and lawyer twice her age. In accepting his proposal of marriage, Ida announced that she would natheless forever love another.

For thirteen years Ida did her duty as an obedient wife and loving mother, despite wildly unfavorable circumstances. Her hapless husband teetered on the verge of bankruptcy and squandered Ida's dowry; the family had to let their servants go, sold their carriages and horses, and, according to Ida, lived for years cold, hungry, and uncertain of their future. Ida supported the family by giving secret lessons in drawing and music—those piano lessons she had hated so passionately. When in 1833 her husband moved to Lemberg for better employment prospects, Ida chose to stay behind with their two sons in Vienna, where her brothers were still running the family business and kindly promised to support her. Ida was thirty-six, and had basically left her husband. She secretly began to study geography and mull over the possibility of traveling.

When her sons had finally finished their schooling and moved out, Ida began to plan the fulfillment of her dream in earnest. Yes, she wanted to *cut loose and make a total change in her life*, but on what pretext could she travel alone to some far distant place without provoking gossip and disapproval? Her solution was genius: a pilgrimage. For centuries religious pilgrimages had been one of the few ways for women to see the world, and no one could criticize a devout, virtuous forty-four-year-old mother and wife (whose husband was too old to travel) for fulfilling a calling to visit the Holy Land once in her life.

To her family, Ida gave a truncated version of her plan: she told them she was going to visit an acquaintance in Constantinople, though in truth she was planning a yearlong journey into politically turbulent regions in the Middle East and northern Africa. Her sons and friends thought even Constantinople an insane, even ludicrous destination: how could she, *a woman*, withstand the strain of travel, the demanding climate, the poor nutrition, and the diseases and insects that lurked everywhere—and alone, to boot! And besides being an entirely unwomanly undertaking, this kind of travel was not really appropriate for someone her age, who ought to retire to live out a peaceful old age. But Ida had other ideas: "I didn't mind deprivation, my body was healthy and robust, I wasn't afraid of dying, and as someone born in the last century I could travel alone." Exactly: an advanced age could even be an advantage, since you didn't need a chaperone to guarantee the chastity of a worn-out old hag.

Prior to her departure, Ida set her household in order and made a will, so that her possible (or even probable) death wouldn't cause anyone any trouble. Other practical arrangements were more challenging: there were no hotels or railroads where she was going, and travelers had to carry everything they needed with them. Thomas Cook would not begin to arrange his tours abroad for another two decades, and precious little information was available about various travel destinations. You could study the copperplate drawings in books, but they were European artists' idealized conceptions of foreign lands—and apart from that, you had to set out on your journey blind. Nor did Ida have much in the way of travel funds: she was financing her travel out of her skimpy savings. As a practical person, she also cut her hair short before she left. This was, in fact, one of her most radical moves: back then, the only women who had short hair were prisoners or mental patients.

In March 1842, Ida boarded a steamship in Vienna. It took her down the Danube to the Black Sea and then across to Constantinople. On the first few days of her trip she suffered from nausea, headache, and fever—the state of shock typical of departures—and she herself noted that her illness was probably due to change of climate, the anguish of parting from loved ones, and nerves. She spent the two-week sea voyage chatting up her fellow passengers, and by the time they arrived in Constantinople she had gathered the requisite information about everything under the sun, from places to stay to how much she should tip. In Constantinople she mounted a horse for the first time in her life, learned to ride, and instantly got to the heart of the traveler's ethos: "Here another world opens before my eyes. Everything is different: nature, the art, the people, the customs, the way of life. One must come here if one wants to see anything other than . . . ordinary life." In May Ida pushed on through Cyprus and Beirut to Jerusalem. Her little pilgrimage eventually stretched out to nine months, and in addition to religious destinations she visited Syria, Lebanon, Egypt (where she climbed the pyramids and rode a camel to the Red Sea), Italy, and other destinations.

When Ida returned to Austria in December 1842, a certain Viennese publisher began working to convince her to publish her travel diary. She wasn't excited about the idea. She had, in fact, written in her diary every evening of her trip, and filled fourteen notebooks with her meticulous notations, but she had intended them for her own use only, or at most to be read aloud to her family. She had no literary ambitions. She did, however, have one nagging problem: money. She was living on support from her brothers, and publishing a book might help her finance her next trip. (Yes, she was already planning to go.) So she edited her notes into the manuscript of a travel book. To be sure, publication legally required permission from her husband, with whom Ida had had nothing to do for years; so Dr. Pfeiffer was brought in to sign the publishing contract, and, after a few dubious passages had been deleted at his insistence, *Reise einer Wienerin in das heilige Land* (translated into English as *A Visit to the Holy Land, Egypt, and Italy*) was published anonymously in 1844. In her preface, Ida profusely begged her readers' forgiveness—*I'm no writer, I've never written anything but letters, my diary is just a simple tale in which I relate everything the way it happened*—but the book was a success all the same, and quickly went through four printings. To the dismay of Ida's relatives, everyone in Vienna knew who had written the book—an annoyance, of course, because this sort of celebrity was wildly inappropriate for a woman. But Ida didn't care: she had discovered an escape from the crushing conventionality of bourgeois Vienna.

With the royalties from her book she did finance her next trip, a six-month journey to Iceland and Scandinavia (she didn't make it to the Grand Duchy of Finland). She prepared for her trip meticulously by visiting museums, learning how to collect samples of plants and animals, studying English and Danish, and learning the rudiments of a new technology, the making of daguerreotype photographs. Setting off was easier this time, as she had "already proved that a determined woman can get along in the world just as well as a man, and that there are good people everywhere"—and she did indeed need to rely on the help of those good people in Iceland, as there were no inns or other forms of public accommodation in the country. When her book about the trip came out, *Reise nach dem skandinavischen Norden und der Insel Island im Jahre 1845* (translated into English as *A Journey to Iceland, and Travels in Sweden and Norway*), Ida's reputation was further enhanced. The book was praised by some reviewers, but awakened disapproval in others: her first trip had been minimally acceptable as a pilgrimage, but there was flat-out no justification for the second—though at the end of her book, Ida listed the plant samples she had collected, as if in defense of the trip. She anticipated this kind of negative reaction, and quoted her imagined judges in her preface: "'Yet another trip,' they'll say, 'and into areas that everyone would rather avoid than seek out. This woman goes on these trips just to attract attention!'" And then she wrote the sentence that makes her perhaps the most radical of all my traveling night women: "*Dear reader, do not condemn me too harshly, instead grant me this pleasure, which harms no one and makes me happy.*" In the end Ida had no excuses for her trips. She traveled only because she wanted to, and dared say so out loud.

She was right about attracting attention: traveling women, silly curiosities that they were, were laughed at in general, but in Ida's case there was the additional burden of her advanced age. In newspaper articles the writers expressed their astonishment that despite her "manly" behavior—meaning she was courageous and decisive—she had managed to retain her outward femininity so perfectly! And, in fact, she invested time and effort in that side of things: in order to be able to keep traveling, she knew her manner of dress had to convey extreme respectability. When I look at her photos, the woman posing in them is truly no emancipated amazon but a thoroughly sober and sensible matron. In her official explorer photograph, Ida is wearing a day dress in the style then popular in Viennese bourgeois circles, with a bonnet tied under her chin—a style of headgear whose symbolic value cannot be overestimated. Looking a bit like a lampshade, the bonnet was also called the *kiss-me-if-you-can* hat: it blocked attempted kisses effectively. It also functioned like a horse's blinkers: by restricting its wearer's field of vision to straight ahead, it emphasized a woman's virtue, fragility, and limited sphere of life. A woman dressed in a bonnet remained obediently inside the confines assigned to her (the home), and without looking to either side she proceeded down the path onto which her male guardian (father or husband) had set her (her family's well-being). On top of everything else, lining Ida's face on the inside of her bonnet is a thick padding of crimped lace, as if to say: *Nothing to worry about, I'm here in my padded little reality, living by the book, precisely as you want me to live*. And it's certainly true that if you pose next to a globe, as Ida does, you have to wrap your head in a padded lampshade if you hope to get any kind of approval from decent citizens.

And the bonnet bunco worked. According to contemporary reports, Ida's whole being seemed to exude so much obedient, hardworking *Hausfrau* that it was difficult to credit her adventure-filled journeys at all.

—

But they were true. Ida spent the rest of her life either traveling or preparing for her next trip. She circumnavigated the globe twice, in opposite directions. She was prodigiously determined, strong-minded, tenacious, and bold, and always most attracted to whatever was absolutely not recommended for a woman traveling alone. She was also a true die-hard tourist, who always wanted to see as much as possible in the shortest possible time; nothing irritated her so much as delays. She was never one to relax in a hammock on some paradisal beach: her sand was always rushing through the hourglass. "If only I were ten years younger," she wrote; "—how I would like to expand the scope of my travels even further!"

To finance those travels, Ida sold everything she owned and wrote travel books for money; but no matter how she scrimped and saved, the royalties were never enough to cover her expenses for trips lasting several years. Had she been a male explorer, she could have launched official expeditions or participated in state-funded scientific expeditions, but none of this was possible for a woman. Ida did what she could. She began to collect plants, beetles, butterflies, mollusks, fish, and ethnological objects that she tried, as her male counterparts did, to sell to museums of natural history in Vienna, Berlin, and London. The museums in Berlin and London did buy objects from her, and indeed several living creatures were named after her, including *Myronides pfeifferae*, a sticklike insect; *Vaginula idae*, a sea snail; and *Rana idae*, a frog found on Madagascar. The academic world in Vienna, however, turned up their noses at her—not just because she had no scientific training, but because women were considered incapable of doing science at all. Even the Austrian finance minister opined at a ministers' conference in 1852 that "it is scarcely to be believed that a woman without scientific training would know how to collect anything of scientific value." And so, after returning to Vienna from her second round-the-world trip, Ida opened a private room where an entrance fee gave visitors the chance to admire the curiosities she had brought back from distant lands, including a whole collection from the Dayak in Borneo (head ornaments, clothes, belts, weapons, and baskets woven from human hair in which the Dayak carry the heads they have cut off their human victims), as well as books and calendars full of exotic writing. Ida also followed the example of male explorers in applying for state assistance and various commissions for her travels, but to little avail: the only official grant she ever received was a miserable 150 thalers from the Austrian government in 1851. (I know, I know. Depressing news: grant rejections.) Outside her native land, however, Ida was regarded much more highly, and especially in Berlin's society circles she was quite popular. The leading scientist of the age, Alexander von Humboldt, was her great admirer, and even introduced her to the King and Queen of Prussia, who in 1856 awarded her a medal for her accomplishments "in the realm of the sciences and arts." She was the first woman to be admitted—as an honorary member—to the Berlin Geographical Society, as well as to its counterpart in Paris. (The doors of the Royal Geographical Society in London would not be opened to women for four more decades, through Isabella's work.) But in her hometown Vienna, "people were quite sparing in their expressing of acceptance," as Ida's son diplomatically put it in his biography.

Ida was never free of the constant worry about a shortage of funds; not once in her life was she able to travel in comfort, let alone without cares. Fortunately, she had learned to live austerely in the officer camps of her childhood home and during her marriage—why should she not be capable of traveling with absolutely minimal funds and luggage? So she traveled alone without servants and with so little luggage that in an emergency she could have carried her things herself. She paid little attention to physical pains and ailments: the malaria she contracted in Indonesia couldn't stop her, and while lying half-dead in Madagascar, as she herself described her own state, she kept planning new routes. She lived abstemiously, even puritanically, traveling on a tiny portion of the proverbial shoestring budget, taking the most modest sailboats or traveling in steerage on steamships, riding mules or, on difficult terrain, going on foot. She lived like the locals, ate whatever she could get (often no more than water and rice), slept in the cheapest inns or in tents or sometimes on her straw mat under the stars. In this way she undoubtedly came in unusually close contact with the ordinary people and their culture. About the only thing that distinguished her from modern travelers was that Biedermeier dress and bonnet. Besides, there were many ways for an Austrian to pinch pennies. Ida's way was smoothed by letters of introduction, which she would carry into European consulates in search of assistance and information—and, implicitly, rides and places to crash for the night. In distant countries, a woman traveling alone was a rare enough sight that her compatriots would give her a princely reception and then equip her for the next leg of her journey. Handiest of all was when she was passed from one host to another—and it did nothing to tarnish her reputation as a fearless world traveler either. She most often traveled on ships that agreed to offer her a free trip, and sometimes she demanded that, for respectability's sake, the shipping company or the gentlemen aboard ship offer this married woman traveling alone meals and maintenance. Once she bragged in a letter that she had traveled a thousand miles without spending a gulden. "If this continues, I'll never come home, since I've decided to keep traveling as long as my funds last, and of course my age (54 years). . . ." She also takes the same kind of pride in her parsimony as modern dollar-a-day backpackers ("travelers like Prince Pückler-Muskau or Chateaubriand and Lamartine would have spent the same on a two-week trip to a spa as would last me, the simple pilgrim, for a two or three-year trip") and is always happy to mock "typical Europeans" who cumbersomely haul their entire household with them on trips (like the "Samsonite tourists" mocked by modern backpackers). Once she became famous, Ida began to expect free services, and could snap and snarl if she didn't get them. Upon returning from a trip she would always thank the people who had helped her in her books, but also mention by name those who had treated her badly—and that may be why shipping companies later began to beg her to accept free trips from them.

After her trip to Iceland, Ida's travels became ever more adventurous, and she roamed farther and farther from the usual tourist routes—sometimes into uncharted territories where Europeans had never before been seen. In 1846, she set off on her first round-the-world trip, which would last two and a half years. The Austrian reading public was able to follow her travelogue "in real time" in the papers, and her travel book *Eine Frauenfahrt um die Welt* (1850; the English translation *A Woman's Journey Round the World* was published in London in the same year) contained comprehensive accounts of "exotic" corners and cultures of the world, people, religions, natural phenomena, plants, animals, local food, customs, dress, prices, and distances, even the conditions of hospitals and prisons.

I ransack the pages of her book looking for night women's advice, those rare personal remarks like gold nuggets.

*

[READER FEEDBACK TO THE PUBLISHER, CARL GEROLD AND SON, VIENNA]

Dear Ida,

The ideal growing conditions of the pepper tree is of course a fascinating topic, but I thirst for your tips on a whole other category of things. What did you pack to take along? What did you do if you got sick? Were you ever afraid, or homesick? I'm especially interested in the following topics: eating, sleeping, the contents of your luggage, modes of transportation, travel clothing, hygiene, health, illness, your strength and mood and ability to keep going, intimate matters like the toilet and menstruation (though I suppose you probably got rid of the last one soon enough), setbacks and dangerous situations, possible affairs with men, and subjects related to being a travel writer, including writing, money, and income. And please don't forget tips on saving!

Hoping you don't consider these topics too trivial,
I remain yours sincerely, M

*

Let's see. In May 1846, Ida, then forty-eight, left Hamburg on a ten-week sea voyage to Rio de Janeiro with the intention of circling the globe to the west. Note that she took a sailing ship, because *a steamship would have been too expensive*. In her diary she noted down tips on what necessities one should take along on an extremely uncomfortable trip like this: among other things, a mattress, a pillow, and a blanket; plenty of eggs, rice, potatoes, and sugar—and families traveling with children *should take along a goat.*

Having survived the sea voyage, Ida spent a couple months traveling around Brazil in the vicinity of Rio. On one of these outings she became the target of a violent mugging attempt by a "native," but *successfully warded off the attack with a sunshade and a switchblade.* Brazil's climate proved ill-suited to her constitution—the humid heat induced nausea—though otherwise she always touted her excellent health. From Brazil she set sail on a three-month journey through the stormy waters off Cape Horn to Valparaíso in Chile, and from there continued on a nearly four month sea voyage to China via Tahiti. As the ship was about to pull out of Valparaíso Harbor, Ida took sick with a severe gastrointestinal disorder—cholera, in fact—but she couldn't stay behind, because *she would have forfeited the ticket she'd already paid for* (note: budget), and besides, the next ship wouldn't depart for months, and Ida hated delays. So instead she fasted for a few days and managed to cure the disease completely *by taking six quarter-hour saltwater baths aboard ship*, which I hereby offer sufferers from cholera as a tip for a cure.

Arriving in China was a dream come true for Ida, and she was proud to be one of the few Europeans able to get to know this "remarkable country." But as she made to push on from China to Singapore, she lost her temper when the steamship company refused to sell her a *third-class deck ticket*, which she wanted to buy to *save money*. According to representatives of the British company, steerage passengers were not "respectable," and besides, they said, the moonlight on deck would be extremely dangerous; nor was traveling in this manner fitting for a European married woman. And so Ida traveled in the more expensive second class, and in her book, in choleric paragraph after choleric paragraph, reported on the conditions and treatment on this *Pekin* ship piloted by Captain Fronson, which were, she railed, *substandard for the price.* "Never in my life have I been so defrauded!" she exclaimed.

From Singapore she continued on to Ceylon and India, where she traveled widely for many months. In Calcutta she was invited to a party for society circles, where to her dismay she only had a simple muslin dress to wear, while the other women were draped in silk, satin, lace, and jewels, but *fortunately they all pretended not to notice* (note: minimal luggage). Departing from Calcutta, Ida was given a taste of truly ascetic travel. She journeyed alone for weeks through territories that were off the maps, mostly in uncomfortable ox-drawn carts (*cheaper than traveling in a sedan chair or on camelback*), and spent the night in squalid clay huts along with the local travelers (she found them *surprisingly well swept*) and ate little (*most often just rice and water, at best rice boiled in milk with eggs*).

Her suffering was rewarded, however, when after a few weeks on the road she reached her destination, Kottah, and the local king, who had received word of her arrival, sent her a basket of fruit and candies, a beautifully decorated elephant to ride in on, and an honor guard consisting of an officer and two soldiers. Onward from Kottah she was forced to travel on camelback (*riding on camels is always unpleasant and troublesome*), and she spent one night in the tent camp of Captain Burdon, whose wife had not seen a European woman in four years. In remote villages where there was no accommodation for travelers, she would *spread her straw mat on a veranda and sleep outdoors*. In the village of Rumtscha she had to make her sleeping arrangements under a shelter in the middle of the bazaar, where half the village gathered to watch her. These villagers also "were able to witness what an angry European woman looks like," for she laid into the camel-drivers, who had allowed *the camels to trudge so lazily* that they had only covered around twenty miles that day, or roughly *the speed of ox-drawn carts*. In Indore, by contrast, where there was a European settlement, she was invited to watch a surgeon who had recently arrived from Europe perform his first operation (to excise a tumor from the patient's neck—but the ether anesthesia failed and the patient began "shrieking fearfully," at which point Ida left the operating theater). Another time she ended up participating in a tiger hunt on an elephant's back, and when the wounded tiger launched a furious attack at the elephants, she valiantly kept her face "so calm that none of the gentlemen had any suspicion of what was going on in my mind." And let us remember at this point that all of the above happened while Ida was gussied up in an ankle-length Biedermeier dress and a bonnet tied under her chin.

In continuing on from Bombay toward the Arabian Peninsula and Mesopotamia, Ida managed to buy *the cheapest possible deck ticket* on a ship. Having checked out her options for a while, our resourceful Viennese matron found herself an excellent place to sleep *under the captain's table*, and *wrapped herself in her coat to sleep*. Unfortunately, during the voyage she came down with a high fever, and by her account it was *painful to creep out of her asylum at mealtimes to make way for the feet of the people at the table*. Still worse, a few days later there was an outbreak of smallpox on board ship, and three passengers died.

When Ida reached Baghdad, she explored her environs, but refused the food reserves her hostess offered her: "My rule in traveling is to exclude every kind of superfluity. Wherever I am certain to find people living, I take no eatables with me, for I can content myself with whatever they live upon. If I do not relish their food, it is a sign that I have not any real hunger." Later, to be sure, she offered the advice that *the traveler should not watch food being prepared if she plans to eat it*.

From Baghdad Ida rode a mule with a caravan to Mosul, though she was warned that the 260-mile trip was far too dangerous for a woman traveling alone. Due to her limited resources, she could not even afford a servant, so she traveled *for two weeks through the dangers of the desert "like the poorest Arab,"* exposed to the blazing sun, *with no other sustenance than water, bread, a handful of dates, and a few cucumbers*. (Because I'm obsessive about food, I pounce on tidbits like this and save them for later study.) Ida reports that the caravan would travel ten hours through the night without stopping, and then rest through the heat of the day—but even then it was often impossible to find shade from the sun. She wrote that she envied missionaries and scientific men their horses, tents, servants, and abundant food provisions. All she had to take the edge off, by contrast, was "lukewarm water, bread so hard it had to be soaked in water before it could be eaten, and cucumber without salt or vinegar. *I did not, however, lose my courage or endurance, nor did I regret for an instant that I had exposed myself to these hardships.*" And she was amazingly buoyant: as soon as she reached Mosul, she wrote that she was "cheerful and energetic," although over the past fifteen days she had eaten only two warm meals, had worn the same clothes day and night, and had suffered horrible heat, constant riding, and all manner of other exhausting conditions.

In Mosul she joined a caravan into even more dangerous territory, through a notorious region of Kurdistan where there were no Europeans. She *mailed her papers and diaries home to Vienna* (note this, travel writers)—that way, if she was robbed and killed, at least her sons would be able to read her notes. From the village of Sauh-Bulak onward there were no more caravans, so she continued alone on horseback, even though she was warned that she would probably be shot—that is, if her throat wasn't slit. She had to pay a guide four times the usual fee, because there was no caravan to provide protection. "In the evening *I prepared my pistol and made up my mind not to sell my life cheaply,*" she wrote before they set off. In the end, the worst things she had to fight were a swarm of locusts and poor food. Once she was about to be robbed, but when the guide explained that she was just a *poor pilgrim*, and *her dress, minimal luggage, and lack of an entourage proved the same*, the bandits left her in peace and offered her drinking water instead. When Ida finally reached her destination, Tabriz, she admitted she was relieved "that the oppressive sense of fear was at the end." A European doctor living in the city, refusing to believe that a lone woman without language skills could have made it through a region like that unharmed, assumed that her "company" had been robbed and killed and she alone had survived to tell the tale.

Nope: this was Ida.

When Ida finally returned home to Vienna from her first round-the-world trip in November 1848, Europe was in the midst of a year of upheaval. There had been a revolution in Austria as well. Ida wanted to get to work immediately on her travel book, for she urgently needed the income from it; but catastrophically the package of diaries had not arrived! (This is every travel writer's worst fear: the painstakingly amassed material disappears.) Feeling desperate, Ida even put an ad in the paper. Finally, a year and a half later, the package suddenly appeared, after wandering about out in the world. She got down to work on it, and *Eine Frauenfahrt um die Welt* was released in 1850 in three volumes. This book finally made Ida a celebrity. Her sensationally popular books were translated and read all over the world. She herself assured readers that they were just "simple tales," and presented herself as "a modest ordinary woman who had happened to be possessed by an insatiable desire to travel," which in a sense was quite true.

She was now fifty-three, and plagued by malaria and some infection she'd picked up in Mesopotamia, but narrow-minded Vienna soon began to feel confining. And so in March 1851, she departed on her second round-the-world trip, this time in the other direction. The journey would last four years and take her, if possible, into even wilder regions. She spent more than a year and a half roaming widely around Borneo, Java, Sumatra, and the rest of the Indonesian archipelago, and in many areas was the first European the locals had ever seen. In Borneo she defied local warnings and traveled deep into the dangerous uncharted interior on the river, there getting to know the headhunting Dayaks. (Ida found them good-natured, honest, and modest, and got along with them wonderfully. She was fascinated by the dried skulls of their enemies that they showed her, and studied them carefully.) She slept *under the stars in the jungle*, sometimes *with a large stone as her mattress*, or *in a Dayak dugout canoe*, if one was available. She traversed great distances through the jungle either *on foot* or *paddling along a river*. She encountered wild animals; suffered from leeches, parasites, and malaria; ate food cooked by the indigenous people (*hunger is the best chef!*); and lived in their villages, where hygienically speaking there was much to be desired. Later she wrote that sometimes it was astonishing even to her that her courage and tolerance never flagged; instead, she *proceeded to the destination she had set her mind on step by step*. "That just proves that *a strong-willed person is capable of doing the almost impossible*," she noted.

I jot down Ida's practical tips in my notebook for future use:

1) *Avoid the African interior. Traveling there is frightfully expensive, for you'll need to obtain a wagon and six pairs of oxen, fit out the wagon for sleep, hire not just a driver but also a teamster and a servant, and buy food and water for the entire trip.* (Check.)

2) *The cost of living in Cape Town is shocking. If you can, bum lodging for the night from the Hamburg consul.*

3) *A recipe that works for malaria-related fever is to dissolve a teaspoon of cayenne pepper and five spoonfuls of sugar into half a glass of good brandy.*

4) *If you encounter hostile cannibals, start clowning.*

That fourth tip comes from Ida's wish to travel into the territory of the Batak tribe in Sumatra. She was warned off that plan, because the Batak were known as cannibals: in 1835 two missionaries had been killed and eaten by them. Ida dismissed the warnings, because she wanted to be the first European to see Lake Toba in the caldera of a supervolcano—although access to the lake was forbidden on pain of death. On the evening before her departure, Ida asked the locals whether it was true that the Batak did not kill their victims immediately, but tied them to a stake and cut off pieces of them while they were still alive. That prospect frightened her a little. But no: she was told that that was a special punishment for especially evil criminals. Everyone else had their throats slit immediately, the blood collected for drinking, or else used to make a tasty pudding to eat with rice. Then the body was cut into pieces—the palms, the soles of the feet, the head meat, the heart, and the liver were considered special delicacies—and the meat was roasted, sprinkled with salt, and eaten.

The journey to Lake Toba was rough. Ida traveled fifteen or twenty miles a day on foot; the dense thornbushes tore her flesh bloody and her bare feet were spiky with thorns (she couldn't wear shoes in the swampy terrain). It rained every afternoon and it was impossible to change her wet and muddy clothes; food was scarce and vague, she couldn't sleep at night for fear of the tigers patrolling nearby, and every morning she thought she couldn't go on. But she did anyway.

In the event that she met hostile locals, Ida had a plan: she believed she would survive if she could just *make them laugh*. When one day she was surrounded by eighty indigenous soldiers who mimed slitting her throat and eating her, she pulled her gun and began to explain to them, half in Malay, half in Batak, rounded out with gestures, that *they probably wouldn't want to kill and eat her, a woman, and an old one to boot, her flesh would be hard and tough!* And sure enough, this crazy woman's comical performance made the soldiers laugh, and they let her through. A couple days later, however, she had to give up just five or six miles from her destination. Hundreds of angrily gesticulating soldiers had gathered in a village to block her path, and now she estimated that her fate was hanging by a thread. Ida turned back—at a run, as her guide recommended. (And here let us not forget that she was wearing a long dress.)

In extremity, the night woman's advice is: *If you can't make 'em laugh, run.*

Having next toured Central America, Peru, Ecuador, and many places in the US, Ida, now fifty-seven, returned to Europe in the summer of 1855 from New York on a ship that had comped the famous world traveler's passage. The next year her massive work *Meine zweite Weltreise* appeared in four volumes, with the English translation *Second Journey Round the World* following soon after. (Four volumes! I can only envy publishers' casual attitude toward book length in those days, as I have spent months and even *years* trying to trim my massive quantities of material to fewer than five hundred pages, as the editor breathing down my neck demands.) The publication of this book was a significant event for another reason as well: for the first time, Ida's name was printed on the cover of the book she wrote. She had become one of the most beloved travel writers of the nineteenth century; her books were translated into English, French, Dutch, Russian, Malay, and other languages. Readers of the fashion magazine *Die Wiener Elegante* (*The Elegant Viennese*) demanded her photo on the cover, and the magazine did indeed print a drawing of Ida in imagined travel clothes, holding a butterfly net in one hand. Other periodicals published lampoons and satirical cartoons of her, for what could possibly be more comical than a woman traveling alone? In one cartoon published in *Wiener Telegraf* (*Viennese Telegraph*) in 1855, Ida is shown on an exploring trip among the Native Americans, holding a telescope in one hand, wearing a veiled hat, and carrying a coffeepot in a basket, as if she were picnicking. "Don't run away, I'm not afraid of savages!" Ida is shouting at a fleeing Native American in the caption. "But I am afraid!" the Native American is replying.

At fifty-nine Ida dreamed of a trip to Australia, and planned to stop over en route in Madagascar, that mysterious island in the Indian Ocean. She was suffering from many illnesses and was no longer young, of course, but set out on the journey nonetheless, making first a quick tour of European cities, raising funds for her trip among her fans. On Madagascar, however, she ran into trouble: the island was racked with political turmoil, and Ida, along with a few other European tourists, was jailed as a spy. They were kept imprisoned for almost two months in primitive bamboo huts, where soldiers closely watched every step they took. As Ida later reported, she was not able to wash or change her clothes for fifty-three days, and when she came down with a fever, she was not allowed to be treated by a doctor. When the prisoners were finally freed, Ida was still dreaming of a curative sea voyage to Australia, but she was so weakened by malaria that she couldn't make the trip. In the end she was brought back to Europe on board ship, and then to Vienna, where at the age of sixty-one, in October 1858, Ida died of complications from malaria—probably cancer of the liver. In her sickbed she worked industriously till the end, and her book on Madagascar was published posthumously.

Thirty years after her death, Ida Pfeiffer was given a memorial monument in the central Viennese cemetery, but then she was forgotten for a century. Her face was on the Austrian schilling in the 1990s, and in 2008 a street was named after her in Vienna, but even my German and Austrian friends have never heard of her—this transgressive author of international best sellers, this middle-aged woman awarded royal medals, for whom a sea snail and a Malagasy frog were named.

When I think of Ida at night, I see her portrait floating in my mind's eye—the one where she sits next to the terrestrial globe in her padded bonnet. *Here you see a respectable matron*, she seems to be saying in the photo. *Yes, and no matter how long you stare, that's all you'll see.*

But in fact, this world is mine. Dammit to hell, I've seen every corner of the globe, and you weren't able to stop me.

*

Night women's advice:

If you want to travel, go. You don't need a reason.

It doesn't matter if you're broke.

Bum everything: trips, lodging, meals.

Skimp. (Money. You can skimp on other things as well, if you like.)

Write books, collect rocks, sleep under a table, if need be—do whatever you must in order to be able to do what you want.

If you find yourself in a place where the food customs differ from your own—say, eating unusual animals, or other humans—don't panic. Eat whatever's offered.

Don't give a damn what other people think.

Be buoyant as hell.

MARY

NIGHT WOMEN'S ADVICE 4

If you're all alone and no one needs you,
you might as well go to West Africa to die,
and laugh all the way.

NIGHT WOMAN #4: *Mary Kingsley*
PROFESSION: *Spinster, later explorer and travel writer. First took care of her parents until they died, then set off for the jungles in West Africa, where she ended up paddling the rivers in her long black skirt and making friends with cannibal tribes and European traders. Wrote two super-popular books, in which she relentlessly pokes fun at herself.*

> *"There are only two things I am proud of: one is that Doctor Günther has approved of my fishes, and the other is that I can paddle an Ogowe canoe. Pace, style, steering and all . . . as if I were an African. . . . I often wonder what are the things other people are really most proud of."* —Mary, upon her return from her second trip to West Africa in 1897

How about Mary, then, wonderful, droll, self-ironic Mary, whom you can't help but love? In January 1894, when sixtysomething Isabella was setting off on her last trip to China, thirtysomething Mary was just returning from her first trip to West Africa. I imagine them passing each other on foot in the Liverpool port, the sun just rising on the one, setting on the other.

There was nothing in the childhood of British Mary Kingsley (1862–1900) that hinted at a future career as an explorer. Her childhood was just as grim and lonely as you can imagine. Her father was a doctor who'd gotten his servant pregnant, and decided at the last minute to marry her; four days after the wedding, Mary was born. For Mary this misalliance was truly a stroke of good fortune, but for her mother I'm not so sure. George Kingsley, you see, was not exactly an ideal husband. He spent Mary's entire childhood and adolescence traveling around the world—Asia, America, the South Seas, and so on—leaving his wife and children at home for months, even years, on a minimal subsistence allowance. Mary's mother, who as a former servant wasn't exactly suited for society circles, withdrew into her chamber with neurasthenia, depression, and other "women's troubles," and never recovered.

And so Mary spent her childhood inside the four walls of her house on the outskirts of London. She was not sent to school, nor did a tutor come to the house; she had no friends or other social life. Her father was out in the world somewhere, her mother lay spectrally in her bed upstairs, and her only company was her younger brother, Charles, their nanny, and the cook. Mary later painted her home life as the valley of the shadow of death, where her family lived as outsiders, isolated from the company of other people. Normally the daughter of an upper-middle-class family would have been taught to read, draw, and play the piano by her mother; but Mary's mother had none of those skills herself—in fact, she could just barely read. And so from a very young age Mary took over the housekeeping and sitting by her mother's sickbed. It seemed that the rest of her life would be devoted to caring for her mother and serving her family.

But Mary was plagued by a trait most unsuitable for a woman: curiosity. It's not known how she learned to read—maybe her little brother taught her, since he was sent to school—but she spent her free time in her father's library. There were well-known authors in her father's family, and the capacious library had books from all disciplines; by devouring them Mary managed over the years to teach herself Latin, physics, chemistry, mathematics, technology, biology, and the social sciences—all subjects in which no Victorian girl would have received instruction. And if her two role models were a weak, dependent, bedridden mother and a learned, world-traveling, explorer father, it isn't difficult to guess which she identified with. Mary admired her absent father and his exciting life above all else, and greedily consumed both the letters her father sent from exotic parts of the world and the explorers' books she found in his library. And perhaps she found on one of her father's shelves Isabella Bird's books—for though Mary didn't know it, once while traveling in the Rockies her father had met Isabella's one-eyed boyfriend, Rocky Mountain Jim.

Jim was bleeding out from gunshot wounds, and Mary's father had saved him from death's door.

But Mary was tied to her mother's sickbed. In her twenties she cared for her mother around the clock: her mother refused to eat food cooked by anyone else, and only Mary was allowed to push her around a nearby park in her wheelchair. In her spare moments Mary studied math, read Darwin, and served as her father's secretary, whenever he was briefly home; for he brought back diaries and notes from his trips that he planned to rework into scholarly articles. Mary had no suitors or romances, nor any other kind of social life. When in 1885 the twenty-three-year-old Mary accompanied a friend's family on a short trip to Wales, she was away from home for the first time in her life—but after only two days, she received a telegram saying that her mother's condition had taken a sharp turn for the worse, and she had to rush home. In the spring of 1888 she went to Paris for a week with another friend, on the first vacation of her life, but when she returned her mother's condition was even worse, and the longest she could be out of the house was an hour or two. In 1890, her mother had a stroke, which made her almost entirely incapable of speech or movement; now Mary fed and bathed her mother and did everything for her. Then in February 1892, her father unexpectedly died, and in April her mother followed. Mary was twenty-nine. She was devastated with grief—and free.

After her parents' funerals, Mary decided to go somewhere to recover. A family friend suggested Madeira, but to Mary that sounded far too civilized. The most obvious destinations, like the spas in the south of France or Italy, she didn't even consider. As she gradually began to grasp the opportunities afforded her by her sudden freedom, she decided to travel to the Canary Islands, in those days a truly adventurous destination. Her sea voyage from Liverpool to Tenerife in the summer of 1892 lasted seven days. She spent many weeks in the Canaries, exploring different islands and among other things climbing to a volcano's crater (and spending the night en route, because she had miscalculated the duration of the hike). For her, however, the most significant benefit of the trip was that all the ships from Europe to Africa stopped off in the Canaries. She got to know traders, missionaries, and officials from the West African coast, as well as those suffering from malaria, yellow fever, or blackwater fever who'd been sent from Africa to the Canaries to recover or to die.

By the time Mary got back to England, she had decided to travel to West Africa.

To Westerners, Africa in the nineteenth century was a land of passionate dreams. Its uncharted territories and natural resources were of great interest to many. The second half of the century was the Golden Age of African exploration—the time when answers were sought to many of the continent's geographical mysteries, such as the location of the source of the Nile. Explorers penetrated from the coasts up the rivers deep into the heart of Africa, where travel was life-threatening: the members of expeditions were plagued by malaria, various parasites, and tropical diseases, each more horrific than the last; the sick were carried through the jungle in field beds, and many died. In 1858, Richard Burton and John Speke located Lake Tanganyika, and Speke found Lake Victoria. In 1864, Samuel Baker and his future wife found Lake Albert. When the missionary, physician, and explorer David Livingstone disappeared while searching for the source of the Nile and the Congo River, the *New York Herald* hired the young journalist Henry Morton Stanley to go in search of him. And so nine-year-old Mary may have read in the paper how Stanley found Livingstone on the shore of Lake Tanganyika in 1871 ("Dr. Livingstone, I presume?"), and then how Livingstone died two years later in a remote Central African village, and how the doctor's two faithful African servants first buried his heart in the ground and then carried his embalmed body to the coast—an eight-month trip on foot—where it was loaded onto a ship and sent to England to be buried in London's Westminster Abbey.

European imperialist dreams peaked in 1885, when Africa was divided up among the European powers at a conference held in Berlin. Not a single African was invited to this absurd conference, where diplomats who had never set foot in Africa sliced the continent up into pieces to suit their own purposes. The economic prospects of West Africa were overwhelmingly tempting, and in addition to explorers, colonial officials, and missionaries, traders began to flood into the region, buying ivory, palm oil, rubber, and cacao, trading alcohol, fishhooks, and glass beads for them. The steamship companies' posters proclaimed "Liverpool to West Africa—Lagos Express—every other week," with a drawing of an African "native" and a European wearing a Roman conqueror–style helmet shaking hands. Around them were depicted elephants, lions, and wooden crates filled with the most desirable commercial goods.

And that's where Mary wanted to go as well.

But Mary's family responsibilities did not end after all when her parents died. As the unmarried sister, she was now required to serve as washerwoman, cook, and housekeeper to her persnickety and demanding little brother, Charles. Fortunately, her brother liked to travel as well, so whenever Charles left on a voyage, Mary rushed to buy passage for herself. Then she had to wait a full year for Charles's next trip; during that wait, they moved to London, where Mary took a nursing course that taught her how to treat snakebites and tropical diseases with first aid.

Mary had decided to travel to the West African coast alone. This was unheard of. In those days if a woman traveled to Africa at all, it was as the wife of a colonial official or missionary. She herself offered several different explanations for her trip: she was following up on her father's anthropological research and finishing the book he had been planning, as if she were driven by pure daughterly duty. Other times she said she found herself for the first time in her life with a few months free, and she wanted to spend it "learning tropics." To a friend she wrote yet a third version of her motives, with that characteristic night-woman style she had:

"Dead tired and feeling no one had need of me anymore when my mother and father died within six weeks of each other in '92 and my brother went off to the East, I went down to West Africa to die. West Africa amused me and was kind to me and scientifically interesting and did not want to kill me just then—I am in no hurry."

Maybe she did truly want to die, or just didn't care whether she lived or died. Maybe her thought was *all or nothing*—that she had nothing to lose.

Me, I would have been terrified. In those days West Africa was called "the white man's grave." Traveling there was like Russian roulette. "Deadliest spot on earth," the doctors joked to Mary, showing her a map of the areas of distribution for tropical diseases. Mary filled a notebook with lists of African dangers, diseases, potential horror scenarios, and things she absolutely had to bring along with her—exactly as I did my own notebook 121 years later. Mary later noted that 85 percent of those who set out for West Africa either died there or returned with their health permanently ruined. Many died of fever, yellow fever, or malaria within a month of their arrival on the coast; others soldiered on longer with their fevers, but then one fine day up and died. A man's—or woman's—fate depended on his or her resistance to malaria, and as Mary noted, there was no getting acclimatized to the Coast.

Even so, in August of 1893 Mary set off on her voyage. (A realist, she made her last will and testament before leaving.) She boarded the cargo ship *Lagos* in Liverpool, which ominously sold only one-way tickets. With her she took photographic equipment, including the heavy tripod and negative plates, formaldehyde bottles for the preservation of fish and insects, and other equipment for the collection of scientific specimens. In addition, she had a black portmanteau and a watertight sealable sack full of clothes, blankets, and other necessities. She also took along two blank diaries (a bush diary for the collection of scientific data and a personal diary) and two books (Albert Günther's *Introduction to the Study of Fishes* and a collection of Horace's poems), as well as a long bowie knife and a revolver—the two last so that in an emergency she could use them on herself. For food she had packed a few tins of smoked herring and crackers, as well as a sufficient store of proper English tea. It later turned out that she had not brought enough hairpins or toothbrushes, which turned out to be popular items for barter. Her travel clothes were precisely the same as those she would have worn in England, for to her mind she had no right to go about Africa in clothing that she would be ashamed to be seen wearing in London. And because after her parents died Mary dressed like a widow for the rest of her life, she packed several long black skirts, a cummerbund, a dozen white blouses, black leather boots, and, of course, corsets—which she had no reason to stop using in the tropics. Some wicked tongues have claimed that Mary took along her brother's old trousers, which she wore under her skirt—if, say, she had to wade across a river, to avoid leeches she tied her trouser legs tight around her ankles and wound her skirt around her waist—but Mary herself flatly denied rumors of this sort.

She only took £300 in cash; she planned to finance her trip by bartering objects. She also planned to live on local food, proceed on foot or by canoe, and spend nights in the mud or thatch huts in the tribal villages, or else out of doors—vastly different from other travelers to Africa in those days, who wouldn't dare enter the jungle without a sedan chair and a long line of porters carrying canned food, tents, tent cots, rubber bathtubs, and portable toilets. Never mind that Mary couldn't afford all that; she also believed that by trading glass beads, wire, fabric, rum, and gin for rubber and ivory, she would strike up conversations with the locals and gather interesting information. For she also had a scientific objective for her trip: she planned to collect fish samples (the director of the Natural History Museum had hinted that such would be useful) and study the locals' beliefs.

When the *Lagos* arrived in the Canaries, its two other female passengers disembarked, leaving Mary aboard as the only woman among the traders and colonial officials. The men were "most kind," but according to Mary all conversations tended to dead-end depressingly in the mention of poor so-and-so who took sick and died. Mary learned that a traveler to Africa had good reason to pack a better outfit—to wear not at dinner parties but at her own funeral. The men also enlightened Mary about the other diseases on offer besides fever and malaria, including the Portuguese itch, abscesses, suppurating ulcers, parasitic diseases, sleeping sickness, yellow fever, cholera, smallpox, and the ominous-sounding craw-craw. Mary summed up the sea voyage cheerfully: "I do not believe I have ever enjoyed myself so much in my life." All expectations to the contrary, she made friends with the traders. Many of these so-called palm-oil ruffians were former slave traders. They weren't particularly cultured, or even necessarily literate, but they were direct and honest—unlike the missionaries and officials, if you asked Mary. They became Mary's most important support network.

The *Lagos* arrived on the West African coast smack in the worst part of the rainy season. It dropped anchor before Sierra Leone in a dense fog, then continued on past the Ivory Coast, the Gold Coast, and the Slave Coast, as those regions were called back then. In early September the *Lagos* finally reached its southernmost port, Saint Paul de Loanda, where Mary set off on a four-month trek north toward Calabar, where she finally boarded a ship home.

Mary discovered that the talk aboard ship had been no empty blather. A yellow fever epidemic was raging in Bonny; in just over a week it had killed nine of the eleven whites living in town. Kakongo was being decimated by smallpox and sleeping sickness. Whole villages had been laid low. Lepers were everywhere. Along the lower reaches of the Congo there had been severe cases of "malignant melancholy" and suicides. As the locals understood things, all of these diseases were caused by witchcraft and evil spirits, which the Europeans found ludicrous, because of course (they thought) the problem was the air. For example, malaria was named for this belief that you caught it from "bad air" (*mal' aria*). But Mary seemed to be Teflon: apart from a minor case of malaria, she never contracted any kind of disease.

The French Congo, nowadays Gabon, became the core region for Mary's journeys, and even on this first trip she spent weeks there, traveling alone into the interior, first in a sedan chair, then by canoe and on foot, with only a few porters, a guide-interpreter, and a cook, without a care for the general attitude that this kind of venture was sheer madness for a lone white woman. Both the whites and the blacks were suspicious of Mary wherever she went; but after initial perplexity she was often offered the village's best reed hut, food, and palm wine. Many Africans had never seen a white person, let alone a lone white woman, and as if refusing to believe their eyes, they doggedly called her "sir." In these regions unmarried women were simply not found: in the nineteenth century you could count the foreign women traveling alone in West Africa on one hand, and single African women were even rarer, for in polygamous cultures a woman always belonged to someone. Even a widow was always inherited by the deceased man's brother. So when Mary arrived in the tribal villages without a male companion, it was impossible for the villagers to understand that she truly did not have a husband. Later, back in England, she would give women traveling alone a useful tip: "I may confide to any spinster . . . who feels inclined to take up a study of [the African] that she will be perpetually embarrassed by inquiries of where is your husband? Not, have you *got* one . . . but *where* is he? I must warn her not to say she has not got one; I have tried it and it only leads to more appalling questions still. I think that it is more advisable to say you are searching for him, and then you locate him away in the direction in which you wish to travel; this elicits help and sympathy."

I make a note of this night woman's advice: *While traveling in Africa, always be looking for your husband.*

When Mary's ship docked in gray, drizzly Liverpool one January evening in 1894, it seemed to her as if she had been exiled. Her old life seemed intolerably dull. "If you are susceptible to its spell," she wrote in the manuscript she began to prepare from her notes, "West Africa takes all the color out of other kinds of living."

Africa had changed her radically. Before she left she'd been a shy, inexperienced, awkward spinster leading a sheltered life and with nothing to look forward to. To be sure, she still suffered from chronic modesty and remained firmly convinced of her own insignificance; but at the same time she had become an independent, fearless woman who made her own decisions. Her goal was to return to Africa as soon as possible to study the fish and the Africans' belief system—"fish and fetish," as she put it. To that end, she began to familiarize herself more deeply with anthropology, that discipline born out of Darwin's theories, and to study ichthyology under the tutelage of Albert Günther, director of the Zoology Department at the British Museum. When Mary showed Günther the samples she'd collected on her trip, he was impressed, but slightly disgruntled at the amateurish way she'd prepared them. And so he procured proper collector's equipment for her, and hired her to find freshwater fish in the region between the Niger and Congo rivers. She also inquired of Macmillan, her father's and writer uncle's publisher, whether they would be interested in her travel diary, and they promised to publish anything she wrote. All this meant that she would set off on her second trip as a professional researcher and writer with the next best thing to a publishing contract in her pocket. While the trip was thus financially secured, however, she didn't plan to travel in greater luxury—just longer.

Twelve months after her return, Mary was at last ready to set off again, and boarded a ship called the *Batanga* in Liverpool the night before Christmas Eve 1894. She was thirty-two. This time in addition to her luggage she had all manner of things that people had asked her to take to their relatives and friends living on the African coast—among them, a tombstone and several pairs of embroidered slippers. She would return to Africa in the middle of the dry season this time, so the sky would be bright blue and cloudless.

Mary had promised to travel with a certain Lady MacDonald, who was moving to West Africa to live there with her husband, and when the ship stopped in Cape Coast and Accra, Mary found herself obliged, very reluctantly, to take part in various unpleasantly upper-class, colonial society events, including horse races and tea parties. In Accra the women were guests of the governor in the vast Christiansborg Castle, and the governor told them that they always kept two graves ready dug for Europeans, for otherwise they could not arrange the funerals fast enough. Lady MacDonald's destination was Calabar, where they arrived in the midst of a typhoid epidemic—and were immediately recruited as nurses. Mary admitted that it required all of her physical and mental stamina to care for those men, and to bind their jaws when they died. (I admit that I wouldn't have the stamina even to start.)

Once the epidemic had eased off, Mary wandered about the rivers around Calabar collecting fish and insect samples. In the jungle she met Mary Slessor, a Scottish missionary who'd lived on the coast for two decades, mostly on her own in the tiny tribal villages north of Calabar. Mary S. was forty-five, a warm, straight-talking woman who with her short-cropped hair and simple cotton shifts (no corsets or hairpins!) seemed to have gone native. She lived in a primitive clay hut, ate only local food (but brought her own tea from England), and sometimes didn't see other whites for months, even years. When periodically she was forced to take a furlough in Scotland, just walking about in the city traumatized her. Mary K. normally didn't like missionaries, since to her mind they were destroying African culture even worse than the colonial government, but Mary S. was an exception. The women became close friends, and these two tea-and-Africa enthusiasts would sit up nights by their steaming mugs of tea in that clay hut, chatting.

When Mary finally arrived in Glass harbor in the French Congo, in May 1895, in the heart of Africa near the equator, she felt she had come home. Here she began to do her job as an explorer. But "Sir Mary" was a strange bird, not only as a single woman but as an explorer as well. At the core of male explorerdom was a certain ethos of, shall we say, *macho penetration*: imperialist conquest and dominion over nature. Mary's motives were entirely different. She wanted to *see* and *understand*. She was interested in the tribal cultures in their own right. She wanted to live like the locals. She began to think of herself as semi-African.

So now Mary hired a guide and two porters and set off up the Ogooué River toward the interior in a canoe. For the next couple of months she hiked or paddled tirelessly in the jungle in her long black skirt, corset, and white blouse; lived with the native tribes in primitive conditions or under the stars—sometimes, when she had no choice, in missionary stations—eating whatever was offered (cassava, coconut, okra, fish wrapped in leaves and fried, snails, rhinoceros beetle elytra, casseroles spiced with bark, plus of course English tea); fought with spiders, snakes, crocodiles, diseases, and the blazing heat; conversed with gestures (she spoke no French either, the language of the local officials), bartered things, and bought cult objects; caught and prepared fish and insects; and every evening wrote down everything she had experienced during the day. "It's only me!" was her cheerful cry whenever she appeared at a remote station in the jungle, so that in addition to "sir" the Africans began to call her "Only-me." Sometimes she was sternly advised to turn back immediately, or else to take her quinine tablets and continue straight to the Methodist missionaries, who were "the only people on the coast who could arrange a proper burial." Mary didn't care. From the traders who drifted through the outskirts of civilization she had learned not only a taxing travel style but a foulmouthed one: she swore like a lumberjack, and referred to herself as a practical seaman.

Mary learned to paddle her own canoe—so well that she later bragged that she paddled like a local. Once a French official stopped her expedition and forbade them to go any farther; he didn't want to be responsible for Mary risking her life on the rapids that lay ahead, and chastised her for setting out on a dangerous journey without her husband's protection. Mary replied dryly that she didn't remember seeing "husband" listed on her inventory of travel equipment from the Royal Geographical Society—and continued on her way toward the rapids with her canoe and Igalwa crew.

From Ogooué to the Remboué River she trekked through rain forest, swamps, and granite hills. Once when emerging from a swamp, she was so covered with leeches that she nearly fainted from loss of blood. Another time, or actually several times, she fell into a pit dug in the path as a trap. "It is at these times you realise the blessing of a good thick skirt," she wrote, penning one of her most famous bons mots.

Once Mary's canoe ran aground in the mud in the midst of crocodiles, and she had to shoo them off with her umbrella: "What little time you have over you will employ in wondering why you came to West Africa, and why, after having reached this point of folly, you need have gone and painted the lily and adorned the rose, by being such a colossal ass as to come fooling about in mangrove swamps."

Whenever Mary was frustrated or out of sorts, she would fish. Fishing was comforting. She could sit in her canoe for hours, drifting freely, holding her fishing rod. While spending the night in missionary stations, she would go for walks in the jungle, clearing her path with a machete, and encountering cobras, boas, or other blue-green or horny-headed slitherers. "I never came back to the station without having been frightened out of my wits, and with one or two of my small terrifiers in cleft sticks to bottle."

Once she mailed Dr. Günther a lily she'd picked on an embankment in Ogooué. (It can still be found today in London's Natural History Museum.)

Evenings Mary would read her damp, dilapidated Horace in order to lull herself to sleep. Sometimes the mosquitoes and fleas would keep sleep at bay. One sleepless night she left her hut and paddled alone to a tiny island, stripped off her clothes, and swam in the river under the starry sky. ("Drying one's self on one's cummerbund is not pure joy, but can be done when you put your mind to it.")

On the rivers she met naked savages in their canoes and spent nights in their villages. Sometimes she would hold a clinic, tending to the villagers' wounds, infections, and parasites: she grew skilled at recognizing tropical diseases, and had also learned the local remedies. She knew, for example, that the roundworm burrowed right into the white of the eye, and that a live guinea worm living in the leg, which could grow to three feet long, should be removed by pulling it out over several days, a small amount at a time, and wrapping the end around a stick of bamboo. (Mary warned travelers against taking a person suffering from guinea-worm disease along on a canoeing trip, because the operation of pulling the worm out a little each morning would seriously delay the trip.)

With her Mary carried a trunkful of goods for barter—as good as money—and traded handkerchiefs, fishhooks, and tobacco for rubber, ivory, food, a night's rest, transport, or unknown fish species. With one tribal chief's wife she traded a red silk ribbon for elephant-hair necklaces. When she began to run out of goods to barter, she began to offer her own things in trade, such as stockings and toothbrushes. "A dozen white ladies' blouses sold well. I cannot say they looked well when worn . . . in conjunction with nothing else but red paint and a bunch of leopard tails." Sometimes when meeting new tribes she lied that she worked for the trading company Hatton & Cookson, because "it's the proper thing to belong to somebody."

It turned out that some of Mary's porters were fugitives from justice due to debts, entanglements with women, wrongs committed by their ancestors, or even murders, and in many villages Mary had to serve as a porter's lawyer. "I used to have to stand hour after hour, dead tired with the day's march, wet through with its swamps and rivers, surrounded by sand flies and mosquitoes, pleading and arguing for their lives." Even so, Mary found her porters enjoyable company. Her favorite guide was Obanjo, of whom she said she knew "that if [he] and I went to the utter bush together, one of us at least would come out alive. . . ."

At one point Mary decided to head into the territory of the Fang tribe, who were known as cannibals. Because they were avoided by both the missionaries and the traders, on the map there was only a blank spot where they lived. As her caravan of canoes set off, Mary wrote, "my hair begins to rise as I remember what I have been told about those Fangs. . . . Why did I not obey Mr. Hudson's orders not to go wandering about in a reckless way!" Her reception in the Fang village was tense: the tribe's men stood silently with knives in their hands, and the children fled in terror at the sight of this white woman dressed all in black. Then the situation deescalated when it turned out one of Mary's men knew one of the Fang. Mary reports that the village was unbelievably filthy. Everywhere were strewn reeking remains of a crocodile that had been consumed two weeks before, fish guts, and stinking hippo parts. Still, she was given the best hut in the village, and one woman gave her a welcome gift of a crushed snail. Mary spent a sleepless night fighting the mosquitoes and lice; when she sought relief by walking to the river, she almost ended up a hippo's midnight snack.

A mutually respectful friendship grew up between Mary and the Fang, and she also hired them as guides. Sometimes she had a hard time keeping up with her guides, so arduous it was to hike through the jungle; but fortunately the Fang stopped every two hours to eat a little meat and smoke a pipe of tobacco, so she was able to catch up. "We had a snake for supper," she wrote in her diary, "that is to say the Fang and I. The others would not touch it, although a good snake, properly cooked, is one of the best meats one gets out here." The alleged cannibalism of the Fang did not seem to Mary to be a threat to a white traveler, but it was a bother sometimes, she said, "preventing one's black companions from getting eaten."

Once while spending the night in the Fang village, Mary couldn't sleep for the intolerable stench. Upon investigating, she found bags hanging from the ceiling containing a human hand, three big toes, four eyes, two ears, and other human body parts. Mary studied the remains calmly, carefully hung them back up where she'd found them, opened the bark door, and stepped out into the fresh air.

Sometimes Mary wrote that she dared not be afraid. She urged anyone traveling in West Africa to assume the most joyful and cheerful attitude no matter what they encountered, as in her experience this was the only way to keep the fear lurking in the back of her head in check.

I jot down this night woman's advice: *While traveling in Africa, laugh all the time.*

*

[LETTER IN A BOTTLE IN THE OGOOUÉ RIVER]

Dear Mary,

When I think of you at night, I think especially of all those basic things in life that you as a single woman had to deal with in the jungle: washing, eating, sleeping, the humid heat, headache, dizziness, fear.

I wonder how I would feel if I was suffering an infernal malaria migraine and all there was to eat and drink were beetle elytra and boiled river water. Or if I happened to wander into the village of the reputedly bloodthirsty Fang while I was on my period? (What did you use for pads, anyway? Tree leaves? Or did you wash your cloth rags at night in some river churning with hippos?) And would my corset start to pinch if the hut I was sleeping in reeked of rotting human hands and eyeballs? Would I start to panic if I was holding the last tin of smoked herring in my hand? Or if I ran out of tea, my beloved Japanese genmaicha, without which I never go anywhere, because its familiar scent gives me a safe, homey feeling and wraps me in a calming bubble in unfamiliar places?

Could I really sustain that unquenchable attitude of joy and good cheer the way you did? Could I remember to maintain a light, self-ironic touch and a sense of humor black as pitch? Could I keep penning droll quips diary page after diary page? Would I be able to view everything I did as if from the outside, and make of it sheer slapstick?

I wish I could!

Your M

*

To cap off her journey, Mary climbed to the top of volcanic Mount Cameroon, though she also joked that she was likely to find "next to no fish there . . . and precious little good rank fetish." Mary had no mountain-climbing experience, or even a map; the weather was bone-crushingly cold and rainy; the climb took seven arduous days, and they had problems getting their food and drinking water carried up; and—horror of horrors—she couldn't even boil water for tea! Mary considered whether she could in good conscience risk her porters' health in conditions like these. "And for myself—well—that's my own affair and no one will be a ha'porth the worse if I am dead in an hour." When at last, exhausted, she reached the 13,000-foot peak, visibility was less than thirty feet: the weather robbed Mary of the view! And that had been the sole reason she'd climbed the damn mountain in the first place. As a modest person she didn't even think it worth mentioning that she was the first (white) woman ever to scale Mount Cameroon.

When she reached the bottom again, Mary sat on the veranda of her lodging in the dim light of the stars, surrounded by fireflies. The lights of the city of Victoria glowed off in the distance. She could hear the waves pounding the rocky shore, the drumming and singing of the natives, all the sounds blending and harmonizing. "Why did I come to Africa?" she asked herself one more time. "Why! Who would not come to its twin brother hell itself for all the beauty and the charm of it!" Precisely, Mary.

In mid-November Mary shipped back home to England from Calabar. She had sent ahead boxes of the fish, lizard, and insect samples she had gathered, but she still had plenty to haul: dozens of bottles filled with alcohol in which floated who knows what exotic critters, piles of fetish objects, figures carved out of wood, musical instruments, masks, fabrics, amulets, baskets for collecting wandering souls, a giant lizard for the London Zoo, and a small pet monkey. (I imagine Mary puttering about with her luggage: *Okay, the swamp rats are in the ethanol jar, the millipedes are in the ziplock bag, I sent the African moles ahead by mail. . . .* Before that she had caught and killed and prepared the creatures, all by herself.) On board ship she heard that the English papers had already been printing stories about her trip, and that several publishers were offering her a book deal. That sounded good to Mary: she wanted to write a best seller to make enough money so she could return to Africa as soon as possible.

Mary arrived in Liverpool Harbor on the evening of the last day of November 1895, after being away for nearly a year. When she disembarked with the monkey on her shoulder, on the dock in the light of the gas lamps she found a reporter waiting for her with a notebook in hand. Her return was written up in the *Times* and the *Daily Telegraph*, but Mary was horrified at the scandalmongering tone of the pieces: they wallowed in the cannibal stories, exaggerated her courage when meeting a gorilla, and, worst of all, called her a *new woman*. According to them, she represented the latest women's liberation craze, in which women sought to mimic male explorers' derring-do and so to experience *manly things*. This went too far, Mary huffed, and before she had even unpacked her luggage she began drafting a riposte to the paper. "I do not relish being called a New Woman," she wrote. "I am not one in any sense of the term."

Argh, Mary, what the hell! Same as with Isabella: don't you realize how irritating this sort of attitude is? But of course, if I think about it, I guess I do have to understand why you reacted like that. Back then the women's movement and "the new woman" had an unsavory reputation, and not many women were willing to identify with those shrieking androgynous freaks who agitated for women's rights while foaming at the mouth and rolling their eyes about in their heads. An unmarried, childless woman was already weird enough; if you wanted to be a credible explorer, it was best to maintain a low profile, dress as respectably as possible, and emphasize in public that your primary activities were preparing meals, darning socks, and caring for sick relatives. And when I study a photograph taken of Mary around then—one of the two I can find of her—I think, *Mission accomplished*: she truly does not look like a new woman. In fact, she looks like the very last person you would ever suspect of paddling a canoe through the West African jungle. While Henry Morton Stanley posed for an official explorer portrait in a pith helmet and khaki pants next to stuffed lions, Mary looks like any ordinary Victorian spinster. She's wearing a black pouf-sleeved corset dress with a bow on her high collar. On her hat-like headgear there are artificial flowers; out of the middle of it protrude long decorations like the antennae of some giant bug. Gloves in one hand, an umbrella in the other; a park scene in the background; a light, harmless smile on her lips.

Back home, Mary fell quickly into her old routines as her brother's housekeeper, and soon it began to seem as if the whole trip had been just a wonderful hallucination. She did try to keep the feeling alive, by heating her rooms to tropical temperatures, filling her shelves with tribal masks and amulets, spreading out maps of Africa on the floor, and starting work on her book—but somehow there was a pall over all of it. Just like Isabella and Karen, and *just like me too after my trip to Africa*—or, well, after any trip—Mary always collapsed upon her return home. In the jungle she had hardly ever used her medical supplies on herself, and had not even let her malaria slow her down; but as soon as she set foot back on English soil she began to suffer from all manner of ailments: influenza, migraine, heart palpitations, rheumatism, loneliness, depression. It was as if she had traveled in Africa with her father's genes, but back home she had morphed into her mother, wasting away in bed.

And at the same time she began to live a crazy double life. She had become a celebrity, and all manner of politicians, public intellectuals, and society ladies bombarded her with invitations to dinner parties and tea. Mary didn't really want to go anywhere—she saw herself as shy and awkward and in social life an "utter failure"—but she understood enough about marketing to know that if she wanted to earn travel money with her next book, she had to keep the public's interest from flagging until it was published. So she leveraged herself out of her hot Africa apartment and propelled herself out into society, accepted those invitations, gave interviews, and hit the lecture circuit. And to her surprise, Mary enjoyed lecturing! She was a brilliant speaker, a kind of ecstatic mix of comedienne, university professor, and preacher, and her lecture tours around Great Britain were huge hits. She calculated that every pound she earned meant five miles in

West Africa, and so kept up a frenetic pace. By year's end she had to hire an agent to handle the lecture invitations and honoraria, and because in between engagements she also had to work on her book, she found herself in a vicious cycle: stress-related anxiety, headaches, insomnia, despair over what to wear and not having enough hairpins.

All year she did work on her book—and, yes, Mary, it all sounds familiar. She had tons of material (*check*), and over and over she despaired of producing a book that would interest both the large public and the experts; but it seemed impossible to fuse her personal travel diary with research data (*check*). Mary suffered from endless insecurity (*check*), because she had no training as an ethnologist—or *any* training, in anything—and she was afraid the experts would catch her out on details, and that would undermine the whole book's validity. Maybe she should publish the book anonymously, using only her initials M. K.? (*Check.*) A couple of years before, the Kilimanjaro exploration undertaken by the American May French Sheldon had been dismissed in the papers because it produced no scientific findings: Sheldon's motive for the trip was just her "feminine curiosity." (*Check.*) Publishing the book under just her initials would solve many problems: her observations could not be dismissed on the basis of her gender, nor could she be accused of unwomanly activities. And how on earth was she to shape her chaotic bush diaries into a systematic and entertaining narrative, given the hodgepodge she found in them of the price of a kilo of onions, the sizes and quantities of the fish she'd caught, recipes, legal cases, genealogies, and local swearwords? (*Check!*) She was by turns afraid that the book would be too humorous and too heavy, and in any case an utterly unreadable "vast word swamp." Tellingly, her own suggested title for the book was *Log of a Light-hearted Lunatic.* (Since Mary ended up not using it, I could borrow it as a title for my own book.) In the end Mary found herself embroiled in an absurd brouhaha with the publisher, because the editor "cleaned up" her style and edited the text so radically that Mary could no longer consider it her own, and so entered into a tense correspondence with them about restoring the text to its original state: "I have got a good character to lose as a practical sea man and an honest observer of facts." As the book project approached its conclusion, Mary grew more depressed than before, and suffered from frequent migraines, insomnia, and exhaustion (*check*). In her preface she spent a whole page begging the reader's forgiveness for the book's weakness and her own incompetence—in so doing raising the art of self-deprecation to new heights.

But her doubts were wasted; her labor paid off. When the book was published in January 1897, with the clearheaded title *Travels in West Africa*, it became an instant best seller and over the long haul a classic in the field. Still today the book is at once laugh-out-loud funny and jam-packed with facts, and its many clever ripostes are so enjoyable that I'd love to give you a page or two of them to enjoy. True, one reviewer complained that "it is a pity that Miss Kingsley has not tried to write in a more ladylike manner," but dozens of enthusiastic reviews proved that her manner worked. And if anyone wonders why there isn't a map in the book to show the route Mary took, let it be known that in those days there *didn't exist* a detailed enough map of the region through which she traveled—and she didn't have time to prepare one herself.

Night women's advice, dear Mary: *Don't underestimate yourself.*

More even than popularity with readers, Mary longed for academic approval—so it was excellent news to her that the vast majority of the sixty-five fish species and eighteen reptiles she'd collected were accepted by the experts. Among them were a few invaluable finds, such as a lizard that the British Museum had lusted after for ten years. Three new species of fish were named for Mary: *Ctenopoma kingsleyae, Pollimyrus kingsleyae*, and *Alestes kingsleyae*.

I admit that I'm bugging out a bit over this fish thing. Just for kicks, I google the fish names, and—incredibly, I know—I find photographs of some of the fish samples that Mary brought back to Albert Günther . . . which is to say, *the actual fish* she caught with her own hands (I think). All in a lather, I load those truly insignificant-looking tiddler pix on my computer and come back to them day after day, to study them closely, as if through them I could project myself into a specific moment on some West African river in 1895. (Hasn't anyone ever noticed the time-window these fish open up?) In the photos, the blankly staring little fish the color of translucent parchment have been laid out on millimeter graph paper, and on this one that I'm looking at right now there is a piece of paper attached with the typed caption "Pollimyrus kingsleyae (Günther, 1896) Holotypus BMNH 1896.5.5:100." To the fish's tail has been attached an obviously older piece of paper, already yellowed, with handwriting on it—maybe (maybe!) in Mary's own hand. I devote the afternoon to zooming back and forth on this tiddler, and think, first of all, that I'm losing my mind (does it really all come down to this one dead fish?), and, second, feeling a little moved, that on one blazingly hot afternoon on the equator, Mary truly caught this individual fish that was born in some bend of the Ogooué River. This very fish she prepared for preservation with equipment that she had in her canoe; this very fish she carried with her through the jungle and finally on a steamship across the Atlantic to distant Liverpool, whence it has wended its way through the following 120 years to my computer screen in a studio apartment in Helsinki. Maybe she talked to it while it was still on the hook (*okay, got you, little guy*), maybe hummed a little while removing the hook from its mouth, or, how do I know, maybe you can't catch a fish this little on a hook, maybe Mary scooped up whole schools of little fish in some bowl carved out of wood. (In any case, I imagine her being cheerful throughout.) Maybe she took one tiddler as a pet—someone to talk to—and gave it a name, Polly, or Myrtle, and took it along with her in a water container at the bottom of the canoe. . . . I think of how just a few days ago I got an e-mail from Olli in Africa with photos of the small emperor moth that he managed to snap on one of his nighttime mothing trips—*can anything in this world be more beautiful*, he wrote—and as a return gift I send him a photo of Mary's translucent tiddler. I ponder the strange things people's passions fixate on: West African fish, moths from the slopes of Kilimanjaro, all manner of night women. Things that to some people are matters of complete indifference, strange or totally without value, are to others matters of life-or-death, for which they are willing to sacrifice everything.

For the next three years Mary kept trying to get back to the West African coast, and kept failing. She had the funding for the trip, but she remained dependent on her brother's schedule, which distressingly kept changing. Although Mary was now a famous Africa-traveler, lecturer, and writer, she still had to meet her obligations as an unmarried woman: cook her brother steak-and-kidney pie, launder his undershirts, and whenever necessary rush off to care for sick relatives. (I would like to know whether a single male explorer's departure was ever delayed by children, siblings, or aging parents. Can you even imagine James Cook delaying his expedition's departure because his contribution to dinner was required in the kitchen?) Mary was planning to leave for West Africa in April 1897, a few months after her book came out, but had to postpone her trip because her brother took ill. After graduating from university her brother had not achieved anything worth mentioning, and I can't help but wonder whether he might have been difficult on purpose, out of sheer envy. (I hate this miserable, whiny brother anyway for destroying Mary's diaries and correspondence after her death.)

With her departure thus delayed, Mary began to write *West African Studies* for an academic readership, and stayed active on the lecture circuit. With her lectures Mary promoted the Africans' cause; as a result, she had gradually become a significant figure in the battles over colonial policy. In some people's opinion she was quite a dangerous figure, in fact, because her views diverged radically from those of the missionaries and colonialists. To Mary the Africans were neither "innocent children" nor "cruel savages" who needed to be "civilized," but people with common sense whose culture ought to be cherished and respected.

The African cause swallowed up everything else, including the feminist cause, and I try to accept that as best I can: that Mary, who had ridden the rapids in African jungles, publicly opposed women's suffrage and admission into the Royal Geographical Society, along with bicycles (dangerous) and buses (total strangers in too close a proximity).

When I think of Mary preaching in her Victorian spinster's uniform, I remind myself of what I read somewhere, that *radical women in all eras have often adopted an outwardly conventional style in order to win a larger audience for the cause they consider most important.*

Yes, Africa was important, but it seems to me that in an interview

Mary might have half-accidentally revealed her *most important issue*, which she did after all promote between the lines. What she said was that she thought it strange that people considered her travels an unusual achievement for a woman, while no one would admire her for continuing to carry out her demanding household duties until she died. "Little account is taken of a woman if she sacrifices herself on the domestic hearth, while should she follow in the track of men—frequently a much easier course—everybody cries 'How marvellous!' "

Mary said she believed that at a deeper level, a woman actually had more endurance than a man. She personally would rather wade neck-deep across a muddy swamp or scale Mt. Cameroon than go through such a treadmill life of any society woman in London with all her social obligations. That workload would have killed Mary, pure and simple.

Mary's second book, *West African Studies*, was released in January 1899, and its first print run sold out in a week. That same year Mary also fell in love—apparently for the only time in her life, and unhappily, with a man who was soon to be sent to Sierra Leone as governor.

That year Mary also finally met Isabella Bird, that esteemed older world-traveler and member of the Royal Geographical Society; their paths had crossed many times, but they didn't meet until February 16, 1899, at a dinner party in London—or at least, Mary stood close enough to her there to hear someone complaining to Mrs. Bird about the unfortunate fact that "books that were amusing were not always accurate," referring, of course, to Mary. Isabella agreed.

Mary, I'm sorry that this meeting of two night women was not more favorable. But I also know that you and she met again a few weeks later. Could you please tell me what you talked about?

In January 1900, the number-one news topic in Britain was the war raging in South Africa, the Second Boer War, in which the British and Boers (of Dutch extraction) fought for control of a huge vein of gold. Mary, feeling she had failed in her political battle on behalf of the Africans, decided to head to South Africa as a nurse. That she could do. On the side, she could also collect fish for the British Museum and possibly report on the war for the English papers—and later push on up to the West African coast, which she had been trying to reach for the past four years.

Mary had a selection of khaki nurses' outfits made up and shipped out to Cape Town in March 1900. When she arrived, she was assigned to the worst possible job: caring for the sick and wounded Boer prisoners, for whom an emergency hospital had just been opened in the old Palace Barracks in Simon's Town. In the last letter she sent home, Mary wrote about the typhoid epidemic ripping through the hospital, and how she had more than a hundred patients in her care. "I am down in the ruck of life again," she wrote. "Whether I shall come up out of this . . . I don't know." I can only imagine the hell of stench, blood, pus, bedpans, and enemas in which Mary cared for her patients, bathing and feeding them. To prevent contagion, she began to smoke tobacco and drink wine in the evenings, and undoubtedly they were necessary for other reasons as well.

In mid-May, Mary came down with a fever and couldn't eat, but assured others that it was just your typical West African fever. In fact, she had all the symptoms of typhoid fever: headache, fever, dizziness, aches and pains—later nosebleeds, stomach pain, diarrhea, and delirium caused by dehydration—and suffered it all alone in bed in her little room.

On the evening of June 2, Mary asked Dr. Carré to promise that she would be buried at sea off the Cape of Good Hope, the most southwestern point of Africa. Then she asked to die alone: she didn't want anyone to see her final suffering. When she lapsed into a coma, her fellow nurses returned to her bedside, and she died on the morning of June 3, 1900. She was thirty-seven.

Mary's coffin was lowered into the sea off the coast of Cape Town. And I think about our comedian heroine's last joke: her coffin didn't immediately sink into its oceanic grave, but bobbed brightly on the waves. I imagine the audience at her lecture howling with laughter as she told about this latest escapade.

When I grieve for Mary, her hilarious report of African diseases from *Travels to West Africa* echoes in my head:

1) *Nothing hinders a man half so much as dying.*

2) *Next in danger to the diseases come the remedies for them.*

3) *Drinking water must always be boiled; just filtering isn't enough. A good filter is a very fine thing for clearing drinking water of hippopotami, crocodiles, water snakes, catfish, etc., and I daresay it will stop back sixty per cent of the live or dead African natives that may be in it; but if you think it is going to stop back the microbe of marsh fever—my good sir, you are mistaken.*

4) *They say that to prevent malaria one should avoid potable water, night air, chills, mental and bodily exertion, nerves, agitation, and losing one's temper. The only one of these that can be avoided is potable water. I would like to know how it is possible to live without air from six-thirty in the evening till six-thirty in the morning. What other air is available in the night than night air?*

One day a couple of months later I'm reading Mary's book, and a piece of wood that I'm using to weigh down the open book marks the page with the red dust of Mkomazi. I wonder whether it will suffice for writing about Mary that I've traveled on the high plains of East Africa, or whether I should foray into her terrain on the suffocatingly hot and humid coast of West Africa. Applications are still open for a Finnish artist's residence there. I imagine standing in Benin on a white sandy beach and watching as Mary's ship glides past.

I don't need to visit the place where Mary died in the end, though, because I've been there already. When ten years ago I spent a few nights in Simon's Town, South Africa, I knew nothing at all of Mary or the prison camp hospital's horrors—I only knew that the place was famous for its three thousand African penguins, and they were what I had come to see. I woke early and sat quietly on the shore surrounded by hundreds of penguins. They stared at me curiously, braying out of tune, swaying and flapping in an official sort of way, or rushing shyly past me. Some dove in the waves or sat brooding on eggs. Later in the day a solitary penguin could be seen swimming along in the shallows of the lagoon among the tourists, or weaving its way through the sunbathers lying on the beach as if on important business. The penguins in all their humanity and sincerity were the most touching thing I'd ever seen; I couldn't watch them without crying. It felt like that predawn beach was a paradise.

I think of how Mary, *dear Mary*, wrote to a friend in a letter in 1899:

I am no more human being than a gale of wind is. I have never had a human individual life. I have always been the doer of odd jobs and lived in the joys, sorrows, and worries of other people. It never occurs to me that I have any right to do anything more than now and then sit and warm myself at the fires of real human beings. . . . It is the non-human world I belong to myself. My people are mangrove swamps, rivers, and the sea. We understand each other. They never give me the dazzles with their goings on like human beings do by theirs repeatedly.

*

Night women's advice:

Don't blame your childhood or your mother. Just go.

While traveling in Africa, laugh all the time.

Having no spouse or kids is not a threat but an opportunity. It's no inconvenience to anyone if you die.

Even if you only have eight years of game time, you can still experience more than many people do in a full lifetime.

If you have a passion, study it. You don't need formal education.

Always wear a long black skirt.

Be buoyant as hell.

V Kyoto, September

> *"Having been recommended to leave home, in April 1878, in order to recruit my health by means which had proved serviceable before, I decided to visit Japan, attracted less by the reputed excellence of its climate, than by certainty that it possessed in an especial degree those sources of novel and sustained interest, which conduce so essentially to the enjoyment and restoration of a solitary health-seeker."* —Isabella Bird in the preface to her book on Japan

I'm packing my suitcase for Kyoto. Isabella's cure for depression clearly works: if at some point I was strangely down in the dumps, just buying plane tickets has worked a miracle cure. It occurs to me that if I'm traveling *for health reasons*, maybe I can get reimbursed for my plane tickets from Social Services?

I've been looking for someone to rent my apartment while I'm gone, and have gotten a reply from a writer I know who needs an office for that same period. So today I passed the keys on to my *secret tenant*: the writer has asked me not to tell anyone about this arrangement, as she wants to work long days in the apartment and knows that the plan won't work if her friends learn that she is in town. The only thing that has helped her survive the ordinary daily chaos of the last few weeks is the thought of this secret office. She isn't even going to give the address to her husband. Every morning she will just disappear—go to a place whose location no one knows. What joy!

I understand completely. One of the most important prerequisites for a writer's ability to write is the ability to hide. Writing, if you plan to get anything done, demands extreme solitude, and it takes superhuman discipline to decline lunch dates, trips to the flea market, and glasses of wine—in short, *life*—for months on end. During the intensive writing stage, you have to have nothing on your calendar for days before it's worth even trying to start—and then for days more you can't talk to anyone, so the fragile half-formed thoughts, rhythms, structures, and causal relations surging about in your head don't dissipate. You have to cling to those vague wisps of thought while waking, working, eating, and sleeping, with only yourself for company. Sometimes the only way it works for me is to flee to my parents' attic (a legitimate reason not to take part in the human race). An even better hiding place is this house I know in Normandy—that is, if I keep my solitary writing retreat to a maximum of six weeks, which is the absolute limit without going crazy.

So, yes, I understand the attractions of a secret office. In fact, my utopia would be always to work in secret. There's nothing worse than well-meaning "how's the book coming along?" queries. "Getting anything done?" (How do you measure that? By the number of pages, or the number of ideas you've gotten after a long dry spell?) "What stage is your book at?" (It's at a stage.) "Are you even halfway yet?" (No idea, because I don't write straight through from beginning to end.) "Are you still working with the same idea?" (With the implication that I should really be changing it?) "But you're making progress, right?" (This is especially deadly if you're struggling with the existential horror of *not* making progress.)

Sometimes I imagine the sheer joy it would be to keep writing my first book, which no one even knew I was writing.

After hiding out with my night women for weeks in my parents' attic, I try to pull myself together and transform myself into a social superanimal—or at least someone who goes through the motions. I fulfill my obligations as a writer: I make guest appearances in reading clubs (in one, the participants are dressed in kimonos and serve sushi); I read passages from my book at the chrysanthemum party thrown by one reader for influential women, an enchantingly elegant soirée devoted to flowers and aesthetics. My mission, like Mary's, is to beef up my travel fund. I calculate that every hardback book I sell personally represents a single many-tiny-bowl lunch in Kyoto. (I also figure that ten paperbacks sold in a bookstore represent one economy lunch in the dining room for lonely men near my lodgings on the slope of Yoshidayama. I'm not exactly rolling in cash here.)

And then I only have a few days to finish my travel preparations for Kyoto: go to the hairdresser, meet friends, clean the apartment. And to top it off, the day before I fly I've agreed to a photo shoot for an interview piece in a women's magazine.

The day is absurd. The journalist had promised that I could just "be myself" in the photos, but the reality turns out a bit different. When I arrive at the photographer's studio in the morning, in addition to the photographer I find the photographer's assistant, a makeup and hair person, a clothing stylist, and the magazine's visuals secretary—all ready to give me a complete makeover. I'm horrified: the stylist's rack is full of businesswomen's power suits that match the magazine's style, big winter coats, fur stoles, button-down blouses, slacks, knitted dresses, felt capes, and sequined spike heels—which is to say, *adult clothes*, the likes of which you'd never find in my closet. That's what I'm supposed to wear? I don't even own a single pair of high heels, not to mention a business suit! I try to squeak out a protest, something about me being just a poor travel writer, but even in my own ears that whole line sounds ridiculous.

The whole photo-shoot day is an out-of-body experience. We drive around Helsinki looking for locations, the makeup artist constantly dabbing more mascara and eye shadow on my face, the stylist patting my collar into place. It's like *America's Next Top Model*. And sure, I realize that these top professionals are doing their top professional work, but what I don't realize is what *I'm* doing there. Fortunately, the photographer is foulmouthed and funny as fuck. She tells me to mince around on the gravelly terrain on some industrial beach in my four-inch heels looking like I've just "beamed down from another planet"—all the while remembering to keep my mouth relaxed, thrust my chin forward in some weird way, and stare *intensely puzzled* at the gravel, which by the way is hard as hell. And as I wobble across some rocks in my sequined spike heels and neon-yellow fur, I complain that I'll never get another grant, because the grant officers will think I'm jetting glamorously around the world in high style. The photographer tells me she was the one who back in the day put leather pants on acclaimed violinist Linda Lampenius, and see, didn't that change Linda's whole career? And think of lawyer and author Jens Lapidus: where would he be without that dark suit? The heels are sweet! Thrust out your chin! Relax your mouth!

At one point I'm posing in an outfit consisting of high heels, pantyhose, a blouse, and a long winter coat—and nothing down below. It's September, maybe seventy degrees, and I'm sweating. As we change locations the stylist takes my coat, and I sit in the car in just my pantyhose, blouse, and high heels. At the next location I climb out of the car, still with nothing but pantyhose below the waist, and go pose in front of this gigantic granite boulder with my chin thrust out. Tourist buses drive past. People stare.

When the shoot is over—the whole operation has taken six hours of working time for five people plus myself—the photographer wants to offer us a late lunch at an ice cream stand. Because all I have on is a blouse and a pair of pantyhose—the long winter coat vanished with the stylist—I wait in the car.

The rest of the day I fret over how the photos will go with the story about a travel writer who abandoned her salaried job and is living on a shoestring budget, dressing herself in clothes I'd theoretically already consigned to the flea market.

The next day I fly to Kyoto. At the airport I'm suddenly excruciatingly aware of how ghastly my travel attire looks. Leggings, flight socks, worn sports sandals, help! I look at all the exquisitely made-up women who will be striding onto the plane in their white rhinestone-decorated plush jumpsuits and high heels.

I keep hearing Mary's voice in my head: *While traveling you have no right to go about in clothes that you would be ashamed to be seen wearing back home!* Besides, even Isabella's travel wardrobe in all its clarity was unquestionably stylish: 1) a tweed dress for cold weather, 2) bloomers for riding, and 3) a silk dress for special occasions.

Should I upgrade the contents of my closet after all?

*

[A HANDWRITTEN NOTE ON THE BENCH AT THE AIRPORT GATE]

Mary!

I remember how warmly you spoke in favor of a long black skirt as a practical travel outfit, and I've been thinking of trying it. An ankle-length skirt made of some robust fabric, a moleskin hat, a white blouse with a high collar, lace-up boots, maybe a red silk tie, wasn't that it? Where might I purchase an outfit like that? I wouldn't mind buying one secondhand, if the price was right. My size is 10, and I'm five foot seven and a half. Please reply as soon as possible. I'm about to step onto an airplane.

Your M

*

Kyoto. My familiar lodgings on the slope of Yoshidayama are unchanged, and Kim has readied for me the tatami-floored room where I've spent more than a year of my life. I greet my roommates (I met Iris from Austria last year), then take my bike in to be serviced; in the grocery store I immediately bump into Rei, a half-Finnish bar owner here (no, I'm not hitting the bar yet today), and in the hundred-yen store I spend a thousand yen to get my living situation up and running.

Kyoto is wonderful, but it's hot and stifling as hell. I muse that if you're looking for a curative climate, it's best not to come here in September.

Why am I here then? It seems to me that I always have to justify traveling to Kyoto: to myself, to friends, to my parents. As I lie here with a headache and jet-lag nausea, I ask myself whether there was any sense in coming here. What exactly have I traveled halfway around the world to do? Nothing special. Work. Most days I'll probably just sit at home writing; occasionally, I'll bike along the river, spend time in organic coffee shops, eat many tiny bowl lunches, enjoy the quiet in tearooms. Maybe I'll go to the Nichibunken to rummage through the books archived there. I'll read Isabella's travel book on Japan, that unbelievably beautiful 1900 edition that I found in the university library, with the gilded script lettering and Mount Fuji bathing in the rising sun pictured on its cloth cover. If there's butoh, kabuki, or *taiko* drumming to be seen and heard, I'll go. I'll restock my tea stores—I've run out of genmaicha, I had to come for more—and go sit in Rei's bar sipping *umeshū*. I'll meet my former roommates and friends, and with Seb and Reina I may take a hike in the mountains and perhaps go to an *onsen*. If my money holds out, I'll go to Tokyo to check out the state of contemporary art. Then I'll go to Nicole's yoga retreat, and while sleeping in the temple I'll remember for a moment how to be a mountain.

Kyoto is its own state of mind. Here everything is possible. Everything is beautiful, strange, exciting: the coffee shops, the gardens, the quiet lanes and temples. I want to understand the life behind the door curtains and the shuttered windows—just a little more on each visit. I want to learn the names of everything sold in the Nishiki food alley.

Sometimes I wonder whether Kyoto's endless mystery isn't just a function of my inability to read the signs. Would everything suddenly look totally mundane if I knew what the words said on the advertising placards and the *noren* curtains hanging in the door openings of the old *machiyas*?

I meet my friend Beatrice around noon in the Tōji temple marketplace. It's a hot, sunny day—I leave my umbrella home, thinking that today at least I won't need it, but en route I remember why I do need it after all: as a sunshade.

Beatrice is German; she was my roommate here three years ago. She's spent the last six months in Kyoto's Nichibunken—the International Research Center for Japanese Studies—working on her art history dissertation dealing with the poetry on Muromachi-era lacquer objects. It seems to me Beatrice has done nothing but sit in the Nichibunken library, living off tofu, nuts, and avocados. She is inconceivably ignorant of Kyoto's sights—for example, she's never heard of Pontochō, one of the city center's famous geisha alleyways. In a week's time she'll be returning to Berlin, so it's about time she made a quick tourist circuit. Since we've paid for full-day bus tickets (Beatrice is extremely practical), we decide to ride from the temple marketplace to Kyoto's National Museum to have our minds blown by the lacquer objects, the gleamingly colorful kimonos, and other historical treasures—my favorite is a lacquered box on whose surface the maker sprinkled gold dust, so that it would look like deerskin. In the museum gift shop I buy a pile of plastic folders, as I always do—nowhere in the world can you buy plastic folders as gorgeous as in Japan. I choose the kind where cranes fly in an ink drawing from the seventeenth century, borne upon lines of poetry in beautiful calligraphy.

After a shabu-shabu dinner, we sit outside on the tiny balcony on stilts at the Atlantis bar in Pontochō, on the bank of the Kamogawa. The evening's warm and I'm feeling a little tipsy on the *umeshū*—it's wonderful to be here with a friend.

Things I love:

Organic coffee shops in Kyoto. Their glorious, slightly overpriced lunches consisting of earth-colored portions served in small bowls on a wooden tray.

Tearooms. A bridge over a narrow canal, a graying bamboo gate, the walls of the tearoom lined with benches from which you can see out into the serene garden. This is a time capsule, a trip you make across the distance of a cup of matcha tea to some distant place.

The last summer days on Lake Biwa, as predicted in the weather forecast.

The Kamogawa. When you bicycle north past the Shimogamo shrine up the western fork of the river, you arrive in another world: the riverbank is wide and quiet, no sound but the surging of the current, the glow of yellow and red flowers in the midst of all the green, the *susuki* grass as soft as down. The cranes stepping slowly through the shallows, and the white ducks . . . the hawks soaring above . . . somewhere under the water the gigantic *kappa* salamanders . . . the long grass populated with turtles, snakes, sometimes deer. I eat lunch in an organic coffee shop, then lie on my back on a bench in the shade on the bank of the Kamo River. I stare up at the hawks, the clouds, and the blue sky. I read a book about the art of growing poor in style that a former professor of mine named Anna gave me as a gift a while ago. It seems to me that happiness like this cannot possibly be legal.

Things I hate:

Stifling heat. This headachy jet lag that I still can't shake.

Making corrections in my interview script for the women's magazine. How is it possible that things like this awaken such visceral self-loathing in me? Why do the things I say come out sounding like I'm some inarticulate nitwit?

Things done in jet lag and headache:

Forgot my bag on the bus. The bag with my computer, camera, calendar, wallet, everything in it. Panicked, felt the cold void exploding in my chest. Wondered where I could call after 6 p.m. speaking no Japanese. E-mailed Kim and Reina, asked them to call the bus station. Went to the police station with Iris (who learned the relevant Japanese phrases just for this trip). Then the next day received the notification: the bag was found in a bus station in a northern district. Traveled to that station with the Japanese phrases I needed written by Iris on a piece of paper, as for some hapless child. Got the bag back with everything still in it. Only the banana peels in the top of the bag had politely been discarded.

Birthday. I've been here more than a week now, but am still weirdly fatigued, headachy, and grouchy. In theory everything's great, of course, but this muggy heat does me in. I have no strength for anything. I complain like Isabella in Australia.

In the afternoon my mother calls, then my nieces sing "Happy Birthday" over Skype. My mother tells me that Grandma, now ninety-seven, went into the bathroom at night and left the hand shower on, then went to sleep under the bed, because "it was raining so hard." That's where the caretaker found her in the morning. The hand shower running all night has wrought havoc, pretty serious water damage, the parquet floor is ruined, a massive renovation lies ahead.

We need to get Grandma into a nursing home. Most likely there's no returning to her own home for her.

In the evening Beatrice and I have dinner at this great yakitori place we've found near the river. Beatrice talks about a love affair she's been having with a guy. To me it sounds like a Greek drama, almost like a dream, and I'm not sure how all of this could actually happen. But then—how did I become a person who suspects people's love affairs, and thinks that falling in love is something requiring treatment?

Maybe I'm the one who needs treatment. Thing is, I've started to wonder whether I might be able to figure out what Isabella, Ida, Mary, and Karen were doing on this very day, my birthday. I wade through diaries, letters, and travel books looking for even a single notation mentioning today's date.

It turns out that on September 28 in 1848, Ida was returning from her first trip around the world, in Russia heading for Vienna. The day before she had boarded a steamship that carted her across the Black Sea, and today the ship docked in Yalta, then a tiny village with a population of five hundred. She would be turning fifty-one soon.

On September 28 in 1873, Isabella had just arrived in Estes Park up in the Rockies, and from the little settlers' log cabin started writing her first letter to her sister. The letter is dated "Este's Park!!! September 28." Isabella, then forty-one, was bubbling with excitement: she had just met Mountain Jim, perhaps the only man she was ever passionately in love with. *It is not easy to sit down to write after ten hours of hard riding*. . . . Mary would soon turn eleven; Ida was already dead.

On September 28 in 1895, Mary was on the West African coast recovering from her conquest of Mount Cameroon. The day before she had returned from the peak—the first white woman ever to scale it. She was thirty-three. In the evening she sat on the veranda of her lodging and thought up her famous quip: *Why did I come to Africa?* . . . By then Isabella was in her sixties and traveling somewhere in China or Korea, or maybe even here in Japan. Karen was ten years old and at home in Denmark.

On September 28 in 2014, I sit on the tatami floor of the house on the slope of Yoshidayama thinking about Ida, Isabella, and Mary, and writing. I can hear the chirring of the cicadas. I'm forty-three.

Then it occurs to me to compare *their* birthdays.

Mary was born on October 13.

Ida was born on October 14.

Isabella was born on October 15.

These three world-traveling women were born on *three consecutive days*. They're all Libras, like me. What does that mean?

Invisible threads and mystical patterns zip about in my head.

I spend my last day with Beatrice, as tomorrow she'll be returning home to Germany. In the evening we go for a walk through the Gion geisha district, in whose traditional teahouses the representatives of this disappearing profession, experts in art, conversation, dance, and song, still entertain their customers. And apparently everyone else is here too: at six in the evening there's an incredible crush at Hanamikoji, tourists gaping at the poor geishas like paparazzi. We see two geishas coming out of a famous old teahouse, and when they climb into a taxi to wait for the rest of their party, the tourists circle them like hyenas, cameras flashing. A Japanese tour guide has brought his group to wait outside another restaurant, and when a *maiko*, a young geisha student, finally comes out, the tour guide screams, shaking his finger: "*Maiko! Maiko!* Teenager! Teenager!" And as the tourists greedily snap photos, he shouts: "Are you satisfied? Teenager!" Ghastly. I'm nauseated. I wonder how geishas can work in conditions like this every day. How do they pull themselves together after monkey-house experiences like this? I can't imagine a greater contrast than the one between the banal group hysteria on this street and the exquisitely refined and elevated beauty that is their work.

And yet here I am too, walking down this street precisely in order to catch even a glimpse of them.

A powerful typhoon is expected to hit Japan, and Kim sends us an e-mail reminder to leave the windows and doors open a crack so that the house doesn't explode with the buildup of pressure in this or that corner. While waiting for the typhoon, I do battle with giant cockroaches, which have invaded the kitchen.

In the evening I read the book about ninjas that Beatrice gave me for my birthday and make an early night of it. It's already raining, and through the open sliding doors roisters a rich, thick, earthy scent. The damp has crept into my futon. I try not to dwell on the danger of landslides on this steep slope.

When morning comes it turns out that the typhoon has missed Kyoto but slammed hard into Tokyo. Flights and trains have been canceled, a metro station is flooded due to a mudslide, schools are closed, and residents have been urged to move to the shelters designated by the authorities. I think—apropos of nothing—of Hiroshige's woodcut number 58 from his series *One Hundred Famous Views of Edo*. In it the citizens crossing the Ōhashi bridge are surprised by a sudden downpour: the whole image is blanketed by a driving rain, through which people trudge canted forward beneath their umbrellas.

I try to keep my travel diary up to date, but it's actually hard as hell, exhausting, really, to discipline myself to write every single evening of my trip, after wearing myself out all day going places and seeing people and being constantly inundated with information—especially when I'm feeling under the weather from the heat and headache.

"It's so hard to write," Isabella too wrote to her sister from Hawaii in March 1873—"I believe I have quite lost the power of describing anything so as to give anyone any idea of it."

And then: "Crater House Kilauea!!!!! Wednesday night June 5th. I am shaking with excitement for everything is happening that could happen. How will this letter ever be written for I am so tired and 'drunk with sleep.'" (Isabella in Hawaii, June 5, 1873.)

"I don't see how letters can be written. After a long day's ride I am so sleepy and wholesomely tired that I really can't write." (Isabella in the Rockies, October 23, 1873.)

"I cannot write about Canton because there is so much to say and I am always either out or too tired to write or 'making myself agreeable' . . . oh I wish I were stronger!" (Isabella in China, January 5, 1879.)

And yet Isabella did write, every evening, as did Ida and Mary. I think of them staying up late, alone, writing by candlelight, when everyone else was asleep—writing with that unrelenting willpower of theirs, just one more page, and one more, and then still one more.

It seems to me that the whole point of traveling is here: *seeing* and *writing down what you've seen*. For in some strange way the world keeps getting more marvelous and more meaningful as you write about it. Only as you write do you begin to *understand*.

Night women's advice: *Write every evening.*

I know, I know. Force yourself.

I decide to do something useful—at least *one* thing!—so I make the tiring hour-and-a-half trip across town to the Nichibunken library to read about a night woman named Ema Saikō (1787–1861). She was a Japanese poet, calligrapher, and artist in the Edo period who lived her whole life unmarried in her father's house near Lake Biwa and occasionally traveled here to Kyoto to meet her male poet colleagues, to hike with them up into the mountains to admire the cherry blossoms, and to drink wine and write poems. She was no radical world traveler, but rather a *quiet radical* who didn't care about what was considered suitable for a woman in that period, but did and was what she wanted. I often think at night about her soothing voice, her personal serenity and tranquility, her dedication to the artist's brush, her solitary trips to Kyoto, her decision not to marry, and the way she was pulled to wine, retreat, and the moon; about her whole life as a woman, which progresses in her poems from youth to middle and old age. I think of her wise awareness that after restlessness comes peace—that no emotion is forever.

One day I'm flipping through a book I found on the shelf at Nichibunken, about women's travel diaries in the Edo period, when a treasure drops into my lap—a treasure disguised as an insignificant detail.

I read that in the Edo period *Japanese women needed a travel permit to move from one city to another*.

The main reason for this requirement was apparently that the samurai government held the wives and children of feudal lords hostage in Edo—what is now Tokyo—in order to ensure the lords' loyalty. An eye had to be kept on the women to make sure they didn't escape back to their home regions. What the women's travel diaries show is that the biggest inconvenience about traveling was obtaining that travel permit, as well as the official inspection arranged for women at special *sekisho* checkpoints. Obtaining a travel permit was extraordinarily complicated: on the application you had to specify among other things the woman's identity, the number of travel companions, the number of means of transportation (horses, oxen, carts), the departure location, the destination, the applicant's name (in the countryside, for example, the application might be made by the temple's high priest), the woman's status, whose mother or daughter she was, possible pregnancy, and whether her teeth were blackened. At the inspection stations, every woman was subjected to a physical examination, including combing through her hair, and interrogated; and if any single detail differed from the one given in the application paper, she had to return home and make a new application. If a woman tried to cross a border wall without a travel permit, her punishment could even be "crucifixion on the spot." Many women complained in their travel diaries about how vexatious it was that once you had obtained a travel permit you could not change your travel plans, even if you fell ill or felt homesick. Toward the end of the Edo period, these inspections did become less common; and around the same time more and more stories began to be told of rebellious women who traveled without a permit. For example, if a woman had decided to add to her itinerary a destination that was not listed on the permit, she would circle around the inspection stations by climbing steep mountain slopes, hanging onto roots and rocks, and paying a guide to lead her around to the other side of the station. The *sekisho tegata* was the travel permit for ruling-class women; ordinary women had to carry a slightly simpler permit listing the bearer's name, place of residence, and whose mother or daughter she was. The permit also included a line requesting a night's lodging in case the traveler did not reach her destination before sundown, and another requesting burial in case she died. Sometimes the permit specified that in case the traveler died, her family did not need to be notified.

The true pearl in this travel permit business, though, is the question about the *woman's status*. The application was required to specify whether the woman was, say, a Zen nun, the widow or sister of a samurai or court noble, or a nun in the shrine of Ise, or perhaps a *ko-onna* or young girl wearing a kimono whose sleeves reached to the ground. Or—get this—whether she was insane, a prisoner, or a corpse.

A corpse!

These past few weeks in Kyoto I have been oddly down in the mouth, without quite knowing why. Of course, I'm tired and listless and moody due to this heat. But I've also been inexplicably frustrated and nettled. I've tried to identify the sources of irritation, and thus to clear the decks of them, but they just seem to keep multiplying. I've regretted coming to Kyoto at all. It feels like I had built up a good head of writing steam back in Finland, which I've now disrupted and dissipated by coming here without a purpose. What am I doing here? I can't afford to be traveling for pleasure, either money-wise or time-wise! And worst of all is when the pleasure trip isn't at all pleasurable!

But now this discovery of women's travel permits in the Edo period gives my whole trip to Japan a purpose. You can't go looking for information like this. You don't know *how* to look for it, because you don't even know that it exists. This revelation struck me serendipitously precisely because I've come to Kyoto without a plan, come to lounge about doing nothing, frustratedly trying to come up with a reason for being here. In order to stumble upon it, I first had to wade through massive quantities of academic studies that seemed to lack all ability to inspire (how can anyone be inspired by anything containing the word "discourse"?) and kept beating myself up because nothing was ever going to come of this.

Now that I suddenly find myself in possession of such a pearl, everything makes sense again. It's that I've followed an emerging chain of interest without having any idea where it might lead. It's that I collect anecdotes and stories, weave them together into a kind of web, a rhizome of night women, a twist of threads crossing decades and continents. It's that I see flashes of Karen on her steamship en route to Africa, Isabella lying awake on the flea-infested tatami in a

Japanese mountain village, Mary bathing in a jungle river, Ida sleeping with a high fever under the ship's captain's table, Ema Saikō with her travel permit trekking toward Kyoto with an inkstone and brush tied up in a *furoshiki* cloth, ticking off her status at the border station: [ ] zen nun, [ ] court noble's widow, [ ] insane, [ ] corpse.

And ultimately the significance of that treasure is this:

I can travel to Kyoto just because I feel like it.

I don't need to get a travel permit from anyone. I'm not held hostage anywhere. I don't have to tick off what I am. The state of my mental health may be up for grabs, but no matter: I still don't have to take circuitous routes around border stations by climbing mountains and hanging from roots. I can walk through airport passport control wearing whatever clothes I happen to feel like wearing.

Women in Edo Japan didn't have that right, and neither did women in many other corners of the world. Many women today still don't have that right.

But at this moment in time, I am free to stay in this city of happiness and bliss and do or not do whatever I want.

And I do.

One day I'm biking without a destination and find a deserted street I've never been down before lined with beautiful *machiyas*—traditional Japanese town houses. In the doorways to the teahouses hang red-and-white paper lanterns, with three red rings on them as the emblem of the Miyagawachō geishas. In between the teahouses are tiny vegetable stores, tofu shops, and hair salons. Old women work out front sweeping the sidewalks, even though they look spotless already. It's quiet; from inside one open door I hear someone plucking a samisen lute and singing—perhaps a *maiko* practicing. This is Kyoto at its best, I think: stumbling by chance on a side-street idyll like this, like a secret no one else knows.

And so in the evening I stand before the *kaburenjō* theater of the Miyagawachō geishas: I've managed to buy a ticket to their show. In the street around me stand elegantly dressed Japanese, distinguished gentlemen and their wives in kimonos, *geta* sandals and traditional hairdos. Everywhere I look there are *geikos* (full-fledged geishas) and *maikos* too, come to watch the performance with their clients. Not a tourist in sight: the contrast between this scene and the Hanamikoji paparazzi hell just a few blocks away is striking. I linger on the theater steps to make a surreptitious study of two sweet *maikos*, those miraculous embodiments of elegance. I don't stare, of course, but apparently my gaze sweeps over them too often, or lingers on them too long, because one of the *maikos* looks me straight in the eye and bows her head in a slow greeting. I'm so stunned—like some stupid elephant or shabby barbarian to whom beauty is shown—that I can't even return the greeting. I cough and jerk my head weirdly (why has no one ever taught me how to behave if a *maiko* greets me!?), and then almost tear up, because that fairy-tale creature actually *sees me*.

The performance is wonderful. At night I think about these last dreamlike night women from a vanishing world.

But more bliss lies in store for me: three days at Nicole's yoga retreat in a Zen temple. As soon as I enter the Daishin-in temple, a deep tranquility settles in and the world disappears. I'm given my own beautiful tatami room with a view of the rock garden. We do yoga and meditate on the tatami floor of the temple's main hall, through whose sliding doors we have a view of the garden, and then also out of doors, on the wooden walkway that circles the hall. The air is fresh, a slight breeze caresses my skin, and the smooth wood is warm under the soles of my feet. For lunch we are served a perfect *shōjin ryōri*, the monks' vegetarian meal: a row of low red tray tables has been arranged on the tatami, on each many small portions in bright-red lacquered bowls. The temple priest's wife serves us the "tea" favored by the monks, hot water in which rice burned on the bottom of the rice pot has been steeped—it has the same aroma of roasted rice as genmaicha. In the evening we bathe in the *ofuro* one by one; before bed I stand for a moment more admiring the moon over the dark rock garden.

At six the next morning, we wake to mediate. The temple priest rings the gong—*bong, bong*—then we do yoga for a while, then we're silent for a while, then we walk slowly around the temple, our socks shushing on the tatami like hospital patients in their slippers. Then we quietly eat our lunch out of our lacquered bowls, chewing our food slowly and carefully with empty gazes, then we sit silent in the tearoom, looking silently out at the raked sand of the rock garden, thinking *I am a mountain, I'm a pebble in the current, serene as a stone, ommm, I'm a gust of wind*, but the outside world seeks entry over the temple wall, somebody's boom box booming, the blare of a megaphone, sounds like some sort of sporting event in progress, emergency vehicles' sirens, the bleating of traffic signals for the blind—I try to concentrate on the humming of the wind and the chirping of the birds, but it's difficult, so deranged does the noise pollution make the external world sound. And that's precisely what this is about: learning not to attach myself to the irritants the world throws in my path, but letting them flow past.

I write in my notebook:

compassion for myself and others

try to see the truth about yourself, even if it's unpleasant

use your energy wisely

don't cling to things either physical or mental

and most important of all:

don't attach yourself to your identity, or imagine that it is unchanging, for it changes all the time.

What a relief it is to think this way: to step outside the shell of my imagined self, drop it like a *nō* mask, be fresh, raw, new—anything at all.

Upon my return to the world, I spend another perfect day with friends. I travel to Seb and Reina's old wooden house on the outskirts of Kyoto, on the shore of Lake Biwa. Seb picks me up at the train station; on the way to their place we make a stop in a little park at the base of the mountain forest, and Seb plays his shakuhachi flute for a while. The piece is called "Deer's Cry," and that's what it sounds like. I notice that Seb has started to dress in traditional monk's clothes, blue cotton jacket and pants, and to speak some mixture of English and French shot through with Japanese words and vocalizations. He looks tired—apparently their year-old daughter, Luna, has been keeping them up at night. I tell him about my temple bliss, and Seb says he dreams of a retreat where he would meditate alone in a cave for a month and someone would stop by once a day with food. I laugh, but he's quite serious. Apparently a retreat of the mountain ascetics is his greatest dream.

Seb and Reina and I drive to a nearby temple village with an abiding old-timey feel. We stop in a little restaurant and eat *kamameshi*, a dish with rice and meat fixed at the table in little cauldrons. Out the window we have a view of a traditional garden with a stream meandering through it; sweet little Luna plays on the tatami floor. The adjacent temple's priest used to live in this house, but no one wants to live in houses like this anymore: it's freezing cold in winter, since the top part of the floor-to-ceiling sliding doors is made of paper.

After we eat, we climb to a nearby shrine. It's a mystical place with a forgotten feel to it; I'm told it has protected Kyoto against evil spirits from the northeast since ancient times. The gigantic trees and Mount Hiei looming behind the shrine make us feel small. Everywhere, in the canals and river, runs ice-cold water off the mountain; behind the shrine a clear waterfall churns; in among the trees squat an abandoned tearoom and a dilapidated inn. The place feels unreal. But there's an energy that permeates it, surging in the cedars that rise high in the sky, in the mountain cavities, in the earth's power fields: I fill my lungs with it.

And then an *onsen* tucked into the side of the mountain, and a late supper cooked by Reina. Friends, the playing of a bamboo flute, many bowls of food, remote mountain shrines, waterfalls, baths in hot springs—the trip's mission accomplished. I am tired and happy when I ride home from the train station in the light of the crescent moon.

On my last day, I pack a box to mail home containing all the *scientific samples* I've gathered on this trip: kilos of fragrant tea leaves, colorful *furoshiki* cloths, books, tea bowls, Kyoto grandmas' quilted haori jackets, wooden trays I've found in the temple marketplace, beautifully decorated plastic folders, shells from the Lake Biwa beach, long pine needles and gingko leaves carefully pressed between the pages of my notebooks. I imagine that package with my name on it racing along in semi trailers for months on end down the Silk Road, across the entire Asian continent all the way to Helsinki. It occurs to me that despite all my passion for them, not one of them will ever be named for me.

The weather is warm without a cloud in the sky. I spend another moment lying on the riverbank looking at the cranes and listening to the Kamogawa's rushing water. I breathe in the bliss that is condensed into the Kyoto air. I wish I could stay here for good.

Out my window on the plane to Helsinki, I see Mount Fuji rising up through a crown of clouds. Waiting for me at home in Finland are the cold, drippy fogs of October and jet lag.

And a few days later, the anxious-making women's magazine hits the stands. The one where I stand in sequined spike heels staring at the gravel with a look of intense puzzlement.

I'm reading the morning paper when I notice a full-page ad for the women's magazine's latest issue. On the cover is the caption: *Fashion designer Mia Kankimäki: "We are a passionate breed."* I choke on my genmaicha. Unbelievable!

It turns out key people were fired this week, and in that turmoil they accidentally left the graphic designer's dummy caption on the ad when the paper went to the printer. The editor-in-chief sends me an apologetic e-mail and asks whether I'm at home, and could she send over a bottle of champagne to make amends? I say I am, and while waiting for the champagne guy to arrive I field queries from my disbelieving friends about my latest, relatively surprising change of careers.

[LETTER TO THE HIMALAYAS, ATTACHED TO THE REFRIGERATOR DOOR WITH A MAGNET]

Dear Madame Alexandra,

I would like to have your digestive system. Or your pancreatic function, or blood-sugar regulation mechanism, or whatever it is that allows you to wander four months in the Himalayas on practically no food at all, whereas sitting here in this studio apartment in Helsinki I'm having to prepare food or a snack at a minimum every four hours if I want to stave off collapsing into bed with a splitting headache or nausea, feeling no good for anything. Maybe a pinch of strychnine would do the trick—maybe the jolt of bug-eyed energy it gave me would help me finish this book?

So please, if you could kindly send me your digestive system as soon as possible—or, if circumstances will not allow that, please ask Monsieur Philippe to forward it posthaste from Tunisia by first-class mail. It would be much appreciated if Monsieur Philippe could also send along a decent sum of money—say, enough to see me through to the end of the year. I realize that my work has taken longer than I expected, but it is essential that I continue writing. *I am just now on the verge of finding a solution.*

Respectfully yours, M—— K——

[TELEGRAM TO NELLIE BLY, NELLIE BLY'S TRAIN; TO BE ACCOMPANIED BY A DOZEN RED PEONIES]

Dear Nellie,

I'm writing this note in haste, for I am off on another journey soon, and the most horrendous moment in that journey—packing my suitcase—is nearly at hand. I can't stop thinking about your handbag. How is it possible that you managed to squeeze everything you needed for a two-and-a-half-month trip around the world in that little portmanteau?

Do you think you might consider arranging packing courses for world-traveling women? I would even come to New York if I could be guaranteed a place in your course and the tuition is reasonable. (And if I can fit my things in my bag.)

Your M

PS Where is New York?

ALEXANDRA

NIGHT WOMEN'S ADVICE 5

Follow the path that opens before you.
Don't use your return ticket.

NIGHT WOMAN #5: *Alexandra David-Neel*
PROFESSION: *Willful feminist, later Buddhist nun, traveler, and writer. In 1924, became the first white woman to enter the forbidden city of Lhasa, disguised as a beggar.*

> *"People whose hearts are not strong and who cannot sufficiently master their nerves are wiser to avoid journeys of this kind."* —Alexandra while trekking across the Himalayas toward Lhasa in the winter of 1923–24

> *"I don't believe in free will. I just follow the path that opens before me."*—Alexandra in a letter sent in 1914 from India to her husband, who was irritated because his wife hadn't returned home.

Since getting back from Kyoto, I've been thinking at night about Alexandra David-Neel. I think with considerable envy of her incredible success at doing what I've always dreamed of, and simply not using her return ticket. I also think about how she made my dream of not leaving the temple—of staying there to meditate and be enlightened—come true for herself. Another thing I think about is how absurdly she realized the wish of many an adventurer to be transformed while traveling as someone else, and how she showed that you can compensate for almost anything, including a balanced diet, with enough willpower (or strychnine).

Some nights I try to chase her out of my head. The problem is that the honorable Madame David-Neel is a bit *too much*. She doesn't really fit the arc of this book. *Take a hike*, I tell her. But Alexandra refuses to go, and I don't know how to delete a night woman like this.

—

Alexandra David-Neel (1868–1969), born in Belgium, grew up a super-energetic, self-willed, headstrong person. She dreamed of wild mountain ranges and impenetrable glaciers, and ran away from home alone while still a teenager, went abroad. At twenty she got interested in Buddhism, then traveled to Paris to study theosophy, Sanskrit, and music, and made her first trip to India in 1891—returning from there two years later, having spent her grandmother's inheritance down to the last penny. Then she decided to try to earn a living as a singer (apparently one of the few even marginally respectable professions with which a twenty-five-year-old unmarried woman could support herself back then), and wound up traveling to Indochina as an opera singer in a touring ensemble. Along with her operatic singing she traveled, gave lectures, and wrote fiercely feminist articles for the papers, and generally lived an entrepreneurial and independent life. She had no intention of burdening her life with a husband, let alone motherhood.

But while performing in Tunisia, she met Philippe Néel, a conventional railroad engineer, and decided to marry him after all. Theirs was hardly a love story, but Alexandra was thirty-five, and a woman approaching middle age did have to ensure her financial security. For a few years she tried to be a good bourgeois wife, but with minimal success: she sank into depression and began to suffer from nausea, headaches, and neuralgia. To her husband she wrote that he was the only person in the world for whom she felt affection, but that she was not cut out for married life.

What she was really burning with desire to do was to learn more about Tibetan philosophy and mystical teachings, and finally her husband suggested a *curative journey* to Asia. Philippe nobly promised to finance a yearlong study trip to India—maybe his wife would get these restless longings for eastern religions out of her system and return home and be a proper spouse? Alexandra latched on to this offer like a stoat and announced that she would be leaving immediately—in fact, she departed via steamship from Tunisia so abruptly one day in August 1911 that she had no time to say good-bye to her husband.

Alexandra poked her way slowly through India, finally ending up in the northeast corner of Sikkim, close to the Tibetan border, where she planned to study Buddhism. But sleeping for the first time in a tent in the Himalayas, and seeing the vast glaciers across the border in the Tibetan high plains and the snowcapped mountains gleaming across the horizon, Alexandra felt as if she had arrived at her true destination. "It felt as if, after a long joyless trek, I had arrived home," she wrote. She was forty-four.

Alexandra didn't return home after a year had passed, as her long-suffering husband had expected, but actually did what so many have dreamed of doing: left her return ticket unused, ignored the commitments she'd made, cleared her calendar, and stayed. And we're not talking about a few weeks or a few months here: she extended her trip to *fourteen years*. And in case anyone is feverishly trying to figure out, as I would be, how such a thing is even financially possible, I'll jot down a night woman's tip: *If you want to extend your journey to fourteen years, hold on to your husband.*

Even though they never again lived together under the same roof as husband and wife, Philippe continued to finance Alexandra's travels until he died. In addition to being her money bag, Philippe was her vital connection to Europe. For decades Alexandra wrote to her husband almost daily. More than three thousand pages of her letters survive—though she decreed that the vast majority later be burned—and from various corners of Asia she was constantly sending large boxes full of her explanations, book manuscripts, and articles to be published in the papers. Although poor Philippe begged his wife over and over to return home—his patience did occasionally seem to be at an end—he continued obediently to send the sums of money and whatever else she requested: her favorite kimono, six pairs of long brown socks, a long thick woolen vest (preferably red), a book of practical medical advice, books on anatomy and gymnastics, her coral and amber jewelry, and other precious and semiprecious stones (she could use them as barter). By return mail, Philippe received endless instructions regarding his health, his diet, his business affairs. It is simply incredible how Alexandra managed for fourteen years to sustain this correspondence marriage that was so beneficial to her, explaining over and over why it was so *important to continue studying*, how she was *on the verge of finding ultimate serenity and the solution to her health problems*, how she was truly making her *great dream* come true. *My dearest Mouchy, a divorce is out of the question, I love you more than ever*. Genius, dear Alexandra.

Back then it was fashionable for Europeans to try to get into Tibet, and that's where Alexandra too wanted to go. The country's borders were closed at the end of the nineteenth century, and the mountain passes were guarded so strictly that many had been thrown in prison or even killed trying to get in. Alexandra tried several times to sneak in from India, but each time was turned back. The whole thing started to chap her hide. So what did our determined night woman do? She vowed she would be the first white woman to enter the forbidden city of Lhasa. She would show the world what a woman's capable of!

It took her thirteen years, but she did finally succeed. In the meantime she immersed herself heart and soul in the Asian way of life. She studied Tibetan and Sanskrit, and began to collect and translate sacred texts and manuscripts. She spent a couple of years in a monastery in the Himalayas studying Buddhism and Tibetan yoga methods, and spent lengthy periods living as a hermit in a cave, practicing an extremely strict form of meditation, finally earning the Buddhist name Lamp of Wisdom. She loved the eremitic life: nothing was as wonderful as living ascetically dressed in nun's garb, cut off from everything, alone in the vast silence of the mountains. (Yes, Alexandra, I understand the attraction.) In the mountain monastery, Lamp of Wisdom also met a fifteen-year-old monk named Yongden, who became her guide and lifelong travel companion, and later her adopted son.

If Alexandra had been thinking of returning to Europe at some point, the First World War made it temporarily impossible. In 1916, Alexandra and Yongden decided to head east: they traveled through Calcutta to Burma, French Indochina, Japan, and Korea, then on to China. Along with them traveled Alexandra's twenty-seven trunks full of travel equipment, books, manuscripts, notes, and photo negatives—obviously even she couldn't free herself of all worldly goods. All through the trip, Alexandra wrote that she was homesick for Tibet, "the country that isn't even mine." In China they settled for two and a half years in the Tibetan Kumbum monastery, where they studied and translated Buddhist texts and Alexandra honed her skills in the Tibetan language until they were perfect. (This too is something I envy: working in peace and quiet in a monastery.) Finally, in winter 1923, they decided to head toward their secret destination, Lhasa, disguised as beggars.

Alexandra and Yongden had had plenty of time to figure out their strategy, and they had decided to go as mother and son: Alexandra would be an *arjopa*, a typical begger-pilgrim, and her "son" Yongden would be a lama, a learned Buddhist, which in fact he was. Their insanely arduous and dangerous trek on foot from Yunnan Province in China to Lhasa through the wintry Himalayas—six hundred miles—took them four and a half months. And let's not forget here that at the time Alexandra was fifty-five years old.

In order to be credible as a beggar, Alexandra could carry only a bare minimum of possessions, and anything that might look suspicious had to be kept concealed under her robe. Her gear included a kettle, two spoons, a knife, chopsticks, one bowl for each of them, tinder, a concealed revolver under her robe, golden jewelry and silver coins hidden in a belt in case they had to pay ransom, a thermometer, a clock, a mini compass, and a Tibetan rosary made of 109 pieces of human skull. Their maps and notes on the route were hidden in her yak skin boots—although it soon became clear that the maps were terribly deficient, since no Western person had ever trekked through this territory before. Alexandra's Tibetan beggar's costume, on the other hand, was a work of genius—she had, after all, learned to disguise herself while working as an opera singer. She dyed her hair with Chinese ink, made braid extenders from black yak hair, colored her face brown with cacao and ground coal, and blackened her hands by rubbing them on the bottom of the kettle. Every backpacker's dream of going native, blending in with the locals, Alexandra took to new heights.

En route, their main goal was not to get caught, so at first they avoided traveling during the day—setting off on their nocturnal journey every day at sunset. They mostly slept out of doors, sometimes under a tree, sometimes in a cave or a tent, whose white cloth was almost invisible against the snow. They had little to eat, and sometimes nothing at all, and their diet was truly simple: one meal a day, either a) Tibetan tea with a little butter and salt mixed in, or b) soup with maybe a piece of dried bacon and a handful of tsampa, a kind of roasted barley flour that was mixed into the salty butter tea or kneaded into a porridgy mass. I tip my hat to you, Alexandra: I can't help but admire you here. Let me confess at once that I'm such a weak woman that under no circumstances could I trek four months in the Himalayas living off butter tea, barley dough, and soup with basically nothing in it but water. I'd collapse the very first day out.

But Alexandra and Yongden pushed on tirelessly, week after week, month after month. Alexandra loved these stark Tibetan steppes and slopes, the mountains' dizzying heights, the eternal snow, the wide-open sky, the blinding light of the horizon, the barren never-green flats, the chaos of imaginatively shaped boulders, and the silence in which the only sound was the singing of the wind. They crossed snowy mountain ranges and gleaming glaciers, forded rivers with the water up to their chests, crossed crevasses hanging off a rope, traversed beautifully blooming valleys, and now and then had to fortify themselves against intolerable cold. Once the snow had wet their tinder and their situation on the nighttime mountain in frigid temperatures was life-threatening, but Alexandra dried the fire-making implements with the *tummo* breathing technique she'd learned from hermit yogis, in which you raise your body temperature by meditating. Another time they got lost in a blizzard and Yongden sprained his ankle, and they had to take shelter in a cave—and by morning, snow had sealed the opening shut. Then they waded knee-deep through the snow looking for the right route, and finally, after fasting for three days, ended up boiling and eating leather intended for soles of shoes. (Add to the night women's advice column: *In an emergency, eat your shoes.*)

Sometimes, awkwardly, they were invited by locals to be their guests, and many times they came within a hair's breadth of getting caught. Yongden had to perform the tasks expected of a lama, such as predicting the future, conducting ceremonies, and giving the dying their last blessings; and in gratitude their hosts offered the lama and his old mother food and lodging for the night. This, naturally, was difficult to turn down. They could not express wonder, horror, or doubt; they had to act as if they'd been born into this world. Every activity, even the most intimate, had to be performed publicly in the local way before all eyes: if eager-to-help youths wanted to come hold the lama's old mother's hands as she squatted on the edge of the rooftop, which served as their latrine, she couldn't become embarrassed or suffer sudden constipation. They had to sleep in the same rooms with their hosts and worry how they were going to manage their morning routines—blackening their faces and hiding their gear. They had to mumble prayers for hours and speak various Tibetan dialects fluently, if that was what was called for. They had to sit calmly on the bare dirt floor, which was speckled with grease, butter, and sputum, and gratefully accept the piece of meat offered them by the women, who had first cut it in their laps on the dresses that they had been using for years as handkerchiefs and kitchen towels and never washing. They had to blow their noses with their fingers, as the poor people did, then dip their fingers in their soup and tea and smile. They had to adjust to the Tibetan custom of never washing their food bowls, just licking them clean; and if they hadn't done a very good job of licking the bowl clean, as was often the case with Alexandra, they had to pour their tea the next morning over the frozen remains of the previous night's dinner. And the fear of getting caught never left them, as when the black color on Alexandra's hands began to wash off into the milk tea, which as beggars they were expected to stir with their fingers. One morning Alexandra had lost her compass and searched for it in a huge panic: if after they left their hosts had found a foreign object, even if they found it in the mountains far from the villages, everyone would have been talking about it, and the authorities would start searching for illegal aliens.

But the sojourners never lost their nerve. Let me jot down, feeling no small envy, some of the comments Alexandra made about various tight situations she found herself in—and note that you'll never find anything like this in any of my travel diaries, no matter how closely you look:

“The morrow was to be the first of a series of eventful days, well qualified to prostrate with nervous breakdown one less strong than myself.”

“There was no time for useless sentiment.”

“I was ready to show them what a woman is capable of.”

“We had not come to these Thibetan wilds to indulge in gastronomy.”

“Emotions may tire me, but can never prevent me from eating or sleeping.”

“For nineteen hours we had been walking, without having stopped or refreshed ourselves in any way. Strangely enough, I did not feel tired.”

I can’t help but wonder what kind of role drugs played in that last one. According to some sources, Alexandra and Yongden kept themselves going with homeopathic strychnine, a stimulant that affects the central nervous system. A tiny overdose causes hallucinations; a larger overdose will kill you.

Finally, in February 1924, more than four months after they set off from Yunnan, the scruffy and exhausted travelers arrived in the forbidden city of Lhasa—Alexandra as the first European woman. She wrote to her husband: “My dearest great friend . . . I’ll tell you at once that I have *completely* . . . succeeded in the ‘promenade’ I undertook when I sent you my last letter. The excursion, considered rough for a young robust man, was pure madness for a woman my age.” She added that she would not undertake that kind of insanity ever again. Besides, she had lost so much weight, she looked like a skeleton. “When I pass my hand over my body, I find only a thin layer of skin covering the bones.”

She wrote to Philippe that the city itself was a disappointment. Of course, Alexandra! Isn’t the dream that comes true at the end of a trip like that always a disappointment? In the collapse that comes as the aftermath of an exhausting trip, one might well write extreme things to one’s husband like *Lhasa is a stupid place*, and anyway that one only came here as a kind of practical joke—just to show the people who had tried to stop her. But later, once the suffering had worn off and been forgotten, Alexandra came to consider those four months wandering through the Himalayas as a free *arjopa*, the happiest of her life.

When the next year Alexandra at last returned home to France, Yongden came with her, and Alexandra adopted him officially as her son. Her husband must have gotten fed up waiting, because Philippe informed her that his house was too small for his wife's travel souvenirs and especially for a certain young man to fit in it; but the whole rest of the Western world received the returning travelers with open arms. Alexandra had become famous. In Bombay, she had received telegrams from French and American papers begging her for articles and additional stories from the trip, and in Paris reporters met their train at the station. Alexandra's book *Voyage d'une Parisienne à Lhassa* (*My Journey to Lhasa*) was published in 1927 in Paris, London, and New York, and *Magic and Mystery in Tibet*, which followed a couple years later, was a cult book for decades. All in all, she wrote more than thirty books about eastern religions, philosophies, and travels. When she turned one hundred she renewed her passport once more, because she was planning a trip to Asia, or at the very least to Berlin to see a doctor who might be able to cure her rheumatism. But that last trip was not to be: Alexandra died in 1969 just before her hundred and first birthday.

The French Geographical Society gave Alexandra a gold medal, and she was named chevalier of the French Legion of Honor, but a strange cloud always hung over that famous trip to Lhasa. Some readers doubted her story to the end. For some reason, it seemed impossible for them to believe that a woman could have made a journey like that. Why didn't she make a map of her route, or at least describe that route in detail, with stops and dates? (Maybe she had better things to do, trying to stay alive on butter tea and dope?) And what about the photographs? Alexandra presumably didn't carry a camera, since that could have exposed them as impostors, but in her travel book there are photographs of Lhasa, which are presented as having been taken by the author. At the heart of the suspicions of fakery is a photo with the Potala, the Dalai Lama's palace in Lhasa, in the background; in the foreground on a lawn sit three people, identified in the caption as Madame Alexandra, Yongden, and a small Lhasan girl. Alexandra is unrecognizable, as her face has been smudged black "according to the custom of the Thibetan women," and where Yongden's eyes should be are white smears, as if he had put cucumber slices over his eyes, or someone had scratched the eyes out in the photo. I don't know what to make of all this. If the photo is a forgery, it was embarrassingly badly done. And if it's not a forgery, who took it?

The shadow of suspicion has clung so tightly to this case that in the biography of Alexandra that appeared in 1987, with a revised edition in 1997, scholars took it upon themselves to marshal documents, maps, letters, previously ignored footnotes, and the top-secret archives of British India to prove that Alexandra did truly visit Lhasa. Yes, a certain British official's notebook records Alexandra's arrival at the border station as she left Tibet; and the secret service archives contain abundant notations about a woman given the code name "French nun," whose movements were followed for a long time. The Potala photograph was probably taken by some Tibetan photographer (there were a few back then). It has been confirmed that Alexandra sent that photograph to her husband as a Christmas present from India in 1924.

When I think of Alexandra at night, I feel a certain anguish about all the conflicting information that's available about her—about how difficult it is to pinpoint even the most rudimentary detail, and indeed how common this sort of uncertainty seems to be with my night women. Nor is the problem just that women are so often ignored in the history books, or that there are so few facts. It's also that the women have themselves blurred and twisted the facts, and censored everything in their stories that might threaten that all-important impression of their *competence*: illnesses, self-doubts, weak moments, travel-financing husbands, photographs obtained from others—all that ordinary human reality that I would like to know.

But in the midst of all this mess, I also think about that inconceivable willpower, that energy that pushes through walls, which seems to be a defining characteristic not just of Alexandra but of all my night women. It shines through all the misremembered dates, misunderstandings, mistranslations, biased interpretations, and disbelieving comments, like a bright, unadulterated, and overwhelmingly enviable light.

And I do in the end find, in the recesses of the Web, at least one concrete, unconflicted, provable thing: a tea named after Alexandra. You can purchase a stylish black tin of Alexandra David-Neel Adventurers Black Tea mixed by the prestigious Mariage Frères tearoom in Paris for 14 euros, plus 17 euros shipping. In addition to floral aromas, it contains pepper, cloves, ginger, cinnamon, and cardamom, and though just between you and me I hate spiced teas like this, I order a tin of it anyway. Maybe some sleepless night I'll boil some with butter and salt, throw in a handful of tsampa, and imagine that I'm trekking across the Himalayas with Alexandra. And if I'm still hungry after that, I'll pop open a can of Liebig's extract of meat.

*

Night women's advice:

If you want to do something, do it.

Seize the day. Follow your passion, even if it means stretching a one-year project into fourteen. Only the results matter—and the trip.

If you want to be enlightened, move into a cave.

Proceed intuitively. Get by on little. Disguise yourself if need be.

If at times things are a little tough or cold, or you're a little hungry, you'll survive.

Don't fret: go. "As a rule things appear much more difficult and terrifying in the course of such discussions than when the moment of action has arrived." (Alexandra on the customs bridge leading to Lhasa.)

NELLIE

NIGHT WOMEN'S ADVICE 6

Invest in coming up with good ideas.
Travel with the single-handbag gambit.

NIGHT WOMAN #6: *Nellie Bly*
PROFESSION: *Journalist, feminist, world traveler, later (having inherited her husband's businesses), industrialist, and inventor. Traveled around the world in seventy-two days with only whatever she could fit in a handbag.*

> *"If you want to do it, you can do it. The question is, do you want to do it?"*—Nellie in 1889, having received the assignment to travel around the world with a day's notice

I confess: I am head over heels in love with Nellie Bly, the American pioneer of investigative journalism who more than a hundred years ago fought passionately for women's rights, and among other things traveled around the world in seventy-two days. First and foremost, Nellie was a genius with creative ideas: *Ten Days in a Mad-House. Around the World in Seventy-Two Days.* "Trying to Be a Servant." "Nellie Bly as a White Slave." Just these titles of Nellie's stories make my blood race. This is a woman who commits to a thing body and soul, and on top of that is a gifted writer—clear, concise, and funny. I wish I were Nellie Bly!

Another reason to fall in love with Nellie is that she was a phenomenal packer—and on certain nights, especially the nights before I'm about to fly out somewhere, I think about her especially hard.

Nellie Bly (1864–1922), née Elizabeth Cochrane, was born into a poor working-class family and received no schooling, but she had a knack for edgy writing from interesting points of view, which soon got her attention and then work as a newspaper writer. The topics her editors offered her—gardening, cooking, fashion, society circles—didn't interest her. She burned with a desire to write about social issues, especially women's grievances, such as the working conditions of factory workers and servants, the status of unmarried women, and the fate of unwanted babies.

This is how Nellie got what was perhaps her most famous idea: One Sunday night in New York in 1888, she was tossing and turning sleeplessly, because in the morning she had to present a story idea to her boss, *New York World* publisher Joseph Pulitzer. (I'd be paralyzed if my boss was *the* Pulitzer.) At three in the morning Nellie cried out in despair that she needed a vacation. *I wish I were at the other end of the earth,* she thought. Click click click. There was the idea: go on a round-the-world trip. Click click. Could she make it around the world faster than Jules Verne's fictitious hero Phileas Fogg in his hugely popular novel *Around the World in Eighty Days*? *Gotta check it out,* thought Nellie, and sank into peaceful sleep.

So first thing in the morning, Nellie got online . . . er, went down to the steamship company's office to grab a pile of schedules, and having studied them carefully decided that it was, in fact, possible to go around the world in less than eighty days. She was buzzing with the adrenaline rush, butterflies in her stomach, her chest jittery—such is the power of a brilliant idea. Then she marched into her editor's office. "Any ideas?" he asked. "Well, one," Nellie replied. "I want to go around the world. I think I can beat Phileas Fogg's record. May I try it?" It turned out the editorial office had spitballed the idea before, but of course the traveler would have to be a man—it would be impossible for a woman to pull off, as she'd require a companion and too much luggage to manage the quick transfers she'd need to make. "Very well," Nellie retorted. "Start the man, and I'll start the same day for some other newspaper and beat him."

In the end, the *World* did decide to send Nellie on the trip. A year later, on a cold and rainy November evening in 1889, Nellie was called into her editor's office. "Can you start around the world day after tomorrow?" he asked. "I can start this minute," Nellie replied. So she had one full day to prepare for the trip. Some might have panicked at this, but not Nellie. Next morning she marched into the stylish Ghormley dressmaker's, to have a travel outfit made: "I want a dress by this evening. I want a dress that will stand constant wear for three months." The dress was ready in four hours. In another shop she ordered an ulster, as well as a thin dress to wear in hot climates. Finally she bought a portmanteau-style leather handbag, into which she would need to pack everything she was taking with her. In the evening she wrote brief farewell notes to her friends and packed her handbag. "Packing that bag was the most difficult undertaking of my life," she wrote. The thin dress didn't fit in, so she traveled around the world in a single dress.

Nellie departed New York on Thursday, November 14, 1889, at 9:40 a.m. (and thirty seconds) on a ship called the *August Victoria*. As travel funds the *World* had given her £200 and a little American currency as well—no one knew whether the American dollar would be accepted out in the world. She packed the gold coins in her pocket and the bills in a little chamois-leather bag that she tied around her neck. Ahead of her lay a 28,000-mile round-the-world itinerary, which she would mostly be traveling alone. Standing there on deck, however, Nellie did not yet feel an ounce of joy: "Shall I ever get back?" she wondered disconsolately. "Intense heat, bitter cold, terrible storms, shipwrecks, fevers, all such agreeable topics had been drummed into me." And soon enough she was seasick. Departures: they're always tough, even for night women.

But after a week at sea, Nellie got up to speed, and the stops flashed by: New York—London—Calais (France)—Brindisi (Italy)—Port Said (Egypt)—Ismailia—Suez—Aden (Yemen)—Colombo (Sri Lanka)—Penang (Malaysia)—Singapore—Hong Kong—Yokohama (Japan)—San Francisco—New York. In London, Nellie bought tickets for at least half the journey from the Peninsular and Oriental Steam Navigation Company. (At this point her handbag was too full to lock.) On the train through France—a brief stop in Amiens, where Monsieur Jules Verne and Madame Verne had asked by letter to meet Nellie (Nellie fretted that she was bedraggled from traveling and could not primp herself in any way, but the meeting went swimmingly in gestures with smiles and nods, and Madame Verne was so sweet that Nellie had to restrain herself from kissing her on the lips). Then back on the train and on to Calais. ("I might have seen more while traveling through France if the car windows had been clean.") In Italy Nellie wanted to wire a greeting to New York, but that proved difficult, as the telegraph operator didn't know where New York was. About the India Express route's ship Nellie remarked that "travelers who care to be treated with courtesy, and furnished with palatable food, will never by any chance travel on the *Victoria*." From that beastly bucket Nellie also reported on a young man who was passionate about traveling and told her that his fondest dream was to find a wife who could travel without luggage. Right: the man himself had nineteen trunks.

Port Said—Suez—Aden—Sri Lanka . . . In Singapore the ship had to sit in the harbor twenty-four hours, and Nellie was desperate: she was already running behind schedule, and if she missed her next ship in Hong Kong, her overall travel time would be days longer! And maybe it was her irritation in Singapore that broke the back of her self-imposed ban on shopping: "I did resist the temptation to buy a boy at Port Said [!] and also smothered the desire to buy a Singalese girl at Colombo [!], but when I saw the monkey my will-power melted and I began straightway to bargain for it. I got it." Well, at least she didn't have to fit it into her handbag.

In Hong Kong Nellie made a beeline for the Oriental and Occidental Steamship Company's office to find out the quickest way to get to Japan. She had been en route thirty-nine days. The steamship company official calmly predicted that Nellie was going to lose. "Lose"?! It turned out *Cosmopolitan* had started another woman on a round-the-world journey on the same day, but in the opposite direction, and now the whole world was on tenterhooks to see who would arrive first. "Did you not know?" the official asked. "She left here three days ago. You probably met somewhere near the Straits of Malacca. She says she has authority to pay any amount to get ships to leave in advance of their time. . . . She intends to do it in seventy [days]. She has letters to steamship officials at every point requesting them to do all they can to get her on."

Nellie was thunderstruck. She had been rushing around the world in the best amazing-race style for thirty-nine days, and now she had a competitor—and had been told nothing! She had been sending reports of her trip to the *World*'s editorial office by telegram and mail (mailed letters took weeks to arrive, so she wasn't exactly online), and they had been published around the world. Tens of thousands, maybe even millions of readers had devoured these "Nellie Bly travel stories." And now it turned out that everyone knew about her competition *with this other woman*—everyone except her!

Nellie got stuck in China for days. Because she only had the one dress, which she'd been wearing for more than a month straight, she refused invitations to the dinners and receptions that people in Hong Kong wanted to arrange for her. She was amazed at how many affluent, good-looking bachelors she saw everywhere there, and urged all young women to take the next ship to Asia. The captain on her next ship was likewise young and handsome, and surprised when he met Nellie, whom he had imagined as "an old maid with a dreadful temper." Fie!

The title of my favorite chapter is "One Hundred and Twenty Hours in Japan." Nellie's assessment of Yokohama, Tokyo, and Kamakura was incisive: "If I loved and married, I would say to my mate: 'Come, I know where Eden is.'" Her only regret was that she hadn't thought to pack a Kodak. Everyone else had one, and these "kodakists" took the most beautiful photographs with them.

Her last leg on the sea was made on the *Oceanic* on its way across the Pacific to America. The crossing was stormy and difficult, and the sailors discussed throwing Nellie's monkey overboard, as they believed it was the cause of the bad weather. The men in the ship's engine room, however, did their best to make it on time: *For Nellie Bly, we'll win or die*, they wrote on the ship's engines.

The ship arrived in San Francisco two days behind schedule, but Nellie found a private special train arranged by Pulitzer waiting for her—it would take her across the continent at top speed. By this point Nellie was famous nationwide: at every station, masses of people dressed in their Sunday best gathered to wave and cheer her on, sometimes more than ten thousand strong. There were quick handshakes and hurrahs, bouquets of flowers and trays of fruits and candies thrust through the train windows, and congratulatory telegrams from all over the country, addressed only to "Nellie Bly, Nellie Bly's train."

Nellie arrived in New Jersey on January 25, 1890, a national hero and example for all women. She had circled the globe in 72 days, 6 hours, and 11 minutes, beating her own expected time by three days and setting a new world record. (The other woman had gotten stuck on a slow ship across the Atlantic, and didn't arrive in New York until four days later.)

But the most heroic part of her achievement was that Nellie had traveled around the world *in one dress and with only a single handbag.* How was that possible?

"I have been asked very often since my return how many changes of clothing I took in my solitary hand-bag. Some have thought I took but one; others think I carried silk which occupies but little space, and others have asked if I did not buy what I needed at the different ports. One never knows the capacity of an ordinary hand-satchel until dire necessity compels the exercise of all one's ingenuity to reduce every thing to the smallest possible compass. In mine I was able to pack two . . . a complete outfit of . . . a small . . . several . . . a liberal supply of . . . and most bulky and uncompromising of all, a jar of cold cream to keep my face from chapping in the varied climates I should encounter. That jar of cold cream was the bane of my existence. It seemed to take up more room than everything else in the bag and was always getting into just the place that would keep me from closing the satchel. . . . After-experience showed me that I had taken too much rather than too little baggage. . . . On one occasion—in Hong Kong, where I was asked to an official dinner—I regretted not having an evening dress with me, but the loss of that dinner was a very small matter when compared with the responsibilities and worries I escaped by not having a lot of trunks and boxes to look after."

When I think about Nellie at night, it should be obvious what I'm thinking.

Top 3 Worst Packers

1) Alexine Tinné

A filthy-rich Dutch aristocrat plagued by wanderlust. Set out to look for the source of the Nile as a twenty-six-year-old in 1862. Took along her sixtysomething mother, her aunt, and two chambermaids as well as a somewhat excessive amount of luggage: thirty-six trunks of luxury necessities, loaded onto three ships. Included were pieces of furniture, hatboxes, tea services (Chinese porcelain), silver dinnerware, sunshades, furs, evening dresses, a whole library of reading material, mirrors, copperplate drawings, five dogs, a piano, tents, tent cots, blankets, mattresses, sheets, a camera, equipment for developing photographs, equipment for collecting and preparing plant samples, an easel, everything else needed for painting, a collection of five revolvers and a pistol, a year's food supplies—chickens in cages, camels for milking, sheep, many pounds of salt, cases of wine, cognac, coffee—and more than three hundred pounds of glass beads for barter, eight hundred bars of copper, and twelve thousand conch shells, and, later, an orphan leopard cub adopted off the bank of the Nile, a porcupine, a monkey, a stuffed crocodile, intermittently slaves (whom Alexine bought in order to free them later), and a hundred and fifty heads of servants, porters, cooks, guides, interpreters and soldiers, plus pack camels, donkeys, and horses.

They had so much luggage that it was literally the death of them.

First, the ship hauling the women's mountain of stuff ran aground in the labyrinthine swampland of Bahr el-Ghazal, where the tall Nile grass and floating water hyacinth islands blocked their passage for days. The rainy season was approaching and the company needed to reach the interior as soon as possible, but it was impossible to find enough bearers in the region to carry that amount of stuff (they would have needed at least five hundred strong men). When they did finally get going, it was pouring down rain, the swampland flooded, the tropical fever and other horrific diseases attacked, it was difficult to find reliable routes and campsites—let alone food—for that huge group of people, and gradually all the pack animals died and their vital goods were ruined in the rain; but those pigheaded aristocratic women in their fancy dresses insisted that they be carried in their sedan chairs along slippery, narrow pathways, with four hundred bearers and a hundred and fifty soldiers and servants behind them, all in appalling shape, sick and hungry.

On that trip Alexine's whole party died: her mother, both chambermaids, a scientist who accompanied them, and later her aunt. Ultimately, the women died because *they had too much luggage*.

When I think of Alexine at night, her tragic power figure glides eternally in my mind's eye along the Nile, first upstream, then downstream, surrounded by her mother, her aunt, and her chambermaids—first alive, then dead. When she finally arrived back in Cairo in December 1864, having buried two of the bodies, she had hauled the other two (and all the luggage) on board ship and by camelback for two thousand miles, over nearly a year and a half. She only missed discovering the source of the Nile by a smidgen.

Alexine herself died a few years later in murky circumstances in the Sahara Desert. Apparently a camel caravan carrying fifty humans and their luggage was too tempting a prize for the local nomads.

2) May French Sheldon

A translator of French literature, businesswoman, and feminist, later an explorer FRGS. Climbed Mount Kilimanjaro in 1891 at the age of forty-three, because she wanted to prove that a woman can do anything a man can do, and even better. A.k.a. Crazy May and Bébé Bwana. In Zanzibar she hired a hundred and fifty bearers, instructed them in the name of decency to put some clothes on for God's sake, and organized her expedition so meticulously that not a single soul would ever suffer hunger or cold. She packed massive quantities of food, weapons, tents, folding tables and chairs, a bathtub, a boat you could assemble yourself, porcelain dishes, silverware, napkins, sheets, many sorts of medical supplies (including instruments for extracting teeth if necessary), a silk dress for dinner, letters of introduction from the sultan, and heaps of rings made specially for the trip with her name engraved on them, which she handed out to the locals she met. Let herself be carried in a cushioned wicker sedan chair that she designed herself, dressed in full-on ladylike attire, a pistol on each hip, and in a waist bag—the legendary "French-Sheldon Medicine Belt"—a first-aid kit for emergencies. She carried a banner with the Latin motto *Noli me tangere* (Touch Me Not), because of course one wants to make a prestigious impression. Whenever she approached a native village, she would don her ball dress (white embroidered with silver and artificial gemstones), a white wig, and the treasures of her jewelry box. Managed to be the first white person to see Lake Chala in a volcano's crater.

3) Me

I cannot overemphasize the importance of having my own supply of tea and accompanying apparatus. That's why I never travel without a small wooden teapot and a selection of tea leaves in ziplock bags—genmaicha in the morning, *pu'erh* or high-quality Japanese *sencha* in the afternoon, chamomile in the evening, and for colds German *Husten und Bronchial* herbal tea. I also pack enough rolled oats and rye bread for the duration of my trip (not because I'm afraid I won't want to eat the local food: on the contrary, so I don't fatten myself up with white flour every morning), as well as energy bars and nuts (all right, maybe I do have a slightly neurotic fear of starving to death). Also in my bag is a headlamp (believe it or not, I always need it), a laundry bag, shoe polish (indispensable!), a Tanzanian *kikoi* cotton cloth (to be used as a scarf, a towel, a picnic spread, or a skirt), countless tiny Japanese cloth bags (for keeping things properly sorted), a thin extra bag (for gifts), and a small roll of duct tape (to be used, say, for fixing the extra bag if it falls apart, or taping up the neck of the half-drunk pommeau bottle, if I want to haul it home in my suitcase from Normandy). Also included are a money belt, a spare pair of glasses, a blow-up airplane pillow, earplugs, a sleeping mask, tissues (those who have traveled in Japan learn that you can never trust the local tissues), and a neurotically extensive collection of medicine, out of which the only thing I ever need is vitamins, oh, and the echina zinc tablets, which in my experience will postpone the onset of flu symptoms almost indefinitely. Then, of course, books, notebooks, Post-it notes, pens, flash drives, my laptop, my camera, my phone, chargers for all those, a power adapter, a travel hair dryer, and of course clothes—everyday clothes, party clothes, home and night clothes, sports clothes, shoes—and finally cosmetics packed in travel-size bottles and then in ziplock bags. A total of fifty pounds checked and eighteen pounds in my carry-on—and I don't even have my own saddle. I am desperately in need of Nellie Bly's packing course.

[NELLIE BLY'S PACKING COURSE]

One dress (wear two and a half months)
Passport and currency (in a chamois bag around your neck)
A silk umbrella (carry in hand)
A handbag, containing the following items:

- *Two travel caps*
- *Three scarves*
- *A tennis blazer*
- *A dressing gown*
- *Underwear*
- *Slippers*
- *Ruchings**
- *Handkerchiefs*
- *Toiletries*
- *Hairpins*
- *Needles and thread*
- *Inkstand, pens, pencils, copy paper*
- *A small flask and a drinking cup*
- *Cold cream***

That's it.

Ruchings are a woman's most important accessory. They can be stitched or buttoned to dress collars and sleeves as needed.
***Will never fit in the bag, so leave it out.*

[MISCELLANEOUS NIGHT WOMEN'S ADVICE]

Travel permit.
Ask yourself whether you want to travel. If you do, issue the travel permit.

Luggage.
Don't pack anything that you'll need to hire ten to five hundred bearers to haul.

Setbacks.
Regard trials as a gift. Everything is grist for the mill.

Online/offline.
Hennie Bird, Isabella's sister, traveled offline in Shetland in 1873: "The tour occupied five weeks, I enjoyed it most thoroughly. All was new, I could not arrange to have my letters sent after me, *so I had no worries! I let all bothers stand over, and had no cares beyond today."*

If you can avoid it, don't arrange to have letters sent after you.

PART III

Artists

[LETTER OF INTRODUCTION]

Dear recipient,

Let me begin by assuring you that the presenter of this letter, Miss M. K., is in every imaginable way a respectable woman. I would be most obliged if you could see your way clear to helping her to secure appropriate lodgings for the night—modest accommodations will suffice, but of course if you are able to offer a higher standard. . . . Full board would be most agreeable, given that Miss M. K. is a single woman. . . . Kindly note that, despite her traveling disposition and unfortunate introversion, Miss M. K. is a thoroughly honorable and quite trustworthy individual. . . .

Sincerely yours,

[signature illegible]

VI Florence, November

Upon my return to Finland from Kyoto, I face a quick turnaround. I have two weeks to get over jet lag, do my laundry, meet friends, and hang out at the Helsinki Book Fair before it's time to pack my bag again. I'm heading to Florence, Italy, in November. I've passionately wanted to visit the artistic treasures of Florence for twenty-seven years, ever since I spent a single hot and wonderfully exhausting day there as a sixteen-year-old. Now I plan to make my dream come true, since I can. I've issued myself a travel permit.

Besides, there must be night women in Florence.

I'm feeling a bit nervous about my accommodations, though. Once again I'm going to stay with a man I don't know—all I know about him is his name. Nino, a former roommate of mine in Kyoto, arranged a crash pad for me with the Florence-based brother of the girlfriend of a childhood friend of his. This Stefano has promised to let me use the larger bedroom in the place, and the only rent I have to pay is half of the electricity and water bills. This is almost too good to be true. I truly know nothing about the man. He may be twenty or sixty—I don't know, and I didn't feel comfortable asking. I picture an unwashed bachelor cut off from the world who awaits my arrival in his helter-skelter man cave like a spider waiting for a fly to land on its web. Maybe I should have bitten the bullet and spent more than a thousand euros on a rental apartment downtown? No: Ida would certainly have accepted the offer.

During breaks from packing I've been reading Anna Kortelainen's book *Hurmio* (exaltation, ecstasy, rapture), and I learn that the French writer Stendhal had his famous experience of rapture in Florence. A little over two hundred years ago, in September 1811, this vigorous young man of twenty-eight jumped out of a stagecoach in Florence and later wrote this description of the experience that shook him to his core in Santa Croce church: "I was moved almost to tears. I have never seen anything so beautiful. When I came out, I had a heart flutter that Berliners call 'nerves': my life force had ebbed and I feared I would fall as I walked. . . . I was all a-tremble for two full hours." He had experienced for the first time what came to be called the Stendhal syndrome—a powerful state of multisymptom confusion provoked by an experience of art.

A foreign city, an unknown man, treasures of Renaissance art, an unformed agenda: I wait for the symptoms to manifest.

Florence, O Florence! I take a taxi from the airport straight to the apartment, and at the door stands a reception committee: a very young, very stylish Stefano, looking the quintessential intellectual; his older sister, Angela (who lives in the same building); and her boyfriend, Benedetto, Nino's old friend. All of them look friendly and completely harmless. Stefano drags my suitcase up to a modern, sparsely furnished apartment with two bedrooms at the top of a narrow spiral staircase. Or, to be precise, a single big bedroom with a double bed and an en suite bathroom with a skylight operated by remote control—and in the hallway to that room, a narrow little excuse for a bed in which Stefano says he'll be sleeping. We're both a little abashed: I really don't know how to react to this kind of hospitality.

Toward evening Benedetto comes to check out my situation and asks whether I'm satisfied with my accommodations. Am I ever! Except that I feel terrible to be sleeping in this huge bedroom while Stefano sleeps in the stairwell. "But you're a wo-oman," Benedetto says with an Italian lilt and a wave of his hand, as if that explained everything.

Soon Stefano starts to cook a welcome dinner for the two of us, pasta and tomato sauce made by his mother; it's delicious and perfectly al dente. He switches on some classical music on an old-fashioned record player—yes, he has one. He tells me he collects old vinyl records; on his shelf I see Pink Floyd, Frank Sinatra, Edith Piaf, and classical—all my favorites. By this point I am feeling like I came to the right place after all: can this be true? His book collection too has classics from Boccaccio's *Decamerone* to Marcel Proust, and on the table I find Dante's *Divina Commedia* ("in the original," of course)—Stefano says he's memorizing it, so he can teach it to the children and elderly in his home village. On top of a cabinet is his great-great-grandfather's camera from the late nineteenth century; on the wall hang an old pocket watch and posters of Kandinsky. "I like old things, combined with new," this shy twenty-two-year-old student says—not, I assure you, referring to me.

I don't feel like sharing with him just yet that to me, Florence, the Uffizi Gallery, and Pink Floyd form an ecstatic holy trinity. That when as a sixteen-year-old I returned home early one summer morning from my larger-than-life trip to Italy, I was so enchanted with cities the color of burnt sienna and with Leonardo da Vinci that I stayed up that whole white night playing Pink Floyd records over and over, staring at Leonardo's beige women in the wall calendar that I'd bought in the bookshop in the Uffizi. Those drawings stayed on the wall of my room for years.

And now I'm here. A fire rushes beneath my skin.

First thing in the morning I take a bus into the old city center and spend the whole day wandering Florence's narrow, labyrinthine streets. I eat lunch at Trattoria Nella and wonder whether the restaurant itself could give me Stendhal syndrome and the attendant ecstasy, as the *sogliola*—sole—and butter-fried spinach are so divine that they bring tears to my eyes.

In the afternoon my feet take me to the Santa Croce church. I feel a little choked up at Michelangelo's tomb—his expression in the bust carved by Giorgio Vasari seems so wise and warm—but this doesn't measure up to any kind of syndrome, no matter how hard I try to squeeze out a little emotion. Michelangelo syndrome, on the other—neck and eye problems brought on by bad working ergonomics, which the artist suffered while painting the ceiling of the Sistine Chapel—does threaten while I admire the frescoes in the side chapels:

I get dizzy, feel a bit nauseated. I tell myself to buck up: my great Florentine fresco project is just getting off the ground!

And then back at home the Stendhal does indeed kick in, belatedly as usual. It feels as if I'm going into convulsions, laughing and crying at the same time—as if something big is trying to burst out of me.

I've just returned from the store when Stefano comes home from the university. He doesn't go to a laptop or start scrolling through his cell phone the way every other young person would do in 2014; instead he lays a vinyl Pink Floyd on the turntable and sits down on the sofa with his Dante. I sit in the kitchen eating chicken salad as the world's longest and most beautiful intro, to the *Wish You Were Here* album, issues from the speakers. I plunge down a rabbit hole in time, as if I'd just swallowed a piece of Proust's madeleine, and I'm again at that choked-up moment at which all was possible. I go tell Stefano my whole sixteen-year-old story with voice a-tremble, but he just laughs. Then I return to the kitchen to resume eating my chicken salad/madeleine with an ecstatic smile on my face.

I've been warned that it usually rains all November in Florence, and I find that that's quite true: it does rain all November. I am, however, a conscientious die-hard tourist, and I do churches, monasteries, museums, and palazzos until my feet are about to drop off. I join guided tours, thinking how much easier it would be if they could arrange your whole life as a guided tour, thank you very much.

I had thought I was coming to Florence to worship Renaissance beauty, this stunningly beautiful city, beautiful frescoes and the beautiful women in beautiful paintings, but I soon begin to realize that architecturally speaking Florentine beauty is rather stark. Not luxurious hedonistic trappings, but severe undecorated façades; palazzos that are like fortresses, forbidding and almost frighteningly medieval (which is not to say that I don't keep falling in love with them), and looming watchtowers from which defenders are preparing to loose a barrage of arrows or dump boiling oil on invaders. There's nothing playful here, nothing entertaining or birthday-cake-like—and not very hospitable either. Church façades are at most decorated with different colors of marble (the white from Carrara, the pink from Maremma, the green from Prato), but often they too are completely unadorned. The Duomo, of course, is impressive—it looms large, absolutely huge in its surroundings—but there's something simplistic about it too, almost animalistic: in the evening dusk it looks a bit like Hayao Miyazaki's Totoro squatting all alone.

Certainly there are beautiful frescoes and paintings here, enough to take your breath away. I imbibe the photographically precise image the frescoes give of their time, their bright or faded colors, their hidden meanings. I learn that the frescoes especially are Florence's treasures (you can only paint them in a specific kind of climate), that the technique is difficult (only for masters), that even the madonnas have the faces of specific contemporary women (even if of prostitutes), and that if one of the peripheral figures in a painting is looking straight at you, it's probably the painter himself. The frescoes in Santa Trinita are my favorites, and whenever I walk by I check to see whether the church is open. I can't tear myself away from the Sassetti Chapel, on whose walls the banker Francesco Sassetti had his whole family painted in the 1480s, in scenes displaying the family's wealth and status. One significant source of income for the Renaissance church was rich families' habit of donating private burial chapels—and it seems still is: you have to drop a coin into the metal box on the wall of the chapel to make the lamp light up to illuminate the frescoes, and the light invariably fades to darkness just as I think I'm about to understand something important.

For the more I look at the paintings in this city, and the more I understand the stories they tell, the more I begin to cling to them, almost to the point of addiction. It feels to me as if just by *looking* at the works long enough, so that I know them almost by heart, so that I truly *see* every millimeter of them, I gain something irreplaceably valuable. It feels like I can *almost* see through the veil, as if I could almost get a handle on what it's all about, life, like a dreamer to whom all is suddenly clear, but who upon waking loses the thread. . . .

Or could it be a simple matter of the experience of perfect harmony having an integrating effect? That some of that harmony is transferred to the viewer?

Of course, the primary target of my pilgrimage is the Uffizi Gallery, the world's oldest art museum and mecca of Renaissance art. As early as the fourteenth century, Florence was one of Europe's most affluent cities; back then it was ruled by various professional guilds, such as the wool and silk merchants, the bankers, judges, and pharmacists, and, in the cultural realm, by the painting pioneer Giotto and the writers Dante Alighieri and Giovanni Boccaccio (and others). But in the fifteenth century, the era of the Medicis began. That powerful family would reign in Florence for three centuries, and to them belongs credit for the Renaissance of art. The Medicis were unscrupulous bankers who buffed up their reputation by building churches and chapels and hiring painters to create numerous religious works. In this way they earned themselves access to heaven—and gave birth to the Renaissance. The entire cream of Renaissance art and architecture in the fifteenth and sixteenth centuries, from Masaccio to Fra Angelico, from Brunelleschi to Donatello, from Leonardo da Vinci to Botticelli and Raffaello, worked under the Medicis' patronage.

The most admired Florentine figure of the late fifteenth century was Lorenzo de' Medici, the charismatic ruler, poet, and patron of the arts who made the city glitteringly wonderful. Lorenzo organized splendiferous parties, hunting expeditions, and tournaments; he dabbled in philosophy, and held a sculpture school in his garden, where one of his pupils was the young Michelangelo. The nobles studied the classical virtues and read Plato, and the artists' workshops produced paintings, marble statuary, architectural drawings, and sketches for frescoes that would become the most beautiful ever seen. On metal bars attached high on the exterior rock walls of palazzos, flags were raised to mark celebrations, but also birdcages were hung there to give their occupants some fresh air; collared cats and pet monkeys would also clamber about up there. In 1490, Lorenzo's garden contained golden pheasants from Sicily, gazelles from Tunisia, monkeys, parrots, and a giraffe that he had been given as a present by the sultan of Babylonia.

Life, however, was not entirely idyllic. If we think of Florentine Novembers in Lorenzo il Magnifico's day, we have to think of the cold, the mud, the pestilences, and the smells. We have to think of the dark, damp nights, lit only by torches fixed to the walls of the fortresslike houses. We have to think of the artists who worked in dark, ice-cold churches in exceedingly difficult conditions, risking tuberculosis. After it rained the streets were muddy and the marketplaces so slimy that the women had to wear high-soled shoes on their trips to market. There was a horrific stench in the streets, because they had no drainage system, and to the reek of actual feces was added, depending on the district, the smelly wastes from dyers, tanners, butchers, chandlers, and silkworm growers. On the Ponte Vecchio there were no gold and jewelry merchants, as there are today; back then stank the stalls of fish merchants and the workshops of leatherworkers. Nor were things particularly idyllic indoors: in November the palazzos grew very cold inside, so their chambers' rock walls were covered with tapestries lined with squirrel pelts, and if the owner couldn't afford window glass, the openings were covered with linen saturated with oil or wax. And while we're on the topic of Florentine smells, we also must remember that the beautiful people in their frigid palazzos never washed. They would certainly never have washed their bodies with water, because they knew that water spread bacteria, at worst the plague; and besides, touching one's own body might awaken impure thoughts. It was believed that even washing your face made your vision deteriorate and caused toothache. . . . Nor were the fancy dresses ever laundered, only at most aired out. Instead the nobles would spritz themselves with perfume, hang nosegays here and there, and while out of doors raise perfume-soaked gloves to their mouths, for perfumes would protect them against pestilence. . . .

Unfortunately, Lorenzo il Magnifico died of gout at a young forty-two, and after him Florence was for a time without a Medici as ruler. During those years, one of the powerful men in the city was Girolamo Savonarola, a severe Dominican friar who preached fanatically against the debauchery and luxury of the nobles. He sent groups of children into the streets bearing crosses, with the task of seeking out signs of vanity and urging citizens to fast and to snitch on each other. Many obeyed: the fashionable ladies began to wear colorless dresses, and silver candlesticks and illustrated books were removed from churches and monasteries. In 1497, a bonfire of the vanities was lit in the Piazza della Signoria; in it burned heaps of scent bottles, hairpieces, fans, necklaces, silk dresses, chessboards, Botticelli paintings, the works of Plato, and books on magic, as well as the portraits of all those beautiful women who had not been portrayed as madonnas. Savonarola's bleakification campaign only lasted a moment, however: he himself was burned to death in the same piazza a year later.

The Medicis returned to power, but died out in 1743, when Anna Maria Luisa de' Medici died childless. But fortunately the family's vast art collection had already been transferred to the Uffizi, which had been built by Grand Duke Cosimo I de' Medici starting in 1560—first as his office, but then his son Francesco I later converted a part of it to an art gallery. It is to Anna Maria Luisa's credit that she donated the family's art treasures to the Florentine people, stipulating that the collection must be kept eternally on display to the public, and that nothing could ever be removed from it.

And here those treasures still are, to be admired by all who have had the stamina to stand in line before the Uffizi for hours—or, like me, arrived in the November rain and walked straight in.

Here are Giotto's madonnas bathing in a golden sea, Filippo Lippi's fresh pastel madonnas, Piero della Francesca's *Duke and Duchess of Urbino*, and Leonardo's astonishing *Annunciation*, in which the twentysomething painter rendered the angel's wings with scientific precision, on the model of birds' wings. Here are scandalous paintings intended for private bedrooms, like Botticelli's *Birth of Venus* and *Spring*, the model for both of which, legend has it, was Renaissance Florence's most beautiful woman, Simonetta Vespucci; or Tizian's *Venus of Urbino*, whose commissioner apparently waited impatiently for it to be finished so the naked lounging Venus could serve as an exemplar and guide to his thirteen-year-old bride. Here is also Michelangelo's *Doni Tondo*, a round panel painting of the holy family, famous as the artist's only such painting. Michelangelo hated painting above all else—compared with sculpture, it was a complete waste of time, he thought—so he only finished two paintings in his life, this panel and the frescoes in the Sistine Chapel. He only agreed to do that latter work through gritted teeth, because he was paid well for it. *Okay, let's slap this up there then*, he snorted, and slapped it up on the ceiling of the Sistine Chapel so fast that later generations have never been able to understand how he did it.

If my purpose has been to find women in Florence, there are plenty of them here on the walls of the Uffizi: madonnas, Mary Magdalenes, Eves, Medici wives and mothers and sisters and daughters, unknown nuns, dignified noblewomen, serving girls rummaging through trousseau chests, artists' girlfriends, devout wives, and seductive Venuses—most of them nameless, representing someone else.

Finding female *artists*, however, is like looking for a needle in a haystack.

Do they even exist?

Stefano decamps to London for a few days, and I begin to hunt for women. I gather my books about Renaissance Florence around me on the big bed in his (former) bedroom and start wading through them. The names of artists, fresco painters, and architects roll about on my tongue like deliciously crackling candies (I read them aloud over and over, exaggerating the Italian pronunciations, taking a strange satisfaction in them). They are undeniably gorgeous (*Michelangelo*), somehow flower-scented (*Fra' Angelico*), or mosaically crisp (*Brunelleschi*), or bring to mind a spinning dance (*Ghirlandaio*), while the names of the wealthy power families—*Sforza, Strozzi, Pazzi, Pitti*—exude strength and mysterious luxury. (I later learn that they mean "force," "strangling," "insanity," and "extortion.")

But they're all men.

I read about the Medici women, the mothers, daughters, and wives, some of whom, like Caterina and Maria, ended up queens in France. I read about the women in the Uffizi, those noble wives who appear in the portraits with ethereal white faces.

I read about the style gurus, the dispensers of beauty tips, and fashion pioneers like Caterina Sforza or Isabella d'Este (later Gonzaga), who had their fingers so sensitively on the pulse that France's King Louis XII urged his wife not to travel to Italy, because the fashionable attire of these "d'Este women" would leave her in their shadow. Isabella was also a passionate collector of art and cultural treasures; in her *studiolo* in Mantua she collected the best artists' paintings, sculptures, cameos, and exquisitely illustrated books, as well as nonpareils from the teeth of strange fish to a unicorn horn—something that was a required object in all collections, because only a virgin could hunt one.

But right now I'm not excited about exemplary beauties, aristocratic movers and shakers, or devout saints. I'm tracking other game.

When you look at the women on the Uffizi walls—the sweet madonnas, the foam-born Venuses, the noblewomen in their radiant dresses—you might think that women were respected in the Renaissance, but it's beginning to be clear to me just how much suffering lay behind all that beauty. Florence was a city for men—and women were their property. The women belonged as virgins to their fathers, as wives to their husbands, and as widows to their sons, and they were expected to adhere at all times to the strictest possible chastity, humility, devotion, and obedience.

Simplifying only slightly, we can say that women in those days had roughly three options: a) get married, b) hie them to a nunnery, or c) become prostitutes. Especially for the daughters of good families, marriage was a must; but given the high cost of dowries, families could often afford to marry off only one or two daughters—any more than that had to be packed off to convents. Poor unmarried girls often became servants, and their fate was, among other things, to offer the man of the house and his sons sexual favors. The offspring from such unions were sent to orphanages, after which the girl in question might become a wet nurse for the heir born to the official wife. In addition to breast milk, poor girls would also sell their hair: men's wigs were made of horsehair, sheep's wool, straw, and the hair of the dead, but the best and most expensive were made from serving girls' curls. To some extent, women worked in artisan occupations as well, for example as weavers, spinners, and slipper-makers, or as wine and oil merchants, wool and silk merchants, innkeepers, and money-lenders; there were also female slaves in Florence, many of them Slavs or Tatars, some Russians, Greeks, or Africans. The asking price for a slave in the market was fifty florins; if a gentleman happened to buy a female slave who had been impregnated by her previous owner, he could demand compensation for damaged goods.

If the lot of poor girls wasn't easy, things weren't much better among noblewomen, even when they found themselves in option a), marriage. The daughters of noble families were married off young, at around twelve or thirteen, as soon as their periods started, because virginity was a bride's most important quality. The father chose the groom from a family with which he needed to strengthen relations, and the groom was typically ten or even twenty years older than the bride. After that, the bride's task was to give birth to as many heirs as possible, and it was quite common for a woman to be constantly pregnant from the age of fifteen on, giving birth to ten or so children, of whom perhaps three or four would survive to maturity. Immediately after birth, the babies were given to wet nurses or sent to the countryside to grow up in healthier conditions; that way the woman could get pregnant again right away, and wouldn't feel so bad if the baby happened to die. But for many women, pregnancies and deliveries were fatal.

If you saw women in the Florence streets at all, they were mainly servants or prostitutes. Noblewomen spent their days at home. Their lives passed in the shelter of the palazzos, because moving about in public was not considered suitable for respectable women, unless to go to church. The only physical exertion allowed them was giving birth. Women were also not allowed to vote or take part in politics or the parades organized by the magnificent Lorenzo, so during feast days they followed the festivities through their bedroom windows. (I decide from now on to focus my search for women on palazzo bedrooms, kitchens, and toilets, for these are apparently the rare portals into the world where generation after generation women did after all live, always giving birth to and then raising the latest crop of significant men.)

But whether she went outside or not, every noblewoman spent

endless time looking after her appearance. The beauty ideal was white skin and light-colored hair, which hardly anyone had naturally. The beauty treatments they used were painful and the substances they contained often harmful, even poisonous. For example, hair color was lightened with a liquid that contained lemon and urine—either one's own or obtained from a horse. With this pee solvent in their hair, the women would sit on the roofs of their palazzos in the hot sun for days, weeks, and even months, protecting their faces with floppy hats with a hole cut out for the hair. Nor was burning their hair blond (or, failing that, strawberry blond) enough—they also had to lengthen their foreheads upward by plucking the hairline higher. A tall forehead was a sign of intelligence. They also plucked out their eyebrows and eyelashes. In addition, they bleached their faces with "maiden's milk" prepared from lead acetate, which made the face look like a mask, but also damaged the skin and made large craters in it. Most fashionable of all was a kind of *corpse look*—a bare, expressionless whiteness. The most perfect representation of that look on the walls of the Uffizi is of Battista Sforza, whose portrait was painted after she died.

And what of option b)? Those daughters of good families who for financial reasons couldn't be married off were sent to nunneries in good time, at the latest at age nine, so there could be no threat to their virginity. Women did become nuns for religious reasons as well, of course; but for the most part those institutions were storage units for unmarriageable daughters, and you ended up in one against your will. And in case one of the nuns might be planning to escape, or to break her vow of chastity, nunneries were conveniently surrounded by high walls. (Clearly this was not enough protection, for in one Florentine nunnery two nuns gave birth in 1460.) In a way, nunneries were like women's prisons. There was, however, an upside: they gave women a rare opportunity for erudition and the creation of art. Many nuns lined their chambers with books, and read and painted. For example, in the seventeenth century the Venetian Arcangela Tarabotti spent more than three decades in a nunnery against her will, and used her time writing. In her writings that survive—especially *Convent Hell* and *Paternal Tyranny*, neither of which was allowed to be published in her lifetime—she zealously defended the female sex, criticized greedy fathers' habit of locking their daughters up in convents when they didn't want to pay their dowries, and demanded freedom and the right to study for women. You go, Arcangela! Night women!

And if the excess daughters of good families ended up nuns, the daughters of the underclasses ended up c) whores. In Renaissance Italy, prostitution was more accepted and more common than ever before or since in human history—Venice was actually known as a "big bordello," with catalogues printed up for the travelers flooding into the city of the most respected ladies of the evening, with their addresses and prices. These were educated women who could converse about Petrarchan sonnets, sing arias, and play the lute—in addition to their skills in the bedroom. But there was no shortage of practitioners of the profession in Florence either, and municipal bordellos began to be built there in the 1350s. In the fifteenth century Florence created a government office that determined prostitutes' prices and decreed "moral protections": working girls were to signal their profession by wearing gloves on their hands, bells on their heads, and high heels on their feet, and to stay as far as possible from convents and monasteries and the districts where respectable women lived.

So, which option would I choose—a), b), or c)?

Would I spend my life sitting on the roof of my palazzo with pee solvent in my hair and my face cratered from lead poisoning—or rather, all that whenever I wasn't giving birth? I'd have beautiful clothes and expensive jewelry, but part of the deal would be a ban on going out in public. I'd probably die in childbed.

Or would I live celibate in a women's prison disguised as a nunnery or convent? I'd be able to read, write, and paint, but I could never have children or men.

Or would I opt for "freedom"? I'd be able to move about in the city, socialize with men, and do everything women were mostly forbidden to do. The only downside would be sex work, venereal disease, accusations of witchcraft, and dying in miserable conditions.

Option d), anyone?

At night I think about Battista Sforza—the beautiful women in the Uffizi paintings have begun to torment me. I saw her today in the gallery, surrounded by a human wall of admirers, and her death portrait has been tattooed on my inner eyelids ever since. In the painting she looks aloof, calm, and perfect. Her skin is lead-pale, her forehead high, and her blond hair has been braided into a bun at her ear. Her pearls and jewels gleam; on her throat there is a dark line, as if from the bottom of the death mask.

The biography of Battista Sforza (1447–1472) swirls through my imagination like a broken record.

Was given a humanistic education rare for a girl,
was talented and smart,
spoke Greek and Latin fluently,
was unbeatable in rhetoric,
was married at thirteen to the Duke of Urbino (a widow twenty-four years older than Battista),
began to give birth,
between thirteen and twenty-three had six daughters,
the seventh was at last a boy,
no longer recovered from her delivery,
died.

While Battista was lying on her deathbed, her husband brought in Piero della Francesca to paint her portrait. The artist succeeded brilliantly: Battista became a beauty ideal, and nowadays the painting of Battista and her husband is one of the most famous in the Uffizi.

But when I think at night about Battista and her career as a baby-making machine, I feel like crying. In the recesses of the Internet, I find a picture of her clay-cast death mask, and there is no idealized pale beauty in it. There's only the face of a very tired dead woman: an ancient twenty-five-year-old Battista ravaged by seven pregnancies, exhausted forever.

I think of Beatrice d'Este at night as well. I think about how people writing about her portrait always focus on her gorgeous jewelry and hairdo—*here is a splendid example of a* coazzone, *a thick braid attached elegantly with a hairnet*, as the explanatory plaque on the Uffizi wall notes. Sure, the braid's pretty, but to my eye she looks a little pissed off. Her mouth is compressed into a pretty-fucking-sick-of-this-shit look, and her eyes stare blankly, seeing nothing. I think her whole being is screaming silently: *Jesus F. Christ*. Or maybe she's just decisive.

Maybe the portrait doesn't do her justice, as according to the stories Beatrice d'Este (1475–1497) was the embodiment of perfect womanhood. She was born into a wealthy family, and was famous not just for her beauty but for her impeccable taste in matters of style, and she and her big sister Isabella d'Este were trendsetters whom all Europe emulated.

Beatrice was affianced at the ripe age of five to Ludovico il Moro, who was twenty-three years her senior. They were married when Beatrice was fifteen, with Leonardo da Vinci in charge of the wedding ceremony—in those days he was attached to the Milan court as a kind of genius-at-large. It is said that Beatrice's diplomatic skills rivaled her husband's, and when she was sixteen he sent her to Venice as his ambassador to promote his ambition to be named Duke of Milan. At twenty, sitting at the table during peace negotiations, she reportedly showed great diplomatic tact and skill. Beatrice and Ludovico's court was a great success, and Beatrice gathered into that court the best scholars, poets, and artists of the day. In addition, she gave birth to two sons, both of whom later became Dukes of Milan. In short, Beatrice was perfect: a beautiful, talented, stylish, highly educated exemplar for all women.

That is, until she was twenty-one. Then she perished in childbed, giving birth to a stillborn son.

The stories of the talented Uffizi women speed by in fast-forward. No wonder they're pissed off.

I sleep badly and wake up in the morning with a headache, so I decide to spend the day doing laundry in a laundromat down the street.

I pop into the corner restaurant to grab a bite to eat and order a truffle pizza, which is gigantic in diameter but thin as paper—I gulp it down almost without stopping to take a breath, as if afraid that if I lay down my fork it'll be snatched away. I wonder whether there's something instantly addictive about truffles, some heroin-type ingredient: the instant you get a taste of it on your tongue, you can't stop shoveling it in till the last crumb has been devoured.

In the afternoon I lie in bed feeling incapacitated. I google news of the Finnish book world and speculate about it with my friend Buz over Skype. I think again what a blessing modern technology is, that I don't need to do what Isabella d'Este's friend living in Ferrara did: put Isabella's portrait in front of her as she ate so she could imagine she was sitting across the table from her. In 1498, Isabella asked her friend Cecilia (who by the way was the lover of that pissed-off Beatrice's husband) to send her the portrait Leonardo da Vinci had just painted of Cecilia, to have a look at. Cecilia promised to send the painting—which we now know as *Lady with an Ermine*—but complained that it was no longer all that realistic: she had aged, and the dress and hairdo in it were no longer in fashion. Isabella too had portraits of herself made so she could send them to her friends, but all too often was dissatisfied with them. In one, for example, she thought she looked fat, and was not at all pleased when her brother-in-law called it an excellent likeness.

I think of all these portrait women I've been running after here: the Uffizi women, the artists' girlfriends posing as madonnas, the young girls in the frescoes who look straight at the viewer. I think of the portable portraits with folding covers; the portraits painted of young noble girls to send all over Europe as advertisements in the marriage market; the portraits painted at the last moment, on the subject's deathbed.

Then I think of the people hawking selfie sticks on the bridge over the Arno. (No, I didn't buy one.) I think of the photo I took of myself in the blackened mirror in a boudoir in the medieval Palazzo Davanzati: the only way I could think to situate myself in these women's world.

I also think of the photographs of Isabella, Ida, Mary, and Nellie:

the gazes, hairdos, clothes, innocent-looking sunshades and globes recorded in their portraits—all the messages those things are designed to send, and the other messages that they are designed to suppress and hide, which nevertheless flicker shadowlike in the background. I think about how a picture often seems to be telling one story but concealing another.

Then I wonder whether I might find, here in Florence, night women who didn't just pose for the gaze of others, but did their own painting. Are there, somewhere, images painted by women? Are there visual stories told by women about the lives of women?

If there are, that would mean that someone did manage to actualize option d).

I do know that female artists have historically been rare as unicorns' horns. If you flip through the thick catalogues of art history, you don't find many in the earlier centuries. Women have always been acceptable as models and muses, of course, but it has always been much harder to actually become an artist: women have not been allowed to study, and the assumption has long been that their creativity is basically suited to handicrafts, such as weaving tapestries and doing embroidery. And while some women have indeed become artists, they have often had to work in secret, and their works have not been publicly displayed. Many times their work has been attributed to men—and many works attributed to men have only been identified as actually created by women in the past few decades. And those women who have in their lifetimes become acclaimed artists have for one reason or another been forgotten, left out of the history books, their works ignored in the corners of museum storerooms for centuries, turning black, at the mercy of rats, pigeon poop, and moisture. In the corridors of the Uffizi, for example, you can wear your feet down to nubbins looking for a single painting by a female artist; and precisely those galleries where works by the precious few female artists should be hanging always seem to be closed for renovations, or else somehow keep magically avoiding my path.

I have, however, managed to see a single work by a single female artist here, a painting of Christ being taken down off the cross by a Florentine nun named Plautilla Nelli. Nunneries, after all—option b)—were among the few places where women could develop themselves, and artistically talented nuns could, for example, paint illustrations in prayer books. Sister Plautilla Nelli (1524–1588) lived in the (now defunct) Dominican Santa Caterina di Siena convent from a very young age, and according to reports was a self-taught and quite productive artist, and evidently also famous, because her paintings of saints were found "in so many Florentine gentlemen's homes that it would be tedious to mention them all," as Giorgio Vasari noted in his *Lives of the Most Excellent Painters, Sculptors, and Architects*. Only a few of Plautilla's paintings have survived, however. One of them is on display in the former convent (now an art museum) on the Piazza San Marco, where it has recently been retrieved from the deeper recesses of the basement and restored. The large painting is colorful and touching; the eyes of the women grieving for Jesus are swollen from crying and their noses are red. Her male figures have sometimes been criticized as being more like women, or else as if assembled from disparate parts, but can you blame her? Life as a nun would tend to place certain restrictions on one's access to naked male bodies. Another surviving work by her, the seven-meter-long *Last Supper*—her true *opus magnus*—should really be world-famous, because it is the *only* last supper known to have been painted by a woman. In addition to the traditional bread and wine, Plautilla also put salad, beans, and a whole roasted lamb on the table, which to my mind not only works as religious symbolism but shows a most excellent womanly feeling for the situation: who would want just bread for his last supper? It's just a pity that this rare work is rotting away on the wall of the Santa Maria Novella convent dining room, where it cannot be viewed by outsiders.

My time in Florence is running short. Returning home one day, I bump into Benedetto—he's standing outside the downstairs door, smoking. I tell him that I only have one week left, and that it would be nice to see "you two" someday. "You can come ring the doorbell anytime," he says. The doorbell! In Finland we don't just go ringing doorbells! "But this is Ita-aalia," Benedetto says with a capacious wave of his hand.

Benedetto also delivers the day's political sermon. In a nutshell: over the past twenty years, Italy has been ruined. The politicians are crooks; it's impossible to get work; the big banks are running the country. He isn't satisfied with his own life either. He graduated top of his class at the university in Milan, and works as a consultant for a multinational insurance company—and hates every second of the work. I ask what he'd rather be doing. "It wouldn't be possible anyway," he says. But in a perfect world, what would his dream be? "I'd like to live in Rome and teach, either in the schools or the university." A fortysomething PhD would like to teach his own subject. As dreams go, that doesn't sound exactly over-the-top.

In the evening Stefano is at home, and we sit in the kitchen, each of us eating our own food. Stefano shows me pictures from his spring trip to New York and plays Frank Sinatra on vinyl. He tells me about his plan to drop out of university and study to be an artisan in the leather industry. He's not particularly excited about the switch, but says it's the most sensible thing to do. He tells me young people in Italy are desperate, because there is no work and study doesn't guarantee you anything, but maybe he could get work in the leather field because of his family background. Then he reveals what he would like most to do: write a novel.

In bed I reflect on how everybody in this world seems to want to do something other than what they're doing right now, and how for various reasons they can't do what they'd like to do. Benedetto would like to teach, Stefano would like to write, the noblewomen in the Renaissance would undoubtedly have preferred to do something other than give birth.

I think of a fact I heard at the yoga retreat in Kyoto: that over the years human cells are renewed so thoroughly that by our forties there is little left in any of us of what we were as children.

Suddenly I realize that cell renewal can be used to explain practically everything. If you want to leave your boyfriend: "Listen, my cells got renewed." Or if you want to become a writer even though you should be accruing your pension, or you want to become the kind of person who goes around ringing doorbells without waiting for an invitation—blame it all on the new cells. Cell renewal makes everything possible: a new life, a new attitude, literal rebirth.

A renaissance.

During my last days in Florence, I start panicking: Where all do I still have time to go? I go back to the Santa Trinita church and drop a coin in the metal box, and the lamp illuminating the frescoes comes on. There again is the whole Sassetti family: the banker himself, his wife, his daughters, his sons and sons-in-law, as well as a selection of the cream of Florence, beginning with Francesco Sassetti's boss, Lorenzo de' Medici, and ending with the artist himself, Domenico Ghirlandaio, the city's most illustrious fresco-maker.

But my eyes are fixed on Sassetti's daughters. I can't stop looking at them. One of them, the youngest, meets my gaze. *I'm next,* she's saying. *I'm ready for impregnation. You can marry me. My tummy's a little round, you see, I've begun menstruating, I can give birth to your descendants. Interested?*

Or maybe she's saying: *Save me.*

And then on my way home, I find it—at last! I step into a bookstore near the Duomo and know instantly that this is exactly what I've been looking for all these weeks. On the bottom shelf in the section of books in English is a book titled *Invisible Women: Forgotten Artists of Florence.* Its author has tracked down every artwork by a female artist on display in Florence and mapped their locations. It's like a map to secret treasure.

Three of them get my heart pounding: Sofonisba Anguissola, a noblewoman from Cremona; Lavinia Fontana, the daughter of an artist from Bologna; and Artemisia Gentileschi, who was born in Rome.

They successfully lived option d).

Their paintings are hidden in this city.

And I only have a few days left to find them.

On the day of the Florence Marathon, there's no one in the Uffizi. I rush through the empty galleries in a fever of excitement, first stopping to greet my old friends on the walls. I note that Battista's hair looks a bit hempy at the ends (sorry, Battista); but I shouldn't be too harsh, after all she's dead. I goggle at Beatrice's jewels for a moment; they nearly tumble out of the painting at me, so realistically are they rendered, and it must be admitted that her hair occupies pride of place in the painting, as if she were sitting there as a hair model. And how have I not noticed the black bags under her eyes before now? I reflect again on how astonishingly different it is to study the actual paintings versus photographs of them. (Things that make traveling worthwhile: to experience artworks live.) I greet Meryl Streep, a.k.a. Maria Bonciani, a Florentine banker's wife whose head is too big and long in the Flemish style—she somewhat resembles a space creature, but is nonetheless strangely fascinating. I cast a longing glance at Filippo Lippi's delectable girlfriend Lucrezia Buti, whom he liberated from a nunnery and here depicted as a madonna. I pass Eleanor of Toledo, who sits in her massive dress with a small boy next to her, a potential Medici ruler—she has apparently performed her reproductive duties successfully. As I walk by I call out *ciao bella* to Simonetta standing naked in a seashell, and think that she must be Florence's most famous woman: when she died of tuberculosis at twenty-two, her coffin was carried around town so that all could admire her beauty, and even today her face travels to all corners of the world with hundreds of tourists on postcards, stamps, fridge magnets, and the covers of every single art book.

But I can't find Sofonisba's and Lavinia's paintings. Galleries 33 and 34, where my treasure map says their work should be, are closed, and I'm only allowed to peek into the gallery of miniatures from the doorway, so there's no way I can see any works by female artists hidden there. No wonder I haven't found them!

Then suddenly I'm in the Caravaggio gallery, in the corner of which hangs a painting oozing with grim violence. Its name is *Judith Slaying Holofernes*; in it a woman in a yellow silk dress has rolled up her sleeves to slit a man's throat with her sword. He's dying; the blood spurts onto the white sheets; another woman, a servant, holds the writhing man down on the bed with strong arms. The strength in Judith and the serving woman roll off them like a shock wave. Their gazes are calm and determined. The man, however, is panicking: the battle is still on. I can almost hear his death rattle. . . .

I glance down at the name plaque. Artemisia Gentileschi.

She painted this here in Florence four hundred years ago.

Hoo! What a night woman.

When I get home, I think feverishly that I must get to the mysterious Vasari Corridor in the Uffizi. According to my treasure map, that's where these night women are, goddammit! That's where the self-portraits are of the few female artists of the Italian Renaissance, rare as unicorns' horns.

The half-mile-long corridor, built over the Arno River and named for its designer, Giorgio Vasari, was commissioned by Cosimo I de' Medici as a private passageway from the family's Pitti palazzo to the Uffizi. Nowadays it holds the Uffizi's massive collection of artists' self-portraits. The collection, which runs from the sixteenth century to today, contains 1,600 self-portraits—93 percent of them male, of course, but I've read that twenty or so women have made it onto the walls. (Heaps of night women huddle about in storage as well—for example, Patti Smith.) I plan to find Sofonisba and Lavinia, by hook or by crook.

I manage to get myself a spot on the exclusive and annoyingly expensive ninety-minute guided tour of the Vasari Corridor—the only way to get in to see the night women face-to-face. The tour begins with a romp through the highlights of the Uffizi, and I stand impatiently through seeing the Lippis, the Botticellis, the Leonardos, the Tizians, and—ooh!—that solitary Michelangelo painting one more time. Then the guard opens a barely noticeable door in a wall, and suddenly we're in the famous corridor. It meanders up and down stairs, sometimes opening onto narrow hundred-meter straightaways with both walls filled with double rows of portraits. Through round barred portholes I can see the river and the Ponte Vecchio, where the sellers of gold jewelry and selfie sticks hawk their wares. Our guide leads us like a herd of cattle down the corridor, now and then stopping to deliver a little lecture on something or other; I listen with one ear while scanning the walls for the women. "The self-portrait collection is arranged chronologically . . ." I hear the guide explaining, but here in the sixteenth century there's nothing, not a sign of a woman. The group moves on and I struggle to keep up, can't be left behind, there are explicit rules against that, and the guard stares in stony warning as I dash back and forth across the narrow corridor from wall to wall. I'm dripping with sweat, but it makes no difference: Zip. Nada. Not a single female artist on these walls!

Then finally I find Sofonisba in the wrong century, surrounded by bewigged eighteenth-century men. The guide and the herd have passed her by without a word (what could possibly be interesting here, the first woman in the last hundred meters?), but there she is, with her big, intelligent eyes, gazing calmly straight into mine.

In the midst of all the pretentious men in wigs, Sofonisba's self-portrait is somehow preternaturally real and human. She's only twenty—she painted her self-portrait in 1550 to celebrate her birthday in Cremona. No pee-bleached hair, no precious stones or embroidered silk dress—just a plain black dress, light-brown hair pulled back, her bare sincere face, a piece of paper in one hand and a palette and brush in the other. *I paint*, Sofonisba says. *You do whatever you like, but I paint.* I stare into her eyes until the guard comes to rush me along.

I've found them. The women who did what they wanted.

SOFONISBA

NIGHT WOMEN'S ADVICE 7

You do whatever you like. I paint.

NIGHT WOMAN #7: *Sofonisba Anguissola*
PROFESSION: *Daughter of a noble family, later the first free woman artist and exemplar for all women artists. Wound up working in the Spanish court. Painted an extraordinary number of self-portraits.*

I fall head over heels in love with Sofonisba. Out of her many self-portraits she always gazes at me with a friendly and peaceful but serenely self-confident look, as if she knows exactly who she is. No wonder: she is the first woman to win fame as a professional artist and support herself with her work.

Sofonisba Anguissola (ca. 1532–1625) was born and raised in a family of the lower aristocracy in the city of Cremona, in what is now northern Italy. It may be that her father could not afford dowries for all six of his daughters, for he settled early on an extremely unusual course of action: to have his daughters educated. Whereas typically the daughters of "good" families were at most given lessons in music and embroidery (both useful not only for future wives but for future nuns), Amilcare Anguissola decided to apply the principles laid out in Castiglione's super-popular *Book of the Courtier* to his daughters and have them study Latin and Greek as well as painting—even if that ruined their chances of getting married.

And so at fourteen the family's oldest daughter, Sofonisba, along with her sister Elena, began studying with Bernardino Campi, a portrait and fresco painter from Cremona who was one of the first to take in female students. The girls lived with Campi's family, and because it wasn't suitable for them to be in the workshop where men were working, they most likely practiced drawing and preparing equipment for painting in Mrs. Campi's kitchen. (Not to disparage kitchens and their resources: a few years earlier, Properzia de' Rossi from Bologna, who dreamed of becoming a sculptor, carved incredible miniature sculptures and full-body images out of plum pits, since no other materials were available.) Sofonisba learned to prime canvas and wood panels, to make a glue base of dried hare leather, to spread thin layers of chalk powder or gypsum on it, to cook oil from linseed or walnuts and lead, and to mix the pigments from mineral ingredients—all very laborious and time-consuming. Because it was, naturally, out of the question for her to draw a nude model, she had to learn anatomy from her own body. But Sofonisba was extremely gifted. At eighteen she painted a canvas depicting Bernardino Campi painting her portrait—in a way, *creating* Sofonisba. It would appear that the process of creation had been completed, and the artist Sofonisba born.

In 1554, twenty-two-year-old Sofonisba traveled to Rome to study with Michelangelo himself, then a seventy-nine-year-old master whose influence on the artists of the day was massive. The trip was arduous: from Cremona it was some three hundred miles to Rome, which in carriages meant about a three-week journey. She was accompanied by the mandatory chaperone and a couple of servants, and took with her a *cassone*, a gorgeously engraved and painted oaken trousseau chest filled with silk and velvet dresses and painting equipment—appropriate, in fact, since she was clearly planning to choose work over a husband. Virtually no information about her time in Rome has survived, but we do know that Rome back then was a pretty shopworn place whose days of restored glory were still ahead: sheep grazed around the ruins half-buried in the Roman Forum; grapes were raised for wine on the Palatine Hill; and the epitome of Rome's degradation was that the great monuments of antiquity were treated as sources of free building materials. (The outer ring of the Colosseum had been half carted away; it was like a great overgrown garden, in which people lived.) Michelangelo for his part was known as an arrogant, difficult, and stingy hermit who never changed his clothes (that would have cut into his working day) and lived in a tiny shack near the Imperial Fora (the vast fortune he'd earned would only become known after his death), so I can't help but wonder what Sofonisba's encounters with him must have been like. But evidently the serenely wonderful Sofonisba made an impression on the genius: Michelangelo gave her drawings to copy, commented on her work, and advised her on problems of anatomy and perspective; and later in a letter, her father thanked Michelangelo for all the praise that the master had heaped on his daughter's drawings. And perhaps Michelangelo's connections had something to do with the fact that at the end of Sofonisba's stay in Rome she delivered a self-portrait she'd painted to the pope himself.

Upon her return to Cremona, Sofonisba continued to practice, industriously painting portraits of her family—in one such portrait her father, Amilcare, and her little sisters exchange sweet looks, and even the family's scruffy dog has an innocent look in its eye. In that same year, 1555, she painted what has become her most famous painting, *The Chess Game*, featuring three of her sisters—Minerva, Europa, and Lucia—playing chess in the garden. Sofonisba rendered the young women with an unprecedentedly relaxed and vivid hand; her sisters' intelligence and sense of humor shine from the painting. The subject was also revolutionary: it is the first known painting to depict family life realistically.

While Sofonisba painted these historical family portraits at home, Amilcare was out working as her manager. Quoting Michelangelo's praise, he marketed his daughter's skill to the Cremona nobles so effectively that many clamored for her to paint their portraits. With her father's connections, portrait orders began to come in from farther afield as well, and Sofonisba traveled to Piacenza, Mantua, Milan, and other places for work. Society circles marveled at a young noblewoman arriving in town with her painting box and canvases. In fact, the whole freethinking Anguissola family caused a stir. Was it possible that women were capable of such things? Or was Sofonisba just some freak of nature possible only in Cremona? In contemporary accounts, Sofonisba was truly regarded as an anomaly, an extreme exception to womankind in general. She was clearly "a male soul born in a woman's body," or else she belonged to some third gender. This was certainly not normal.

Many of her self-portraits from this period survive—to be precise, thirteen—and it's the self-portraits that make me love her. Her big eyes gaze straight at me out of the paintings, curious and modestly self-confident. In the self-portraits of her youth, Sofonisba always appears in a simple black dress with her hair braided back: no makeup, no jewelry, no fancy dresses, no breathtaking hairdos, or dogs to symbolize marital fidelity, or anything else hinting at vanity. Her natural appearance is the opposite of the highly decorative feminine ideal of the time. It's almost as if Sofonisba were emphasizing what she knew too well: that she was an exception. In some self-portraits she has painted herself holding a brush and palette; in others she is next to an unfinished painting; in some she is playing the clavichord; and sometimes the self-portrait is just a tiny and extremely accomplished miniature on a medallion. On the paintings she did in her younger years she wrote the advertisement: Sophonisba Anguissola, a virgin from Cremona, painted this herself with the aid of a mirror, and she was indeed a sensation worthy of being advertised. The self-portrait as an independent artistic genre was still a fairly new and rare thing—Albrecht Dürer had painted the first such just a few decades earlier. And in fact, the kind of proper mirror that one needed to paint a self-portrait was a new technology as well: while mirrors made of polished metal had been around since antiquity, it wasn't until the turn of the sixteenth century that the glass artists on the island of Murano in Venice had come up with the idea of adding a compound of tin and mercury to the surface of a sheet of glass, thus creating a precise reflection. It was with the help of such a rare gizmo that Sofonisba was now painting. It was worth emphasizing that a woman had painted her self-portrait with her own hand; it was even more important to sign the painting as a "maiden," as if to assure the viewer that this unmarried daughter of a noble family was, despite her unusual pursuits, nevertheless chaste. In fact, she often painted her self-portraits for marketing purposes; the miniatures especially were well suited as calling cards to potential clients. In one miniature self-portrait, Sofonisba holds her family shield in her hand, as if to advertise the female wunderkind of this Anguissola family from Cremona; in another the marketing text is written on an open book that Sofonisba is holding. I can't help but envy the skill with which this novice professional marketed herself, and how knowledge of her expertise spread through the network that joined the noble families from different cities—without the Internet! *Brava*, Sofonisba.

In 1558, twenty-six-year-old Sofonisba traveled to Milan to paint the portrait of the Duke of Alba, and this trip changed her life. The duke was so impressed with this unusual noblewoman's skills that he wrote about her to the King of Spain, and urged Sofonisba to send a painting to the court as a sample. Sofonisba painted a palm-size self-portrait and put it in the mail. The painting served as a persuasive job application: King Philip II of Spain invited Sofonisba to come to Madrid as soon as possible to join the court. He needed this sort of artistic companion for his fourteen-year-old fiancée, Elisabeth de Valois, who would soon be arriving from Paris.

Sofonisba almost certainly received this invitation with mixed feelings: it was of course a great honor to be invited to join the court of Europe's most powerful ruler, but Madrid was a long way away. On the other hand, she also had to consider the financial implications: as an unmarried woman she was still her father's property, but a place at court would transfer the responsibility for her upkeep to the King of Spain, and thus reduce her father's financial burden for his six unmarried daughters. Amilcare traveled to Milan to consider the matter, and then wrote his approval to the king in September 1559: "However, at the same time, it was a great sorrow to me and my family, to see my beloved daughter go so far away. . . ." Though perhaps Amilcare wasn't so sad after all—this may, in fact, have been precisely the hoped-for outcome toward which he had been striving in having his daughters educated: a well-paid job in a royal court, dowry on the house, one daughter taken care of.

And so Sofonisba packed her painting gear in her *cassone* and sailed to Spain—and didn't see her family again for twelve years. The royal wedding was held in the Guadalajara palace, and the history books report that Sofonisba, that "Cremonese woman who paints," made an impression in the torch dance, which conjured up a memorable magical atmosphere in the dark of the night. And what do you know, Sofonisba and the young bride, now Queen Isabel, hit it off right from the start.

There were hundreds of workers in Queen Isabel's household, almost a small city of them: from stable boys, servants, cooks, and scullery maids to tapestry weavers, embroiderers, goldsmiths, physicians, musicians, butlers, confessors, and ladies-in-waiting. Sofonisba's position in the court was unique: she had been invited as a court painter, but since her status as a noblewoman was higher than her status as an artist, she was also given the title lady-in-waiting. She did not sit around making idle conversation, however; she was a busy, multi-skilled professional who worked as a lady-in-waiting, art teacher, and portraitist. She played the clavichord with Isabel, taught her to draw and paint, and helped design the queen's sumptuous dresses. Both women felt a passion for expensive Italian fabrics, the purchase of which Isabel sometimes entrusted to Sofonisba, and it became Sofonisba's trademark to paint the dresses in portraits with exquisite detail. Because, yes, she did paint. When the pope sent a letter asking for a portrait of the charming young Isabel, Sofonisba painted it and sent it to the Vatican. When Isabel's mother, Caterina de' Medici, missed her daughter in Paris, Sofonisba painted another portrait and sent it off. Sofonisba was paid handsomely for her work—though sometimes her salary was paid in jewels and fabrics, for silks embroidered with gold or silver thread, brocades, and silk satins were as good as cash. Beginning in June of 1560, Sofonisba was paid 100 ducats a year for herself and additional salaries for her lady's maid and stableboy, as well as money for candles, laundry services, and feed for a horse or mule (apparently the equivalent back then of today's company car). For painting King Philip's portrait, Sofonisba was granted a lifetime pension of 200 ducats, paid to her father; and for painting the portrait of the prince, she was given a diamond worth 1,500 scudos. All in all, she did the work for which she was trained and was paid a salary for doing it that made her rich and enabled her to support her family in Cremona—an unheard-of thing for an unmarried noblewoman in the Renaissance. Unfortunately, she didn't sign the paintings she did at court, so many of them got mixed up with the paintings of male court painters, and ended up lying forgotten in random places, their glory ebbed.

Sofonisba spent nine years in the court with Isabel, until the queen died of complications from a miscarriage in 1568 at the age of twenty-three. This was Isabel's fourth pregnancy. She had given birth to two daughters previously, who were two and three years old at her death, and lost twins in an earlier miscarriage—and now she was dead as well. This was the life of a noblewoman on fast-forward, option a). I can only imagine how Sofonisba felt. She was thirty-six. Would she have liked to have kids and a family herself, or was she just relieved that her unusual career-woman status helped her dodge the baby-making-machine bullet that dropped so many women into the grave decades before their husbands? She did grieve for her friend and employer, Isabel.

After Isabel's death, the king began to consider marrying Sofonisba off. As her caretaker, he had a duty to find her a suitable husband; and because Sofonisba had requested that this man at least be Italian, a certain nobleman was given the task of finding a husband candidate in Cremona. Wonderful Sofonisba had had plenty of suitors in earlier years, but now the task proved difficult—maybe the image of a fortyish career woman scared the men. Messengers brought a steady stream of discouraging reports: *So-and-so was interested in the above-mentioned lady before, but no longer. . . . Marriage is out of the question. . . . The gentleman in question would be interested in marrying this Sofonisba if he were given the governance of Novara* [which was declined]. . . . *In order to bring this matter to an expeditious conclusion, I would like to know what exactly Your Highness intends to give the man who marries this Sofonisba. . . .* While these messages were flying back and forth between Italy and Spain, Sofonisba concentrated on caring for Isabel's tiny daughters, and painting the girls on canvas with their pet dogs and birds. And finally in 1573—after four years of searching—a husband was found for Sofonisba in Don Fabrizio de Moncada, a Sicilian prince. The wedding was arranged in the royal chapel (the groom wasn't able to attend, but sent his representative), and then Sofonisba traveled to her new husband's hometown, Palermo. As a dowry Sofonisba received the 1,500 maravedis and massive trousseau (including not only linen and clothing but jewels, silver, and furniture) decreed in the queen's last will and testament, and a sizable pension from the king, which was granted to her personally. The marriage only lasted five years, however, as her husband unexpectedly died in 1578.

Sofonisba was now forty-seven and a widow. King Philip tried to entice her to return to the Spanish court, but she preferred to travel to Cremona to her mother, sisters, and brother. So Sofonisba sailed from Palermo to Livorno, and what do you know, fate inserted its finger en route. The ship's captain, a younger Genoan nobleman named Orazio Lomellino, fell madly in love with his "famous passenger" (yes, Sofonisba was famous the length and breadth of the Italian peninsula)—or else Sofonisba fell madly in love with Orazio, since in some retellings she proposed to him rather than the other way around. (Others claim the whole thing was a marriage of convenience, so Sofonisba would not have to return to the court, which would have meant going back to drudgery.) Explain it however you like: the marriage lasted more than forty years, until Sofonisba's death.

But let's stop for a moment in Livorno, where Sofonisba arrived with her captain. She decided to break her journey for a rest in Pisa, in the Santo Mazzeo convent, and on December 18, 1579, she wrote to Grand Duke Francesco I de' Medici in Florence to request that she not be required to pay import duties on the goods she was bringing with her. She also mentions that the journey had been arduous. Because she had been seasick? Or because her husband had only recently died? Or because she had so much to think about?

I imagine Sofonisba in that wintry convent, reflecting on her situation. She was forty-seven, childless and husbandless, and had left a secure job—sounds familiar, right? She was a renowned and acclaimed artist who earned good money, but who up until that point had lived her life under male ownership: owned first by her father, then by the King of Spain, and for the last few years by the husband chosen for her by the king. Now that she was a widow, the right of ownership would be transferred to her younger brother, unless she returned to the Spanish court. Or unless she married. And now she had met a man. For possibly the first time in her life, Sofonisba was able to make a real choice. She had spent nearly two decades in the court: that was definitely a been-there-done-that. If Orazio seemed nice and was in love with her to boot (he was younger, and who knows how good-looking), maybe that was her best bet? Never mind that she had met with some resistance on that front: Francesco I de' Medici had urged her in a letter to reconsider, and her brother was dead-set against it, possibly because he was in financial trouble and would have been quite happy to have Sofonisba's hefty pensions transferred to him. Not particularly tempting to her. As a sea captain's wife, she might be able to live the most independent and autonomous life of all? After all, her husband would be constantly away at sea! Besides—let's mention this again—the man was younger, and who knows how good-looking. Did Sofonisba lie awake in the wee hours in that Pisan convent calculating her odds and trying to choose the financially and socially smartest move? Maybe. But when I study her self-portraits and the calmly self-confident and earnest eyes that gaze out of them, it doesn't seem to me that she would have done anything that she didn't truly want to do.

And so a couple of weeks later, this night woman had made her decision, and Sofonisba and Orazio were married in Pisa without further ado. On January 14, she wrote to Grand Duke Francesco that her new husband would soon be arriving in Florence to pay his respects—and maybe she went with him? Maybe they were invited to the Pitti Palace for a ceremonial dinner? Or maybe Sofonisba was given a tour of Francesco's art collection—the one that would soon be displayed in the upstairs gallery of the Uffizi? Maybe she was enraptured by the Renaissance treasures of Florence, as I was, or at least studied her colleagues' techniques with interest? And then they continued on to Genoa, where Orazio had his own palazzo.

I think Sofonisba made the right choice. While Orazio was off captaining his ship, she had plenty of time to paint, and for the next few decades her studio became a gathering place for both artists and the Genoan aristocracy. She was Europe's most famous female artist, "the beautiful and talented Sofonisba," a *natural wonder* whose paintings were imitated by artists all over the country. (Even Caravaggio himself used a drawing Sofonisba had made in her twenties as a model for one of his paintings.) And she herself was a role model, especially for those north-Italian female artists whose careers were rising in her wake—for Lavinia Fontana and a few others. It was as that kind of exemplar—straight-backed, calm, knowing her own worth—that she painted herself in 1610, in her late seventies.

The couple spent the last years of her life in the south, in Palermo, where Sofonisba was visited by several artists, including the young Flemish painter Antoon van Dyck, who later said he had learned "from this blind old woman more than from all the Italian masters." Van Dyck drew Sofonisba in his sketchbook in 1624, when she was ninety-two—the last surviving portrait of her.

Sofonisba died in Palermo at the age of ninety-three in November 1625, when the plague killed half the population of the city. In 1632, in honor of her hundredth birthday, Orazio, her grieving husband—younger and who knows how good-looking—erected a marble tomb in her memory. Sofonisba had no children, but she left us her paintings.

Sophonisba Anguissola, a virgin from Cremona, painted this herself with the aid of a mirror.

When I think of Sofonisba at night, I think above all of her self-portraits, those remarkably delectable calling cards with which she so skillfully marketed herself and her talents. Their recipients were able to see in them for the first time a creative, intelligent, and proactive woman, an independent agent, a woman who looked them directly in the eye. I think about how brilliant it was for her to present herself always a) in a simple black dress, and b) as a virgin. Back then it was mostly noblemen who dressed in black, and—perhaps insolently—that's what she looked like in her self-portraits: a person who was free to do what she wanted. And maybe in Sofonisba's mind, virginity too meant something other than chastity: maybe to her it was a kind of manifesto of independence.

And what force those paintings of her dressed in black still wield today! Lying in Stefano's bedroom, I wonder whether I shouldn't have bought a selfie stick on the bridge over the Arno after all, and Sofonisba-style taken a marketing pic of myself hard at work. I'd be wearing an outfit that would awaken clients' respect, holding a pen or airplane tickets, something that would symbolize the significance of my work. I'd look at once intelligent, cultured, curious, and somehow sweet, and across the top of the photo I'd write (all in Latin of course): M--K--, Virgo Helsinkiensis, took this photograph herself with a selfie stick in Florence anno domini 2014. Though actually I'm not a Virgo: I'm a Libra.

Then I'd post the pic to Instagram, send it to grant juries and possible clients, and money and jobs would start to flow in from all over the world. I'd be given big fat pensions and a king's ransom with which to feed my mule.

The only problem with that vision is that here in Florence I don't have a desk to sit at stylishly. I lie in Stefano's bed surrounded by piles of books, and the T-shirt I'm wearing says Super Dry.

I bump into Sofonisba by surprise once more. Two years later, on an October day in Helsinki. I have been writing about her all day. In the evening I head out and walk to the national museum, where a friend of mine is giving a lecture; while I'm waiting for it to start, I glance through the exhibit of Renaissance art, planning to come back with more time to view the paintings. I walk through the galleries looking at the portraits of aristocrats, the women painted as madonnas, Raffaello's self-portrait as Jesus, and the Florentine trousseau chests—the kind that Sofonisba had too—until I come to the next-to-last gallery.

First I see a portrait of a young girl, set in a glass case. I look at the name plaque: it says LUCIA ANGUISSOLA. For a moment I'm at a loss. Then I shift my eye to the name of the painting: *Europa Anguissola*. Lucia and Europa, wait, this can't be—this is a portrait painted by Sofonisba's younger sister Lucia of their youngest sister, Europa. And when I turn, I see on the opposite wall a portrait of a Dominican brother, and I know immediately that it was painted by Sofonisba. I don't really care for the bearded friar, though he looks quite gentle; I just stare down toward the bottom of the painting, where on a dark-green background, over the shoulder, I can just barely make out twenty-four-year-old Sofonisba's handwriting. Sofonisba Anguissola, Virgo Coram Amilcaris Patre Pinxit MDLVI. Right here, her own holographic signature, so close I could touch her brushstrokes.

I think: *Sofonisba has traveled to Helsinki, almost as if she wanted to come meet me.* The Anguissola wunder-daughters, Sofonisba,

Lucia, and Europa, have traveled in stealth mode, without warning, not knowing that at this very instant I'm thinking about them at night. They have boarded an airplane, Sofonisba in the window seat, Lucia on the aisle, Europa in the middle seat, clutching tickets reading CRE–HEL, DEP 1556 – ARR 2016 (FLIGHT TIME 460 YRS)—unless they were bundled unceremoniously into the hold, where they spent the whole flight sitting awkwardly on the floor among suitcases; after all, it would not be suitable for noblewomen to walk about being stared at by all and sundry. Or perhaps they have squeezed themselves into a full-length trailer behind a semi and roared up the autobahns across all of Europe, south to north, munching on Cremonan cheese and bread in truck stops while they stretched their benumbed legs; or maybe they were packed in a container and loaded onto a container ship, I don't know: in that case they would have sailed through the Mediterranean and up the European shoreline, avoiding pirates, and then across the Baltic before dropping anchor in Helsinki's harbor.

Ciao, night women. *Benarrivate*.

*

Night women's advice:

If you know what you want to do, do it.

If no one you know has ever done it before, so much the better.

Mark everything you do in big proud letters: I did this.

Advertise your skills. Distribute your calling cards.

In the pictures, look straight at the camera. Be sincere, calm, self-confident, and wonderful.

LAVINIA

NIGHT WOMEN'S ADVICE 8

Do you want to combine family and a career? No problem. You can have everything.

NIGHT WOMAN #8: *Lavinia Fontana*
PROFESSION: *Artist's daughter, later wife, mother, and career woman. Supported her large family by painting. Branded herself the favorite artist of noblewomen and earned like a man.*

If Sofonisba devoted her life to painting alone, we can consider it the heroic labor of Lavinia Fontana (1552–1614) from Bologna that she succeeded—inconceivably for the time, four centuries ago—at combining work, family life, and motherhood. Lavinia was the first professional female painter who didn't work at court or in a convent but competed on a level playing ground with the city's male artists. She carved out an exemplary career and painted a couple hundred paintings—commissions came in from the Medicis in Florence, the pope in Rome, and the Spanish court—all while giving birth to *eleven* children.

Lavinia was the second daughter of Prospero Fontana, a Bolognese fresco painter. No sons were born to the family, so at some point the aging Prospero began to fret about who would inherit the family business—could it be Lavinia? In those days Bologna was an exceptionally open-minded city, and women had been allowed to study in Europe's oldest university since it was chartered in 1158. Making art was, however, still strictly a man's profession, and as artisans painters belonged to the same guild as saddlers and swordsmiths. But, thought Prospero, could Lavinia do what that universally admired noblewoman and artist Sofonisba Anguissola was doing, and become sophisticated, famous, and successful? After all, the Anguissola girl had been invited to the court of Spain to paint, and was sending home to her father what rumor had it were heavy bagfuls of gold.

Prospero may not have been the most illustrious painter in town, but he was a skilled networker, and he decided to aim high for his daughter. Lavinia received an education that was unusually good for an artist's daughter: her letters testify to her beautiful handwriting and refined diction, and she may even have received instruction in mathematics and geometry. It's not known where the young Lavinia studied painting, but one thing is sure: if the idea was to transform her into a *gentildonna,* it wasn't in her father's workshop, alongside the butcher's son.

Lavinia's first signed painting that survives—a portrait of an aristocratic boy—is from 1575, when she was twenty-three. Lavinia was already alarmingly old to be still unmarried, and the question of her marrying had to be settled quickly if she was to make a career for herself as a painter. The fact was that a female painter, if she wanted any kind of respect at all, could not work—say, paint portraits of male clients—if she didn't have a husband. Who would negotiate her fees, sign her contracts, handle her legal affairs? Only a man could take care of those things, and at sixty-seven Prospero could not be that man forever. If Lavinia hoped to a) protect her reputation, b) expand her business, and c) succeed in her career, she would need a husband—one who was open to certain unconventional arrangements.

Normally marriage meant that the bride left her childhood home and moved with her dowry into her husband's household, but Prospero did not want Lavinia to go anywhere—he needed her to give him and Lavinia's mother comfortable retirement years—nor could he afford the level of dowry that would have tempted high-quality suitors. What he needed, therefore, was a man who would accept a wife who was a career woman and a painter, who would be satisfied with a modest dowry, and who would move in with them and ensure Lavinia's status as a respectable married woman. The miracle he found was a young man named Gian Paolo Zappi, the son of a family from the lower gentry in Imola, and Prospero began to negotiate the marriage with the young man's father, Severo. When the future father-in-law came to Bologna to inspect his son's bride candidate, his assessment of the twenty-four-year-old Lavinia in a letter he sent to his wife was that she was an honorable and virtuous young woman with lovely manners. Lavinia also "looked as a woman should, neither beautiful nor ugly, but somewhere in between," which was in fact what the age considered ideal: she wouldn't be vain or flirtatious like a beautiful wife, but neither would she be unbearable to look at. Severo also mentioned that Lavinia had given him two small self-portraits, which he would bring home to Imola.

And it is those self-portraits that Lavinia painted in 1577 that I think about at night. They were marketing images painted for her future father-in-law, and to that end they were brilliant. In one of them—the one that has survived—Lavinia is playing the clavichord as a virtuous *gentildonna* should, and the maidservant standing behind her is handing her a folder of sheet music. Lavinia is beautiful, calm, decisive; she is wearing the kind of elegant dress that Bolognese noble brides wore, with a lacy frilled collar, pearls, and coral. Across the top of the painting is a text in Latin—the language of learned humanists, following Sofonisba's example—announcing that the subject of the painting is Lavinia, virgin daughter of Prospero Fontana, and that she herself painted the image using a mirror, which is to say that the image is honest and veracious. Though in a sense it wasn't, quite: Lavinia was not a noblewoman, as the painting implied, and most likely didn't have a personal servant at home, let alone an expensive instrument like a clavichord. She was just an ordinary fresco painter's daughter. But Lavinia had seen Sofonisba's self-portraits and decided to emulate her night woman. In the background Lavinia also painted an easel and an open *cassone* to indicate that she could support her family, and that her career as a painter would be her dowry. In short: Lavinia looked like a chaste and cultured noblewoman, and was a good investment to boot. No wonder Severo decided to sign the marriage papers on the spot.

And so Lavinia and Gian Paolo got married. In the marriage contract there is a condition according to which they must live in Lavinia's father's house on the Via Galliera in Bologna, and specifying that their painting-related income would go to Prospero, who would in turn see to their food and clothing. (If Gian Paolo had thought that his seventyish father-in-law would probably die soon, he had another think coming: Prospero lived another twenty years.) Gian Paolo's role is a bit unclear, but it's possible that he was a painter too. Some biographers believe that he gave up his own modest career as a painter and began to assist Lavinia by painting backgrounds and the folds of drapery in her portraits; but others insist that the minutely detailed depiction of luxurious fabrics was Lavinia's forte, and the reason she could later charge astronomical fees for her paintings, so that there was no way she would delegate such an important job to her bored husband. According to some sources, Gian Paolo must have been mentally deficient, simpleminded in some way, to have agreed to a marriage like this—househusband to a career woman. But maybe he was actually smart: he would later inherit Prospero's whole workshop. And if Gian Paolo felt underappreciated next to his successful wife, no textual evidence of that feeling survives. They lived together until Lavinia's death.

So now at twenty-four Lavinia was supporting the whole family. She was responsible for the livelihood of many people: her husband, her parents, her future children. Her father and Gian Paolo would handle the contracts and payments, since it wasn't suitable for women to ask to be paid for their paintings, but in the end everyone's lives depended on Lavinia's artistic contribution and ability to attract paying clients. (Asking to be paid for the work you do seems to be difficult for many women still today; I confess that in my literary negotiations, I envy Lavinia her managers.)

And Lavinia certainly could deliver the goods. In the early years of her marriage, she mostly painted Bolognese scholars, churchmen, poets, and bankers—men who wanted their portraits done for a reasonable price. But soon her reputation began to spread beyond Bologna. In an age in which exotic and wondrous objects were collected with great enthusiasm, a portrait painted by a woman was a sought-after novelty. One collector commissioned a self-portrait from Lavinia so that he could place it right next to the beautiful and talented Sofonisba in his collection. Lavinia sent it off in May 1579; later it ended up in Florence, in the collection of miniature portraits in the Vasari Corridor, where I finally find it in the home stretch of my sweaty run through the guided tour. *There's Lavinia, microscopic!* Ignoring the glowering guard, I stop reverently to study the painting. Painted on a copper plate the size of a postcard, the self-portrait is precise as a photograph; the lacy frills on the dress are perfectly airy and translucent; the tiny pearls and jewels glitter and gleam dimly. (Note to self: *Add a magnifying glass to the explorer's packing list!*) The fresco painter's daughter, who has painted herself as an aristocratic scholar, looks out self-confidently from her seat by the table in her *studiolo*, and well she might: she truly had the knack of self-branding.

In 1584, the thirty-two-year-old Lavinia was commissioned to paint an altarpiece for the chapel in the Imola City Hall—a significant commission in that this was the first time a female artist had been commissioned to paint a public work. And when Laudomia Gozzadini, the daughter of a noble Bolognese family, commissioned her to paint a family portrait—now a famous painting—commissions began to flow in for Lavinia from the city's wealthy noblewomen. Nothing like this had ever been seen before in Bologna, and everywhere people were talking about this "rich and virtuous noblewoman" [*sic!*] who only accepted commissions through personal recommendations. Women competed for Lavinia's favor; they all wanted to spend time with her. She became such a major celebrity that just seeing her in the street was something to tell friends about. Soon Lavinia was able to charge such astronomical fees for her paintings—fees equivalent to those paid to Europe's best male court painters—that no one but aristocrats could afford to commission them.

And so Lavinia painted. Every day she traveled by carriage from Bologna's Via Galliera to the other side of town, where the noble families' palazzos stood, and set up her easel in her clients' rooms. She painted young brides in their red dowry dresses to display the family's wealth, around their waists on a chain a jewel-studded sable fur or gilded paw, symbol of fertility. She painted aristocratic wives in their sumptuous gowns, holding expensive *cani bolognesi* in their laps—those ultrafashionable dogs that represented marital fidelity. She painted widows, but not of the sort normally portrayed in paintings back then—toothless and apathetic old ladies who had withdrawn from life, wearing nuns' habits and holding prayer books in their hands—but rather glamorous women in velvet and brocade dresses and black veils decorated with pearls, holding handkerchiefs in their hands as signs of tears. Lavinia painted the silks, satins, brocades, taffetas, gold-thread embroideries, and pearl and lacy adornments of the women's dresses with meticulous detail; sometimes she took her subjects' gemstone, pearl, and gold jewelry home in order to paint each stone's gleam and glow with careful attention in her studio. (Various types of contracts were written up to ensure the safe return of these expensive items.) Lavinia was also commissioned to paint family portraits featuring both the quick and the dead, newborn babies in their luxurious cradles, and small children in their stiff Sunday best. There is even a portrait of a "monstrous child," a little girl whose face is completely concealed behind long fur. Lavinia also produced altarpieces for families' private chapels and smaller paintings for bedrooms; ever popular were images of the sleeping baby Jesus and other beautiful people, as it was believed that gazing on such would promote safe childbirth. (It was thought that the birth of the deformed or "monstrous" child had been caused by the mother looking at something ugly or malformed during pregnancy, such as a tortoise or a harelipped beggar; staring at beautiful images during conception would promote favorable fetal development.)

So Lavinia's business flourished, and she was smart enough to use the situation for upward mobility: she made friends with many of her clients and, smartest of all, asked them to be godmothers to her own children. Each successive godmother brought her expanded influence and connections in society circles, and in 1588, she and her family were able to move to the other side of Bologna, to the Via della Fondazza, near where her new social circles lived. And there she continued to paint until 1604, when she received an invitation from the pope to join him in Rome. At fifty-two, Lavinia packed up her aging mother, her husband, and four of her children, and spent the last ten years of her life painting portraits and altarpieces for the pope, the Borghese family, and other VIP clients. When Lavinia died in Rome at the age of sixty-two, in 1614, she had scaled the mountain and reached the peak.

What have I learned from Lavinia? At least how a woman living four centuries ago could fulfill twenty-first-century self-help manuals' advice on how to achieve success. One such manual suggests that to get what you want, you must act as if you've already gotten it. If you want to be a successful, wealthy career woman, you must dress as if you already were a successful, wealthy career woman. If you want to be rich, you should carry around a picture of a million-dollar check in your wallet and imagine that it's the real thing. If you want to be a writer-explorer, you have to write on your calling card *Literary Exploring and Human Experiments*, no matter how damn silly that sounds. And if you want to paint portraits of scholars and aristocrats, you have to paint a self-portrait as an aristocratic scholar, and act like one. Genius, dear Lavinia.

But above all, in the midst of the hundreds of paintings, the portraits, the altarpieces, the astronomical fees, the success, and the praise, I think about this: the baptismal record kept by Lavinia's husband.

In January 1578 she gave birth to a daughter named Emilia.
In November 1578 she gave birth to a son named Horatio.
In November 1579 she gave birth to a second son named Horatio.
In January 1581 she gave birth to a daughter named Laura.
In May 1583 she gave birth to a son named Flaminio.
In January 1585 she gave birth to a third son named Horatio.
In June 1587 she gave birth to a son named Severo.
In October 1588 she gave birth to a daughter named Laudomia.
In December 1589 she gave birth to a son named Prospero.
In December 1592 she gave birth to a second son named Severo.
In April 1595 she gave birth to a daughter named Costanza.

I think about how from age twenty-five to forty-two—all those years during which Lavinia was building that remarkable career described above—she was nearly constantly pregnant. Over a period of seventeen years, she gave birth to eleven children. Only three of them survived into adulthood. Eight she buried, some only days old, some a little older. Sometimes she gave the next child the name of the previous one who had died, hoping that *this* Horatio or *this* Severo would survive.

Often only a month or two would pass after a delivery before she was pregnant again—and busy painting. For example, in January of 1578, when Lavinia was giving birth to her first child, her nervous husband reported in a letter to his parents that his wife's life was in danger: over the past few months "not enough care has been taken," he wrote, meaning perhaps that Lavinia had been working too hard. Barely a month after the delivery, in March of 1578, Lavinia was pregnant again, and starting to work on larger altarpieces for private chapels—at least three such pieces were signed in 1578. In late November she gave birth to Horatio number one. In early January 1579 there's a mention in another letter that Lavinia had given birth a month previously but was already at work again. Either Lavinia was a workaholic or she couldn't afford to rest.

I wonder how she could have done it, and how it felt. Constantly pregnant, battered by hormonal storms and morning sickness or waddling about with a big belly, back aching, legs swollen, sleeping badly, and then going through and recovering from childbirth . . . Presumably she didn't have to breastfeed the babies—they had wet nurses for that—which also allowed her to get pregnant again more expeditiously. It seems scholars always pass over the large number of Lavinia's childbirths on the grounds that in those days it was usual to be constantly pregnant; only a single art historian mentions in passing that Lavinia probably didn't paint frescoes because in her condition it was too difficult to climb up onto scaffolding. And it's true that back then women typically had a dozen-plus children—families needed workers and heirs (just boys, *per favore*), and because infant mortality was high, you had to be continually giving birth so that some of your babies would survive into adulthood. But just because this was "typical" doesn't trivialize the experience for any individual woman. Babies didn't plop out of sixteenth-century women more easily or routinely than today, as on a conveyor belt, or in a sped-up cartoon—childbirth, plop, childbirth, plop, baby died, *oh no, what a shame, just pop another bun in the oven*, plop, plop, plop. On the contrary: every female body had to go through the process concretely, tangibly. Pregnancy, childbirth, hormones—everything slammed into the woman's body just as powerfully then as it does today, only worse, because medical assistance was minimal, and the most reliable way to guarantee a safe childbirth was to adorn your belly with a book about Saint Margaret, the patron saint of childbirth—though to be sure, mandrake root, coriander seeds, or concoctions containing ground snakeskin, hare's milk, and crab might help as well. Every pregnancy was a potential death sentence to a woman: Will I survive this one? And this one? And now this one? (Many didn't.) And in between, in the tumult of pregnancy hormones, the deaths of tiny daughters and sons. *And the whole time, Lavinia kept painting.*

I can't help wondering whether Lavinia did this of her own free will. Was she in the end an exemplary night woman who fulfilled her own deep ambitions as an artist, or was she just slave labor for her father and husband, a money machine burdened with both supporting and reproducing the family? I don't know. But when I think of her at night, I think that at least she wasn't a miserable slave. She was a powerful woman. She *had* to have been strong as a horse, enormously determined, with nerves of steel, not to mention prodigiously talented, industrious, proud, brave. There's no way she could have produced two hundred paintings if she hadn't been those things. And who knows, maybe Lavinia loved her work. Why wouldn't she? Maybe her lust to paint was so great that she *had* to get up from childbed to work at her easel just as soon as she was able. Maybe she was such a crazy workaholic that even her father or husband couldn't hold her back! *Gian Paolo! Could you, please! Mommy doesn't have time. Mommy's painting.*

Or maybe Lavinia was like so many women today: a passionate, supernaturally hardworking and capable career woman who could do it all—work, kids, husband, and her own aging parents—just with a few more kids, is all.

A couple of years after my Florence visit, I'm in Bologna and peer through the keyhole at the expansive courtyard inside Palazzo Gozzadini. I think about how somewhere on the other side of this gate, Laudomia Gozzadini, a thirtyish noblewoman, confessed her harrowing life story to Lavinia, a story of a childbirth competition between two sisters, which Laudomia lost, and with it her inheritance and marriage. Lavinia painted Laudomia's story based on her subject's hopes, and the result became one of her most famous works.

To see the stupendous *Portrait of the Gozzadini Family*, the explorer in quest of night women must first trek all the way across the city of Bologna, past the labyrinth of medieval alleyways, the reddish-orange glow of the palazzos, the crumbling double towers, through the light and shadow of the arcades, through the whole fierce and disheveled city that is so redolent of old wealth and culture, so full of sequestered private gardens, black-clad students, drunks, homeless people, and the descendants of powerful families. Then she has to walk through room after room of paintings by men in the Pinacoteca Nazionale, endless lines of crucifixions and all manner of holy folk slithering along through paintings many meters long, and wonder why Lavinia isn't even mentioned in the museum's brochure in the list of great masters and attractions. But when she does finally locate almost the only paintings in the museum a) by women, and b) with secular themes, they are prominently displayed at the back of a large gallery, on a raised dais, glitteringly fresh as the water in a clear mountain stream.

When you study the messages brilliantly hidden in Lavinia's gigantic family portrait—the ugly face of the dead sister, the gesture revealing the father's preferred daughter, the treacherously lurking husbands, the black dog slinking about in the background—or its meticulous detail, such as the silken lynx stole resting on proud Laudomia's lap, the earrings on the lapdog, the silks and gossamer-thin lace of the sisters' dresses, and the golden necklaces and stiffly starched lace cuffs, as well as the refined lace blanket on the aristocratic baby lying in the luxurious cradle pictured in another Lavinia painting hung on the adjacent wall, you begin to realize something.

Lavinia has decided not just to excel but to shine. She has decided, dammit, to nail this painting thing, because she's damned good at it. Yes, Lavinia lusted after this job. She *loved* painting all these details. Look: everything is perfect, brilliant, absurdly virtuosic, like these embroideries here, every fraction of every inch of which screams passion and the burn of perfectionism.

I think: *No one paints like this just because her father or husband makes her do it. Not like* this.

And okay, so maybe nothing in this city has been named after Lavinia except the crummy little dog park at the end of Via Fondazza, so be it: that's trivial compared with what I see, namely, that she painted out of passion.

*

Night women's advice:

If you want a glorious career, make it.

If you plan to give birth to eleven kids while doing so, find yourself a man who's up to it.

Follow your night women. Brand yourself. Paint yourself the way you'd like to be.

Bond with women but earn like a man.

Be industrious as hell.

Work out of passion.

If you suffer horrific losses, keep going.

ARTEMISIA

NIGHT WOMEN'S ADVICE 9

Deal with your trauma.
Slay your Holofernes.
It's all grist for the mill.

NIGHT WOMAN #9: *Artemisia Gentileschi*
PROFESSION: *Artist's daughter, later artist. Had her reputation ripped to bits in a rape trial, later had a brilliant career in Florence, Rome, Venice, and Naples. Raised one or two daughters as a single mother. Painted naked women and strong amazons who did what they wanted.*

Back to Artemisia, whose blood-spattered manslaughter painting I saw on the wall at the Uffizi.

It turns out that Artemisia Gentileschi (1593–ca. 1654) is the most famous of my Florentine night women: she has become a symbol of the strong and free fighting woman and an idol of feminist scholars. Much scholarship and several novels have been written about her; cinematic dramas and erotic thrillers (inspired by her paintings) have been made; perfumes, art galleries, and hotels for women have been marketed in her name. And it must be admitted: even if you aren't crazy about the baroque aesthetic of her paintings, you have to admire her sheer guts. The woman had nerve.

Artemisia was born in Rome, the oldest daughter of an artist named Orazio Gentileschi. Her father worked mostly as a fresco painter, and Artemisia got to work as his assistant from an early age. Her mother died in childbirth when Artemisia was only twelve; at that juncture most girls would probably have been married off or shipped off to a nunnery, but for some reason her father didn't do the usual thing. Instead, he started to teach Artemisia to paint. In seventeenth-century Rome, Orazio's decision raised eyebrows, because artists' workshops were a man's world, but Orazio was different in other ways as well and had a reputation as a difficult person. Most likely he wasn't projecting a glorious career for his daughter as a respected historical painter: back then that would have meant roaming about the city painting statues from antiquity and copying the works of the Renaissance masters, which was out of the question for a girl. But maybe in addition to grinding pigments, Artemisia could help her father with commissioned work, and in that way contribute to the family's income? In so doing she would also surreptitiously become part of the vast demimonde of artists copying the masters, mass-producing paintings, and painting cheap portraits and religious subjects at the market. You didn't need much in the way of an education, or even minimal literacy, for that. And Orazio could also occasionally use Artemisia as his model: nude female models were hard as hell to come by, as the practice was illegal.

And so Artemisia toiled away as her father's apprentice in the family's cramped rented apartment, which doubled as Orazio's workshop. She was only allowed to go outside on Sunday to attend mass, since the neighborhood was unsafe, even violent: the blocks between the Piazza del Popolo and the Spanish Steps were inhabited by a motley crew ranging from monks and log-driving "river pigs" to chamberlains, churchyard builders, artists, and prostitutes, all of them often moving from apartment to apartment—as did Orazio himself.

In those years Artemisia's father noticed his daughter's astonishing talent: she painted better than any of his three sons! When at sixteen Artemisia painted her first signed work, *Susanna and the Elders*, Orazio knew that he had taught her everything he himself had learned from his own teachers. And so he hired his colleague, the fresco painter Agostino Tassi, to come in and teach her perspective. That was a mistake. One day, when Artemisia was seventeen, Tassi raped his student.

The rape seems to be at the core of everything that is written about Artemisia these days. A quick history of the events would go like this: Agostino Tassi had been obsessing about Artemisia for a long time, and finally on a day in May 1611 managed to trap the target of his lust. After the rape Tassi made vague promises to marry her, the usual recompense for the deed back then, because an unmarried woman who had lost her virginity was damaged goods and thus unfit to marry anyone but her rapist. (Another possible recompense for besmirching the family's honor would have been to pay a considerable dowry sum.) When Tassi did not make a formal proposal of marriage, however, Orazio decided in early 1612 to file a lawsuit against him for stealing his daughter's maidenhead and thereby ruining her chances of marriage. The scandalous trial lasted seven months, and was extremely humiliating for Artemisia—among other things, she had to suffer gynecological exams to prove her loss of virginity, and she was tortured with thumbscrews. Tassi was convicted in the end, but Artemisia's reputation had suffered a massive blow. And so her father married her off quickly to a talentless young artist (the first who agreed to take her), and in 1613 the couple moved to the groom's hometown, Florence.

Incredible as it seems, Artemisia's court records have survived. The document, eighty pages long in English translation, is confusing, circuitous, and exhausting to read. But there it is, Artemisia's voice, exactly as it would have been heard four hundred years ago: the testimony she gave in March 1612 can still be read word for word.

In cross-examination, Artemisia described the rape itself in detail. On that day in May 1611, she reported, she'd been at home on the Via della Croce, painting "for her own pleasure," when Agostino Tassi had entered without permission. He had flirted a little with her at first, then pushed her into the bedroom, locked the door, shoved her onto the bed, thrust his knee between her legs, held a handkerchief over her mouth, and penetrated her, which hurt. Artemisia had tried to scream for help, scratched his face, torn at his hair, and grasped his penis so hard that skin came off, none of which had restrained him. After the rape Artemisia had run to the dresser, seized a knife, and threatened to kill him. "Go ahead," Tassi had said, and opened his jacket, and Artemisia had tried to stab him with the knife, but had only managed to inflict a tiny cut on his chest. Then Tassi had buttoned up his jacket, Artemisia had wept, and to console her he'd promised to marry her once he'd resolved all the messes he was in. Having received this promise (one can't quite call it a proposal, right?), Artemisia had felt a bit more at peace. The judge wanted to know whether Artemisia had bled, which would have been evidence of losing her virginity, but Artemisia said she'd been menstruating, so it was difficult to determine where the blood came from. "Maybe the blood was redder than usual," she said. Later Artemisia agreed to have sex with Tassi several more times: he had, after all, promised to marry her.

Oh, Artemisia. Rape, breaking your hymen, the desperate attempt to stab him with a knife, your tears, the humiliating promise of marriage, the use of that promise to extort more sex, the analysis of the color of your menstrual blood . . . testifying to all this in court, in public, and having every ghastly detail recorded and reprinted in the works and analyses of acclaimed art historians hundreds of years later . . . this is way more intimate information than I ever wanted to know about the life of any talented female artist who lived four hundred years ago—or for that matter about the life of any woman living today.

Nor was that the end of Artemisia's humiliation. Next to be cross-examined were Tassi and the witnesses he had recruited. Agostino Tassi assured the court, his eyes brimming over with sincerity, that he had *never laid a finger on said Artemisia*, hardly even knew her. He said he had paid a visit to his colleague Orazio's house only because he had been asked to teach the girl perspective, and had never even spoken with her alone. Tassi claimed that Orazio had had all manner of problems with his daughter, who was "wild and was leading a bad life." When Tassi had urged Artemisia to be a "good girl," her answer had been that her father had driven her to this state, and in addition "used her like a wife." "Never have I had carnal intercourse, nor tried to have it with the said Artemisia," Tassi insisted, adding that she had taken numerous other men into her bed, including a certain stonecutter named Francesco, with "whom one couldn't trust a female cat." "It is well known that Artemisia is a whore." "Everything she says is a lie." As his crowning evidence, Tassi proclaimed that Artemisia's "mother and aunts were famous for their bad reputation and that" . . . [there is a hole in the paper] . . . "is and has been a known public whore." Whores, the whole bunch of them!

After the testimonies of Artemisia and Tassi, an endless series of relatives, neighbors, serving girls, launderers, tailors, churchmen, innkeepers, fellow painters, mixers of ultramarine, pilgrims who had sat as Orazio's models, and barber-dentist-bloodletters took the stand and gave their jumbled accounts of what each had heard or seen out of the corner of one eye, what someone had looked like coming out of some room or another, and what had happened at some mass or on some carriage ride or in some vineyard or just in the artist quarter on the Via Margutta or the Via della Croce. Images from four centuries ago flash before my eyes, but it seems impossible to know what's true and what isn't. It's clear from the judge's comments that he doesn't believe Tassi's lies either, but still it's the honesty of Artemisia's testimony that they have to test with the *sibille* torture. "Whatever is necessary," Artemisia says in consenting to the thumbscrews—though these are the fingers with which she will earn a living.

And what did the said Artemisia do after all this humiliation? She certainly didn't curl up in bed depressed. Immediately after the trial, in November 1612, nineteen-year-old Artemisia married Pierantonio Stiattesi, who was ten years her senior. The day before the wedding her rapist had been revealed as a total scumbag, convicted, and sentenced to exile (it's unclear whether the sentence was ever executed), and Artemisia's reputation was at least partly restored. The couple moved to Florence, and their first child, a boy, was born in September 1613. As her calling card Artemisia took along the powerful painting she had painted during the trial, in which Judith beheads Holofernes—and it became her ticket to success.

Contrary to all expectations, once she was in Florence her career as an artist took off like a rocket. Back in July of 1612, Orazio had sent a letter to the widowed grand duchess in Florence singing his daughter's praises: she had, he wrote, become "so skilled that I dare say there be none to compare." Back then there wasn't a single female artist in Florence, so Artemisia was unique, and something to marvel at. Her painting of Judith and Holofernes stirred up considerable controversy; none of the city's art experts could believe that such a powerful and violent painting could have come from a woman's brush. Michelangelo the Younger, grandnephew of the famous Michelangelo, immediately commissioned a piece by Artemisia for his palazzo, Casa Buonarroti; after that she began getting commissions from others as well—*A rarity! A talented female artist!*—such as Grand Duke Cosimo II de' Medici. In the Medicis' court Artemisia got to know the city's influential poets and dramatists, as well as Galileo Galilei, with whom she continued to correspond until the astronomer's death; and Michelangelo the Younger became a family friend, possibly even godfather to her son—at least he paid her generously for the painting, three times more than he paid other artists. In 1616, Artemisia was so highly regarded that she became the first woman admitted into the prestigious Florentine Accademia del Disegno. This was not only unprecedented, but a crucial turning point for her career: membership in the art academy gave her an autonomous status, independent of the guilds and the male members of her family, something that no woman had experienced before. After that she could buy pigments without her husband's or father's permission, sign contracts, and travel alone; and she began to haggle on commissions like a man, since she could—not bad when you consider what had happened to her in Rome. It's not known whether Artemisia availed herself of the instructional opportunities at the academy—the curriculum included not only drawing nude models and anatomy but mathematics and natural science, and Artemisia was just barely literate—but it is known that as a woman she was uniquely positioned to avail herself of nude female models, and she began to specialize in painting female figures.

While working away on her paintings, of course, Artemisia also made babies. In November 1615, a second son was born; in August 1617, a daughter named Prudentia followed; and in October 1618, a second daughter came along, but died at eight months of age. Maybe she gave birth to other babies as well, but they didn't live long enough to be christened. In any case, by 1620, only one child, three-year-old Prudentia, was still alive.

In early 1620, Artemisia began to plan her return to Rome. She wrote a letter to Cosimo II describing the many troubles she had had at home and with her family (her fourth child had recently died); to recover from them, she wanted to spend a couple months with her relatives. Not least among her troubles were the financial ones. Despite her constant work and success, the family spent more than they earned, and the bills piled up, from the carpenter, the apothecary, the baker, and the tailor; the ounce and a half of ultramarine obtained to paint her *Hercules* had not been paid for; nor had the stretchers and a walnut panel. Every now and then the creditors would descend upon them and confiscate her household supplies to cover the unpaid bills. Artemisia doesn't seem to have been a particularly incompetent businesswoman, and Michelangelo the Younger seems to have lent her money; maybe it was her no-good husband who was the problem. He not only earned nothing with his painting, but was drowning in debt, and even spent Artemisia's dowry without permission. Artemisia for her part had been pregnant at least four times in the past seven years, which must have had a negative effect on her work pace; and they'd had to pay funeral costs for three children.

So little information about Artemisia has survived that every microscopic crumb of evidence has tended to get blown up to colossal proportions. Scholars have reconstructed "economic portraits" of Artemisia based on those few randomly surviving receipts, bills, and dunning letters, and the image they paint of the artist's life is brutal—but also inevitably distorted. I have no idea what Artemisia thought about her marriage, say, or her children, or her painting; but I do know that during her pregnancies in Florence she spent so much money on laxatives and candy that she couldn't pay her bills. What should I do with information like that? Isn't it somehow intrusive to know so many physically intimate details about her, on top of all the scandalous stuff from the trial? I try to imagine what some greedy-eyed scholar four hundred years from now would conclude about my life if he got his hands on my purchase records for pharmacies and other stores and noticed that I've been hauling home unnaturally large amounts of cheese, books, painkillers, and sleep-inducing natural products lately.

And yet here I am, still mucking about in the same swamp, feverishly studying every surviving yellowed scrap of paper and imagining that it opens some new depth of understanding for me. Aha, Artemisia may have suffered from constipation during pregnancy! Oh no, she might have been driven into bankruptcy by the same monk-run cosmetics shop in a Florentine monastery that I too love! (For your information, the Officina Profumo Farmaceutica de Santa Maria Novella sells a divine camphor-scented foot cream at an astronomical price.) Oh no, she had to buy ultramarine on credit! Artemisia's ultramarine situation also tells me that a certain Florentine nobleman named Francesco Maria Maringhi guaranteed her debt with the pigment dealer and in that way saved her from having it confiscated. I also know that when she left Florence, Artemisia sold her entire household goods to said Maringhi for 165 ducats. And because that inventory dated in February 1621 survives, I can imagine myself peering into Artemisia's home—yes, I can imagine that *Artemisia invites me over*, maybe even to that inventorying of her household goods, in the flurry of her move. I'd sit there on a little wooden stool against the wall, sipping wine and nibbling a torn-off chunk of bread, and little three-year-old Prudentia would squat in the stairwell staring shyly at me. . . . *I'm changing scenery*, Artemisia would think, *what does it matter if some woman from the twenty-first century sees my home? Let her look*. And so now, somewhere here in the narrow streets of Florence, maybe near the Santa Maria Novella monastery, or in the hovels of the seedy Piazza dei Ciompi, or up on the hill near the base of the San Miniato church, looking out over the views below, I step into Artemisia's house, which contains among other things:

2 large walnut chests

3 Venetian walnut-veneered chests

1 large walnut cupboard with shelves

12 walnut stools with backs

4 chairs upholstered with various-colored damask

4 wool mattresses

4 rough linen mattresses

4 straw mattresses

76 golden and green leather hangings, Spanish size

1 turquoise blanket, trimmed with green taffeta, another with rose-colored cloth

1 turquoise-and-white cotton canopy, Turkish style

2 feather cushions

4 small feather cushions

1 embroidered down-filled blanket

1 wooden bed-warmer

3 small wooden tables

1 wooden cabinet with drawers
1 large pot
1 cauldron
1 large pan for starching
1 vessel for cold water with brass dishes
1 small brass bucket with handle
1 bucket
1 copper pan
1 chain for the fireplace and 1 pair of fire tongs
3 three-legged stools
3 round tin plates
2 brass candlesticks
3 iron oil lamps
1 pair of brass candle snuffers
1 lamp holder with an iron candlestick
5 Pistoian stools
4 wooden stools
4 easels
1 large canvas (half-painted)
1 painting of clothed Magdalene (2 braccia high)
1 painting of the Madonna (2 braccia high)
1 painting of Magdalene, just begun (2 braccia high)
1 portrait of a woman, in a walnut frame
3 small paintings on copper
4 walnut palettes for colors
15 stretchers for paintings, large and small
1 crucifix
1 mortar and pestle
1 large vessel and clay strainer
140 gold and red common leather hangings and 13 turquoise and gold cotton ones, decorated on the top and the bottom
24 majolica dishes, large and small, and other clay utensils for the kitchen

But why, dear Artemisia, I think quietly over in my corner, *why are you selling your easels and all those half-finished portraits of women?*

Are you that hard up? Or are you planning to change professions entirely—staging a renaissance in your own life?

Before her departure for Rome, however, Artemisia painted a larger version of her *Judith Slaying Holofernes*, a commission from Cosimo II. This painting is the one that nowadays hangs in Gallery 90 of the Uffizi, before which one can only gulp. Artemisia was twenty-seven. She had been raped and humiliated in court, lived with useless men, and delivered and buried several children; with her own labor she had earned fame in Florence and achieved an independence as an artist almost impossible for a woman in that era, and now was painting this gloomy but forceful Caravaggio-esque power painting, six and a half by five and a half feet in size, in which two women carry out the slaughter of a man in the dark of night, calmly and with determined faces. Studying the painting in the Uffizi, where it has been hung next to Caravaggios, I have to admit it's ferocious. In the eighteenth century, Anna Maria Luisa de' Medici regarded the painting as too horrific to view, and hid it away in some dark nook of the museum; it was not publicly displayed in the Uffizi until 2000, almost four hundred years after it was painted. The blood, the bed, the dark bedroom, the wrinkled bedsheets, the force, the violence, the sword . . . the symbolism and the execution are perfect. Artemisia knew that the brilliance and cruelty of the painting would stir up controversy, so as a precaution she signed it along the bottom *Ego Artemitia / Lomi fec.*, as if to say, *Yes: I, a woman, made this*. It may be that she was driven to paint it by the trauma of humiliation and a thirst for revenge; and certainly she deliberately portrayed Judith as a mature, strong woman who knows what she's doing, not as some timid, fearful damsel as, say, Caravaggio did. She already knew what her strengths were, and how her technical virtuosity and "wrong gender" needed to be exploited. And maybe she wanted to give her viewers a lesson in what women could and could not do. *Here, dammit. See what a woman is capable of.*

And Artemisia certainly was capable. Upon her return to Rome, she settled with her daughter, Prudentia, and a single servant in her old stomping grounds in the Via del Corso. She was now an autonomous artist and single mother, for—as the residence records reveal—around this time the husband dropped out of the picture. But the rise to fame that had begun in Florence continued for Artemisia in Rome; over the next thirty years she succeeded in carving out a brilliant international career. In the 1620s and 1630s, she painted commissioned works for the King of Spain and aristocrats all over Europe; achieved fame in Rome, Venice, and Naples; and worked with her father in the royal court in London, where they painted the ceilings in Queen's House. Her works were praised, and she herself became an admired, charismatic power figure represented on canvas in portraits and on a fashionable bronze medal struck in her honor, with her profile featured. In Venice, the city's poets wrote dozens of poems and letters in praise of her—more than of any other living artist—and later the verses of Neapolitan poets too testified to her talent, intelligence, and beauty.

Somewhere around 1629, at thirty-six, Artemisia moved to Naples, where as far as we know she lived out the rest of her life, and probably had another daughter, this one out of wedlock. Earning a living was not easy in a big city like Naples, which suffered from overpopulation, a weak economy, epidemics, starvation, and riots. Artemisia received commissions, but she constantly had to go begging her clients to pay up. The most devastating blows to her finances came from her daughters: around 1637, at forty-four, she almost went bankrupt as she tried to put together a dowry for Prudentia. (In the same period she sent out an inquiry to find out whether anyone knew about her ex-husband, whether he was alive—perhaps she was hoping for help paying the dowry.) Despite her success, her resilience, and her business sense, Artemisia never shook off her money troubles.

Twenty-seven of Artemisia's letters survive from her years in Naples, and those letters are the reason I think about her at night. If Artemisia is a power figure for women who have experienced sexual violence, slut-shaming, or just mundane aggressions and domination, she is also a figure for any writer or artist struggling to stay financially solvent.

Her letters were sent primarily to her clients and patrons, such as Duke Francesco I d'Este in Modena and Don Antonio Ruffo in Messina. At least she had learned to write—or had she? In 1649, she warned one recipient not to wonder about "the different handwritings, because I dictate my letters while I am painting." But her voice resounds through the letters, and it is the complete night woman's voice. She is direct, intelligent, and exacting in business matters, with a sense of humor; sometimes raging, sometimes despairing, and if necessary flattering, court-style. She does not philosophize in the letters, but very pragmatically informs her recipients that a painting will be arriving on a certain date, or will be delayed; she haggles on fees, requests new commissions, or hopes for recommendations to new clients. Artemisia knows how to wheel and deal: she sets a fee and will not budge from it; she refuses to finalize a fee until the work is finished; and she doesn't send sketches in advance of the work itself, having learned the hard way that clients will use them to get the work done more cheaply elsewhere ("if I were a man, I can't imagine it would have turned out this way"). The fee for a painting was determined by the number of human figures it had in it, and she often notes that using female nude models is extremely expensive and difficult, a real "headache." Sometimes she would send paintings as gifts in order to woo new clients or hold on to old ones; some of these had perhaps been done for other clients, with whom it had proved impossible to agree on a fee or the painting's subject. Once she sent a patron a work done by her daughter: "As she is a young woman, please don't make fun of her."

In October 1635, Artemisia wrote to Galileo Galilei, asking him to inquire after two paintings that she had sent to Florence for Ferdinando II de' Medici. She knew the grand duke had received them, but had had no word since, which was humiliating—after all, the kings and rulers of Europe had all thanked her with praise and gifts for her work. Those thank-you letters were extremely important. They were like letters of recommendation, or like reviews in a major paper. It was essential that they be kept, and sent along with requests for money, or shown to clients in the hope of new commissions. Artemisia was furious that the grand duke had not sent his appraisal: "So

I cannot believe that I have not satisfied His Highness," she wrote to Galileo. "Therefore, I wish to learn the truth from you, including every detail. . . ."

In 1649, Artemisia turned fifty-six. She had health problems and money troubles, but at least she had found a good client in Messina, Don Antonio Ruffo. In early 1649, she wrote to Don Ruffo to say that she had sent the painting he had commissioned, and apologized for not being able to come down on the fee, for she had asked for and received 100 scudos per figure everywhere—in Florence, Venice, Rome, and even Naples, back when that city was still flush. If the Most Illustrious Lordship had considered her arrogant and presumptuous, she hoped he would feel differently once he saw the painting: "A woman's name raises doubts until her work is seen. Please forgive me . . . if I gave you the reason to think me greedy. . . . If Your Lordship likes my work, I will also send you my portrait, which you may keep in your gallery as other Princes do." (January 30, 1649)

Don Ruffo became a regular client, and their correspondence in 1649 was energetic.

"As soon as possible I will send my portrait, along with some small works done by my daughter, whom I have married off today to a knight of the Order of St. James. This marriage has broken me. For that reason, if there should be any opportunities for work in your city, I ask Your Most Illustrious Lordship to . . . keep me informed, because I need work very badly. . . . I shall not bore you any longer with this womanly chatter. The works will speak for themselves. And with this I end with a most humble bow." (March 13, 1649)

"I wish to express how greatly obliged I am to you for your concern in trying to find work for me, which is very scarce these days." (June 5, 1649)

"I am compelled by two circumstances—first to finish your painting soon, and, second, not having enough money to finish it. . . . [I'm asking] Your Most Illustrious Lordship . . . to send me a note for fifty ducats. . . . The expenses for hiring nude women [models] are high. Believe me, Signor Don Antonio, the expenses are intolerable, because out of the fifty women who undress themselves, there is scarcely one good one. And in this painting I cannot use just one model because there are eight figures, and one must paint various kinds of beauty." (June 12, 1649)

"As for my being able to finish the painting by the tenth of next month, it is impossible, because this painting requires three times as much work as the Galatea. I work continuously, and as fast as I can, but not so [fast] as to jeopardize the perfection of the painting, which I think will be finished by the end of August." (July 24, 1649)

"I received [your] . . . most kind letter with the bill of exchange that was paid to me immediately, and for this I thank you especially. . . . The painting is coming along well and will be finished by the end of this month, with eight figures and two dogs, which to me are even better than the figures. And I will show Your Most Illustrious Lordship what a woman can do, hoping to give you the greatest pleasure." (August 7, 1649)

"It will seem strange to Your Most Illustrious Lordship that the painting is taking so long, but this is due to my desire to serve you better, as is my duty. While painting the landscape, establishing the [vanishing] point of perspective, it became necessary to redo two figures. . . . Please forgive me because, with the excessive heat and many illnesses, I try to keep well by working a little at a time. I can assure you that this delay will be of the greatest benefit to the painting." (September 4, 1649)

"My Most Illustrious Sir . . . I was mortified to hear that you want to deduct one-third from the already very low price that I had asked. I must tell Your Most Illustrious Lordship that this is impossible and that I cannot accept a reduction, both because of the value of the painting and of my great need. Were this not so, I would give it to [you] as a present. And I am displeased that for the second time I am being treated like a novice." (October 23, 1649)

"[The price] must be no less than 400 ducats, and you must send me a deposit as all the other gentlemen do. . . . I swear . . . that I would not have given it even to my father for the price that I gave you. . . . I am sure that when you see it, you will say that I was not presumptuous. . . . I only wish to remind you that there are eight [figures], two dogs, and landscape and water. . . . I will say no more, except . . . that I think Your Most Illustrious Lordship will not suffer any loss with me, and that you will find the spirit of Caesar in this soul of a woman." (November 13, 1649)

When I imagine Artemisia writing those letters, quill scratching, and hear how the rage in her voice keeps growing, I think about how absurd it is that nothing has changed in four centuries. Money matters, deadlines, working conditions, finding clients, marketing yourself, constant worries about workload, maintaining your ability to work, and how your work is received: all the same today as back then. Week after week and month after month I write, agonizing over the progress of my work, and over why I've reached the end of another month and the thing still isn't finished, despite my expectations. I worry about whether I'll have enough money, and where the hell I might get some more, and why it seems like all the work available should be done either gratis or for a nominal sum. I worry about what readers will think of the finished product, and whether I've painted these women who have undressed for me well enough. Way too often I lie in bed with a headache, cursing the loss of a working day. And then I try to think of Artemisia: *You won't be disappointed. You'll find the spirit of Caesar in this soul of a woman.*

Caesar's spirit kept Artemisia going for a few more years: the last surviving bit of information we have about her—a bank receipt—is from 1654. After her death she was plunged into historiographical twilight, but she was restored to well-deserved grace in the 1970s, when the works of forgotten female artists began gradually to be rediscovered. Feminist art historians found in Artemisia an early supporter of women's liberation who sent battle signals to her sisters-in-arms through her paintings. She became a cult figure worshipped by feminists and female artists.

And to be sure, it is tempting to view her paintings through feminist lenses. In an era when the rare women artists limited their subjects to portraits and still lifes, Artemisia became known for large-scale baroque works featuring the strong heroines, female sacrifices, saints, and warriors of the Bible and Greek and Roman mythology, from seductive, freethinking Cleopatra to penitent Mary Magdalene. She specialized in depicting nude women, using as her models *actual female bodies* (unlike the male artists); the result was a series of female-dominated paintings exuding atmospheric strength. Among her roughly fifty surviving works we find a total of seven Judiths, seven Bathshebas, six Mary Magdalenes, three Susannas, three Madonnas, two Lucretias, and two Cleopatras. Another inventory counts eleven of her paintings in which a woman controls or is attempting to control a man, fifteen in which women are subjected to male control or lust, twenty-nine with implications of sexuality, and nineteen featuring female nudes. Nor do the subjects of the paintings leave the modern viewer cold: *Susanna and the Elders* depicts sexual harassment from a woman's point of view. In *Lucretia*, a virtuous Roman wife is in despair after being raped, and to spare herself the shame is about to commit suicide with a dagger. Cleopatra, the symbol of the dangers of a woman in power, kills herself with the bite of a poisonous snake in order to avoid the shame of imprisonment.

It sends shivers down my spine to reflect on when Artemisia painted her most famous paintings. *Susanna and the Elders* was painted in 1610, when Artemisia was only sixteen, shortly before she was raped in May 1611; it could stand as a personal representation of how Agostino Tassi's sexual harassment felt to her. *Lucretia*, in which a raped woman is about to kill herself, was painted in 1611, the same year Tassi raped Artemisia. The first version of Judith and Holofernes was painted in 1611–12, precisely during the period when justice was being sought for the wrong that had been done to her—as in fact was *Judith and Her Maidservant*, in which the women carry the head they've lopped off Holofernes in a basket. But how personal were those paintings, in the end? Some scholars argue that Artemisia consciously constructed her works as feminist interpretations of a woman's experience, but others insist that these were just ordinary commissioned paintings—after all, Artemisia was barely literate! Besides, the subjects she chose were extremely popular in that era, and there are dozens of versions of the same scenes by male artists, including Caravaggio and Artemisia's own father. It is simply not possible for Artemisia to have painted such large-scale works purely as personal therapy: the materials were expensive, and if she wanted her paintings to sell, she had to think of the client's taste.

Still, even if the paintings were commissioned, Artemisia had the experiences listed above *at the same time* as she was painting them. Even if she couldn't choose her subjects, she certainly could choose how she painted the women in them.

For example, Susanna as depicted by Artemisia is not the seductive maiden that the male artists of the day painted: she's violently apprehensive at the men's stares.

Judith, for her part, is mature and self-confident and utterly focused on her murderous task—no shy or frightened maiden embarrassed or confused about the situation in which she finds herself. Her maidservant too, whom Caravaggio for one portrayed as an old hag standing around cluelessly, at the end of Artemisia's brush is all the way in, as if to show what women are capable of if they join forces.

Nor are Artemisia's later women weak or vulnerable. They are strong, serious, and determined. They have life experience; they act. Their strong arms lift a tub of water in which to bathe a newborn baby, or carry a basket with the severed head of Holofernes. They are no idealized beauties or sleeping Venuses; they are what women are in real life, with ordinary faces, hefty bodies, a bit rounded in the belly. They have other things to do than to be the object of the male gaze.

And if Artemisia was not the theoretically reflective feminist that some scholars have imagined her as, she certainly was that on the practical level. Yes, she demanded the same treatment, respect, and pay for herself that her male colleagues received. Yes, she painted strong and tragic female figures, and made her own decisions how to portray them.

And no, Artemisia did not sign her works as a virgin like her female colleagues, because the whole world knew she wasn't one. She let it all hang out.

And this is the portrait I have now painted of her. If I've learned anything from Artemisia, it's that art historians around the world still argue over her. New paintings are discovered, and the attribution and dating of the ones already found are still contested. Did Artemisia serve as her father's nude model, or would that have been simply out of the question? Did she remain illiterate till her death, or did she ultimately find her way into sophisticated circles? Was Artemisia's rape as traumatizing an experience as we assume, or was its significance somehow less personal back then, because the self-concept of a seventeenth-century person was different from ours? And which of her paintings were self-portraits? Her facial features and body shape have been identified in the Judiths, the Susannas, the Cleopatras, the lute-players, and the helmeted Amazons—but on the other hand, it has been shown that in Italy in her lifetime, she could not have had access to a mirror big enough to allow her to paint her whole nude body. And why does the style of her paintings change so much? Was she a mediocre artist who lacked her own powerful vision, or does the ability to adapt to each city's local style demonstrate both artistic and marketing genius? The truth about Artemisia is still being reconstructed piece by piece, and every new bill of exchange, purchase receipt, and poem carrying her name is still being scrutinized meticulously, until the entire night woman is illuminated.

One possible surviving self-portrait by Artemisia was painted in the 1630s. In it she is thirty-eight, or maybe forty-five, the single mother of two daughters, and if she isn't in Naples, she's in London helping her father with the ceiling-painting project. In the image Artemisia is totally focused on her painting. She's wearing a green dress with broad, frilly sleeves—a bit too fancy to be working in—with a small mask pendant hanging around her neck on a golden chain, a brush and palette in her hand. Her dark hair is pulled back into a bun, but it's starting to escape: she hasn't had time to doll herself up. Artemisia isn't looking at me. She doesn't have time for that. She's otherwise engaged.

*

Night women's advice:

If you know what you want to do, do it.

If you've been humiliated or wronged, if you've suffered, don't get trapped in those experiences. Forge onward. Go to Florence. Or Rome. Or Venice. Or Naples.

Transform your wounds into your strengths. Paint them on a big fucking canvas for all to see.

If there's something you don't know how to do, like reading and writing, learn.

Imbibe the spirit of Caesar and hold it close.

Demand the same pay that the men are getting.

Don't sell yourself cheap.

Learn to negotiate.

Don't grovel.

[A THEORY ABOUT FATHERS, WORD-FILE]

Sometimes at night I think about how behind all these female artists there seems to be an exceptional father wielding his influence in the background, deciding against all precedent to get his daughter an education. I would, of course, like to think that the fathers of Sofonisba, Lavinia, and Artemisia were wonderful fathers, *wise and progressive supporters of equality between the sexes, men who sought in an exemplary fashion to promote the liberation of the female gender—but it may well be that their motives were considerably more banal than that: money. What should we think about that? Were these female artists after all not* truly exemplary women *who pursued their own passions? Did they just obey their fathers' ambitious agendas?*

I'd like to think both views are true. For how do we know which family member came up with the novel idea to educate daughters, and who called the shots in each family? We can't be sure that Sofonisba's father had his daughters taught to paint just to earn their dowries; perhaps it was also because *the daughters* wanted it themselves. We *can't be sure that Lavinia didn't* beg her father please-please *to let her learn to paint, since Sofonisba was allowed to. And maybe Artemisia agreed to sit as her father's model* on the condition *that she be allowed to paint as well.*

Maybe these women were daddy's girls, or at least knew how to wrap their daddies around their little fingers. Maybe they went through their options in their intelligent little heads, trying to figure out how to do the work they wanted to do, and realized that all possible pathways to that end ran through their fathers. Maybe they were able to escape the patriarchy's prison cell only because they were smart enough to slip through the door as their fathers' shadows.

Nor is the importance of fathers evident only in the life stories of female artists: Karen, Isabella, Ida, Mary—it seems as if behind al-

most every successful night woman there is a father who in one way or another encouraged his daughter to chart an extraordinary path. A heroic father who could be admired above all else (Karen); a strict father who educated his daughter like a son (Ida); an absent father whose approval was sought and whose life's work was continued (Mary).

And, somewhere in the background, the shadowy mothers: conventional, slaving in the kitchen, bedridden, ill, dead.

VII Kallio–Mazzano, Winter–Spring

The winter is horrendous. In January, I hole up in my doghouse-size apartment in Helsinki to write, and almost go crazy. I try hard, really I do: I've spent the whole last year collecting material, chased down night women on three continents, kept a journal, and waded through scads of source books—now it's time to buckle down and rework that material, edit, and write.

I set myself up by turning the dinner table against the wall as a desk (no more eating or dreaming in this apartment, this place is for working) and getting a proper desk chair (my father's old broken-down office chair) and a notice board, to which I fix my night women's pictures: middle-aged women in respectable black dresses, a pinup girl riding a zebra, Karen as a young woman surrounded by lion carcasses and as an old woman with Marilyn Monroe, the white-faced Renaissance women from the Uffizi, Artemisia hacking through Holofernes's neck. On the corner of the desk I lay out pieces of wood dyed red by the Mkomazi sand. I fill Post-it notes with encouraging words for myself, like *natural evolution, voyage of discovery, jazz structure, poetic license, lightness, play, joy*. I impose a lunch-date ban on myself and tell everybody of my plan to keep my calendar empty until May—to embalm myself for weeks and months in my lonely bubble and just write. No social life, no writer visits, no googling travel destinations to get my blood churning, nothing. Just putting the pedal to the metal as if blasting across the Olduvai desert, scarf over my mouth, no looking to the left or the right. Book or bust, buckies!

The first week goes okay. I sit at my desk from nine in the morning till five in the afternoon. I don't meet or talk to anyone. By the second week I'm already longing to beg someone to force me out of this studio apartment, lest I go completely nuts. Every day I start coming up with some reason to walk to the nearest grocery store, so I can exchange a few words with the cashier. In the third week I flip through dozens of files containing my notes, forward and backward, a cold panic slowly spreading through my chest. Then I can no longer get out of bed in the morning; the thought of even turning on my computer makes me want to vomit. It feels like I'm alone in a black cave; the winter darkness weighs on me like a pitch-black blanket. *Lightness-play-joy*, my ass. What if nothing comes of all this? Is this the dread second-book syndrome?

All winter I slog through that swamp day after day, still without a clue to how I should be writing this book. I'm so frustrated I could scream. I try to focus on what my painter friend Jyrki said—that this stage of the work, what is called *slinging the shit*, is an unavoidable part of the process, and the key to the whole profession is how you get through it. I'm obviously not getting through it. And because I've voluntarily isolated myself in a total social vacuum, I lie there evenings watching TV in a state of advanced self-loathing. It's almost as if I'm depressed. But how the hell could I be depressed? I'm living the fucking *dream*!

I scoff now at that ridiculous moment of overweening hubris when I defined the noble method of my work as *human experiments*. Sheesh. I'd had another kind of human experiments in mind—you know, adventures to distant uncharted continents, freedom's wind in my hair, time travel back to past cultures—but apparently I have to gulp down the whole foul mess: loneliness, isolation, the frustration swelling in my gut, the feeling of being blocked, of failing, doubts about my own mental health and the existence of any kind of meaning in my life—everything that my night women have all experienced before me, and the kind of experience that used to have women like them committed to the loony bin, with HYSTERIC stamped on their foreheads. That would be me soon. I need a night woman more than ever.

So one night, desperate, I ring up Frida Kahlo. I find her phone number in the facsimile edition of her address book, which I bought early on, when I was first gathering information about my original group of exemplary women. Frida wrote her number down in red ink, in her curly hand:

Frida Kahlo 195221. Diego Rivera ~~239121~~ 147121.

I ask myself at what stage it's possible to say for sure that someone is completely around the bend. Would it be the stage at which she stands in her doghouse-size Helsinki apartment on a winter's night in January, dressed in long underwear and a thermal shirt, and actually picks up the phone and dials Frida Kahlo's number?

She doesn't answer. *The number you have reached is no longer in service*, a woman's voice tells me.

I've got nothing to say to Diego.

One day I receive notification that I've been accepted for a writer's residence in the medieval Italian village of Mazzano, near Rome, for the month of May. In theory that's great, of course, but because I'm neck-deep in the black swamp, I'm horrified: it's going to be survival camp, lonely, lonelier, loneliest. In the instructions included in the e-mail, I'm told that the village is in the middle of nowhere, on the verge of a gorge swarming with snakes ("if you go for a walk, take along a stick"); that there are no transportation links; that you can only get a phone signal "in the front left corner of the terrace," and worst of all, they don't even have an Internet connection. To some mother and wife living the most hectic years of her life, I'm sure that would sound like heaven. Me, I couldn't stand the isolation and loneliness for another second.

But maybe once I've bought the plane tickets, I'll be able to breathe again.

And that is in fact what happens. At the end of April I arrive in Rome, where I'll be spending a few days with my parents before burying myself in Mazzano. I've rented my doghouse-size Helsinki apartment to a young man who's just arrived from Kuala Lumpur, and my parents and I have rented some Italian man's huge, high-ceilinged, old-timey digs a two-minute walk from the Pantheon. On both sides of the grand old building's entrance someone has spray-painted the initials *M*, *I*, and *A*. I stare at the letters in disbelief: What are the odds that out of all the dozens of rental apartments I looked at, I happened to choose this very one, where my name is written by the door?

Ah, eternal Rome! Mornings I creep along at the frustratingly slow snail's pace set by my parents—that's the price I have to pay to eat heavenly three-course lunches with them, meals I wouldn't bother to order by myself. Then I set off on my own to visit the streets and the museums, to devour history and culture. For a few moments I forget all about the book project and feel drunk on everything: Rome's golden light, the beautiful colors of the exterior walls of the houses, the stratified ruins that make me feel like the map of the city should be drawn in three dimensions, with dotted lines marking hundreds of levels on top of one another, the archaeological history of the human race. I'm drunk on the verdant summer, the lilac bushes and the flowering horse chestnut trees, the quiet mood of the side streets. The views from the rooftop terraces out over the city. How Saint Peter's gleams surreally through the gaps in the wall in the evening's misty backlight, and how I catch my breath every time the two-thousand-year-old Pantheon appears out of nowhere. And the food, of course: the artichokes, the deep-fried zucchini flowers, the truffle rabbit patés, the grilled calamari, the saltimbocca (properly prepared), the spinach fried in butter, the *puntarelle*, the calf tongue and salsa verde, the pine-nut pies and Sardinian white wine—and the Tiber at dusk, evening walks past the Colosseum as it turns orange in the setting sun, and the gold-tinted shadows of the pines leading there. And the gloomy Caravaggios, the treasures in Raffaello's rooms, the gold and lapis lazuli excesses of the Jesuit churches, the ancient bent-over nuns who come up to my waist as they take me to a deserted choir loft to look at the remains of a fresco painted in the thirteenth century—the glorious colors fading on its walls, the radiant rainbow-like wings of the angels—and then doze off on a bench while they wait.

I think of my night women, whose shades flicker here and there about the city. I walk around in Artemisia's old seventeenth-century stomping grounds, in the blocks where the artists lived; and I try to find Lavinia's self-portrait in the gallery at Accademia di San Luca, with no luck. Of course not. When was any female artist's work easy to walk up and view?

On our last evening in Rome, May Day Eve, I walk once more to the Pantheon. The moon glows nearly full over its gigantic form, which looks safe, like some great animal.

I post one last message to Facebook: *My next month I'll spend in the land of medieval communication. Homing pigeons and smoke signals okay, maybe the occasional Web or phone, telepathic broadcasts safest of all.*

Mazzano, Mazzano Romano. What to say about it? A dilapidated medieval village on a mountain slope. The residence in the seven-hundred-year-old city wall, the key in a mailbox, from the window in the residence and the rooftop terrace a dizzying view straight down into the waves of green primeval forest and the gorge that cleaves it. Down there live wild pigs, foxes, turtles, snakes, and scorpions. Through the open windows I can hear the rapids roaring through the gorge, but can't see them. The chirping of birds, the swallows and jackdaws swooping over the walls, the mangy one-eyed cats in the narrow cobblestone alleyways, the steps that meander hither and yon up and down the hill, and the unlit arched corridors and latched wooden doors under the arches reminiscent of stalls or dungeons. I'm told the place is haunted, and am not surprised—where else would ghosts live if not here?

The first residents arrived in this village in the tenth century, around Sei Shōnagon's time. They were monks. In the fourteenth century the wall up the vertical slope was built to protect the town, and within the wall houses were built—including my home. Next to the ruins of the church stands the palace of the feudal lord del Drago; from its windows you can look out over the whole village and valley. On the gate to the wall is the stone shield of the dragon lord—a serpent wound around a scepter—and right behind the gate there used to be a moat and stables for horses and mules. Outside the old wall, the houses were built in later centuries; they rise up toward the other hill, and the higher you climb up the winding road for cars, the more modern the houses become. Up on top of that hill, in new Mazzano, is an entirely ordinary world stocked with cars, bus stops, variety stores, and ATM machines.

But here in the old village it feels as if I've found myself in the middle of an ancient book of fairy tales with decorative illustrated letters. Once upon a time, long, long ago, in a certain distant corner of the realm, at the end of a long and difficult journey, behind forests, hills, rivers, and walls, there was a tiny village whose inhabitants had been forgotten there for centuries to live their own quiet lives. How they first landed there, no one remembered. Perhaps they were born from the dragon seeds brought by the ancient monks; perhaps the seeds became wedged in the vertical cliff face, where they began to grow painfully, twistedly, in circumstances not lacking in hardships.

Everything here is sort of approximate: the people, the houses, the animals. Out of the windows hang clotheslines sporting faded, tattered laundry; on the steps and rooftop terraces, potted gardens emerge from the gray stone full of plants wilting in the heat. Everywhere in the houses' gray walls there are strange pits, broken steps leading nowhere, broken gates, and mossy cavities, and if a car occasionally wanders accidentally into the central square, it's probably missing its hood. Faded pictures of the Madonna are everywhere in tiny recesses in the stone walls. In the small square there's a small grocery store and Vittorio's produce shop, selling what the local farmers grow. (I suspect that the owner is actually French actor Jean Reno, who keeps this store in his spare time under the pseudonym "Vittorio.") There's also a tiny chapel, where men sit with the priest evenings near the medieval fresco, and of course the Caffe del Falco—the Falcon Bar—with depressingly dirty plastic tables at which the one-eyed mangy owners of the one-eyed mangy cats sit, including a darkly bronzed, cowlick-haired man who glares about him feverishly but otherwise looks remarkably like Keith Richards.

And it's to the Falcon Bar, "that horrible bar," that a Finn living in the village, eighty-four-year-old Cai, takes me the evening after I arrive. He comes to the residence just as I'm making a minestrone soup out of ingredients I've bought from "Vittorio," presses the button, and yells into the door intercom, "Any Finnish writers here?" It's Cai's tradition, he tells me, to take newly arrived occupants of the residence to this bar and buy them a *caffe corretto* or "corrected coffee," which is to say an espresso sambuca; but because I don't drink coffee, I get sambuca in tea, though Silvia behind the bar says she can't guarantee the result. A normal espresso costs eighty cents, the corrected version a euro. As we drink, Cai tells me the history of the village, and as he walks me home he shows me a secret pitch-dark shortcut through an arched passageway reeking of cat pee and mold—a route that'll take me home, if I manage not to dwell on the ghosts and the horrific stories he's told me about the village's past. Then he teaches me the proper Italian way to kiss somebody on the cheek, and heads off for his own place, which is on the same narrow, mossy Savior's Alley just a few doors down.

A few days later I write:

At first you think, what godforsaken place is this, with its busted houses, collapsed churches, and junked cars? The taxi driver from Rome couldn't find the whole village on his GPS! Then after a day or two, when you've found food, slept well, sipped your own Japanese tea, and read a book under the sun up on the rooftop terrace, listening to the river rushing by below, you start watching the swallows that so passionately swoop around the ruins in the evening, and a warm, homey feeling begins to sneak up on you. Then you start studying the broken-down gates and the steps that dead-end in walls; soon you're photographing the weeds growing on top of the stone wall, the bumpy exterior house walls given multicolored surfaces by centuries of remortaring and tuck-pointing, the out-of-square shadows and arches of the narrow alleyways, the only splash of color the laundry hanging on the line. Then you find that you've fallen in love with those swallows that swoop and dive through the glow of the setting sun, and with the fresh morning light, the dizzying scent of the morning flooding in through the windows, and with the jackdaws; and on the third day you start to count how few the days are till you have to leave—only twenty-four! It occurs to you that you don't want to take that one early-morning bus to Rome after all. It's not that the 7 a.m. departure is too early, but that the day trip to Rome no longer seems all that attractive. Why would you want to go anywhere else, even to the new village just a six-minute walk up the hill? You just want to stay here inside this gray town wall in the small labyrinth of these houses, and walk the three routes it's possible to walk through it; you want to listen to the quiet rustling of this wall, which may be the sound of the river coursing through the valley. You want to sequester yourself inside this wall, in the vast space that hides within.

Now I'm writing instructions for my next twenty-four days.

Before sundown: always go out and watch the swallows.

Always go out to listen to the rustling of the wall.

Hot day: 80 degrees in the shade. I tell myself to get busy with the book, but I'd much rather sit for a moment in the sun, up on the rooftop. Then I climb up to the upper village to buy fresh calamari at the fish market, and on the way back stop at the Falcon Bar to drink a grapefruit juice. As I'm walking home through the dim labyrinth, I run into the people living in the artist residence. "Hey, I know you!" the man says in Finnish. Turns out he's my little brother's childhood friend Markus; he's with his artist wife, Aura, and their three sons. All of them seem incredibly nice. Aura says I must come over to their place for dinner some evening, and go for an exploratory walk in the forest together. They drove down from Finland in their car and are planning to spend an enviable two months here.

That evening Aura comes over to read her e-mail with my dongle (it works after all!) and we chat for a while. She mostly paints in watercolors and lately, she tells me, has been painting a lot of early Christian female saints, like Agnes and Cecilia. I know Cecilia—I saw her marble body in Rome, in the Santa Cecilia Basilica in Trastevere. Aura tells me how Cecilia guarded her virginity in the third century, fasted, wore sackcloth against her skin, even drove her husband out of her bed, and converted four hundred Romans to Christianity, in punishment for which she was sentenced to be beheaded. But though the executioner swung his sword twice, her head was not severed from her body, and Cecilia lived, bleeding, for another three days. Agnes's specialty was long hair, down to the ground, sort of like Aura herself. She lived in the fourth century, and avoided suitors until one of them ratted her out as a Christian. As punishment for that, she was sentenced to be stripped naked in the Stadium of Domitian, nowadays the Piazza Navona, so that the crowd could shame her with their gaze. Miraculously, however, her hair grew to the ground in an instant and covered her body, so that she retained her chastity.

Aura is herself like these sainted women she paints. She has all manner of hunches and feelings; sometimes, she tells me, when she meets a new person or senses a powerful mood, she faints. About me she says she knew instantly that I'm a Libra, like herself, whatever that means. In addition to painting, she's a performance artist, and many of the performances she and her partner Linda stage deal with historical women. Once they arranged a social service where a client could meet Marie Antoinette, Anna Karenina, Sue Ellen Ewing, or the Virgin Mary. Both Aura and Linda have grown long hair for their performances, so that the two of them might be indistinguishable.

Later that evening I google the painting Aura did of Saint Serena. It looks like Aura, just sadder, like someone who already knows her fate, with watercolor shadows under her eyes, while Aura herself is full of smiling energy. One day I invite Serena-Aura to drink a glass of wine on the rooftop terrace; we sit out there chatting about saints and night women and staring out at the ancient forest spread before us, in whose recesses molder the ancient graves of the Etruscans and Falisci.

Mazzano in May is one long heat wave. I don't know what I was thinking when I was packing for the trip—probably that I'd be cold in medieval stone buildings—because I'm finding piles of cashmere knits and Bambu long underwear, but the two summer dresses, which I really do need here, I went and removed at the last minute.

Add to the chapter on packing a suitcase: *Never decide against a summer dress*. It's as light as a feather and takes up the space of a handkerchief. Right, Nellie Bly?

One day Mazzano is throwing a village party. I've reserved the morning for writing, but just as I'm about to start, the door intercom buzzes. It's Cai asking whether I'd like to join his wife and him for coffee at a nearby village—a tradition they have, taking the residence people on this sort of trip. "Let's meet in a quarter of an hour up in the Piazza Antisa." I ask where that is, as the only piazza name I know is Umberto I in the old center. "Well, okay, I'll come to this door then," Cai huffs, and I hear him complaining as he switches off the intercom, "Jesus, a woman who gets lost in Mazzano. . . ." It turns out Piazza Antisa means the area in front of the church ruins. It's maybe twenty steps from my door.

We climb in their car and head toward the medieval village of Nepi. Cai's wife, Christel, is an intelligent and extremely competent woman with a great sense of humor. She had a long, illustrious international career, and has lived in Italy since the year I was born. She explains the things we see out our windows nonstop: the distant Apennines (skiing in the winter), the hazelnut plantings (wine and olives don't do well here), the oaks (seven different species), the ivy (I make the mistake of admiring it, but in fact it kills the trees and is destroying the village wall), a building in ruins (a former movie studio that made spaghetti westerns), a spring (where the Nepi mineral water is bottled), the Nepi aqueduct (only a one-inch drop every three feet). In Nepi she gives Cai decisive instructions on where to park (if you were Italian, you'd park *there*). It's market day in Nepi; in front of the church a group of children in white gowns have gathered for their confirmation, and when the village band arrives, the children follow it through the ancient streets. It's like something out of Fellini. We browse the cheese-sellers' wares (choosing pecorino), I buy moisturizing cream (made from an ancient Etruscan recipe, containing olive oil), and Christel buys me a piece of licorice root, a dry-looking stick that I obediently suck all the way back to Mazzano. We finally sit down for coffee/tea (I'm told that to order iced tea, I should say *tè freddo*), and Christel tells me about her impressive career. Cai says that when he is in Helsinki, he is constantly stopped in the street for kisses on the cheek, and he never has the faintest idea who is kissing him, except that the person has something to do with Mazzano. Over the last twenty years, twenty Finnish writers and artists have been in residence here each year—they all remember Cai, but how could he possibly remember them?

I eat lunch at home and try to write for a moment, then have to rush to the village party. It seems like the whole village is working away in the food-preparation tent put up in front of the church ruins. A dark-skinned woman who looks like an ancient Etruscan is baking pizza with flour on her face; "Vittorio" putters about in his apron; Keith Richards, who usually parks himself in the Falcon Bar at 7 a.m., is frying hamburger patties on the grill with precisely the same passion and gestures as his exemplar would display flailing the guitar to a packed stadium, elastic hair band around his forehead, a cigarette hanging off his lip. Long tables have been set up in the square, and Aura and her boys and I eat everything on offer: *pizza fritta*, deep-fried artichoke, *fave e pecorino*, homemade lemon pies. A Finnish artist named Mari joins us: she came here for an artist's residence twelve years ago, met a man, had a daughter, and stayed. As the evening darkens around us, a local youth band set up in the ruins plays all the requisite pieces from Guns N' Roses to Nirvana's "Smells Like Teen Spirit," and the long-haired guitarist moshes shyly.

I'd imagined myself coming to this isolated village for a quiet writer's retreat, getting stuck here without transportation links, phone, or Internet access, and at the very least plunging, over the month I'm here, into miserable cabin fever—but life in this supposed hick town that God supposedly forgot is more hectic and more social than my life in Helsinki was all winter. I haven't written a word of what I was hoping to have written, but I have learned that I need to get my morning activities out of the way by nine, because you never know who's going to ring the doorbell and what the day may bring. I've also learned that this kind of community life is way more wonderful than a lonely hermit camp in a doghouse-size Helsinki apartment in the January darkness.

Fixing food Mazzano-style: go to "Vittorio's" and stand around there for a while looking clueless until one of the old guys hanging around outside comes in to lay his best recipe on you. "You know how to fix these?" asks a sly-looking old Calabrian in astonishingly good English, pointing to the pea pods. Then he explains how to make Sicilian *pasta fave*: boil the peas for ten minutes in salt water, sauté diced onion in oil, then throw the boiled peas and a little of the water in with the onion, and if you want to make a truly Sicilian impression, add a little bacon; then serve with short pasta—*short, not long*, the old man stresses with a shake of his finger. Price of ingredients: one euro forty. Then he asks where I'm from, and tells me he has circled the globe himself: "Once my car broke down in Guatemala and I was stuck there for fifteen years." I ask whether his car broke down here in Mazzano too, and he says, "Something like that."

The person who handles the practicalities of the Mazzano residences is a woman named Carla. Carla has promised (for a fee) to take me on outings into the surrounding region, so I'll see a little of the world. One hot day we drive to Lake Bracciano; another day we head into Rome. (Carla's car is in the shop, so her eighty-three-year-old neighbor with a nasal cannula up his nostrils drives us in and picks us up to bring us back.) A third day Carla and I drive to Viterbo, a larger medieval city near Mazzano. As we're walking along the shopping street, Carla glances at my sports sandals (I still haven't gotten rid of them) and opines that one should *never ever* wear such things. I think it best to stop into the next shoe store and buy the Italian-style leopard-patterned leather sandals that Carla recommends, so she doesn't have to be ashamed of me one second longer.

We eat lunch in a small piazza under a green pergola, then walk to the palace to which the pope fled from the inflamed situation in Rome back in the thirteenth century. We walk about in the palace museum, where the glass cases are filled to bursting with holy relics. No one even knows any longer where they're all from, but behind glass walls there are dozens of bones, twists of hair, pieces of teeth, and fingerprints. As we study the contents, Carla mentions in passing that Jesus's foreskin, *prepuzzio*, used to be kept near here in the village of Calcata, but it was stolen.

I stare at Carla in disbelief: *Jesus's foreskin—in Calcata—was stolen*. Every element in this hysterically funny sentence is utterly absurd. First of all, how likely is it that Jesus's foreskin was even saved, and if it was, how and where? (Though how do I know, maybe it's some kind of cultural custom, like the tooth fairy; I'm told some mothers keep their newborns' umbilical cords in a box.) Second, how likely is it that of all the possible places for a holy relic like Jesus's foreskin to end up it should land in Calcata, Italy, that dreamy stone village perched on top of a hill that I visited with Aura's family one day? And third, who would have stolen it, and why? What's the going rate for a theoretical messianic foreskin on the Catholic holy relics market these days? Are there a lot of fake foreskins in circulation?

My questions are answered that evening, when I go over to Aura and Markus's for dinner. Somewhere between the deep-fried polenta and the *cantuccini*, Markus brings up the mythical foreskin, about which he has learned the following:

Legend has it that Charlemagne gave Jesus's foreskin *as a Christmas present* to Pope Leo III in the year of our Lord 800. Charlemagne happened to have it because it was dropped into his reverent hand by an archangel—though a slightly more believable story would have it that it was given to him as a wedding present by the Byzantine empress. In any case, Pope Leo took his Christmas present to the Sancta Sanctorum chapel in Rome for safekeeping—after all, it was a pretty consequential object: the only piece of Jesus's body that survived. So consequential was that foreskin, in fact, that there were indeed many competing *fake foreskins* circulating around Europe, each with its own chapel built to house it and its own brotherhood founded to protect it.

That "original" foreskin was lost, however, in the chaos of 1527, when the troops of Holy Roman Emperor Charles V attacked Rome. At that point a soldier stole the foreskin, but he was caught near Rome and held prisoner in Calcata, where he stashed the foreskin. It was not until three decades later that the foreskin was found, and beginning in 1557, it was stored in the village church. Pope Sixtus V granted the honorers of the foreskin absolution of their sins, and Calcata became a popular destination for pilgrims. Thus if, say, Sofonisba or Lavinia had happened to conceive an overpowering enthusiasm for the foreskin, she could have gone to see it—but somehow I doubt it.

When, in 1610, Galileo Galilei discovered the rings of Saturn with his telescope, the Vatican librarian published a study of the holy foreskin, *which he speculated had been transformed into the rings of*

Saturn upon Jesus's ascension into heaven. (It occurs to me to wonder whether Galileo and Artemisia discoursed upon this subject at the dinner table in the Medici court in Florence.) Later, in the nineteenth century, people began to demand proof of authenticity for the foreskin kept in a certain French monastery, and an end was finally put to the decades-long controversy by a 1900 Vatican decree levying a punishment for anyone who ever spoke or wrote about the holy foreskin again. But it wasn't until 1962 that the Vatican finally removed the day honoring Jesus's foreskin from the liturgical calendar, thereby, they hoped, silencing the Foreskin Flap once and for all.

In the sixties, however, the hippies who moved to Calcata decided that worshipping the foreskin and carrying it reverently in the New Year's parade sounded like just the thing, and the tradition they developed then survived until the eighties, at which point the Calcata vicar decided to intervene and put a stop to the shenanigans, which had become something of an embarrassment. Just before the new year, he admitted to *taking the foreskin home in a shoebox and putting it in his closet*, from which it was then "stolen." The thieves were never caught and the foreskin was never found, but the clues point to the "butcher's shop"—which is to say, the Vatican's secret objects department.

At night, lying in my bed, I reflect once again on the mysterious pathways of human passions: holy foreskins, night women, whatever else we decide to worship. And who am I to laugh at holy relics? Who knows into what raptures the discovery of a twist of Sofonisba's hair or Artemisia's authentic fingerprint might plunge me?

They're predicting another hot day, so I'm planning on staying in. I wash the dishes, do my laundry, make lunch, then try to bring my journal up to date—to reach that Shangri-la, the present moment. The guilty thought crosses my mind that I'm not even riding a camel across the Sinai Desert, and yet I haven't found time to write in days. The research notes I've piled up in dark corners of my computer's hard drive are still awaiting their write-up too. At this rate I'll never finish this book. I recall with envy how inconceivably hardworking all my night women have been, and how much they've achieved. If this book were being written by Lavinia or Artemisia, let alone Isabella or Ida, it would already have been sent off to the publisher! They wouldn't be flitting about on the hill hereabouts, looking for the ancient graves of the Falisci, which are completely irrelevant to the book project: they'd be sitting at home hard at work.

But then I think: if the mercury's showing mideighties, maybe it's permissible to lie down for a second on the cool sofa with the windows shuttered and watch Fellini's *La Dolce Vita*. What more perfect place to watch it than here, where Fellini's movies suddenly feel like documentary depictions of ordinary life?

It seems to me like I'm right where I ought to be. The rest of the world is somewhere far away, behind a misty veil—and with it, this book that wants me to write it.

A representative of the residence foundation comes for a visit, and Carla organizes a dinner in honor of the visit in the cantina, down in the basement of my unit. Carla has been cooking up a storm since six in the morning, and the tables groan under the weight of the delicacies—omelets, pasta salads, bean stews, eggplants drenched in oil, heaps of grilled chicken filets, cheeses, salamis, olives, lupin beans, tiramisu. Everybody is busy pouring prosecco into their own and others' glasses and the mood is wonderfully loud and boisterous; many different languages are being spoken on top of and mixed in with each other: Finnish, English, Italian, Estonian, and even Swedish. The guests include the foundation representative, Jyrki, and his girlfriend; their friends—a couple who have just fallen in love; Aura, without her boys; the residence photographer, Karel, from Estonia; then Mari, Cai, and Christel; Cai's daughter, who arrived yesterday with her husband; and Carla and her husband, Paolo. Jyrki is loud and funny; he's wearing a bright-yellow T-shirt that's too small for him and has Beach Life written on it—completely inappropriate for his personality but somehow indicative of his sense of humor. He bought it in the marketplace in the upper village. Cai doesn't join in the conversation, but runs his eyes across the row of young women sitting in front of him, looking happy. Carla doesn't sit down at the table at all—she doesn't even seem to have a chair—because she keeps cooking more dishes and watching the rest of us eat with a satisfied smile. This is precisely the kind of crazy dinner I was hoping for in Florence; to my surprise, it's here, where I expected to be living the life of a lonesome hermit, that I get one. At the table, people tell stories about earlier residence guests. Some have apparently locked themselves in their apartments for the whole month and then complained later about what a horrible place this was. Others have not set foot outside the village, except at most a few strides into the forest. One had wound up by mistake in the Mazzano near Milan; another had gone to Nazzano instead. One had called Carla in a panic on the first night and claimed the apartment was haunted; fortunately, another apartment had happened to be vacant just then, and the resident had moved in there—after Carla had inspected it for supernatural entities. Jyrki is clearly pleased when I say I've fallen in love with Mazzano.

Around midnight everyone goes home, the tables are cleared and wiped, the borrowed chairs returned; and once I've walked the twenty steps or so home, I pour myself a glass of Vermentino di Sardegna from the fridge and go up to the rooftop terrace to stare up at the starry sky and listen to the mute rustling of the ancient forest.

On my last day, Aura paints me.

She's asked me before whether I'd sit for her, and of course I go. She paints on the floor of her studio, where the light floods in through the high windows; I sit before her and pretend to read a magazine to give her peace to work. She draws a sketch on watercolor paper with a long stick dipped in black ink, then paints with watercolors, blue and black, many images, paper after paper, from different angles, from closer in and farther away. She warns me that she doesn't do representational images; I already knew that—in the paintings on the studio table, the women's faces are partly or completed smudged; many have the body of some animal, or some other figure peeks out from behind the woman's shoulder like a shadow. The works have a strong feeling of strangeness and presence.

It's wonderful to watch Aura work. Talk bubbles up constantly, joyfully, as the dark, strange images appear on the paper. She paints quickly, never stopping to fix anything; if some image doesn't please her or goes somehow wrong, she throws a water wash over the top of it with a big brush, or else paints it all black. The watercolors spread on the damp paper, and Aura wipes some off my face with a piece of cloth, so that my face becomes messy, halved, as if sunken beneath the water in a black pond. In one image I look like a three-year-old child, in another like a young boy, but in several I am quite recognizable. It's somehow touching to see yourself on paper, through someone else's eyes, though Aura insists that artists always paint themselves into their pictures. On the last paper, a big one, she paints many faces side by side and stacked on top of one another, different versions, flickering negatives, or like after archaeological excavations.

She gives me two of the sketches to take along, leaving the biggest for herself; she plans to continue it, perhaps until it becomes a finished work. She says she's working on an exhibition with the working title *Women Running in the Desert*—there will be animal figures among the images, sometimes just a hint or a glimpse of them, sometimes as a threat outside the image, so that it's never quite clear whether the women are running with them or away from them.

I know immediately what she's talking about.

The flight is more beautiful than ever. We rise into the air over Rome, curve over green hills toward the shore of round Lake Bracciano; I can make out the point of the peninsula above the village of Anguillara and the Castle of Orsini, and then we dive into a cloud and on through it to the other side, and float up above the soft cotton, into the blue kingdom of the sun.

The intolerable parting sadness of the past few days is behind me now; all I feel is an incredible joy and gratitude. I reflect on how amazing it is to be able to fly over all this, to travel in this way that my night women could never have imagined. I think about all the people I've met on this trip, this unexpected and inspiring feeling of belonging I've had. I think about Carla and her family, the gleam in Paolo's eye, and the daughter dressed in black—always-laughing Carla, who is sometimes so angry she could *kill* someone, and who would like to travel with me to Sardinia. I think of the joy radiating off Aura, her hunches, good-natured Markus and their boys. I think of enigmatic, marvelous Mari, who is en route to big changes and is full of fierce creative power. I think of sweet, silly Cai, who kept calling me "honey" as if I were his grandchild, and to whom I could for that very reason not give as a thank-you card the nude portrait of La Fornarina that I bought in Rome—who knows what he or the immeasurably competent Christel would have thought of it. I think of the villagers, the forest and forest spirits, and the Etruscan women and their ancient graves. I think of Rome, with which I am heart and soul in love, eternal Rome, to which I want to return a hundred more times. It occurs to me that for the past month I have been nothing but happy, because of the city and this tiny village, and the people who have crossed my path, and hope that it isn't all just the effect of the prescription medicine for tension headaches I've been taking, which is said to have a positive effect on mood as well.

Finland. Why does the hat I bought in Rome, which in Italy looked stylish as hell, immediately look in the bathroom at the Helsinki-Vantaa airport like I'm some Hanoi Rocks guitarist?

VIII Rome–Bologna–Florence revisited

Two years later I return to Italy to revisit the cities of my night women. It seems to me something has changed—as if the women may have finally, gradually, begun their slow journey from closed galleries and forgotten storerooms toward the light of day.

In Rome I find lodging in the seventeenth-century artists' quarter, near the street where Artemisia was raped. My high-ceilinged room is whitewashed and beautiful; lying in my bed, I can see the dark rafters of the old grain warehouse that this building use to be. I lean out of my second-floor window and look down at the narrow street—behind those buildings is the Via della Croce, where Artemisia lived in 1611. Whenever I open the window, the street noise floods into my room, but in the evenings so does the sound of passersby singing opera, accompanied by the voices of groups of people looking for dinner; in the mornings my room fills with the buzzing of Vespas, the noises of garbage trucks and street-sweeping vehicles, and the bonging of church bells. I might even hear Artemisia's cries for help from her upstairs bedroom in the Via della Croce.

If four centuries ago these streets were dangerous and violent, full of menace and murder, they still aren't entirely safe. Rome's *teste di cazzo*—peckerheads—robbed me of two days' worth of my travel budget on the Metro one day. But here in Artemisia's bedroom, life is wonderful. The feather-light curtains wave gently by the open window. I hear the sounds carried up from the street. A serving girl brings my breakfast tray to me in my room.

I tour Artemisia's addresses in the local streets, and when I wander through the labyrinthine exposed-beam rooms on the second floor of the white house on the corner of the Via del Babuino—now an atelier-café—it feels as if I'm walking through her childhood home.

And maybe I am. On the Via Margutta, by contrast, the ivy-covered palazzos have swallowed up all the older and smaller dwellings; and the Via del Corso, which in Artemisia's day was still part of the artists' quarter, is these days inundated with the thousands of tourists and Romans who flock here for the pedestrians-only shopping streets to buy cheap clothing, sports shoes, and cell phones—the identical stores you can find in every city in the world. I also walk to the Santa Maria del Popolo church to see the Caravaggios that Artemisia saw there at her mother's funeral. The Caravaggios are a national treasure, and they're cordoned off with retractable woven belts, the guard only allowing a set number of tourists in at a time. While I'm awaiting my turn, I stare unseeing at the cordon belt, until I finally realize what's written on it: ARTHEMISIA ARTHEMISIA ARTHEMISIA, along its entire length.

Then I walk across the city to the Piazza Navona. On the exterior wall of a museum on the edge of the square hangs a gigantic blowup of Judith slaying Holofernes. Inside the museum, Judith slays Holofernes twice more, Susanna suffers the harassment of the elders, Lucretia commits suicide, Danaë gets showered in golden coins, and blue-lipped Cleopatra dies over and over, as the work of Artemisia's hands is on display in gallery after gallery.

Yes: this is the first time I'm seeing a night woman's paintings featured in a special dedicated exhibition.

On my list of things to track down in Rome is also Lavinia's famous self-portrait, the one she painted for her father-in-law in 1577 and which these days is hidden away in the storeroom of a Roman art academy. I've tried to get in to see Lavinia in the Accademia di San Luca gallery on many previous trips, and I've never succeeded; but now, after all those failed attempts and the exchange of numerous e-mails and phone calls in English and Italian, I have managed to arrange a meeting with her. I'm nervous, and feel a bit like an impostor: I've neglected to mention that I'm not a *real* art historian, just a fan in pursuit of night women.

But this time there's no problem. A museum employee named Fabrizio disappears behind the storeroom door and reappears less than a minute later with Lavinia hanging from his hand. He stands Lavinia up on a gallery table on top of a piece of Styrofoam, leaning against a plywood cube, and then heads off to take care of other matters. Suddenly I'm alone with Lavinia.

The painting is small, of an easily portable size, and again a totally different color from the reproductions I've seen in books or online. Lavinia's Bolognese bride's dress is a *lilac purple*, and everything is exquisitely detailed and delicious: the open trousseau trunk, the easel, Lavinia herself. I glance up at the security cameras, then quickly bend over next to Lavinia to take a selfie of the two of us. Inside the frame are also my notebook, pen, and map of Rome.

Then Fabrizio returns to take the painting away. He's in a hurry, so I don't have time to ask any questions, such as why the hell is Lavinia kept in storage? But mission accomplished nevertheless: the fake scholar has successfully tricked her way into the proximity of the object of her invented study, and one night woman lying awake in the darkness of the storeroom has been exposed to the light of day for a few moments.

In Florence I stay in a boardinghouse in the old city center. It decidedly busts my budget, but the view out my window is of the Arno River, and I tell myself that for once in her life a person has a right to a Florentine *room with a view*. The slant golden light of morning tempts me, but I head off to the Uffizi. The crush is horrific; it makes me nervous. Everywhere there are huge crowds of tourists standing like walls in front of precisely the paintings I'd like to see. Only Beatrice stands hogging the limelight all by herself in an empty gallery—I almost laugh to see her there, looking so totally pissed off.

In the evening I visit the Uffizi bookstore once more, since there's no longer a line to it. I decide to take a quick pass through the galleries as well—just over a half hour left till closing time—and glance at the women I wasn't able to see over the walls of people this morning: Battista, Simonetta in a seashell, and the others. Upstairs I notice that a small special exhibition has been opened today—wait, can this be true?—of Plautilla Nelli, Sister Plautilla, *Florence's first woman artist*, the nun who painted in the sixteenth century. What I've read is that only a few works by her have survived; but as I race from painting to painting, I realize that they must have found new works by her, and they've been wonderfully restored. The saints in the exhibition exude a fresh tenderness—apparently Plautilla churned these out in her convent workshop, running an art factory staffed by nuns. I also learn that Plautilla's magnum opus, the seven-meter-long *Last Supper*, the only painting of that subject ever done by a woman, long cracking and flaking in the monks' refectory at the Santa Maria Novella monastery, is now being restored, and will be placed permanently on view in the monastery.

Nor is that all: suddenly it seems that a whole renaissance of women artists has been launched in Florence. I learn that the new director of the Uffizi has taken it upon himself to rewrite the canon and—finally—bring the works of women artists from the back storerooms out to the gallery walls. There will be other exhibitions of artists like Sister Plautilla, and there are plans to collect the portraits of women hidden in the Vasari Corridor and place them on display in their own gallery in the Uffizi. Sofonisba, Lavinia, Artemisia—all the works that I so passionately sought out two and a half years ago will soon be displayed for all to see. The line printed on the exhibition plaques is balm to my night woman-plagued soul: *According to the new understanding, women artists are a vital part of the Renaissance.*

The Uffizi is closing and the guards chase me out, so I walk to the Santa Trinita church to gather my thoughts and share the amazing changes happening out in the world with Sassetti's daughter, who stares at me out of her fresco with searching eyes and a round belly. Then I get dinner at a tiny restaurant kept by two sisters; from my table by the window, I can see the black water of the Arno and the countless layers of lights reflected on it from the palazzos.

On my way home I run into a demonstration on the Ponte Vecchio, and stand there on the narrow cobblestone street watching the mass of people flowing by. The procession goes on and on—and all of the marchers seem to be women, young women, middle-aged women, older women. . . . Is this some kind of women's march? Wait a second: today is International *Women's* Day! That's why the Plautilla exhibition was opened today! What a crowd, what a carnival! The women just keep coming, carrying placards with drawings of ovaries on them, captions demanding self-determination, *autodeterminazione*, the right to make decisions about their own bodies, the right to refuse to become baby-making machines and Sassetti's daughter.

Then I finally get it, what this all means: *anno Domini* 2017, the women of Florence have finally taken to the streets, left the bedrooms, the kitchens, the cellars, and the storerooms—and it's all so wonderful I can hardly catch my breath.

[GRANT APPLICATION, DICTATED TO A SCRIBE]

Honored Don Antonio Ruffo,

I am writing to you once more to apologize that my work is still not finished. I understand your impatience; you have been expecting it since last year, at least. I must confess that the work has taken me many times longer than I had anticipated. There are so many women to depict, all different, and each model must be studied and investigated meticulously; this has required far more time than I had planned. In addition, many times closer scrutiny has revealed flaws and deficiencies in the women, or else suggestive hints that have led to new investigations . . . and from the vast selection of women, I have had to choose only the most suitable—what a headache that has been!

As for the many travels I have undertaken to further my study, they have brought me to the verge of bankruptcy. My funds are exhausted; to be frank, I have been flat broke for some time now, and so I request that Your Most Illustrious Lordship kindly send me another 500 ducats, that I might bring this work to a close. I work continuously, and as fast as I can, but unfortunately headaches and other complaints that I shall not trouble you by listing here periodically confine me to my bed. Another problem is nausea brought on by excessive brain strain; when it comes over me, I am unable even to look at the work at hand, and the only remedy is time—if I spend a week or two working on other tasks, I can return with renewed enthusiasm to the work which Your Most Illustrious Lordship so eagerly awaits.

I cannot express the full extent of my gratitude to Your Most Illustrious Lordship for your understanding, and beg yet a little more patience. I can assure you that this delay will be of the greatest benefit to the work.

On this—— day of the month of——, MMXVII

Respectfully yours, M—— K——

[LETTER WRITTEN WITH A QUILL IN TRIPLICATE]

Dear Sofonisba, Lavinia, and Artemisia,

I am writing to thank you most humbly for the many pieces of valuable advice you've given me. I believe that your encouraging example would inspire many women, and I'd like to arrange a seminar to which I would respectfully invite the three of you as speakers. You don't suffer too horribly from stage fright, I hope? If needed, I can offer you some beta-blockers. Please send me your honorarium requests, and I will pass them on to Don Antonio Ruffo.

The topics to be covered at the seminar include:

1) How to represent yourself professionally
2) How to win clients
3) How to market your skills
4) How to negotiate fees and prosper
5) How to succeed in a male-dominated profession
6) How to combine family and work
7) How to rise up after massive setbacks
8) How to work efficiently: night-womanhood as a resource

I'm also considering future seminars on the following topics:

—A workshop for fathers: how to further your daughter's career, and cautionary examples
—A workshop for husbands: experiences of being married to a career woman
—A workshop for patrons: make and pay for commissions properly

—A course for directors of art museums: get to know your storerooms

Collaboratively,
M—— K——

IX Normandy, September

The village of Villerville, Normandy. I've come here to the Atlantic coast with my friend Buz to stay in this old, narrow, dark house. We're planning on holding a two-week two-person writing camp here, and I'm thrilled with the sheer genius of the idea. If writing is a constant balancing act between the requisite isolation and the debilitating effects of cabin fever, the perfect solution must be precisely this: a writing camp with a colleague.

The Normandy invasion has been exhausting. I first spent the night at Buz's place, because my apartment's tenants came the previous day. Reveille at 6 a.m., then helsinkiparislisieuxtrouvillevillerville, and then, on the verge of starvation, the final trek hauling suitcases up into the cold, damp house. (No, I still haven't gotten around to taking Nellie Bly's packing course.) With our last ounce of strength, we order a pizza for dinner and eat it with red wine on the steps to the levee. It's a beautiful evening: low tide has exposed the mussel catch, and the beach is crawling with mussel-harvesters in their rubber boots and buckets.

The next day we head over to the nearby village marketplace to stock up on food. We stuff our bags with squid, fresh sausage, artichokes, kale, peaches, figs, goat cheese, duck-liver pâté, pommeau, cider, Sancerre. For lunch we have blue mussels on the villa-lined boulevard hugging the contours of the sand beaches in Trouville, and dessert in a yellow *crêperie* on the corner. In the evening the sky is a line of purple clouds marching against a purple backdrop; the tide pools on the mussel beach each glint silver and ice with breathtaking beauty.

I post the picture we took of the two of us in the magical light of the solarium to Facebook and write: *Things that make everything feel more wonderful: a colleague.*

And then we get to work.

In the morning I climb up the spiral staircase to the small bedroom on the second floor. There I find a cherry vanity from the last century that will work as a desk. Sitting at one end of the table, I can see myself and the silver top of my computer in the cloudy mirror. I take a deep breath. I tell myself that this is a woman who knows how to write this book. I mentally include myself in the group of traveling and writing women: Karen, Isabella, Ida, and Mary—and those as well whose creative implement was a brush.

I can almost see them here, their figures in dark dresses merging with my reflection in the these blackened, decoratively framed mirrors. I can almost hear them in this house, surrounded by all the bronze-vine-covered lampstands, the many-armed chandeliers, the silver tea pitchers, the marble women bending to wash, the brass-headed and -footed beds, the claw bathtubs, the ink-bottle stands, and the escritoires. The chivalry-themed Gobelins, the lush forest paths in the landscape paintings, and the grand old sailing ships in the copper engravings: I may look out of place in my fleece hoodie, but my night women fit like a glove.

From my desk I can see into the solarium, through the lace curtains on the window. The sun- and salt-air-faded wicker chairs are coated with a thin layer of dust and mold, and the thin iron garden chairs are rusted, like everything here. Everywhere on little shelves, in basins, and on trays are clam shells, gastropod shells, and starfish collected from the beach—right, scientific samples. A plaster boy on a side table is playing a violin with a shy smile, and the books on the shelves—*Sea Shore of Britain & Northern Europe; Rocks and Minerals, Fossils*, and *Shells* from the Eyewitness Handbooks series; and a collection of coffee-table art books—have all faded till they're almost colorless, translucently white.

As the sun sets, I stand ankle-deep in the tide pools on our home beach, in rubber boots. The sky darkens from pink to a deep aquamarine, unreal as a watercolor. My reflection stares up at me whole from the mirror-still surface of the water, while on the horizon sparkle the billions of Le Havre's glittering gems in a long thin ribbon like a dream.

Each day passes in a matter of seconds. We come up to start writing immediately after breakfast, take a quick look at the beach after lunch, work till dinner, then a quick look at the sunset and off to bed. The hours zoom by so unnoticed at the computer that before I know it I'm hungry again, *again* it's mealtime. Sometimes during the day we carry the beach chairs down to the crushed-seashell sand and enjoy the warmth and the sun for a while. One day we spend in the nearby village of Honfleur, visiting an antique market and eating oysters, snails, and duck drumsticks, and then climb onto an ornamental antique hundred-year-old carousel and snap pictures of each other as the calliope plays. I sit on a giraffe's back, surrounded by a tiger, an elephant, and a white horse, pretending to ride like the wind.

Buz seems quite efficient. The page numbers she racks up each day are enviable. Yesterday, she tells me, a scene appeared in her novel in which the protagonist descends in a hot-air balloon onto the unreal lunar landscape of the Normandy beach at low tide. Today Amanda is trying to escape a women's mental asylum island in the southwestern Finnish archipelago across the ice, and in the afternoon Buz plans to write a section dealing with winter graves. Meanwhile, I'm plodding along with my endless notes about explorers and trying to organize the topics I'm dealing with into at least provisional wholes. This is the absolute worst phase of writing, I know. It's something I'm just going to have to get through.

In the wee hours, things get blown out of all proportion and my whole existence comes to feel like such an agony that I want to scream. The things my night women say drift about in my head in a tangled skein, banging rhythmically around the same loop over and over till I can't tell whether I'm asleep or awake.

. . . if, for instance, he had eaten something, he might not have lost courage, for starvation is known to reduce courage . . .

. . . it is quite a mistake always to travel first class, for then one only hears the talk of foreigners, which is apt to be vapid and stale . . .

. . . take along one especially beautiful nightgown, so that you won't be embarrassed if you are laid low by fever; learn to prepare a good curry for emergencies . . .

. . . the bathroom was another horror . . . for dinner I had a bottle of tepid beer, two Equanils and a sleeping pill; the intention being to pass out as fast as possible . . .

. . . I remember the things I have seen by the light of a hurricane-lamp better than others . . .

. . . travellers are priviledged to do the most improper things with perfect propriety . . .

. . . I have also taught myself to plow, so that I did not need to feel inferior to Tolstoy in a photograph . . .

There's too much stuff in my head. I have too many women to think about at night. Also, I'm constantly being stressed out by all the applications I have to submit during these weeks for grants and residences (*honored Don Antonio Ruffo . . .*), the unexpected writing requests I have to field, and the invitations dropping into my e-mail inbox to appear in public, give e-mail interviews, and provide video greetings to award ceremonies—everything that's part of the job but that I have such a weak stomach for. Beneath all that slithers a chilling terror: What if I can't finish this book after all? What if I just don't know how to write it? What if I can't transform these fifty-one files I have stored on my computer into a smoothly flowing manuscript?

Besides, I'm starting to think that that whole "human experiments" method is no good. My thought was to do *the same kinds of things* that my night women have done. I should have literally followed in their footsteps, paddled through the jungle, dragged myself half-dead across the desert, journeyed through uncharted territories, lived on butter tea, and survived for three months with only a handbag.

Instead, I'm the person sitting on the back of the carousel's pretend giraffe and thinking about the women who did something for real.

We head to Paris. Our plan is to spend a few days there before Buz flies home and I return to my Normandy village. On the morning of our departure, I accidentally see myself in the dresser mirror in the bedroom wearing only my underwear and a flesh-colored money belt. The sight is shocking. FYI: If you as a traveling woman should ever feel the need for a chastity belt to ward off situations leading to physical intimacy, a flesh-colored money belt will work just as well.

In Paris it's raining cats and dogs. We take a taxi to our hotel, which turns out to be tucked away in the recesses of the Passage Jouffroy, then grab lunch at dome-ceilinged Chartier in the same block—an institution that has been feeding workers for little since 1896. (Back then the workers arrived at the food line with their own plates and spoons.)

In the afternoon we're walking in Saint-Germain-des-Prés when the clouds burst again. We decide to go to Les Deux Magots for an aperitif—of course there, because it's a famous writer's café and the birthplace of existentialism, as is the Café de Flore next door. Each café gives out its own literary prize. The Flore's annual prize, I'm told, is 6,000 euros and a glass of Pouilly-Fumé every day for a year—a hint I hereby pass on to coffee shops in Helsinki.

As dusk falls we walk across the Pont Neuf, where I gaze at the boxes of books laid out along the river by the bouquinistes, now closed up for the night, and wonder whether there is another city in the world where a major thoroughfare is lined night and day with old books. Books rule this city. They stand dignified guard over its shores. The wisdom they emanate floats in the air like an intoxicating, inspiring infusion.

In honor of our last evening in Paris, I try to order a glass of an extremely expensive wine, but the server exclaims, "Oh, it's very, very complex," and refuses to sell me any. "So am I," is what I should have retorted, but I confess that the cheaper wine the server recommended was also excellent. Its name was *Who am I.*

Then I return to my writing village, alone. I go for a walk along the awe-inspiring beach at high tide, in such a strong wind that my lips begin to taste salty. In the evening the purple sunset is reflected on the tide pools at low tide, and I seem to be looking down at the flaming crust of the moon.

The next day I get back to work.

Msabu, do you believe yourself that you can write a book? Kamante's words echo in my head.

But what you write is some here and some there. When the people forget to close the door it blows about, even down on the floor and you are angry. It will not be a good book.

[A NOTE ON THE NIGHTSTAND]

I'm M. I'm forty-three years old. I've been writing my second book for six hundred days.

I confess: there are too many women to think about at night. I could never have imagined how many of them I'd find, once I started looking. They stand at my bedroom door, in the stairwell, in the attic, in the winter garden of this house in Normandy, and in the salty wind on the narrow road that leads to the Atlantic beach. I stuff them in the desk drawer, because this book has to be finished somehow, but the drawer won't hold them, their voices leak out of it like a fog, or like the rich scent of roasted coffee, insinuating themselves into every nook and cranny in the house, clinging to my clothes and being carried into my body on my breath, being absorbed into my tissues. I sleep in their presence, my notebooks are heavy with them, I wake mornings to their utterances, which dissipate like smoke the instant I try, half-awake, to write them down. The desk drawer bangs, so I tape it shut. But they pour out of it anyway, forcing their way out, their voices echoing everywhere.

What should I do with this night-woman avalanche?

YAYOI

NIGHT WOMEN'S ADVICE 10

Dive into what you're afraid of.
Work like crazy.

NIGHT WOMAN #10: *Yayoi Kusama*
PROFESSION: *Avant-garde artist, million-dollar brand, manically exemplary worker. Lives in a psychiatric hospital in Tokyo.*

> *"I make a pile of soft sculpture penises and lie down among them. That turns the frightening thing into something funny."*
> —Yayoi's coping strategy, according to her autobiography

> *"Happy people needed for Kusama's happening. Come to Kusama's studio 404 E. 14st 3 floor Jan 21 Sunday 6 pm."*
> —Handwritten note at Yayoi Kusama's exhibition at the Helsinki Art Museum, January 2017

> *15. November 1955.*
> *Dear Miss O'Keeffe,*
> *Will you please forgive me to interrupt you while you are very busy. . . . I am a Japanese female painter and have been working on painting for thirteen years since thirteen years old. . . . I should like to ask you would you kindly show me the way to approach this life. . . . I'm going to send you, under separate cover, my several water paintings to you. Would you please see those?*
> *Yours faithfully,*
> *Yayoi Kusama*

I first heard of Yayoi Kusama in Los Angeles in the spring of 1998. I was twenty-six, newly graduated from university, and working at my first job in a small publishing house. My little brother was learning to play the bass in Hollywood, and I had traveled to see him. I fell instantly in love with Los Angeles, as it was the most absurd place I'd ever been. The city's size alone was ludicrous: to get from the Hollywood hills to the beach, you had to spend hours winding around in traffic through half the city. I learned quickly that in LA no one walks, and there are no metro lines (well, there's one, but no sensible person ever sets foot in its trains), and the only people who ride the bus are crazies, drug addicts, and me. While my brother was at school, I would spend my day at the bus stop waiting hours for the broken-down old rattletrap that, when it finally came, would jerk and snort along at an irritatingly slow pace, carrying us freaks from Hollywood to some other part of the city, downtown, say, or Santa Monica. On these endless strange bus trips of mine, I wrote a whole series of stories in my diary, with the title "The Crazies on the Buses in LA."

One day soon after I arrived, I rode a bus like this to LACMA, the Los Angeles County Museum of Art. I had no idea what exhibition they were showing—there was no Internet, so how would I have found such a thing out?—but when I got there I learned that the museum was filled with a retrospective of some Japanese woman I'd never heard of. In the galleries were endless series of polka-dotted paintings, colorful abstracts, and, in black-and-white photos from the sixties, naked people with polka dots painted on their skin. What made the biggest impression on me were the handbags and dresses covered with different shapes and sizes of macaroni—and I must have seen the shoes and armchairs overflowing with "soft sculpture penises," though I have no memory of them. Despite the killer jet-lag fog through which I was viewing these artworks, I was impressed: I had never seen anything like it. And, well, in retrospect it strikes me that there is no better way to get to know Yayoi than through a reality-softening hangover-like jet-lag fog.

As a souvenir of the exhibition I bought a postcard, in whose red-tinted photograph a young Yayoi dressed in a kimono has campaign-type badges over her eyes with LOVE FOREVER written on each. For some reason that I didn't understand for a long time, that postcard became a kind of totem object for me—it's the only image that has remained framed on my wall for twenty years, moving with me from apartment to apartment and from one phase of my life to the next, right up until the present moment. For some inexplicable reason, when I look at that photo it always seems as if some liquid inspiration were being injected straight into my vein. It makes life feel fresh, deliciously tingly, and full of surprises.

The Yayoi on that postcard became one of my first night women.

Yayoi Kusama was born in 1929, into a wealthy and respected family that had amassed a fortune with a seed business in the small town of Matsumoto. Though Matsumoto, in the middle of the Japanese Alps, was an idyllic town, Yayoi's childhood was anything but. Her father seduced their maids and frequented geishas and prostitutes, and her mother, who was inclined to hysteria, first made Yayoi spy on her father and then spanked her for it. At twelve Yayoi began to hallucinate—to see things that weren't there, and to hear plants and animals talking. She didn't tell anyone about it, but began to draw and paint her visions. Her mother was not pleased with the drawing, since in those days rural artists lived a desperate life, begging money for drink and eventually hanging themselves, so she figured it was best to beat the artistic impulse out of her daughter. Getting married, on the other hand, would have been fine, and her mother showed Yayoi a series of new kimonos, beautiful dresses, and the photos of potential bridegrooms. But Yayoi could not have been less interested. She only wanted to paint.

When Yayoi was nineteen, she talked her mother into letting her enroll in an art school in Kyoto. When she got to Kyoto, however, she hated the archaic and hierarchical art world at the school, and didn't attend classes at all, but spent her days in her rented room in the eastern mountains sitting on her tatami floor manically painting pumpkins. And "manic" describes her working style from then on as well: when at twenty-three she held her first exhibition in Matsumoto, she had 270 works on display; in her second exhibition six months later, there were 280 new works. At this point, in 1953, Yayoi received some treatment for her neuroses, and based on her exhibitions her doctor proclaimed her a genius. It was Professor Nishimura's considered opinion that Yayoi should also get as far away from her mother as possible—out of Japan entirely, was Yayoi's view.

America was her own choice, but back then you couldn't just go there: in addition to a visa, you had to have a letter from a sponsor guaranteeing lodging and upkeep. Whom could Yayoi ask for advice on her way to becoming an artist in America? She had only recently, in a used bookshop, happened upon an art book with paintings by the famous American artist Georgia O'Keeffe. O'Keeffe was sixty-eight then, and one of the country's most important modernists, living the eccentric life of a hermit in the New Mexico desert. Yayoi was enchanted with the buffalo skulls and desert flowers she'd seen in the book, and decided on the spot that this was a woman who would help her get to America. So she took the train six hours down to Tokyo and marched into the US Embassy, where she flipped through *Who's Who* with trembling fingers until she found Georgia's address. Then she wrote Georgia a letter: *Dear Miss O'Keeffe, Will you please forgive me to interrupt you while you are very busy.* . . . It's a typed letter, with some of the letters jumping up a line, but in surprisingly good English. Yayoi was twenty-six.

And incredibly, Georgia replied—in her big, beautifully swooping, artistic handwriting

Abiquiu, N. M. 12/14/55.
Dear Yayoi Kusama,
your two letters came to me and your watercolors also came . . .

Yes, the paintings were interesting, but Georgia lived in the country now, and wasn't up to speed with the New York art scene. But if Yayoi wanted, she could send the paintings to an expert. Would Yayoi like to sell them, and if so, for how much?

Yayoi and Georgia exchanged letters for several years. Georgia did, in fact, show Yayoi's paintings to her art dealer and managed to sell one. (Years later, it turned out that she had sent the remaining paintings back to Japan, but the ship transporting them had sunk and taken the paintings to the bottom with it.) When Yayoi did finally leave for the United States in 1957, Georgia wrote her a letter wishing her well. And when Yayoi was just barely keeping body and soul together in New York as a penniless hungry artist, Georgia wrote that she was welcome at her ranch in New Mexico anytime—that she would gladly offer the young artist a work space and full room and board. (Yayoi didn't go. A ranch in the middle of nowhere wasn't her thing.)

A few years ago I was in Japan writing my first book and ran into an exhibition of Yayoi's work in Tokyo's Watari Museum. There for the first time I saw, displayed behind glass, those letters that the young Yayoi had sent Georgia. There was something amazingly enticing about the correspondence, and I circled the letters for a long time before I realized just what they were.

They were *letters to a night woman*, and *the night woman's replies*.

I thought: *Is it all just that simple?*

If you want something, ask a night woman's advice. The night woman will reply, never fear.

The letters to Georgia did indeed draw Yayoi to America. In 1957, a relative of hers managed to get her a visa on the pretext that her works were going to be on display at an exhibition in Seattle. Yayoi packed sixty silk kimonos and a couple thousand drawings and paintings, which she planned to sell to live on, since back then you were only allowed to take a tiny amount of cash out of Japan. In addition she smuggled—sewed into her clothes and in the toes of her shoes—the million yen she had illegally exchanged for a couple thousand US dollars. Before she left, she burned all her remaining sketches and paintings—which, had she not destroyed them, would now be worth hundreds of millions of yen.

Yayoi arrived in America in November 1957, at the age of twenty-eight. After her exhibition trip to Seattle, she settled in New York, where, having quickly run through all her money, she surrendered to life as a starving artist. Her ambitious goal was nothing less than a revolution in art—but everything was a struggle. The windows in her studio were broken; her bed was an old door she'd found in the street and a single blanket. She was cold and hungry and hallucinating. Some days her only food was a handful of chestnuts; sometimes she collected fish heads from the fishmonger's cleaning buckets, or half-rotten cabbage leaves from the produce seller's dumpster; the soup she boiled from those ingredients would keep hunger at bay till the next day. And she worked, constantly. She sank every penny she raised into painting supplies, and soon her studio was full of canvases painted full of nets—friends asked her, worried, why she kept painting the same subject. Sometimes she would first paint a canvas full of nets and then continue painting the image on the table, the floor, and her own body, repeating the pattern over and over, until the nets expanded to infinity: surrounded by nets, Yayoi could forget herself, or, as she later explained, they helped her *obliterate herself*. But one morning the nets began to move, and to crawl up onto her skin; Yayoi had a panic attack and an ambulance had to be called.

Yayoi continued painting manically, many times neither eating nor sleeping for days. And in October 1959, her dreams finally came true: a private exhibition in New York. *Obsessional Monochrome* in the Brata Gallery was a success.

In November, I head to Japan in pursuit of Yayoi. The killing darkness of the Finnish winter is approaching, and I'm tottering on the verge of the black pit; I'm spinning out of control on the night women's carousel, and the ominous polar-night prostration's on the prowl. I can't stop thinking about the living conditions and state of health in which Yayoi was able to work—if she could do it, so must I!

I decide to write to Yayoi, whose e-mail address I've found on the Web. The big problem with my night women so far has been that they're all moldering in their graves, leaving eighty-six-year-old Yayoi the only one I could in theory meet in person. *Konnichiwa*, I begin my e-mail awkwardly, for all of a sudden I have no idea how you begin a letter in Japanese—and then I ask my question.

Yayoi never answers.

I decide to travel over to Tokyo for a few days from Kyoto. In Tokyo I fret over whether to hang out in Shinjuku near the private psychiatric hospital where Yayoi lives. I know that she has a studio in a building next door to the hospital, and I've read that she always walks over there mornings, works all day, then returns to the hospital in the evening. Could I see her by accident, crossing the street? And what if I did—what would I do next? I read somewhere that Yayoi absolutely does not want to meet anyone, that the hospital is her refuge, and she is too afraid even to go to the store by herself, so some tourist shouting at her in the street would probably scare her to death. But what if I honored her performances, stripped naked and stood in front of the hospital with polka dots painted all over my body? Would she then wave at me from her window? Maybe they'd commit me too to the psychiatric hospital, and I could get the room next to Yayoi's! *Ohayō gozaimasu, sensei*, I would say in the morning as we toddled side by side in our light-blue hospital gowns down for our blood tests.

In the end I settle for studying the hospital through the lens of Google Earth from my hotel room. The psychiatric hospital is in the middle of an ordinary, homey residential area. I have no idea which of the neighboring buildings on those narrow streets houses Yayoi's studio, but I squint at people, doors, mailboxes, flowerpots, bikes left in yards, trash bags, and even laundry—everything that the Google Earth photographer happened to record that day—in a state of growing agitation. In some streets I see people too: workers, an old man with a shopping bag, neighbors stopping to chat at an intersection, and a young woman coming out of a building with a sunshade. No sign of Yayoi.

Embarrassment washes over me: studying the streets around the hospital over the Net feels like stalking. It would be humiliating if Yayoi found out about these obsessive pursuits of mine, that I'm huddled here in this Tokyo hotel room zooming in on what may be her trash bags. And it occurs to me: What if she sees me out some window? Am I there or not? I shut down the website quickly, beating down shame. I'm clearly more in my element with all those women who died at least a hundred years ago.

Yayoi and Georgia finally met in 1961, just once. One day the seventy-four-year-old Georgia O'Keeffe appeared unannounced at Yayoi's studio in New York. *You must be Yayoi*, she said. *How's everything going?* Yayoi found Georgia's face unbelievably wrinkled. She had never seen anyone whose skin was so lined. Yayoi would have liked to take a photo of the two of them, but her camera was out of film (of course), and there was no time to go out and buy some. Then Georgia had to leave.

There is no picture of Yayoi and Georgia. Night-woman encounters: never what you expect.

I can, however, travel with a good conscience to Matsumoto in the Japanese Alps, Yayoi's birthplace, without seeming like some creepy stalker.

And right in front of the Matsumoto City Museum, I come across signs of Yayoi: the whole yard is filled with an installation of gigantic polka-dotted tulips, and in front of the entrance are red-polka-dotted vending machines selling Coca-Cola in red-polka-dotted cans. Inside, the museum's red-polka-dotted banisters lead the visitor up to an exhibition where the polka-dot mania continues. I leave Yayoi a message on top of the polka-dotted Coke machine.

I spend the night in a cheap, old-fashioned *ryokan* by the canal; for breakfast, the old ladies who keep it serve me salt-grilled river fish with tofu, miso soup, pickles, and rice. I take a bath in the inn's wooden *ofuro* bath box, whose water is so hot that a quick dip is enough. Then I wander through the narrow streets wondering where Yayoi's childhood home was, and sit for a while in the moon-viewing pavilion in the nearby samurai castle. The pavilion is built to give visitors three poetic views of the moon: in the sky, reflected off the surface of the moat, and in your cup of sake. In the evening I wind up in an *izakaya*, where the cook grills whatever I order behind the counter: yakitori chicken skewers, chicken skin, wasabi vegetables, deep-fried tofu.

It's been pouring down rain all day, but after dinner on a whim I walk through the dark city to see once more the castle rising up inside the moat. The fog makes the sight unreal: the illuminated samurai castle gleams white in the darkness, and its form is reflected whole in the black mirror-smooth water of the moat. Through the black water float two swans.

The swans don't show up in the photograph I take. But no one would believe in their reality even if they did.

In January I'm in Copenhagen, settling my accounts with Karen, and on the same trip I hope to launch one more search for Yayoi. It's Saturday, and as soon as I enter the Louisiana Museum of Modern Art I realize I've made a horrible mistake in my choice of days to visit. Outside the museum before it even opens there is already a long line, and inside the crush is insane. The whole place is full of happily noisy families with children come to spend their weekend appreciating this Japanese woman artist's much-praised exhibition, which will be coming to Helsinki next.

I squeeze in with the crowd and move slowly from work to work in a cacophonous racket. I dodge the children pelting through the middle of the polka-dotted flaccid penises, trying ferociously to sink into a focused Zen state in which only Yayoi, my notebook, and I exist. The letters to Georgia rest in their glass case, and I hover in the line moving toward them like a hawk focused on its prey. The lines into the special rooms, like the mirror room, where the red-polka-dotted phallus field extends in all directions to infinity, or the space room, with its magical euphoria-inducing flashing lights, are impossibly long, winding through several galleries; and after waiting an eternity in those lines, you can only remain in each room for ten seconds at most. And when I want to watch the ninety-minute documentary *Yayoi Kusama: I Adore Myself*, that undertaking takes a five-hour bite out of my day. By the time I finally reach the museum's much-touted sea-view café, it's already dark, I'm starving, and above all I'm seething with rage, primarily because a) the director of the Yayoi doc gave it such a silly, dismissive title, and b) the delicious-looking lunch buffet ended a quarter hour ago, as the server definitively informs me. I stand in line for twenty minutes to get the last remaining sandwich—which, sigh, is tiny.

But Yayoi is just as joyous as ever: the white infinity-net paintings (painted while starving), the magical-mirror rooms, the pumpkin obsession, the staring eyes, the pink cosplay wig. There's a whole room full of my favorites, the everyday household objects bursting with soft penises: the white phallus armchair, the army of phallus high-heeled footwear, the phallus ironing board, the phallus kitchen stool, the phallus stepladder, the phallus suitcase. The penises stuffed in the high heels look revolting, like bunions or tumors that make walking impossible. The suitcase is so tightly stuffed with flaccid penises that it can't be closed—what a pain it must be to drag it! The biggest penis forest is growing out of the ironing board; and the overhang on top of the kitchen stool looks like a big ol' penis birthday cake. I wonder how on earth all these everyday objects have sprouted so much added encumbrance, like some kind of massive space mold, making life that much harder to live—the whole domestic realm, a woman's traditional life space, has been taken over by those Hattifatteners. Everything a woman does in this home, she does with a phallus in her field of vision. They're always in the way—how inconvenient if you try to iron some clothes! It seems like that symbol of male power has invaded everywhere, marking and obstructing every woman. You can't even sit in a chair in peace without something poking you from somewhere; and if you were thinking you might escape by climbing the kitchen stepladder, forget it, it too is covered with those fast-growing overhangs! (Someone has tried: a pair of high-heeled sandals squished by phalluses has been left on the steps.) Better to surrender completely. Over there is Phallus Girl with a cheerful penis straw hat on her head and, so to speak, with her ear cocked to her audience. Also available are a phallus dress, a phallus handbag, and my old favorite, the macaroni-coated golden handbag—here's a woman locked up in the cooking dungeon!

But why all this? Yayoi reports that people have interpreted her penis art as a sign that she is sex-crazy, but in fact, she says, it's the opposite: she's *afraid* of sex, especially of that grotesquely ugly male organ, and the wild proliferation of these silly hand-sewn cloth soft penises is her way of *coping with her fear*. And it's true: if you pose lying naked on a phallus sofa you've made yourself, your body painted with polka dots, wearing only high heels, you've made considerable progress in your fear-management project. (You've also given that symbol of women's oppression by men a harmless happy hint.)

The exhibition also features an abundance of photos and videos of Yayoi's performances, the ones where she painted polka dots on naked people in the streets of New York. In 1967, Yayoi had been in America almost ten years; she was thirty-seven, and had achieved a name as a visual artist—and now she threw herself into the free-sex and antiwar current of the hippie movement. In the first *Body*

Paint Festival happening that she arranged in January of 1967, Yayoi got the naked hippies to burn American flags in front of a Manhattan church during Sunday mass, and herself tossed Bibles and draft cards into the flames; then the hippies started kissing, and some even had sex. And all of a sudden Yayoi was famous. Her official mission was to promote the sexual revolution and thereby bring about world peace and happiness, and in the name of all that she began to arrange free-sex events. Yayoi served as "high priestess" of these happenings, painting the participants' bodies with polka dots—but she herself had no interest in sex at all. She also founded the Kusama Dancing Team, made up of young gay dancers who performed naked and lived in her studio in the East Village; she arranged gay weddings and orgies, in which the naked polka-dotted participants could express themselves; at happenings in the park, she called on the audience to get naked and let their bodies be polka-dotted, at least until the cops got there.

You have to admire Yayoi's ability to work the media. She founded a company called Kusama Enterprise to oversee her projects, and hired lawyers to advise her on how to carry out public performances without incurring criminal charges that would land her in jail. She produced press releases—those brilliant mixtures of advertisement, artistic manifesto, and social satire—as if on a conveyor belt, with topics ranging from fashion to sex and politics. In support of the antiwar movement, she sent President Richard Nixon an open letter in which she suggested that they "forget themselves" and paint each other polka-dotted. (*Gently! Dear Richard, calm your manly fighting spirit!*) She began to publish a weekly *Kusama Orgy* newspaper dealing with "nudity, love, sex, and beauty," which was sold nationwide. When she decided to design utopian "orgy wear" with holes in strategic revealing places, she sent out a press release announcing the founding of the Kusama Fashion Company. Another press release proclaimed "Priestess of Nudity, Yayoi Kusama, opens fashion boutique" on the occasion of her opening a clothing store on Sixth Avenue (her clothes were even sold at Bloomingdale's). The company was behind the creation of the Homo Dress, with a hole over the buttocks; a women's evening gown with holes over the breasts and derrière; Party Dress, which could be worn by up to twenty-five people at a time; and the exclusive See-Through and Way-Out outfits, which society women enthusiastically ordered at an exclusive price. (By the way, Yayoi hasn't lost one shred of her business sense—in the 2000s she has collaborated with Louis Vuitton, Issey Miyake, Coca-Cola, and others.)

In 1972, Yayoi got her name into the US *Who's Who*. She had spent sixteen years in New York and had become a major star of avant-garde art. In Japan, however, her dancing around in the nude was not understood at all: in her native land she was a national disgrace. Her father stopped sending her money, and her mother wrote that she wished Yayoi had died of the laryngitis she'd had as a child.

Even so, in 1973, at the age of forty-four, Yayoi decided to travel to Japan, and to everyone's surprise the short visit she'd planned became permanent. In Tokyo her health collapsed: she began hallucinating and having panic attacks again, suffered depression, and went over and over to stand on the platform on the Chūō train line—the famous suicide line—and considered jumping in front of a train. She committed herself to a hospital in Shinjuku, and finally, in 1977, moved permanently into an open ward in a private psychiatric hospital specializing in neuropsychology and art therapy. She has lived there ever since.

But neither illness nor hospitalization has shut down Yayoi's career as an artist, or slowed her working pace—on the contrary. Next to the hospital she built a studio where she still works every day, and is more productive than ever. In addition to creating thousands of paintings, sculptures, and installations, Yayoi has written twenty-odd books and composed songs—and there's no end in sight. On display in the Louisiana exhibition there were huge paintings that she had done just two years before, at the age of eighty-five. Word is she started that series at seventy-nine, and her original plan was to paint a hundred works; but because she's now exceeded that number by a large margin, she's raised the goal to a thousand. Her working style remains somewhere between workaholism and mania. For example, in writing her first novel, *Manhattan Suicide Addict*, published in 1978, she sometimes wrote a hundred pages a day. The whole novel was written in three weeks and was published without edits.

After her return to Japan, Yayoi was forgotten in the art world for twenty years, but then she made an impressive comeback. She walked into my life in Los Angeles in the spring of 1998, and I wasn't the only one so affected: the retrospective *Love Forever: Yayoi Kusama 1958–1968* stirred up a regular Kusamania. Yayoi cemented her status in the art world, and nowadays her early works may sell for more than $2 million each.

In the Louisiana Museum of Modern Art, I finally meet Yayoi face-to-face—on screen. The documentary *Yayoi Kusama: I Adore Myself* records Yayoi's day-to-day life over a year and a half. I keep noticing minor details—Yayoi's office building has Tadao Ando–style concrete walls, and the studio building is white, supposedly important clues to guide my Google Earth voyeurism. And, what the hell—I've imagined Yayoi living the lonely hermit's life, but this is a full-blown Kusama Factory, with numerous office workers and assistants handling her affairs! Did no one really have the time to answer my silly *konnichiwa* e-mail?

It's true, though, that Yayoi is not a social person. I read somewhere that the documentary-maker had been filming Yayoi for a year before she began to take note of her as a person with a name, and not just as an annoyingly buzzing camera. In the film, eightysomething Yayoi is crabby; now and then she declares she "feels bad" and so stares straight ahead without saying a word; she toddles like a sick old lady (which in fact she is) and just wants to paint her circles in peace. "Don't talk to me," she tells the photographer, "I can't concentrate when you're here." At the table she keeps drawing the same circular pattern, mechanically but with focus, without thinking or evaluating the work, day after day. Huge paintings are finished, raised for her to look at, then set aside so a new one can be started. Yayoi admires her own work. "Of course I'm a genius," she says when the creature holding the buzzing camera asks.

Yes, Yayoi is self-centered. She concentrates only on her own work; nothing else moves her. She's pleased with the fruits of her labors—more than that, they're brilliant, she *loves* them. When the photographer asks, "Who's your god?" Yayoi answers: "I am myself. I like myself a lot. I love myself." (She doesn't mention her night woman Georgia.) Occasionally she flips admiringly through magazines and books containing and discussing her paintings. (I can only envy her ability to do that without a shred of self-loathing.) When at one event she is asked what writers influenced her literary work, she doesn't understand the question: "I'm not interested in books written by anyone other than myself," she replies. (In fact, her tiny hospital room is full of books, and she reads constantly.) In addition to her own paintings Yayoi loves photographs of herself: she is always in the photos taken of her works, part of the artwork. Her pink-haired, staring-eyed figure is now a Japanese national icon, mascot, and million-dollar brand—and that brand is going to keep working until she takes her last breath.

Yes, Yayoi is self-centered and self-satisfied, but why the hell shouldn't she be, at eighty-six years of age? She has succeeded in transforming all the line items in her complex medical history—the fears, the compulsions, the anxiety disorders, the nervous disorders, the depressions that have plagued her throughout her life—into a *successful working career* that supports both her and many others financially. *Buraboo*, I say. Brava. Imitate her if you can.

When I think of Yayoi at night, I don't think of her ubiquitous polka-dot paintings or soft penises, or the performances or eternal orgies of the naked hippies.

I think of two things: 1) Georgia O'Keeffe, and 2) the psychiatric hospital.

I think of how Yayoi decided to become an artist as a young girl and wrote to Georgia O'Keeffe to ask for advice—how by writing a single letter she extended a hand to her night woman and made her dream come true.

I think of how later, having shaken up the New York art world in the sixties, she returned to Tokyo and asked to live in a psychiatric hospital. I think of how she never let her weaknesses and diagnoses slow her down, how instead she took charge of them and used them as an eternal fountain of her art.

I think of how she has lived in that psychiatric hospital *more than forty years*, and worked the whole time. How she is pushed in a wheelchair along the hospital's long corridors, how she grabs a pill from a nurse, lets her take a blood test, then gets dressed and heads to work, to add to her series of a thousand paintings.

*

[A TYPED LETTER]

Dear Miss Kusama,

Will you please forgive me to interrupt you while you are very busy. . . . Could you kindly tell me what the pill is that the nurse gives you in the morning?

Love forever, M

*

Night women's advice:

Play the cards you're dealt. Illnesses and weaknesses are grist for the mill.

Surround yourself with what you fear. Laugh at it.

Ask the night women for advice. They'll reply, never fear.

Arrange your living conditions so that they're livable for you—even if that means a psychiatric hospital.

Keep working.

Still.

[MISCELLANEOUS NIGHT WOMEN'S ADVICE]

Perfect working conditions:

Live in a hospital.
Live with a relative who cooks for you.
Live in a Tibetan monastery.
Move into a German castle with full room and board.

X Magic Mountain

I arrive at Magic Mountain in bone-chilling late-winter fog. The castle, or I guess actually the mansion, is in a rural area of the former East Germany in the middle of nowhere, and the plan is to spend the next four months of my life in this artists' residence. From the taxi, all I can see in every direction all the way to the horizon is flat gray fields, occasionally punctuated with a windmill, dilapidated industrial buildings, and abandoned brick buildings with broken windows. In the deserted-looking villages we pass, the doors and windows of the houses are barred with metal. Everywhere I look there's an East German feel: poverty-stricken, stark, severe.

At the castle, the Frau Direktorin is waiting for me. She has a silvery-gray bob haircut and a strange sense of humor. She takes me to my room in the old horse stables; from the window I have a view of the beautiful main building and the castle's garden. I think of Hans Castorp arriving at his own magic mountain in the Berghof tuberculosis sanatorium high in the Alps, and then instead of the three weeks he'd intended to stay getting sucked into the strange atmosphere of the place, so alienated from life, and staying seven years. *Welcome to our sanatorium, Miss Castorp*, an imagined voice says inside my head, *have you come as a patient, may I ask? How long are you planning to stay? Yes, aha, well, you'll see that your sense of time will change here. . . .*

Staying here this spring there will be around twenty of us patients—er, artists and writers, and in my Thomas Mann imaginings we would be carrying our chaise longues over there into the garden, under the massive oaks and tall horse chestnuts, and lying there wrapped in blankets waiting for our next meal. The nursing staff would be puttering quietly around us, seeing to our health and comfort. In the misty reality of Magic Mountain, time would fade, and it would become harder and harder to imagine the rest of the world as having any kind of real existence, because everything would seem so far away, so far. . . .

How ugly those green emergency exit signs are—who would ever want to leave here? I hear Frau Direktorin saying in my mind's ear. *In winter we send the bodies down the bobsled run into the valley. . . .*

We quickly settle into a daily routine. I write during the day. I step out of my writing bubble briefly for lunch and dinner, when my patient-colleagues and I drain into the dining hall. In the evenings I do yoga or go for walks in the woods. Sometimes I head out along the roads leading away from the village until all I see before me is a straight road all the way to the horizon, lined with black fields and oaks. One weekend I bike seventeen miles, along the way checking out five different villages. The most momentous sights on the whole ride are four sheep and a spotted horse.

But there's social life here too. In the weekly artist introductions, each of us in turn must vivisect his or her soul under the watchful eye of the directoress. Ines, a fiftyish roller skater from Berlin, reads her translations from Bulgarian. Stefan S. presents his disturbingly strange paintings, which he slaps onto gigantic aluminum bases with a burning cigarette hanging from his lip. Across the table in her studio, Riitta lines up rows of the pieces of birch bark she has painted with watercolors. She has mailed a whole box of the birch bark here from home in Finland. Peter holds a preternaturally magical concert in which the instruments he plays are bike stands, plastic tubing, stones, paper, and the wall. I sit through hours of readings, in which Annick, Martin, Markus, Malte, and Stefan P. read their German texts aloud in a singsong voice, or Nathalie lectures on the redheaded Irish model who sat for the painter James McNeill Whistler: how the whole golden age of nineteenth-century painting and the world of Parisian art salons would not have existed without those women, who had the guts to stand there under the artist's gaze and stare self-confidently out through the paintings.

Some evenings we play Ping-Pong in the atelier. Sometimes we watch movies together, or art videos based on Malte's or Stefan's poems. Sometimes we walk to the only bar in the village, where a gnomish old lady with a limp pours stale beer into steins; and sometimes after an evening like this Anu and I read our books aloud in Finnish. Once Annick teaches us acting techniques, and I try to be Karen. (Strangely, the right side of my face begins to feel flattened and numb, as if I had lain too long on my side in bed, staring up at the Ngong Hills.) One day I take part in Peter's audio project by reading Sei Shōnagon's texts in Finnish into a microphone. In return he gives me an interview with a six-hundred-year-old Vietnamese tortoise recorded on vinyl.

My spoken German begins to return in fits and starts. I'm told I sound like a German who has lived abroad for many years and forgotten all the words.

Sometimes at Magic Mountain there's this strange sense that fairy-tale creatures are stretching their hands out from the recesses of the forest, village fools are riding bikes on the empty forest paths, lost deer panic in the castle garden, and cats have used up their last lives. Then I walk out into Little Red Riding Hood's forest to Grandmother's house, to a dingy forest opening with a forgotten air. I walk along every possible forest path, past the gloomy spruce wood and the dizzying pine heath, but I dare not step off the path, lest I get lost in the maze of trees. A black woodpecker rat-a-tat-tats; somewhere I hear swans and cranes crying—I need little white stones to mark my return path.

But I always find my way back for dinner. I eat traditional German foods like *Milchreis* (rice pudding), *Knödel* (boiled dumplings), *Maultaschen* (sort of like German ravioli), or potatoes and quark (a German curd cheese). In asparagus season we eat white asparagus. Sometimes there are brats and sauerkraut; Sundays we get roasts. Sometimes there's a white egg soup that is hard to swallow.

There is no phone reception at Magic Mountain, and Internet access is sporadic. There's no way to leave, except by hitching a ride with the caretaker on Monday or Friday. But every few weeks, whenever my thoughts start whirling about ominously in my head, I ride into Berlin. The instant I climb aboard the train, my head clears as if shaking off a fug. I go to museums, galleries, theater festivals, bookstores, and coffee shops, wander down noisy streets and eat Vietnamese food. Upon my return to the castle after a couple days of that, I lie in bed in a state of collapse, recovering from overstimulation, as if I'd just returned from some grand voyage.

Sometimes the local villagers come to stare in amazement at us. Reporters interview us and publish stories in the local papers in which we describe how wonderful everything is here.

Sometimes a piano trio plays Brahms in the castle atelier. It's so supernaturally beautiful that I feel like weeping.

One day in the formal garden the boarded-up baroque statues are released from their confinement, and all about the castle appear rows of Greco-Roman mythic figures—Zeuses, Aphrodites, dwarves. Then the trees begin to bud, and suddenly everywhere there are hundreds of frogs, who have hopped up out of the pond to look for spouses. The gray that has surrounded and inhabited us turns green, yellow, red, white, blue, lilac. The endless fields begin to wave with grain, rapeseed, corn, poppies, and cornflowers, and our bike rides become passages through paradise. We haul sun chairs that look almost like official TB sanatorium-approved *Liegestuhlen* (chaise longues) outside, and I lie under a massive oak reading the last pages of Thomas Mann's novel. The tree sighs, it's warm, the castle's deaf cat, Schiller, lies about in patches of sun.

The apple trees are ready to burst into white flower. The lindens are laden with blossoms and resonant; we can hear the clouds of insects buzzing inside them from dozens of yards away. In the evening the frogs' chainsaw-like concert in the pond is deafening even in my room.

Then, finally, the orangery winter garden is opened, and I move out to write in a vast glass-walled paradise shaded by ten-foot-tall potted palms.

There I sit thinking about my night women.

In honor of Properzia, I eat tiny plums and arrange their pits in rows.

I boil Alexandra's tea and drink.

I examine Mary's fish to remind myself that any kind of passion can be meaningful.

I think of Isabella, who always felt better when she had tickets in hand for a sea voyage.

I think of Yayoi, who accepted life's limitations and made money off them.

I think of Sofonisba, who sat in her cabin belowdecks on a sailing ship en route to the court of Spain, her *cassone* filled with painting equipment.

I think of Ema Saikō with her travel permits at the checkpoints, who'd rather go to Kyoto to drink sake and write poems than get married.

I think of Lavinia in childbed, longing to hold a brush in her hand again, and Artemisia taking things in hand in a series of new cities.

When I lie in bed with a migraine, I think of Karen and all the things she suffered through a hundred years ago, in Africa, alone.

When I feel the pinch of dwindling finances, I think of Ida.

And when it comes time to pack my suitcase, I try very hard to think of Nellie.

I think of the terrestrial globe around which all the routes taken by these women are drawn in rhizomes of light, first slowly, then picking up speed—on the surface of the great ball the light intensifies, then dims, and soon it's flashing by so fast that the eye can only make out a white blur as the days go by, and the weeks, and the years, the centuries, human lifetimes. Then I slow time down and think of the modes of transportation the women used to trek across the surface of that globe: the ox-drawn carts, the horse-drawn carriages, the mules, the camels, the wooden ships, the steamships, the canoes carved from single trees, the old-timey cars, the small planes, the whistling steam trains with women riding along in them. Then I think of their luggage, their black dresses and corsets, their hats and hairdos, the thoughts in their heads, their fears and their bravery. They're all there at once, along with their writing implements, their diaries, writing paper, letters of introduction, requests for money, paper money sewn into clothing, their travel permits, their calling-card paintings, their painting equipment, cameras, laptops, food supplies (canned meats, energy bars, teas), their travel chests, saddles, tents, ransom money, and objects for barter, their disguises, the pants they supposedly wore secretly, lucky charms. . . .

I think of them (us) all at once, and of the fact that not one of us ever travels alone.

One evening in May I go out to admire a lilac bush whose branches bend down with the weight of the flowers. Behind the atelier I run into Christoph, who is trying to fire ceramics in a kiln he lifted from an abandoned house—and just then blowing on the struggling fire with a hair dryer. He offers me a marshmallow, and I roast it on the tip of a stick.

In June, Malte finishes his book. We ask him enviously how it feels now, but he just shrugs with a shy smile: "*Es geht,*" it feels okay. And then it's someone's going-away party again, so we sit on the terrace drinking wine and playing a round of *petanque*. Malte shows us his notebook, every page of which is filled with an unbelievably tiny and precise script, edge to edge, no margins. On a whim I ask whether he has many other notebooks like this one, and he says he does, fifty-seven of them, all of them numbered, each with an index at the end. With some embarrassment I show him my tattered spiral notebook that I bought at the Muji store, palm-size, mostly used for shopping lists.

Then in our last week, everything crescendos in a summer party, a great public event in which we present our skills like trained monkeys. For the party, Anu's and my Finnish texts have been translated into German, and as the translator reads my segment into the microphone, I think that life cannot get more absurd: I'm sitting on the terrace of a German castle listening to some man reading my journal to the audience in German.

On the warm evenings of our last days, we sit around a campfire drinking wine. Our time is short; life seems to be one never-ending going-away party, always for someone else. I already know that I'm going to miss them all. Bike-ride conversations with Annick, Ines's warm solidarity, Peter's sincere ability to see beauty in the least significant details in the world. The power of Stefan P.'s kindness and soft voice to make me happy, Stefan S.'s warped sense of humor, Nathalie's unbribable critiques. Hanna's glowing skeleton room, Anu's consciousness-exploding fresh LGBT-vegan-techno-rococo world, the open space of Riitta's atelier, with the dried stalks arranged on windowsills, the tree leaves set in shimmering surfaces like nature altars.

It feels like I've been somehow cured at Magic Mountain. As if I've understood that it's possible to live like this—that this is how artists and writers live. That this is how this work is done, each of us doing it in her or his own way, each wrestling with her or his own demons, each in her or his own workroom, corner of the world, historical slice of time. And yet in a way all together as well: the rhizome of all those letters, brushstrokes, right and wrong notes on the piano, reciprocal inspirations, utopian formulations, depths opening from this or that surprising idea, dozens of systematic or chaotic notebooks, gropings in the dark, misfires and nights spent lying awake in despair moving inexorably over our days like a cloud, or a dream, or like a great chunk of ice crashing onto the shore, irresistibly pushing each person's work forward.

*

Night women's advice:

Whatever you do, find yourself a magic mountain.

Come, Muses,
leave your golden (house)

Acknowledgments

Alfred Kordelin Foundation
Jenny and Antti Wihuri Foundation
The Foundation to Promote Journalistic Culture
Kone Foundation
Otava Book Foundation
Finnish Cultural Foundation and Künstlerhaus Schloss Wiepersdorf
Finnish Institute in Rome Villa Lante
Association of Finnish Non-Fiction Writers
Arts Promotion Center Finland
Väinö Tanner Foundation

Thanks to my mother and father for providing me a room of my own in the attic of their house in Vihti, along with full board. To my brother O-P, my sister-in-law, Hanna, and their two little girls, just for existing, and to Hanna for her analyses of the history of nineteenth-century dress. To Buz, my friend and colleague, without whom this book would not have been finished (either). To Olli and Flotea for their warm hospitality, larger-than-life experiences in Tanzania, and permission to write them into my book. To my guide Fazal, Tony Fitzjohn, Hilkka and Harri Hyrkkö, and Zimbabwean writer Petina Gappah for the general encouragement that gave me permission to write about Africa, uttered at the Helsinki Lit event in May 2017: "Come to Africa and write nonfiction with humility." To Stefano for giving me the use of his bedroom in Florence and general hospitality, which still surpasseth understanding, as well as Angela, Benedetto, and Nino. To Aura and her boys as well as Carla, Mari, Christel, and Cai, without whom my month in Mazzano would not have been so wonderful, and to Marika Räsänen for her comments on Italian history (yes, the picture I've painted of Florentine women is still simplistic). To my colleagues and friends at Magic Mountain: Anu, Riitta, Hanna, Ines, Nathalie, Annick, Insook, Sukyun, Stefan S., Stefan P., Christoph, Peter, Markus, Malte, Andrea, Bettina, and the others. To my Kyoto friends, including Seb, Reina, Iris, and Nicole, and to Beatrice in both Kyoto and Berlin. To Raisa Porrasmaa for her help with Japanese spellings. To Anna and Leo for writing retreats with a sea view, and to Liisa, my ikebana sensei and a real-life night woman, who thus receives at least one mention in this book too. To my many skilled friends at Otava Publishing, especially Lotta Sonninen, Piia Aho, Mari Mikkola, and Ulla Luukkonen. And to all my beloved friends who have put up with my endless cave isolations, grouchy tones when I answer the phone, and unmeetings.

Thanks to my night women—all those brilliant points of light in the nighttime sky with whose help an ordinary fearful woman can find her way by dead reckoning on sleepless nights.

And an especially warm thanks to all the amazing people who have worked around the clock to usher my night women out into the world on the Helsinki–New York–Hong Kong axis: the Elina Ahlbäck Literary Agency and Rhea Lyons, my translator Doug Robinson, and my editor Carina Guiterman and all the other wonderful people at Simon & Schuster.

The sections dealing with Karen Blixen, Isabella Bird, Ida Pfeiffer, Mary Kingsley, and Alexandra David-Neel rely largely on their own works, but are also heavily indebted to the excellent biographies by Judith Thurman, Evelyn Kaye, Gabriele Habinger, Katherine Frank, and Barbara M. and Michael Foster. The chapters on Sofonisba Anguissola, Lavinia Fontana, and Artemisia Gentileschi are based on pioneering scholarship by Ilya Sandra Perlingieri, Maria Kusche, Caroline P. Murphy, R. Ward Bissell, Mary D. Garrard, and Jesse M. Locker, and the rest of the sources mentioned in the Bibliography. The information about Yayoi Kusama's life comes mainly from her own autobiography.

Translation Acknowledgment

Simon & Schuster gratefully acknowledges the financial assistance of FILI—Finnish Literature Exchange.

F I
L I

Bibliography

Adichie, Chimamanda Ngozi. *The Thing Around Your Neck*. New York: Knopf, 2009.

Amoia, Alba, and Bettina L. Knapp, eds. *Great Women Travel Writers: From 1750 to the Present*. New York: Continuum, 2005.

Anderson, Monica. *Women and the Politics of Travel, 1870–1914*. Vancouver, BC: Fairleigh Dickinson University Press, 2006.

Bal, Mieke, ed. *The Artemisia Files: Artemisia Gentileschi for Feminists and Other Thinking People*. Chicago: University of Chicago Press, 2005.

Barker, Sheila, ed. *Women Artists in Early Modern Italy: Careers, Fame, and Collectors*. Turnhout, Belgium: Harvey Miller, 2016.

Beard, Peter, ed. *Longing for Darkness: Kamante's Tales from Out of Africa*. With photographs and captions by Isak Dinesen (Karen Blixen). New York: Harcourt Brace Jovanovich, 1975.

Bird, Isabella L. *The Hawaiian Archipelago: Six Months among the Palm Groves, Coral Reefs, and Volcanoes of the Sandwich Islands* (1875). Online at http://www.gutenberg.org/ebooks/6750.

———. *A Lady's Life in the Rocky Mountains* (1879). Online at http://www.gutenberg.org/ebooks/755.

Bird, Isabella L. (Mrs. J. F. Bishop, FRGS). *Unbeaten Tracks in Japan. A Record of Travels in the Interior, Including Visits to the Aborigines of Yezo and the Shrines of Nikkō and Ise* (1880). London: George Newnes, 1900.

Bissell, R. Ward. *Artemisia Gentileschi and the Authority of Art*. University Park, PA: Pennsylvania State University Press, 1999.

Blixen, Karen [Isak Dinesen, pseud.]. *Last Tales*. New York: Vintage, 1993.

———. *Letters from Africa 1914–1931*. Edited for the Rungstedlund Foundation by Frans Lasson. Danish originals *Breve fra Africa 1914–24* and *Breve fra Africa 1925–31* (1978). Translated by Anne Born. London: Weidenfeld & Nicolson, 1981.

———. *Out of Africa*. London: Putnam, 1937.

———. *Seven Gothic Tales*. London: Penguin, 2002. (Original publication 1934.)

———. *Shadows on the Grass*. New York: Random House, 1962.

———. *Winter's Tales*. New York: Vintage, 1993. (Original publication 1942.)

Bly, Nellie. *Around the World in Seventy-Two Days*. New York: Pictorial Weeklies, 1890.

———. *Ten Days in a Mad-House*. New York: Ian L. Munro, 1887.

Borzello, Frances. *Seeing Ourselves: Women's Self-Portraits*. London: Thames & Hudson, 2016 (1998).

Broude, Norma, and Mary D. Garrard, eds. *Reclaiming Female Agency: Feminist Art History after Postmodernism*. Berkeley and Los Angeles, CA: University of California Press, 2005.

Castiglione, Baldesar. *The Book of the Courtier*. Edited by Daniel Javitch. Translated by Charles S. Singleton. New York: Norton, 2002.

Christiansen, Keith, and Judith W. Mann. *Orazio and Artemisia Gentileschi*. New York: Metropolitan Museum of Art, and New Haven: Yale University Press, 2001.

Chubbuck, Kay, ed. *Isabella Bird: Letters to Henrietta*. Boston: Northeastern University Press, 2003.

Cohen, Elizabeth S. "The Trials of Artemisia Gentileschi: A Rape as History." "Gender in Early Modern Europe," special issue of *The Sixteenth Century Journal* 31, no. 1 (Spring 2000), 47–75.

David-Neel, Alexandra. *Magic and Mystery in Tibet*. Introduction by Aaron Sussman. Original French title: *Mystiques et magiciens du Tibet* (1929). London: Allen & Unwin, 1984.

———. *My Journey to Lhasa*. With a new introduction by Peter Hopkirk. London: Virago Press, 1983 (1927).

Donelson, Linda. *Out of Isak Dinesen in Africa: Karen Blixen's Untold Story*. Foreword by Don Mowatt. Afterword by Anne Born. Iowa City, IA: Coulsong, 1998.

Ema Saikō. *Breeze through Bamboo: Kanshi of Ema Saikō*. Translated by Hiroaki Sato. New York: Columbia University Press, 1998.

Ferino-Pagden, Sylvia, and Maria Kusche. *Sofonisba Anguissola: A Renaissance Woman*. Washington, DC: National Museum of Women in the Arts, 1995.

Finlay, Victoria. *Colour: Travels through the Paintbox*. London: Hodder & Stoughton, 2003.

Fischer-Defoy, Christine, ed. *Frida Kahlo: Das Private Addressbuch* [The Private Address Book]. Münster-Berlin, Germany: Koehler & Amelang, 2009.

Fister, Patricia. "Female *Bunjin*: The Life of Poet-Painter Ema Saikō." In *Recreating Japanese Women, 1600–1945*. Edited with an introduction by Gail Lee Bernstein. Berkeley and Los Angeles: University of California Press, 1991.

Fitzjohn, Tony. *Born Wild: The Extraordinary Story of One Man's Passion for Lions and for Africa*. With Miles Bredin. New York: Viking, 2010.

FitzRoy, Charles. *Renaissance Florence on Five Florins a Day*. London: Thames & Hudson, 2010.

Fornaciai, Valentina. *"Toilette," Perfumes and Makeup at the Medici Court*. Translated by Catherine Burnett. Livorno, Italy: Sillabe, 2007.

Fortunati, Vera, Jordana Pomeroy, and Claudio Strinati, curators. *Italian Women Artists: From Renaissance to Baroque*. New York: Skira & Rizzoli, 2007.

Fortune, Jane. *Invisible Women: Forgotten Artists of Florence*. Florence, Italy: Florentine Press, 2014.

Foster, Barbara M., and Michael Foster. *Forbidden Journey: The Life of Alexandra David-Neel*. New York: Harper & Row, 1987.

Foster, Shirley, and Sara Mills, eds. *An Anthology of Women's Travel Writing*. Manchester, UK: Manchester University Press, 2002.

Frank, Katherine. *A Voyager Out: The Life of Mary Kingsley*. Boston: Houghton Mifflin, 1986.

French Sheldon, May. *Sultan to Sultan: Adventures among the Masai and Other Tribes of East Africa, by M. French Sheldon, "Bébé Bwana."* Introduction by Tracey Jean Boisseau. Manchester, UK: Manchester University Press, 1999 (1892).

Gallen-Kallela, Akseli. *Afrikka-kirja: Kallela-kirja II* [The Africa Book: The Kallela Book II]. Porvoo, Finland: WSOY, 1931.

Garrard, Mary D. *Artemisia Gentileschi: The Image of the Female Hero in Italian Baroque Art*. Princeton, NJ: Princeton University Press, 1989.

Gellhorn, Martha. *Travels with Myself and Another: Five Journeys from Hell*. London: Allen Lane, 1978.

Habinger, Gabriele. *Eine Wiener Biedermeierdame erobert die Welt: Die Lebensgeschichte der Ida Pfeiffer (1797–1858)* [A Viennese Biedermeier Lady Conquers the World: The Life of Ida Pfeiffer]. Vienna: Promedia, 1997.

Harris, Ann Sutherland, and Linda Nochlin. *Women Artists: 1550–1950*. Los Angeles County Museum of Art. New York: Random House, 1976.

Hayden, Deborah. *Pox: Genius, Madness, and the Mysteries of Syphilis*. New York: Basic, 2003.

Hemingway, Ernest. *Green Hills of Africa*. New York: Charles Scribner's Sons, 1935.

Hibbert, Christopher. *Florence: The Biography of a City*. Harmondsworth, UK: Penguin, 1994.

Ireland, Deborah, ed. *Isabella Bird: A Photographic Journal of Travels Through China 1894–1896*. In association with the Royal Geographical Society. Tampa, FL: Ammonite Press, 2015.

Johnson, Geraldine A., and Sara F. Matthews Grieco, eds. *Picturing Women in Renaissance and Baroque Italy*. Cambridge, UK: Cambridge University Press, 1997.

Johnson, Osa. *Four Years in Paradise*. Mechanicsburg, PA: Stackpole, 2018 (1941).

———. *I Married Adventure: The Lives of Martin and Osa Johnson*. Bunkyō, Japan: Kodansha, 1997 (1940).

Jørgensen, Lærke Rydal, et al., eds. *Yayoi Kusama: In Infinity*. Humlebæk, Denmark: Louisiana Museum of Modern Art, 2015.

Kaye, Evelyn. *Amazing Traveler Isabella Bird: The Biography of a Victorian Adventurer*. Boulder, CO: Blue Panda, 1999.

Kingsley, Mary H. *Travels in West Africa (Congo Francais, Corisco and Cameroons)*. National Geographic, 2002 (1897).

———. *West African Studies*. London: Macmillan, 1899.

Kortelainen, Anna. *Hurmio: Oireet, hoito, ennaltaehkäisy* [Ecstasy: Symptoms, Treatment, Prevention]. Helsinki: Tammi, 2009.

———. *Levoton nainen: Hysterian kulttuurihistoriaa* [The Restless Woman: A Cultural History of Hysteria]. Helsinki: Tammi, 2003.

Kusama, Yayoi. *Infinity Net: The Autobiography of Yayoi Kusama*. Translated by Ralph McCarthy. London: Tate, 2011. (Japanese original 2002.)

Lapierre, Alexandra. *Artemisia: A Novel.* Translated by Liz Heron. New York: Grove, 2000.

———. *Women Travelers: A Century of Trailblazing Adventures 1850–1950*. Edited by Christel Mouchard. Translated by Deke Dusinberre. Paris: Flammarion, 2007.

Lasson, Frans, ed., and Clara Selborn, text. *Isak Dinesen: Her Life in Pictures*. Original Danish work: *Karen Blixen: En digterskæbne i billeder* (1969). Rungsted, Denmark: The Karen Blixen Museum, 2009.

Locker, Jesse M. *Artemisia Gentileschi: The Language of Painting*. New Haven, CT: Yale University Press, 2015.

Mahon, Elizabeth Kerri. *Scandalous Women: The Lives and Loves of History's Most Notorious Women*. New York: TarcherPerigree, 2011.

Mann, Judith W., ed. *Artemisia Gentileschi: Taking Stock*. Turnhout, Belgium: Brepols, 2005.

Mann, Thomas. *The Magic Mountain*. Translated by John E. Woods. New York: Vintage, 1996.

Markham, Beryl. *West with the Night*. New York: North Point/Farrar Straus Giroux, 1983 (1942).

Marttila, Olli. *The Great Savanna: The National Parks of Tanzania and other Key Conservation Areas*. Helsinki: Auris, 2011.

———. *Norsuja tiellä!: Vuosi Tansaniassa* [Elephants in the Road!: A Year in Tanzania]. Helsinki: Tammi, 2002.

———. *Safaripassi: Pohjois-Tansania* [Safari Pass: Northern Tanzania]. Helsinki: Auris, 2008.

McEwan, Cheryl. *Gender, Geography, and Empire: Victorian Women Travelers in West Africa*. Farnham, UK: Ashgate, 2000.

McVicker, Mary F. *Women Adventurers 1750–1900: A Biographical Dictionary, with Excerpts from Selected Travel Writings*. Jefferson, NC: McFarland, 2008.

Middleton, Dorothy. *Victorian Lady Travellers*. London: Routledge & Kegan Paul, 1965.

Middleton, Ruth. *Alexandra David-Neel: Portrait of an Adventurer.* Boulder, CO: Shambhala, 1989.

Murphy, Caroline P. "Lavinia Fontana and Female Life Cycle Experience in Late Sixteenth-Century Bologna." In Geraldine A. Johnson and Sara F. Matthews Grieco, eds., *Picturing Women in Renaissance and Baroque Italy*, 111–38. Cambridge, UK: Cambridge University Press, 1997.

———. *Lavinia Fontana: A Painter and her Patrons in Sixteenth-Century Bologna*. New Haven, CT: Yale University Press, 2003.

Navarro, Fausta, ed. *Plautilla Nelli: Art and Devotion in Savonarola's Footsteps*. Livorno, Italy: Sillabe, 2017.

Netzley, Patricia D. *The Encyclopedia of Women's Travel and Exploration*. Phoenix, AZ: Oryx, 2001.

Pelensky, Olga Anastasia. *Isak Dinesen: The Life and Imagination of a Seducer*. Columbus: Ohio University Press, 1991.

Perlingieri, Ilya Sandra. *Sofonisba Anguissola: The First Great Woman Artist of the Renaissance*. New York: Rizzoli, 1992.

Petäistö, Helena. *Pariisi* [Paris], *Versailles, Giverny*. Helsinki: Otava, 2014.

Pfeiffer, Ida. *A Lady's Second Journey Round the World: From London to the Cape of Good Hope, Borneo, Java, Sumatra, Celebes, Ceram, the Moluccas, etc., California, Panama, Peru, Ecuador, and the United States*. Vols. 1–2. New York: Harper & Brothers, 1856. Online at https://archive.org/details/aladyssecondjou02pfeigoog/page/n7.

———. *The Last Travels of Ida Pfeiffer: Inclusive of a Visit to Madagascar, with an Autobiographical Memoir of the Author*. Original German title: *Reise nach Madagaskar*. Translated by H. W. Dulcken. New York: Harper & Brothers, 1861.

———. *Meine zweite Weltreise* [My Second Trip Around the World]. Vols. 1–4. Vienna: Carl Gerold's Sohn, 1856. Online at https://archive.org/details/meinezweiteweltr121pfei/page/n6.

———. *Nordlandfahrt: Eine Reise nach Skandinavien und Island im Jahre 1845* [Nordic Journey: A Trip to Scandinavia and Iceland in 1845] (1846). Edited and with a foreword by Gabriele Habinger. Vienna: Promedia, 1991.

———. *Reise nach Madagaskar* [Journey to Madagascar]. Vienna: Carl Gerold's Sohn, 1861.

———. *A Visit to Iceland and the Scandinavian North*. Original German title: *Reise nach dem skandinavischen Norden* (1846). London: Ingram, Cooke, 1852.

———. *A Visit to the Holy Land, Egypt, and Italy*. Original German title: *Reise einer Wienerin in das heilige Land* (1844). Translated by H. W. Dulcken. Online at http://www.gutenberg.org/ebooks/12561.

———. *A Woman's Journey Round the World*. Original German title: *Eine Frauenfahrt um die Welt* (1850). Online at http://www.gutenberg.org/ebooks/11039.

Pope-Hennessy, John. *The Portrait in the Renaissance*. The A. W. Mellon Lectures in the Fine Arts, National Gallery of Art, Washington, D.C. Bollingen Series 35, no. 12. Princeton, NJ: Princeton University Press, 1979.

Robinson, Jane. *Wayward Women: A Guide to Women Travellers*. Oxford, UK, and New York: Oxford University Press, 1990.

Setälä, Päivi. *Renessanssin nainen: Naisten elämää 1400- ja 1500-luvun Italiassa* [The Renaissance Woman: Women's Life in Fifteenth- and Sixteenth-Century Italy]. Helsinki: Otava, 2000.

Shiba Keiko. *Literary Creations on the Road: Women's Travel Diaries in Early Modern Japan*. Translated with notes by Motoko Ezaki. Lanham, MD: University Press of America, 2012.

Siljeholm, Ulla, and Olof Siljeholm. *Resenärer i långkjol* [Travelers in Long Dresses]. Stockholm: Carssons, 1996.

Stevenson, Catherine Barnes. *Victorian Women Travel Writers in Africa*. New York: Twayne, 1982.

Strohmeyr, Armin. *Abenteuer reisender Frauen: 15 Porträts* [Adventures of Traveling Women: 15 Portraits]. Munich: Piper, 2012.

Tatehata, Akira, Laura Hoptman, Udo Kultermann, and Catherine Taft. *Yayoi Kusama*. London and New York: Phaidon, 2000.

Thurman, Judith. *Isak Dinesen: The Life of a Storyteller*. London: Picador, 1995.

Trzebinski, Errol. *Silence Will Speak: A Study of the Life of Denys Finch Hatton and His Relationship with Karen Blixen*. London: Heinemann, 1977.

Vasari, Giorgio. *The Lives of the Artists*. Translated by Julia Conaway Bondanella and Peter Bondanella. New York: Oxford University Press, 2008.

Weaver, Elissa B., ed. *Arcangela Tarabotti: A Literary Nun in Baroque Venice*. Ravenna, Italy: Longo, 2006.

Willink, Robert Joost. *The Fateful Journey: The Expedition of Alexine Tinne and Theodor von Heuglin in Sudan (1863–1864): A Study of Their Travel Accounts and Ethnographic Collections*. Amsterdam: Amsterdam University Press, 2011.

Winspeare, Massimo. *The Medici: The Golden Age of Collecting*. Translated by Richard Fowler. Livorno, Italy: Sillabe, 2000.

Permissions

Quotes from Isak Dinesen's *Letters from Africa 1914–1931*, Karen Blixen's *Out of Africa* and *Shadows on the Grass*. Rights granted by Rungstedlund Foundation.

Excerpts from *Isak Dinesen: The Life of a Storyteller* by Judith Thurman. Copyright © 1983 by Judith Thurman. Reprinted by permission of St. Martin's Griffin, an imprint of St. Martin's Press. All rights reserved. (Print rights.)

Excerpts from *Isak Dinesen: The Life of a Storyteller* by Judith Thurman. Copyright © 1982 by Judith Thurman, used by permission of the Wylie Agency LCC. (Digital rights.)

Quotes from *Longing for Darkness—Kamante's Tales from Out of Africa*, collected by Peter Beard. Rights granted by Peter Beard Studio/Art+Commerce, www.peterbeard.com.

Quotes from Alexandra David-Neel, *My Journey to Lhasa* and *Journal de Voyage: Lettres à son mari, vols. 1–2.* (Translations from Foster & Foster, *Forbidden Journey: The Life of Alexandra David-Neel.*) Rights granted by Maison Alexandra David-Neel.

Excerpts from *Orazio and Artemisia Gentileschi* by Keith Christiansen and Judith W. Mann, originally published by the Metropolitan Museum of Art, New York. Copyright © 2001. Reprinted by permission.

Quotes from *Artemisia Gentileschi—The Image of the Female Hero in Italian Baroque Art* by Mary D. Garrard. Rights granted by Princeton University Press.

Quotes from Yayoi Kusama's *Infinity Net—The Autobiography of Yayoi Kusama.* Rights granted by Tate Entreprises, Ltd. Other quotes by Yayoi Kusama, rights granted by Yayoi Kusama Inc.

About the Author

Mia Kankimäki is the author of two bestselling books that blend travelogue, memoir, biography, and women's history. After earning a master's degree in comparative literature at the University of Helsinki and working diligently in Finnish publishing, she left her job in 2010 and traveled to Japan to write her first book. Her second book, *The Women I Think About At Night*, was inspired by her travels in the footsteps of inspirational, historical female figures in Tanzania, Kenya, Italy, and Japan. She currently lives in Helsinki, Finland, whenever she's not traveling for her next book project.